THE IDES OF MAY

JOHN WILLIAMS

The Ides of May

THE DEFEAT OF FRANCE

MAY–JUNE

1940

NEW YORK

Alfred · A · Knopf

1968

THIS IS A BORZOI BOOK
PUBLISHED BY ALFRED A. KNOPF, INC.

FIRST AMERICAN EDITION

Copyright © 1968 by John Williams. All rights reserved under International and Pan-American Copyright Conventions. Published in the United States by Alfred A. Knopf, Inc., New York. First published in Great Britain by Constable & Company, Ltd., London. Distributed by Random House, Inc., New York.

Library of Congress Catalog Card Number: 68-23946

Manufactured in the United States of America

Acknowledgment is hereby given to the following publishers for permission to reprint from their works:

G. P. Putnam's Sons for *Sixty Days That Shook the West—The Fall of France: 1940* by Jacques Benoist-Mechin, translated by Peter Wiles. English translation Copyright © 1963 by Jonathan Cape, Ltd.

Holt, Rinehart and Winston, Inc. for *Blitzkrieg to Defeat: Hitler's War Directives 1939-1945,* edited by H. R. Trevor-Roper.

Houghton Mifflin Company for *The Second World War,* by Sir Winston Churchill.

FOR SONIA

THE IDES

in the Roman calendar,
the fifteenth day of certain months,
including MAY.

Foreword

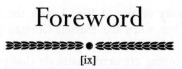

THIS IS THE HISTORY of the defeat of the French Army in the battles of May and June 1940. It is a story of unrelieved catastrophe in which the whole fabric of France was involved. As the wavering French formations moved toward collapse in early June, disintegration began to grip people and government alike. Millions of refugees herded down the roads of France. Paris was abandoned without a struggle. The government, torn with disagreement about whether or not to continue the fight, retreated in growing confusion from Paris to Tours, and from Tours to the final chaos of Bordeaux. Here, the military disaster paved the way for the defeatists who, led by the aged Pétain, overthrew Paul Reynaud and his followers and sought the armistice for which they had been steadily working.

When the cease-fire took effect on June 25, the French Army had been in action for forty-six days—but it was already beaten by the middle of May. The battle for France was irretrievably lost on the sixth day of Hitler's main offensive in the West. This was the date—the fateful fifteenth of May—when the German panzer spearheads broke out from the Meuse and began their race to the Channel to cut the Allied front in two and seal off the bulk of the Franco-British forces in Belgium.

On the outbreak of war in September 1939, France and Germany were approximately equal in men, weapons, and armor. Yet when, after eight months of inactivity in the West, the armies finally clashed in May 1940, the French crumpled under the violent German assault in a matter of six weeks. Amid all the controversy as to who or what was responsible for the *débâcle*, it was clear that the primary blame for what was, after all, a military defeat, lay squarely with the French General Staff and High Command. The generals and the operational planners went to war in 1939 still thinking largely in terms of 1914–18. Staking their faith on the old doctrine of the defensive, they continued to see warfare as static. They rejected the new theories of mobile war based on the concentrated use of tanks and aircraft and, instead, perpetuated the trench mentality of World War I with the immensely costly Maginot Line. Thus when the massed German panzers and dive bombers struck westward on May 10, the French were at the mercy of a fast-moving armored onslaught that proved irresistible.

The fall of France in June 1940 was a tragedy of lost military opportunities: lost during the eight months' lull in the West when the French army chiefs might still have revised their strategic and operational planning to counter the coming mechanized attack; and earlier, during the whole two decades from 1919 when they persistently refused to read the signs and continued to envisage and prepare for a type of war that was obsolete. There was admittedly some pretext for this defense-mindedness and cautious, static thinking. France had twice been invaded by Germany, in 1870 and 1914, and she had suffered losses in World War I from which she had never recovered. Thus, behind the defensive thinking of the French High Command lay a nationwide hatred of war and a strong desire to avoid it. Other factors—the unstable politics and weak and indecisive government of the interwar years, even a latent defeatism—played their parts. The result was that France went to war totally unready for the struggle. Yet the universal cry in September 1939, *"Il faut en finir,"* seemed to express the grim determination of the French people. But Frenchmen—soldiers and civilians alike—had no conception of the task awaiting them, or of what inadequate means they had for performing it, thanks to the outdated planning and preparations of the High Command and General Staff.

Easy hindsight, however, should not go too far. In her war-making capacity France was suffering from the handicap that affects all democratic nations. As General Gamelin points out in his book, *Servir,* his country's political principles ruled out the idea of taking the military initiative and waging aggressive war: unlike a totalitarian or dictator state, France could take up arms only in self-defense, after war had been forced on her. This limitation, he implies, conditioned her strategic and tactical planning, and was even basically responsible for her rejecting the novel theory of armored warfare first put forward by De Gaulle in 1934.

This book is divided into two parts. Part I, covering the years from 1870 to the outbreak of World War II, describes the events and influences which shaped the nation that went to war in 1939: defeat in the Franco-Prussian War; the rebirth of French patriotic spirit and military pride with the introduction of conscription; the swing from defensive to offensive military thinking; the challenge and nearly overwhelming ordeal of World War 1; the exhaustion and then the growing disillusion of the postwar period, as hopes of peace and security dwindled and Europe moved once again toward war. Part II, the main portion of the book, deals with World War II and covers in particular the months of May and June 1940 in which the French Army faced the full force of the German onslaught. The detailed military picture is shown against the background of civilian France. The scene is one of almost total dissolution at front and rear. But as France, led by the aged Pétain in place of Reynaud, bows beneath the heavy terms of the armistice, one figure emerges to rally the forces of resistance—General Charles de Gaulle.

Note: All dialogue reproduced in the book is taken from fully documented sources, to which references are given.

J. W., October, 1967

ACKNOWLEDGMENTS

M OST OF THE RESEARCH for this book has been done at the London Library, the libraries of the British Museum, Imperial War Museum, Ministry of Defence (Central and Army), Institut Français, London; and the Bibliothèque Nationale, Paris. My thanks are specially due to the staff of the Imperial War Museum Library for their ready assistance, and to various individuals with whom I have spoken or corresponded, and who have answered queries and given help and advice. Among these are General Sir Edward Spears, K.B.E., who has also allowed me to quote from his book, *Assignment to Catastrophe* (1954); Lieutenant Colonel W. B. R. Neave-Hill, Narrator, Ministry of Defence Library, who suggested possible lines of research; Lord Keyes, who provided valuable information from his private papers on the circumstances of the Belgian surrender; Miss Margery Weiner, who brought to my notice some interesting material pointing a parallel between the campaigns of 1870 and 1940; Mr. Gordon Waterfield, author of *What Happened to France* (1940); General de Grancey, Governor, Les Invalides, Paris; Monsieur Pineau-Valenciennes, Paris; and General André Beaufre, Director of the French Institute of Strategic Studies, who, as a staff officer at French GHQ in May and June 1940 was in daily contact with the French military chiefs and observed from close quarters the central direction of operations, and whose book, *Le Drame de 1940* (1965), vividly describes his experiences. I am grateful to General Beaufre for permitting me to quote from his book, and in particular for personally discussing with me the campaign of 1940 and its conduct and background, and giving me his impressions of the leading French commanders.

I would acknowledge also the help of the Meteorological Office, which has furnished me with detailed statistics for May and June 1940, proving the truth of the legend that the weeks of Hitler's Western offensive were marked by unusually dry and brilliant weather—a factor that contributed notably to the success of the

German *blitzkrieg* tactics, based as they were on the massive use of dive bombers and swift-moving tanks.

Not least, I would thank the anonymous French workman who clandestinely conducted my wife and myself into the dark, dank, and disused underground casemates at Vincennes, which in May 1940 formed the headquarters of General Gamelin.

Finally, I am immensely indebted to my wife for devoting many long hours to the expert retyping, correction, and arrangement of my MS.

A visit to the Belgian Ardennes around Bouillon, on the river Semois, and the Meuse battlefields around Givet, Fumay, Monthermé, and Sedan—scene of the defeat of the French 9th and 2nd Armies—has afforded me a striking picture of the defensive and offensive problems respectively facing the French and Germans in this key zone of the Western campaign.

CONTENTS

[xv]

ILLUSTRATIONS

[xvii]

Armistice negotiations in progress: General Huntziger,
Field Marshal Keitel
Imperial War Museum, London

France's new leader, Marshal Pétain, June 1940
Radio Times

MAPS

MAPS

PART ONE

THE
YEARS
BEFORE

Chapter 1

➤➤➤➤➤➤➤➤➤● ◄◄◄◄◄◄◄◄◄◄

THE ARMY IN WAITING,
1870–1914

"Devotion, self-sacrifice, discipline, patriotism."
(President Grévy)

i

IN THE AUTUMN of 1895 the French Army was engaged, in eastern France, on one of its periodical maneuvers. In a wide triangle from the Langres Plateau in the Haute-Marne to Mirecourt and Neufchâteau in the wooded uplands of the Vosges, 150,000 troops, under the direction of General Saussier, vice-president of the Conseil Supérieur de Guerre, wheeled, deployed, advanced, and retired in the biggest army exercise ever held under the Third Republic. According to the theme, an enemy from the east, having captured the key fortified positions of Belfort, Toul, and Épinal, was advancing westward toward Chaumont. Among the crowd of foreign military observers was the Russian General Dragomirov, veteran of the Russo-Turkish War and Commander in Chief of the Kiev District. Dragomirov had a special interest in the maneuvers, for by a treaty of 1894 France and Russia were military allies; and what he saw gave him considerable satisfaction. In March 1896 he reported in Russia's official military journal: "The general has been struck by the uncommon endurance of the French soldier. . . . He declares that the present French Army produces an excellent impression. . . . One is now in the presence of a balanced army."[1]

Less impartially, France's own leaders had expressed similar

---

[1] E. Simond: *Histoire de la Troisième République* (1921), Vol. III, p. 394.

views at other recent maneuvers. "Nobody doubts today," proclaimed M. de Freycinet, Minister of War, "that we are strong. We shall prove that we are wise."[2] And President Grévy declared: "The people know what they owe to this valuable school of devotion, self-denial, discipline and patriotism, which has become the school of everyone."[3]

"Devotion, self-denial, discipline, patriotism"—these, through the last quarter of the nineteenth century, were the watchwords of a nation that was only now emerging from the shadow of defeat in the Franco-German War. Some of the conditions imposed by the Treaty of Frankfort had been onerous enough: the huge indemnity of one billion dollars; and the triumphal German entry into Paris in March 1871 when two Prussian and one Bavarian army corps, led by the Duke of Coburg, the Grand Duke of Mecklenburg, and three princes, marched past the Arc de Triomphe and down the Champs-Élysées, "on a day," noted a London *Daily News* correspondent, "kept throughout Paris as one of mourning."[4] But what had never been forgiven or forgotten was the wresting of Alsace and part of Lorraine from France. After the cession, France's Republican leader, Gambetta, kept in his study a figure of captive Alsace as a reminder. And in the heart of Paris, among the twelve seated figures around the obelisk in the Place de la Concorde, that representing Strasbourg, capital of Alsace, was draped in black—to remain so until the city's deliverance in 1918.

Alsace, easternmost province of France, bounded by the Rhine and the Vosges Mountains, and its northwesterly neighbor Lorraine, had had a checkered history. They originally belonged to neither France nor Germany but were long fought over by both. Alsace had been won from Germany at the Peace of Westphalia in 1648 and Lorraine had finally become French at the Peace of Vienna in 1735. In annexing them in 1871 Bismarck was depriving France of her natural frontier, the Rhine. He was also bringing under German rule three million Frenchmen, and acquiring the two great fortress towns of Strasbourg and Metz. In 1870 King William of Prussia told Empress Eugénie, wife of Napoleon III,

---

2 Ibid., Vol. III, p. 148.
3 Ibid.
4 *The Daily News* (London): *Correspondence of the War between Germany and France, 1870–1871* (1871), p. 583.

that Germany had seized Alsace-Lorraine solely in order to be better prepared to resist France in the event of a further attack. William might have added that the departure point of his own forces—should they launch an assault on France—was correspondingly pushed forward.

Weeping deputies at the National Assembly at Bordeaux in 1870 protested against the cession. Bismarck had gained two French provinces but he had lit an unquenchable flame in French hearts. Alsace-Lorraine acquired a sacred aura, feeding the dangerous urge to *revanche*. One of the basic tenets of the League of Patriots, formed in 1882, was that what had been lost by arms could only be retaken by arms. When the statesman Jules Ferry suggested to Paul Déroulède, the League's founder, that it might be best to forget the loss and seek compensation elsewhere, Déroulède cried: "So! I have lost two children, and you are offering me twenty servants!"[5] The grievance burned on into the twentieth century, keeping alive a sense of mission. "For forty years," wrote Alexandre Millerand, the Minister of War, in 1913, "the army's leaders have worn the mourning of the defeats they have suffered, and for forty years their spirit has been directed towards a single aim: to be worthy . . . to regain the place of their ancestors —to be ready."[6]

Germany's triumph in 1870 had been sealed by the proclamation of the German Empire in the Hall of Mirrors at Versailles. To remind France, and the world, of her military prowess, she had raised a mighty monument in a romantic Wagnerian setting. On the wooded, vine-clad slopes of the Niederwald, high above the Rhine opposite Bingen, stood the giant figure of *Germania,* with Imperial crown and laurel-wreathed sword, "erected," stated Baedeker, "in commemoration of the unanimous rising of the German people and the foundation of the new German Empire."[7] An elaborate bas-relief, signifying *"Die Wacht am Rhein"* was adorned with the image of the Emperor on horseback, surrounded by princes, generals, and representative troops—Prussian infantry-

---

[5] J. and J. Tharaud: *La Vie et la Mort de Déroulède* (1925), p. 26.
[6] A. Millerand: *Pour la Défense Nationale* (1913), p. 409.
[7] K. Baedeker: *The Rhine from Rotterdam to Constance* (1900), p. 135.

men, Bavarian fusiliers, Rhenish grenadiers and cuirassiers, Saxon sharpshooters, Hessian chasseurs, Baden dragoons, Brunswich hussars and the rest; "all Germany in arms!"[8] declared Houssaye. In the foreground, next to the Emperor, stood the two architects of victory, Bismarck and the Prussian Chief of Staff, Von Moltke.

The grandiose *Germania* celebrated a militarily well-deserved victory. France was defeated because she faced a highly perfected and efficient war machine with an army unprepared and poorly organized. For three years Germany had had detailed plans ready for the invasion of France. The enthusiasm of the Paris crowds who, on the outbreak of war, shouted *"À Berlin!"* and *"Vive la guerre!"* was not enough. Nor were the doughty fighting qualities of France's professional troops. People and Parliament had refused to take the German threat seriously. Well-meaning bodies like the League of Peace and the Peace Union blinded Frenchmen to the true situation. In 1867 Gambetta even demanded the suppression of standing armies. The pleas of Marshal Niel, Minister of War, for army reforms, including universal service, were ignored. The Chamber rang with woolly, idealistic appeals. "The strongest nation is the one that can disarm,"[9] said one member. Another asserted: "Armies, mountains, rivers, have had their day. The real frontier is patriotism. The *levée en masse* is adequate for everything."[1]

These fine theories were blown sky-high in the smoke of Sedan and the war's other reverses. At the Inquiry into the defeat ordered by the National Assembly, General Chanzy, one of the French commanders, said of the levies hastily raised as reinforcements: "Ah, the *Gardes Mobiles*. They were perfect soldiers, but they were not *encadrés!*"[2] For war in the 1870's the *levée en masse* of patriotic, untrained citizens, the glory of the revolutionary struggles, was an anachronism. Even the French five-year system for regulars was inferior to the Prussian two-year system; for while the Prussians made allowance for reserves to supplement their first-line troops, the French did not. Hence they had no trained formations to fall back on once their main force was committed.

---

[8] H. Houssaye: *La Patrie Guerrière* (1913), p. 318.
[9] Ibid., p. 384.
[1] Ibid.
[2] Millerand: *Défense Nationale*, p. 8.

The "Nation in Arms" idea, so stirringly proclaimed in the decree of 1793, was a noble gesture but it lacked one vital element: conscription. The conscription that was introduced five years later soon fell into abeyance. "The greatest misfortune that could happen to our people," Marshal Niel told the Assembly in 1869, "would be to suffer an outrage in a state of unreadiness."[3] Only in the bleak aftermath of the war was this truth appreciated. In defeat, France looked at last to her army. At Longchamps, in July 1871, Marshal MacMahon, the French Commander in Chief, led 120,000 troops in a great march attended by Louis Adolphe Thiers, chief of the Provisional Executive, and watched by a huge, applauding crowd. Afterward, as the two men embraced, Thiers is said to have openly wept. One year later the newly created Third Republic introduced universal conscription: five years' service for all able-bodied men. "France had risen again," wrote a later historian. "She never rose more buoyant, more hopeful, more resolute than from the war of 1870."[4]

Basic differences between Right and Left, on the nature and make-up of the army, seemed happily resolved. The Right (which included traditionally conservative army opinion) had distrusted conscription because it armed the people. Thiers told a friend that he wanted a professional army, not a compulsory service that would arm every Socialist with a rifle. Moreover, the army held that soldiers could not be properly trained in a few years and had little faith in conscript reserves. The Left, on the other hand, suspicious of military *coups d'état,* pledged itself uncompromisingly to a people's army, the sure means of unity in national defense. From Thiers to the twentieth-century Socialist leader Jean Jaurès, the issue was never quite dormant. "Between these soldiers of the truly popular army, and the people," wrote Jaurès on the eve of World War I, "between these officers—of whom a number are attached by many links to the common people—and the common people themselves, all conflict will appear as a scandal."[5] But after 1870 France needed more than hope and resolution. With Alsace-Lorraine gone—including the great fortress of Metz—she needed a

---

[3] J. de la Tour: *Le Maréchal Niel* (1912), p. 289.
[4] V. Duruy: *A Short History of France,* trans. M. Carey (1927), Vol. II, p. 524.
[5] J. Jaurès: *L'Armée Nouvelle* (1915), p. 361.

new defensive bulwark in the east. "There is no hiding the fact that now, if there is a European power exposed to invasion, it is France,"[6] declared the Director of Engineering at the Ministry of War. The director's name was General Seré de Rivières. He was now to do for France what Vauban had done in the time of Louis XIV, and what André Maginot was to attempt in 1930. Commissioned by the École Supérieure de Défense to provide a fortified barrier against attack from the east and north, he planned two main eastern defensive zones, covering 130 of the 170 miles of the common frontier with Germany, from Belfort to Épinal, and Toul to Verdun, taking advantage of the heights of the Meuse and the Moselle; and in the north, along the Belgian border, a line Maubeuge-Valenciennes-Lille. In Germany, the Emperor took uneasy note of this bastion guarding the heart of France. Even Von Moltke now suggested that caution would be necessary before Germany contemplated staging an offensive. For General de Rivières, his eastern barrier remained a lifelong preoccupation. On his deathbed he murmured with his last breath: *"La frontière . . . la frontière!"*[7]

Napoleon had asserted that a fortified frontier offered an inferior army protection against a superior army, and gave it opportunities to attack with advantage. De Rivières had left in his eastern defense chain two openings, the Charmes Gap and the Verdun Gap, to channel an invading force that could then be counterattacked; or conceivably to allow the egress of French troops moving to the offensive. But for two decades and more, "offensive" was a concept rigorously ruled out of the army's operational plans. It was the fortifications in the Rivières Line, not the gaps, that reflected the French Army's function in relation to Republican France. Despite the warlike urgings of patriots like Gambetta and Déroulède, the fact was that the French Army—deprived of its splendid natural frontier in the east, facing a victor with a larger and more rapidly growing population, and fully occupied in reorganizing itself—was committed, psychologically and strategically, to the defensive.

The famous French *élan vital,* expressed in the death-or-glory heroism of the massed bayonet charge, was in eclipse. The trend

---

[6] F. Engerand: *Le Secret de la Frontière* (1918), p.132.
[7] Ibid., p. 135.

was shown in an Infantry Regulation for 1875, which stressed the preponderant importance of fire and the consequent need for advancing front-line troops to adopt open order. It extended to the army maneuvers of 1879, on which Captain (later General) Cardot reported that, in contrast to the Prussian infantry, the French were concentrating on using every available piece of cover to avoid losses. They no longer valued, he said, the spirit, energy and boldness that were vital for decisive actions.

ii

Shorn of its imperial glamour, France's military machine became *"La Grande Muette"*[8] of President Grévy's era (1879–87). But the new Ministry of War in the rue Saint-Dominique, with its thousand rooms, bespoke a new professionalism. Senior staff training took on a fresh lease of life when the École Supérieure de Guerre replaced the old École d'État-Major. Situated in the mansion where Napoleon received his military instruction, the École was to become the fount of French military theory and doctrine. At first it founded its teaching on the lessons of the late war, especially the strength of the firepower that had caused such bloody losses at Metz. Later it was to range farther back in its quest for the true principles. "Its claim to base a 'doctrine' on the analysis of past events," wrote General Charles de Gaulle, "was to a great extent arbitrary, for the interpretation of history and the value of action are both dependent on non-recurring contingencies."[9] The historian Francis Engerand saw in the École "the disposition to view the battle from an office and not on the ground," but conceded that it "prompted serious-minded spirits towards the study of administrative tasks hitherto regarded as somewhat dull."[1] But it was not only the studious officers of the École de Guerre who typified the changing army. A revival was running through the whole officer corps.

In camp and barracks, officers took up military studies with an enthusiasm unknown before. In the days of the Second Empire,

---

[8] Houssaye: *La Patrie,* p. 325.
[9] C. de Gaulle: *France and Her Army,* trans. F. L. Dash (1945), p. 78.
[1] Engerand: *Le Secret,* p. 139.

when polish was more important than brains, Marshal MacMahon had threatened to stop the promotion of any officer who stooped to writing a book. Now, new service journals were appearing and, in a messroom atmosphere that invited criticism and discussion, there was an increasing flow of military works by officers. The graduates of Saint-Cyr and the Polytechnique even began to look different. In place of the pointed imperial beard they were affecting a sweeping mustache *à la gauloise,* "the moustache," as one writer claims, "of *the revenge* which Frenchmen, feeling and wishing themselves to be Gallic, mean to take on their German conquerors."[2] Inspired by the mustache of the ancient Gallic warrior Vercingetorix, it became the pride of every ambitious officer —including the young Lieutenant Philippe Pétain, who adopted it as a twenty-year-old cadet at Saint-Cyr. Less luxuriant, the mustache survived upon the faces of senior officers in 1914, a continuing symbol of Gallic revenge.

Change of another kind was affecting the officer corps. Gambetta had claimed that the army stood aloof from politics; and later General Boulanger, on becoming Minister of War, was to issue a circular banning political activity in the army. But in practice, the army was inseparable from politics. Republicanism, in breaking down old social barriers, was enabling its supporters to fill administrative and official positions hitherto largely reserved for aristocratic and conservative families. Debarred from such posts in the new regime, the members of these families were increasingly seeking careers in the army, thus strengthening the Rightist element in the officer corps. The antirepublican bias was increased by the prevailing "co-optive" system of promotion, which depended on family connections and political and religious ties. Time was to sweep this privilege away. After the notorious Dreyfus Affair a War Minister, General André, stated bluntly that promotion was in the hands of Parliament.

But now, army and nation were firmly united in the noble concept of *La Patrie.* In a sense not true before, the army *was* the nation. Every year some 140,000 young Frenchmen were reporting at the depots for military service. In their double-breasted blue tunics and baggy red trousers they were being disciplined,

---

[2] J. Plumyène: *Pétain* (1964), p. 10.

drilled, instructed, marched across garrison parade grounds at
the regulation 115 paces a minute with their new-style black knap-
sacks and Gras rifles (a modification of the famous 1866 chasse-
pot), recruits from the four quarters of France being inducted into
their Republican duty of national defense. It was a novel experience
for France, and thinking men, conscious of the army's new place
in society, wondered if these conscripts were being properly in-
doctrinated. The right person to do this was seen to be the regimental officer. "Compulsory service, which passes the entire nation
through the hands of the officer," wrote an anonymous contributor
to the *Revue des Deux Mondes* in 1891, "has enhanced in the
highest degree his role of educator."[3] For this, the officers themselves needed to be educated, said the writer, so that they could
"participate . . . in the general movement which induced en-
lightened youth to understand better the social role reserved for
its activity in the evolution of modern society."[4]

But France's basic problem was to turn civilians into good
soldiers. To Republican patriots like Léon Gambetta, Jules Ferry,
and Paul Bert it was a question less of social role than of military
spirit. Fearing that universal service might endanger the old martial
traditions, they had pressed for paramilitary teaching in the schools.
They held that every child should be imbued with the great patriotic
ideals. Ferry wanted the soldier's crusading mission stressed. School
military instruction, Bert maintained, was the strongest means of
preserving moral standards. To this end the Minister of Public
Instruction formed school battalions and issued patriotic literature
to schools. Classroom walls were adorned with war pictures and
portraits of great soldiers. A Ligue de l'Enseignement en Sainte-
Alliance du Patriotisme was founded, with the motto "By Book and
Sword."

Meanwhile, the black-draped figure of Strasbourg stood in
the Place de la Concorde as a perpetual reminder of France's
humiliation. Impotent in the face of Germany's strength, she
patiently nursed the thought of *revanche*. For a brief period popular imagination was caught by the colorful, ambitious General

---

[3] "Le Rôle Social de l'Officier," in *Revue des Deux Mondes*
(1891), p. 459.
[4] Ibid.

Georges Boulanger, former War Minister and army reformer whose calls for a war of revenge and the recovery of Alsace-Lorraine made him a public hero and who, as a deputy for Paris in 1889, appeared about to stage a *coup d'état* that would make him dictator of France. (Fleeing from a charge of high treason, Boulanger committed suicide in Brussels in 1891.) France's grievance continued to fester like a running sore in the body politic of peaceful Europe. Across the Rhine, Bismarck declined to ease matters by granting the lost provinces full autonomy. He saw Alsace-Lorraine as a buffer against a nation bent on retaliation. He also viewed with concern France's swift economic recovery and the potential threat of her growing army. Determined to isolate her in Europe by depriving her of Continental allies, he hoped she might derive consolation from colonial expansion. With Tunis in mind, he told the German ambassador in Paris, Prince Hohenlohe, that "we ought to wish that France succeeds in Africa. We should be pleased that she should find satisfaction elsewhere than on the Rhine."[5]

Bismarck was unwittingly benefiting the French Army. The rough outposts of the colonial empire that France proceeded to build in Africa and China provided a magnificent training ground for officers. Colonial service became a sure road to promotion. In the decade before World War I senior Home Army appointments were increasingly filled by colonial officers, and in 1914 most of the leading generals from commander in chief downward —Joffre himself, Gallieni, Mangin, Guillaumat, Franchet d'Esperey, and others—had soldiered in the overseas stations.

At home, by contrast, the keen and dedicated spirit that inspired officers in the seventies and eighties was wilting in the lengthening years of peace. Only the eternally guarded eastern marches of the Vosges offered any hope of action. Regimental officers languished in dull garrison towns, performing meaningless routines. Pay was meager and promotion slow, owing to the small turnover of officers; and the prestige of the officer corps sank low enough for a humble postal clerk to declare: "Officer? What a rotten job. No liberty, no money. I prefer my pen-pushing!"[6] Henry Houssaye summed up the mood of the younger officers around

---

[5] J. Bainville: *Bismarck et la France* (1907), p. 70.
[6] Houssaye: *La Patrie*, p. 328.

1900: "They reflect on their sterile efforts and fruitless labours.
. . . They still love their profession and persevere in it . . . but
this is not the passionate love their elders had."[7]

The fall in military prestige was measured by decreasing
officer recruitment and re-enlistment of N.C.O.'s. At Saint-Cyr
alone, in the fourteen years to 1911, the intake fell by sixty per
cent, a drop similar to that among N.C.O.'s from 1900 to 1911.
The days when the army was the glory of a patriotic nation seemed
past. A long peace might be one cause: another was the Dreyfus
Affair, which scandalized the country and catastrophically damaged
the army's reputation.

In 1894 a Jewish officer, Captain Alfred Dreyfus, was convicted—on the flimsiest evidence—of offering military secrets to
the Germans and was sentenced to life imprisonment on Devil's
Island. The case roused furious controversy between those who
claimed that a grave injustice had been done and those who maintained that the honor of the army must be defended at all costs.
Liberals and Republicans ranged themselves behind Dreyfus, and
Clericals and Monarchists supported the army. Only when the
leakage of secrets continued after the imprisonment of Dreyfus
did the weakness of the army's case become apparent. In 1898
another officer, Major Esterhazy, was charged and court-martialed,
but acquitted. This led the writer Émile Zola into violent protest.
In the newspaper *L'Aurore* he published his famous open letter,
"J'Accuse," addressed to the President of the Republic. Prosecuted
for libel at the instance of the Ministry of War, Zola was found
guilty and sentenced to a year's imprisonment. Amid intensifying
dissatisfaction and increasingly insistent calls for revision of the
case, the head of the Army Intelligence, Colonel Hubert Henry,
confessed to forging documents in order to incriminate Dreyfus,
was arrested and committed suicide in his cell. After a retrial the
army authorities still refused to exculpate Dreyfus, merely reducing
his sentence to ten years. Now, however, the President, Émile
Loubet, himself intervened to quash the sentence and release
Dreyfus. But the army kept up its vendetta against him, until finally
in 1906 he was completely exonerated on the evidence of newly
discovered documents. Not only did this unsavory episode—with

---

[7] Ibid., p. 326.

its ugly taint of anti-Semitism—bring the army into a disrepute that took a long time to live down; by discrediting the Clericals and Monarchists and allying the Socialists and Radicals in a common cause, it served to strengthen the Third Republic.

Paradoxically, another factor in the army's decline was the Franco-Russian Alliance, completed in 1894 with a military agreement for mutual assistance in the event of an attack on either power. The Triple Alliance of Germany, Austria-Hungary, and Italy was now faced by a Dual Alliance that made Germany look east as well as west. Whether or not France was to enjoy a new security, Bismarck's aim to isolate her was defeated. The idea of such an alliance was not universally popular. When Déroulède asked the radical ex-Communard Henri Rochefort to write an article advocating it, Rochefort protested that this would mean proposing union with an "autocrat"[8] and denying his whole past. But the magnificent review at Châlons, which celebrated the alliance, was greeted with fervent enthusiasm. "In the crowd, among the troops," wrote Houssaye, "passed a breath unknown for thirty years. . . . In the Russian Alliance they acclaimed something more than a buckler."[9]

But patriotism thrives on the sense of national danger. With the German threat seemingly minimized, Gambetta no longer stirred French hearts so powerfully. The old "bourgeois" nationalism was confronted by a potential new rival, the Russian export of international Marxism, which preached that the only war worth fighting was the class war. Fresh preoccupations and ideas were weakening the memories of 1870. Under the impact of material prosperity and a feeling of increased security the traditional ardor for *La Patrie* cooled. In a rejection of old values, mild antipatriotism and antimilitarism reared their heads. *"La Patrie, cela n'existe pas!"* blurted out a bearded student in the Latin quarter to the astonished André Siegfried.[1] The Ligue de l'Enseignement suppressed its patriotic motto. There was a move to banish pictures of great soldiers from school classrooms. One teacher arranged with his publisher to expunge war illustrations from his *History of France,* and a scholastic editor refused to reprint a book by the

---

[8] Tharaud: *Déroulède,* p. 47.
[9] Houssaye: *La Patrie,* p. 387.
[1] A. Siegfried: *France: A Study in Nationality* (1930), p. 50.

Republican Paul Bert, declaring, "We mustn't talk about patriotism."[2] But in one stronghold at least the martial past was sacrosanct. In a modest room in the Invalides, the newly formed Musée de l'Armée displayed the "glorious souvenirs of France's ancient armies,"[3] organized by a devoted general.

Russia's recent war record made the military value of the alliance doubtful. In any case, the General Staff could not rightly afford to discount the growing power of Germany. In 1890 Germany's population, equal in 1872 to that of France, exceeded France's 38 million by 12 million. France's policy of maintaining parity between her army and that of Germany entailed a proportionately greater strain on her manpower, and her reduction of military service from five to three years in 1889 increased her disadvantage. The widening gap was such that in 1896 France's "effectives" numbered 505,000 to Germany's 550,000. In Germany the Emperor himself carefully watched over the army (retiring 546 generals in seven years), while in Republican France the General Staff had to contend with 16 War Ministers in eighteen years. Without a continuity of policy the army suffered. Whereas Germany's war budget was steadily rising, France's was diminishing. In 1897 (the year after Russia's General Dragomirov had admiringly watched the army maneuvers), the *rapporteur* of the war budget gravely announced to the Chamber: "We are spending hardly more, that is relatively much less, in 1897, to maintain 558,000 men than ten years ago to maintain 464,000."[4]

It was a situation that clearly demanded continued reliance on defense, a waiting strategy firmly anchored to the Rivières Line. But "always in France sentiment dominated reason," declared the historian Engerand. "Collective passions . . . give full play to the theorists, the dreamers. . . ."[5] The spirit of revenge could not be contained forever behind a defensive wall. Plan XVII, which launched the 1st and 2nd French Armies against Lorraine in August 1914, was no sudden strategic innovation. It had its roots in France's deep-seated military pride, and in particular in the

---

[2] Houssaye: *La Patrie*, p. 393.
[3] E. Simond: *Histoire de la Troisième République* (1913–1921), Vol. I, p. 415.
[4] Ibid., p. 395.
[5] Engerand: *Le Secret*, p. 207.

volonté of men like the young lieutenant Ferdinard Foch. Witnessing a show of Bavarian brutality in German-occupied Metz just after the Franco-German War, Foch made a solemn resolution: "Alsace and Lorraine must and shall be retaken; France must not remain a conquered country; I must be one of its liberators."[6]

Before Foch arrived at the École de Guerre to expound his offensive doctrine in the later nineties, the offensive concept was already established in staff circles. Other military minds had revolted against the fortress mentality that denied the greatness of Napoleon and the best of French fighting tradition. The pendulum had in fact swung from prudent caution to extreme rashness. An Infantry Regulation of 1887 ordained that brave and energetically led infantry could move under the heaviest fire, even against well-defended trenches, and capture them. The gauntlet was squarely thrown down by the military theorist Captain Gilbert, who (in his *Military Studies*, 1892) asserted that France was beaten in 1870 because she abandoned Napoleonic methods and failed to take the offensive at the start. Gilbert was crippled by paralysis, and had not long to live. In his fiery advocacy of the offensive he strangely resembled Colonel d'Alenson, who, dying of consumption, egged on his chief, General Nivelle, to the disastrous Aisne assault of 1917.

Brighter spirits in the École de Guerre jumped at Gilbert's ideas. Defensive was forthwith discarded in favor of offensive doctrine. The École switched for its inspiration to the Napoleonic campaigns. Movement, maneuver, the destruction of the enemy became its guiding principles. A recent trend toward the *méthode expectative,* which allowed the enemy the initiative and relied on careful exploitation of opportunity, was reversed. "The defensive was admitted," explained a military commentator, General Fonville, "only if it could subsequently lead to a well-prepared and potentially successful offensive."[7] "*La force morale* was all," wrote Engerand. "The fortress theory was replaced by the dogma of '*corps humaines.*' "[8]

The precise date of the "replacement" can be put at 1899, when the War Minister, De Freycinet, ordered the stoppage of

---

[6] A. de Maricourt: *Foch* (1920), p. 118.
[7] Engerand: *Le Secret,* p. 142.
[8] Ibid., p. 147.

maintenance (on the grounds of expense) on the forts of the Rivières Northern Line, guarding the Belgian frontier. One voice was raised in protest—and dire prophecy. "With our tendency to destroy our northern defences," said General Béziat, a colleague of De Rivières, "the violation of Belgian neutrality is no longer merely a rational possibility, it becomes a fatal certainty (*elle devient fatale*)."[9]

Forts abandoned, army theorists dazzled by "offensive" dreams: in the face of France's real need for a defensive strategy to bolster her geographical weakness and counter superior German strength, French military policy was sowing dangerous seeds. And the "offensive" champions themselves gravely underrated the new master of the battlefield: firepower. From the eighties onward, weapon after weapon was introduced which gave the defensive increasing advantage. Smokeless powder, the Lebel magazine rifle, above all the machine gun, loaded the dice more heavily against advancing troops. The devastating superiority of the machine gun over the rifle was demonstrated in the Russo-Japanese War. A French General Staff report to the War Ministry conceded that machine guns had literally mown down the attackers. The Hotchkiss machine gun, a French invention, was dismissed by a senior officer as ineffective, and for years ignored by the Directorate of Artillery. Gruesomely nicknamed by the Japanese "the devil's watering can" and by the German General von der Goltz "the hyena of the battlefield," in France it was called the "coffee grinder."[1]

In 1897 France produced her famous 75-mm. gun, the answer to the German 77-mm., firing up to three times as many rounds per minute with a faster muzzle velocity. But a decade later a General Staff spokesman told the Chamber of Deputies, concerned about German heavy artillery, "thank God we have none. French strength depends upon the lightness of her cannon."[2]

iii

Amid all the theorizing and misconceptions, the army still awaited its true doctrinal prophet. The mantle fell upon the

---

[9] Ibid., p. 397.
[1] Ibid., p. 233.
[2] De Gaulle: *France*, p. 84.

shoulders of the vigorous, volatile southerner Lieutenant-Colonel Ferdinand Foch, who at forty-one became a professor at the École de Guerre. Foch had passed through the Polytechnique, won rapid promotion in the artillery and shone as a student at the École, from which he graduated in fourth place. The vow he had made at Metz twenty years before, now entered into the spirit of his lectures. Covering the battles of Napoleon and the war of 1870, he electrified his audiences with his brilliant analysis. General Messimy, then one of his students, tells how, against all the traditions of the École, his listeners burst into applause after his lectures. Foch's articles of faith can be summed up as: initiative, flexibility, *sûreté, volonté*. He claimed that victory was a matter of will. The pith of his teaching was contained in the foreword of his *Principles of War*: "The offensive of manoeuvre overcomes all resistance. The passive defensive cannot avoid defeat."[3]

On his appointment as the École's director, Foch's ascendancy was complete. But one heretical professor dared to express other views. A little-known lieutenant-colonel, Philippe Pétain, put the case for the defensive. The cautious, practical Pétain, born of northern peasant stock, was the antithesis of Foch. Coldly realistic, he placed material above moral factors, held that the arbiter of modern war was firepower, and based his military teaching accordingly. A French general, De Négrier, had prophesied that with quick-firing weapons there would be more difference between the next war and that of 1870 than between 1870 and the wars of the First Empire. In Pétain he had a firm supporter. Years later, on being admitted to the Académie Française, Pétain delivered a final thrust at Foch. "Without regard for the evolution that modernity imposes on war," he declared, "the army concludes that the attack is the primordial instrument of strategy. Along with his generation, Foch was influenced by these ideas."[4]

Pétain's arguments had no effect. He was addressing officers intoxicated by a headier doctrine. When military service was reduced from three to two years in 1905, General Pédoya protested to the Chamber that the defensive was an ineptitude and that the best form of defense was attack. The peril of this attitude was

---

[3] Plumyène: *Pétain*, p. 14.
[4] G. Suarez: *Le Maréchal Pétain* (1940), p. 17.

seen when, in the hands of a fanatic, the whole offensive concept ran out of control. In 1911 Colonel Loyseau de Grandmaison, chief of the Operations Branch of the General Staff, addressed two conferences on "The Engagement of Large Units." "It is always necessary in battle," he said, "to manage to do something which would be *impossible* for men in a state of cold blood. For example, movement under fire."[5] He asserted that, to overcome the enemy, "there is no other means than immediate and total attack."[6] He dismissed his audience with the exhortation: "Let us go to excess, and perhaps even this will not be enough."[7] This was nothing less than the *offensive à outrance,* a suicidal rush toward the enemy, without Foch's *sûreté* and exposed to the lethal effects of modern defensive firepower. Startled officers emerged from the conference room approving and otherwise. Among the latter was the outspoken General Lanrezac, who spluttered, "Attack, let us attack. . . . It is crazy!"[8]

But on the General Staff, and in the École and the new Centre des Hautes Études Militaires (a senior offshoot of the École), De Grandmaison's thesis acted like a revelation. It was forthwith embodied in official doctrine, to leave its fateful impress on Plan XVII and the *Field Regulations* of 1913, which, said Engerand, "apply Napoleonic methods without Napoleon."[9]

"The conduct of war," the Regulations began, "is dominated by the necessity to give a vigorously offensive impulse to operations. . . . The French Army, returning to its traditions, from now on acknowledges no operational law but the offensive."[1] The Regulations stressed that battle, once engaged, should be pressed to the limit; and that the defeat of the enemy could not be achieved without heavy losses. Attack must be violent and relentless, and demanded continued effort and extreme energy. It was emphasized that the weapon that overcame final resistance was the bayonet. The defensive was dismissed as secondary to the offensive. Forts

---

[5] L. de Grandmaison: *Deux Conférences, Février 1911* (1912), p. 69.
[6] Ibid.
[7] Ibid.
[8] H. Contamine: *La Revanche, 1871–1914* (1957), p. 178.
[9] Engerand: *Le Secret,* p. 226.
[1] Ibid., p. 228.

and fortifications were relegated to the role of assisting the operations of the armies in the field. Artillery was no longer to prepare an attack, but to destroy obstacles in the path of the attacking
troops.

The European situation in 1913 suggested that de Grandmaison's principles might soon be put to the test. Amid sharpening
international rivalries, mounting tensions and crises from Agadir
to the Balkans, Europe was steadily moving toward war. Once
again France faced the risk of conflict with Germany, a nation with
an unsurpassed army and a population now over a third greater
than her own. Stiffening herself to meet the threat, she extended
military service to three years, not without opposition from Left-
wingers like Jean Jaurès, who still dreamed of a national militia,
fit to take the field after a brief training. In the deepening emergency, France's slumbering patriotism was reawakened. "*La Patrie*
is not a worn-out notion," declared Jaurès. "I have always been
sure that the common people would not subscribe to a doctrine
of . . . national servitude."[2] Millerand, War Minister in 1912,
sought to revive the army's old glamour with reviews and torch-
light parades. New encouragement was given to the Societés de
Préparation Militaire, physical-culture clubs for pre-military training, which by 1913 contained 732,000 members. With a patriotic
flourish Millerand gave these the motto: "*La France avant Tout!*"[3]

In girding herself for war, France experienced all the usual
difficulties of a democracy and, in addition, had to contend with
French character. "If the Frenchman is . . . a warrior," wrote the
historian V. Margueritte, "he is in no degree a soldier . . . nor even,
at heart, belligerent."[4] After forty years of peace, *revanche* was
no longer the same burning issue; but there was a basic toughness
in the peace-loving Frenchman. "When called upon to defend their
country," said André Siegfried in reference to these years, "the
people respond to a man, and we can ask what we will."[5] In eastern
France, where four corps were now on permanent guard, the sense
of urgency had never lessened. Describing life in the frontier gar-

---

2 Jaurès: *L'Armée,* p. 361.
3 Millerand: *Défense Nationale,* p. viii.
4 V. Margueritte: *Au Bord du Gouffre* (1919), p. 44.
5 Siegfried: *France,* p. 49.

risons, Henry Houssaye wrote: "The officers are exalted by the intensity of military existence that prevails there. The battalions and squadrons are always on a war footing." When a night alarm proves false, "more than one man is sorry, for it is in the hope of this moment that the troops have mounted guard on the frontier for so many long years."[6]

These men were not only fired by old memories, they still wore the time-honored *képi,* blue tunic, and red trousers of imperial days. While the British Army had accepted the realities of modern war by adopting khaki and the Germans were changing to field gray, in France the concession to ancient glories lingered on. When General Messimy, appointed War Minister in 1911, tried to make changes, he was opposed by press and Parliament. "To banish all that is colourful," protested the *rapporteur* of the war budget, "all that gives the soldier his gay and spirited appearance . . . is to go against both French taste and military needs."[7] From another War Minister, Étienne, came the heart-felt plea: "Suppress the *pantalon rouge?* No! The *pantalon rouge* is France!"[8] Not until the eve of World War I was prejudice overcome and *horizon bleu* adopted.

Messimy's critical eye picked out another anachronism: the number of elderly, unfit officers clinging to senior posts. Determined to retire them, he appointed eight as umpires in the 1911 maneuvers, with strict orders not to use cars, which left them to the tender mercies of the horse. "You'll send him to the grave!" complained a friend of the chief umpire to Messimy, who replied that he only wished to send him to the reserve.[9]

A still graver defect was France's lack of heavy artillery. Despite increased credits from 1905 onward, French armament expenditure was still only half that of Germany. Political shortsightedness was partly to blame; but from the end of the Russo-Japanese War (1905) French artillery chiefs steadfastly discouraged the adoption of anything heavier than the 75-mm. gun. Against Germany's plentiful 150-mm. and 105-mm. howitzers, France had none; and she could oppose the German 210-mm. howitzer and long-

---

6 Houssaye: *La Patrie,* p. 401.
7 A. Messimy: *Mes Souvenirs* (1937), p. 118.
8 Ibid., p. 119.
9 Ibid., p. 94.

barreled field guns only with thirty-year-old, short-ranged fortress guns and a few 155-mm. pieces. In his brief tenancy of the War Ministry, General Messimy fought a frustrating battle to correct the situation; but in January 1914, the Inspector-General of Artillery had to admit that as regards siege and garrison artillery, nothing had been done for the past forty years.

Looming over all these matters was the most important problem of all: the choice of a commander in chief to head the army in the event of war. Such was the state of the High Command in June 1911 that the Comte de Tréveneue complained to the Senate, "at the present moment the army is headless, without a leader . . ."[1] General Michel, who as vice-president of the Conseil Supérieur de Guerre, was commander-in-chief designate, did not inspire Messimy's confidence, who found him lacking in authority. But other factors were against Michel. Alone among the General Staff, he foresaw the probable direction of the main German assault on France. Germany would bypass Lorraine, Luxembourg, and the eastern Franco-Belgian frontier, he predicted, and make an enveloping sweep southwards through western Belgium. To counter this he proposed a defensive plan which involved the massive use of reserves. On both these counts the unfortunate Michel fell foul of the powerful De Grandmaison school, which hated reserves— as lacking the offensive dash of active troops—almost as much as it abhorred a defensive strategy. "Michel is a national danger,"[2] one of his colleagues on the Conseil de Guerre told Messimy. "He is no leader,"[3] said another. The opinions clinched Messimy's decision to look elsewhere for a commander in chief.

The three most likely candidates were all colonial veterans: General Gallieni, academic-looking in his pince-nez, famous as Governor-General of Madagascar; the small, popular, fierce-mustached General Pau, whose mutilated arm testified to service in 1870; and General Joffre, the eupeptic and imperturbable Engineer. Messimy first interviewed Gallieni, who declined and proposed Pau or Joffre. Pau in his turn was ready to accept pro-

[1] Ibid., p. 73.
[2] Ibid., p. 75.
[3] Ibid.

vided he could choose the generals under him. Unable to agree to this, Messimy then summoned Joffre, who asked for twenty-four hours to consider, and then accepted. But he too imposed a condition. "I ask you to give me as deputy General de Castelnau, who has worked for a long time on the General Staff," he said.[4] Reluctantly Messimy consented, and in 1911 Joseph Jacques Césaire Joffre, aged fifty-nine, the cooper's son from the Pyrenees, was elevated to lead the French Army in war.

Portly and avuncular, Joffre gave a reassuring impression of dependability and solidity. After service mainly in Indochina, West Africa, and Madagascar, he had returned home in 1900 to appointments that culminated in his nomination to the Conseil Supérieur de Guerre in 1910. As an expert in fortification and railway building, his actual soldiering experience consisted of one colonial expedition, and he had no knowledge of higher command or military studies. Politically he was a "safe" man, being a good Republican. He himself summed up his qualifications when he told General Messimy, "I believe I have a methodical mind and the capacity for hard work, and I am familiar with the general organisation of the army."[5] His appointment as commander in chief well suited the "Young Turks" of the De Grandmaison faction. In the words of the historian Liddell Hart, "he . . . proved a solid shield behind which subtler brains could direct French military policy."[6] But to Joffre can at least be given the credit that while he gave the "offensive" planners their heads, he methodically proceeded to transform the army from a peace to a war footing.

The politicians were less helpful and clear-sighted. Having passed the three-year law in 1913, six weeks before the outbreak of war the Chamber was calling for a return to two-year service. Only the President, Raymond Poincaré, the Prime Minister, René Viviani, and a few others realized the true situation. In the early summer days of 1914 the French people seemed oblivious to the approaching war. Even to most of the official world of Paris the first real hint of crisis came only at the end of June. On Sunday, the twenty-eighth, fateful news struck a chill of presentiment into

---

[4] Ibid., p. 77.
[5] Ibid.
[6] B. H. Liddell Hart: *Reputations* (1928), p. 19.

the glitter and gaiety of the Longchamps Races. In the afternoon sunshine the fashionable and elegant crowd strolled on the lawns, and a large gathering of ministers and members of the Diplomatic Corps packed the official stand, before the start of the fourth race. A messenger approached President Poincaré with a note. Poincaré looked at it and quickly passed it to Count Szecen, Ambassador to Her Apostolic Majesty. The Count read it, hesitated, and took hasty leave of the President. Very pale, he hurried from the stand without speaking. Soon the news was circulating that the Archduke Franz Ferdinand and his consort had been assassinated that morning at Sarajevo.

Five weeks later the French Army marched to war against Germany. It was an army badly handicapped by the mistakes of the General Staff, which had committed it to a fallacious strategic doctrine, misjudged German offensive intentions, underestimated German strength and ignored the need for heavy artillery. But on the other hand it was sustained by a morale and a patriotic feeling that had not been higher since the 1870's. *Revanche* at last acquired a reality and became a possibility. This was the climax of forty years' waiting and preparation. In a flight of French oratory that always rises to the great occasion the Prime Minister, Viviani, addressed the Chamber on August 2. "Now let us prove ourselves equal to the glorious memories of our History," he said, "let us face our destiny, let us be men and, standing erect once more, let us acclaim immortal France."[7]

---

[7] G. Samné: *Raymond Poincaré* (1933), p. 144.

Chapter 2

>>>>>>>>>>● <<<<<<<<<

[25]

THE TEST OF BLOOD,
1914–1918

"Their gaze seemed set in a vision of dread."

(General Pétain)

i

BEHIND THE FRENCH ARMY, as it went to war in August 1914, stood a nation signally unready for that war. After forty years of peace, in which preoccupation with the potential enemy and anticipations of an eventual clash were never absent, France was at the moment of emergency a divided country. She was torn by political dissension, social unrest, labor troubles, and strong defeatist and antimilitarist elements. But, as always, national danger proved a potent uniting factor. Superficially at least, as war broke out discord vanished overnight. Political parties sank their differences in a *Union Sacrée*, labor closed its ranks, antiwar agitation was silenced, and all conflicting interests were merged into a single-minded effort against the aggressor. *La Patrie* was menaced and 40 million Frenchmen rallied behind the tricolor. Viviani's government responded to the mood by withholding orders for the arrests of over 2,000 possible troublemakers listed in the famous police dossier, Carnet B, some of whom were suspected of planning to sabotage mobilization. The chief of the Sûreté, advising against the arrests, confidently predicted that the troops would follow the regimental bands. The optimism was justified, for of nearly four million men mobilized the defaulters numbered hardly more than one per cent, a tenth of the official estimate.

The war to which the army marched was the war of the "Plans"—Plan XVII *versus* the Schlieffen Plan (as modified by the younger Moltke). It was to be fought out by six German armies against five French armies and the B.E.F., over the broad arena of northern and eastern France in a vast, mutually offensive operation of movement and maneuver, the main weight of attack being in each case against the adversary's left wing. It was, as everyone thought, to be a short war, possibly over by Christmas. It was expected to be war on the classic pattern, with no great surprises and casualties not unduly heavy. That was the feeling at the beginning of August. Three months later, in mid-November, the firing died down on an entrenched battlefield stretching from the Channel to the Swiss border, stabilized at a cost of losses running into hundreds of thousands. The Plans had clashed, and both had ostensibly failed. The old conception of war had died with the bloody battles of the Marne; and across the Aisne the opposing armies confronted each other in deadlock, with winter coming on and the hopes of an early peace shattered.

For France the inspiration of Napoleon, the lessons of 1870, the doctrines of Colonel de Grandmaison all seemed irrelevant to the military problems now before her. Paris had nearly been captured; and with the enemy firmly lodged on French soil, a sixth of France's population in German hands, and much of her richest coal and other northern industrial and agricultural resources lost, she faced what could now only be a long war under huge handicaps. As 1914 closed, General Joffre gloomily reviewed the situation. "It was not enough that we had prevented the enemy winning the war," he recorded. "It was essential to achieve a complete victory over him. This was the heart-breaking problem which faced me."[1]

One by one, the prewar blunders and misjudgments of the French General Staff were coming home to roost: its disregard of warnings about Germany's offensive plans, abandonment of de Rivière's northern fortifications, disdain of heavy artillery, mistrust of reserves. This latter bias cost the French dear in the first weeks of the war, when the General Staff badly underestimated the use of reserves on the German right wing. And in the final months of 1914 another truth was apparent: the inadequacy of

---

[1] J. C. C. Joffre: *Memoirs,* trans. T. Bentley Mott (1932), Vol. I, p. 320.

the whole offensive theory taught in the lecture rooms of the École which, in essence, pitted human valor against metal. The attitude reflected the spirit of the French Army in 1914, a spirit nearer to 1870 than to the realities, already beginning to be so grimly evident, of twentieth-century war. The dash, reckless attacking tactics, and antiquated red-and-blue uniforms belonged to battles of the past, less dominated by withering firepower and the need for caution and cover. Even the studied gallantry of the officers had a romantic Old World flavor. "Let us swear that we will go to battle in parade uniform, with plume and white gloves!" cried a cadet at Saint-Cyr on the outbreak of war.[2] As a result many young Saint-Cyrions led the charge, and died, in their parade-ground finery. On the green and open battle grounds of France that autumn, not yet reduced to the stark, static wilderness of later years, the legendary *élan* of the French soldier had virtually its last chance to make a showing before the mud and disillusion of trench warfare closed in.

In a brief moment of triumph amid the setbacks of August 1914, historic aspirations were rewarded by the French re-entry into Alsace. But already the war was exacting a heavy toll in French casualties; and by the end of the year the total of killed, wounded and captured was 965,000. The officer corps was particularly hard hit. In August alone, officer casualties amounted to nearly 4,500, over 10 per cent of the total commissioned strength. Along with the casualties there was the shock to morale of an army trained to the offensive and confident in its efficiency suddenly finding itself forced into a headlong retreat. General Joffre wondered anxiously whether his troops would be able to hold out "under this terrible strain."[3] He had other worries too. There were weaknesses in command which he had to handle sternly. Within a month of the outbreak of war he had dismissed fifty generals, including two army commanders. Supporting his action, General Messimy telegraphed him from the War Ministry: "The only law in France is to win or to die."[4]

---

[2] P.-M. de la Gorce: *The French Army*, trans. Kenneth Douglas (1963), p. 93.
[3] Joffre: *Memoirs*, Vol. I, p. 189.
[4] Ibid., p. 186.

"Win or die." As autumn passed, it was clear that France's one alternative to defeat, or sole hope of victory, lay in a long war, which under modern conditions meant total industrial mobilization. In expectation of a short war, France had not begun to mobilize her industrial resources, which in any case were relatively weak; and in Germany she faced a nation which, after America, was the world's strongest industrial power, and whose industry had been ruthlessly geared to war. The loss of her northern coal mines, and the iron ore of the Briey Basin, greatly accentuated France's difficulties. And behind the production problem lay the specter of manpower inferiority, which had haunted her ever since 1870. Against Germany's population of 65 million, she mustered 39 million; and with nearly 4 million troops mobilized at the outset, she was making a proportionately greater call on her manpower than any other belligerent.

Though France's war organization was a task for the politicians and bureaucrats, the man to whom she looked now was Joffre, who bore immense prestige as victor of the Marne. He sat at his uncluttered desk at his headquarters at Vitry, uttering his characteristic expression of optimism, "*Ça va bien*," ate his regular meals with excellent appetite and slept his untroubled sleep, a leader who, if nothing else, inspired confidence in emergency.[5] His faith in the teachings of the École de Guerre remained unshaken. Despite the lessons of 1914 on the costliness of offensive operations without proper artillery preparation and in the face of massed automatic fire, he prescribed for 1915 "a renewal of the offensive as soon as possible."[6] Resisted by Foch, now his right-hand man, but supported by De Castelnau and the "Young Turks" at GHQ, he had his way. Thus was born, out of the ruins of the conventional, mobile warfare that had ground to a halt in 1914, a new type of war, much deadlier for the attacker, against static and entrenched positions: war of attrition, *guerre d'usure*. And in the "offensives" of 1915 and following years, the French Army was to undergo well-nigh crippling damage.

Champagne, Artois, Verdun, the Somme, the Chemin des Dames; over the years the battle grounds of attrition claimed their

---

[5] E. Herbillon: *Du Général en Chef au Gouvernement* (1930) Vol. I, p. 145.
[6] Joffre: *Memoirs*, Vol. II, p. 328.

growing toll of casualties, sometimes by full-scale frontal assaults, sometimes by the smaller operations that Joffre called *"grignotage"* (nibbling). Results were rarely apparent except in losses. After an inconclusive attack in June 1915, Viviani, the Prime Minister, exclaimed in exasperation: "We set off with mad hopes and are stopped by the same obstacles. Then everything has to be begun again!"[7] The aim being to exhaust the German forces, propaganda had to pretend that attrition worked only one way. Joffre fully realized that the Allies too would suffer heavy wastage and conceded "that this intense static warfare was sufficient to weaken the steadiest nerves";[8] but "in war," he pointed out, "it is the final battalions that bring victory."[9]

But who would possess the final battalions? With French casualties in 1915 exceeding 1,400,000 (a figure that included 50 per cent of the army's regular officers), the Western Front was steadily consuming France's manhood. The situation was not lost on the Germans. Considering German plans for 1916, Falkenhayn, Chief of the German General Staff, determined, as a preliminary to dealing with the chief enemy, Britain, to eliminate France in a final battle of attrition. His plan was to attack the great fortress of Verdun, the bastion (then forming an awkward salient 140 miles east of Paris) that traditionally barred the invader's road from the east. Falkenhayn believed that France would never yield Verdun, symbol of national pride and honor, while she could still fight: to defend it, he estimated, she would throw in all her forces.

ii

For France, Verdun was the great traumatic experience of the war. She accepted the German challenge and her troops stood fast, but at a grievous cost. The wooded, fort-dotted hills flanking the Meuse and protecting the main citadel of Verdun were the burial grounds of the flower of the French Army. Under unprecedented bombardments that transformed the ground into a water-logged desert, men became dazed automatons, somehow summoning the courage to endure and fight back. After Verdun,

---

[7] Herbillon: *Du Général,* Vol. I, p. 157.
[8] Joffre: *Memoirs,* Vol. II, p. 393.
[9] Ibid., Vol. II, p. 452.

no one could doubt the valor of the French soldiers. Hardened and stoical veterans of twenty-five, in their mud-stained *horizon bleu,* they went up to the line "with a firm step towards their destiny," recorded General Pétain, in command of the Army of Verdun (2nd Army), "fully aware of the fate awaiting them."[1] Watching the depleted columns returning from the front, he wrote: "Their gaze seemed set in a vision of dread."[2] As the Germans edged forward, themselves suffering huge casualties, Verdun became a supreme contest of national wills, a struggle of prestige that neither side could afford to lose.

By July the Germans had shot their bolt and the assault was called off. Verdun was saved; but "how shall we ever be able to forget at what price?" asked President Poincaré.[3] In terms of men, French losses in the four months' battle were 362,000, German losses 337,000. Falkenhayn, dismissed soon afterwards, had learned that attrition was a two-edged sword. For the French people Verdun was to become a legend of heroism and sacrifice, but for the High Command it carried the lesson of another military blunder. Warnings of the coming offensive had been discounted and Verdun's defenses were neglected and undermanned (the result of the Command's change of mind about the value of defensive strategy). Once again, as in 1914, the soldiers were left to bear the consequences of the errors of the generals.

But at least France's war factories were now in full production, and the guns and supplies rolled uninterruptedly along that single narrow road to be long remembered as the *Voie Sacrée.* Along that road, too, moved no less than two thirds of the French Army, a huge turnover that lessened the strain on individual formations as it provided, largely on Pétain's insistence, a rapid rotation of fresh troops in the line. Nevertheless, the heavy cost of Verdun, and the additional losses in the subsequent Somme battles, brought deepening disillusion to a nation now facing its third winter of war, with the enemy immovably entrenched on its soil. Seeking responsibility for Verdun, government and press turned on Joffre, the leader whose reputation had never been the same

---

[1] P. Pétain: *La Bataille de Verdun* (1929), p. 86.
[2] Ibid., p. 79.
[3] R. Poincaré: *Au Service de la France* (1931), Vol. VIII, p. 210.

since 1914; and in December Joffre relinquished his command to become a Marshal and—honorifically—chief military adviser to the government in Paris.

Amid toppling reputations and fading illusions, after two years the most obvious product of the war was destruction. Resigned to the devastation, somehow tolerating the continued carnage (which produced 900,000 more casualties in 1916), the French Army was buoyed up by one hope. "Our soldiers fancied at each offensive," recorded a French staff officer at the time of the Somme, "that the enemy would be driven out of France."[4] But beneath this optimism, so often disappointed, lay a growing exhaustion. By the beginning of 1917, with the hardest winter in memory settling on the Western Front, the strain was beginning to show. Hope was being too long deferred: for the French troops the war had degenerated into a pointless exercise with no forseeable conclusion. What they wanted above all was an end to the grinding attrition, some prospect of quick and tangible results. They would still stalwartly respond, as they soon showed, to a call that offered real hope of shortening the war. That call was now forthcoming from the new Commander in Chief, General Robert Nivelle.

Nivelle was the new star in France's military firmament. An artilleryman, he had made his name at Verdun, where his successful aggressive tactics had singled him out in the eyes of Aristide Briand's government as the successor to Joffre, in preference to senior generals like Foch, Castelnau, and Pétain. "We have the formula!" he had proclaimed on taking over from Pétain at Verdun. Now, on a wider battlefield, he still believed he had the formula. Reshaping the prearranged Allied offensive plans for 1917, he projected a massive assault—in its final form, a three-army attack on the powerfully fortified heights above the Aisne, including the Chemin des Dames, between Soissons and Reims— which he claimed would produce a breakthrough within forty-eight hours. Here, once again, was the true Grandmaison touch, appealing in its boldness to all the legendary dash of the French

---

[4] J. de Pierrefeu: *French Headquarters, 1915–1918* (1924), p. 80.

soldier but, in the context of 1917, carrying within it the seeds of disaster.

Every experience of the last two years suggested that such a direct frontal assault would break itself against the well-prepared defenses with heavy casualties. Nivelle's own generals, Haig, the British Commander in Chief, and the French government greeted the plan with doubt and skepticism. Pétain bluntly stated that he did not believe in the success of an all-out offensive. But Nivelle was impervious to all objections. At a tense meeting in the presidential railway coach at Compiègne shortly before the attack was due, he dominated the assembly of dubious or hostile ministers and generals with his forceful arguments on why his plan must succeed. Amid the almost total mistrust of Allied military and civil leaders, Nivelle was staking the French Army on its biggest gamble of the war.

But at least he carried the troops with him. He inspired them so successfully with his own optimism—and that of his Chief of Staff, the fanatical Colonel d'Alenson—that by April, on the eve of the attack, the low morale of three months before had been replaced by an enthusiasm perhaps unsurpassed at any time of the war. At last the French *poilus* had an object worth fighting for: in place of endless stalemate they had been promised a breakthrough, with the possibility of early victory. Nivelle's intensive morale-building encouraged the wildest hopes. Postal Control, reporting a few days before the assault, recorded a remarkable firmness of spirit in the troops' letters. In confident fighting mood (whatever the misgivings of the commanding generals) the men of the French 5th and 6th Armies, supported by the 10th, went in to the attack in the dawn of April 16, 1917.

Even without the experience of Verdun the morale of the French Army might not have surmounted the failure of Nivelle's Battle of the Aisne. Within days the offensive had ground to a halt, and the hopes raised by the Commander in Chief had foundered on the impregnably defended heights all along the forty-mile front. Bad security, inadequate artillery preparation against the massed barbed wire and honey-combed machine-gun nests of a reinforced and thoroughly prepared enemy, and atrocious weather had all contributed to doom the offensive from the start. Instead of the promised breakthrough, Nivelle's troops gained a few miles of ground at a cost of nearly 200,000 casualties; and their exalted mood of the sixteenth changed with suddenness to stupefaction, fed by a bitter sense of betrayal and the realization that this was not, after all, the decisive clash. The much-tried French Army, subjected to one ordeal too many, broke under the strain and mutinied.

Between late May and mid-June, men from fifty-four divisions deserted, disobeyed orders, paraded with red flags, called for peace, threatened or attempted to march on Paris. Though impetus was given to the mutinies by the news of the Russian Revolution, which startled the world in March, they were in essence the gesture of an army that had reached the end of its tether. "Now there is a sort of moral nihilism," commented Lieutenant Henry Bordeaux, reporting to GHQ on the state of one rear division. "It is an army without faith."[5] From the fighting men themselves came a chorus of impotent despair mingled with biting criticism of the High Command. Fortunately the revolt was confined to rear formations: in all cases the front-line troops stood firm. Even more providentially, by an outstanding feat of military security, news of the troubles was so rigorously guarded that almost no one outside the zone of the armies (including the Germans) knew of them. At one time only two entirely loyal divisions stood between the enemy and Paris, seventy miles away. On no occasion in the war did France and the Allies lie more open to disaster.

In the spring of 1917, the French home front, like the army, was undergoing its own crisis of morale. Civilians as well as troops had built extravagant hopes on the success of Nivelle's offensive, and its failure had produced acute disappointment in every level of the nation's life, from Parliament to the humblest household. It was one more blow to a country which from the first had been psychologically and materially ill-prepared for prolonged and total warfare, and which now, with vital territories occupied, her manpower and resources overstretched and her losses disproportionately heavy, was under greater strain than any other Western belligerent.

---

[5] H. C. Bordeaux: *Histoire d'une Vie* (1959), Vol. VI, p. 63.

With the clear-cut patriotic ideals of 1914 long since lost, Frenchmen were animated at best by dour determination and the yearning for a quick ending. Even the political unity proclaimed at the outbreak had split apart as Socialists reverted to their old pacifist leanings and increasingly criticized the conduct of the war. By mid-1917, as the Socialists clamored to be represented at the international Stockholm Conference, France's war-weary and disillusioned population faced a new threat, the intensified propaganda of the Paris defeatists and peacemongers. Thanks to the government's original decision not to arrest suspects named in Carnet B, these cliques had gradually emerged again and were now exploiting the Nivelle *débâcle* to the full. They were vigorously attacking the French war effort by speeches, pamphlets, and articles in illicit news sheets. Their task was aided by the government's reluctance to act against them for fear of antagonizing the workers; and, more ominous, by the tolerance or active cooperation of Malvy, the Minister of the Interior, and high public officials. France at this moment was fighting not only Germany but enemies within the gates: a canker of treason and corruption was eating into her public life, whose extent was to be revealed in the sensational traitors' trials of this and the following year.

Inevitably, the saboteurs' best hunting ground was among the disaffected troops in the camps and barracks behind the Aisne front. How instrumental they were in promoting and spreading unrest among the already demoralized army is uncertain. French GHQ maintained that the revolts were the fault of the government, which had consistently failed to suppress the troublemakers; whereas the government, only too ready to find a scapegoat in the High Command, saw the disorders as a purely military matter, the result of Nivelle's abortive offensive. But in any case the defeatist groups were assailing, with some success, the whole French war effort at a highly critical moment. The troubles at the front were matched at home by demonstrations and strikes. In Paris and elsewhere, unease was widespread. At the beginning of June, President Poincaré sorrowfully confided in his diary: "The fever is spreading. Must we await a new victory of the Marne to be healed?"[6]

---

[6] Poincaré: *Au Service* (1932), Vol. IX, p. 153.

iii

No repetition of the Marne was forthcoming. Instead she found two new leaders: Philippe Pétain and Georges Clemenceau. Between them, the cool calculating soldier and the fiery civilian restored the nation's spirit and brought her back into the fighting line in time for the last great battles of the war. The somewhat unpopular appointment of seventy-six-year-old Clemenceau—the *enfant terrible* of French politics with a stormy career going back to the birth of the Third Republic—to the premiership in place of Paul Painlevé late in 1917 was the final alternative to some Socialist solution of the war that would bring less than outright victory. At a late hour France was choosing discipline in place of perhaps fatal disarray. It was her tragedy that she had had to wait over three years for the kind of leadership she had needed at the beginning, when Clemenceau was a mere voice crying in the wilderness through the columns of his *L'Homme Libre* and *L'Homme Enchaîné*. None of the succession of prime ministers, the eloquent Viviani, the liberal but unforceful Briand, the elderly Ribot, the mild and humanitarian Painlevé, had possessed the strength to override faction and conflicting interests and command a united war effort. Before Clemenceau, none had been able to appeal to the historic spirit of France. This ungainly, pugnacious man with the ragged mustache, uncompromisingly Radical and a merciless denouncer of inefficiency and slackness, was the embodiment of French patriotism and will to victory. Now, on becoming Prime Minister and also Minister of War, he bluntly stated his aims: "Home policy? I wage war! Foreign policy? I wage war! All the time I wage war!"[7] It was Clemenceau who started the purge of traitors and defeatists with a fierce attack on Malvy in the Senate in July. In the same remorseless spirit he continued now to root out France's internal enemies, silence the doubters, revive national self-confidence and unity, and marshal all the forces of the nation toward the one goal of victory.

Less belligerently but equally effectively, Pétain was doing the same for the army. Amid a reverberating command crisis Ni-

---

[7] D. W. Brogan: *The Development of Modern France (1870–1939)* (1940), p. 532.

velle had departed in May, to be replaced as Commander in Chief by General Philippe Pétain. The heretical peacetime champion of the defensive at the École de Guerre, who had started the war as a fifty-eight-year-old colonel on the verge of retirement, was now the man to whom the government turned in France's moment of emergency. Having proved his mastery of defense at Verdun, he was being called in again, in the highest capacity of all, to clear up the wreckage of the Grandmaison conception run wild. It was a belated admission that the cautious as well as the aggressive military mind had its place in modern war.

Pétain was always candid about his unheroically defensive views. When President Poincaré and Joffre visited him during a crucial phase at Verdun, Poincaré sought his reassurance that he would not retire to the left bank of the Meuse (and thus abandon the citadel). "Monsieur le Président," replied Pétain, "great leaders have only become famous for their prudent withdrawals. If this measure seemed necessary, I should not hesitate to consider it."[8] He disconcerted Poincaré still more during another presidential visit to Verdun. After listening to Pétain's opinion that only a presidential dictatorship could solve the munitions problem, the shocked President asked: "But, General, what about the Constitution?" "The Constitution," answered Pétain, "oh, to blazes with it! (*La Constitution, oh! moi je m'en fous!*)."[9] According to Pétain's *chef de cabinet,* Colonel Serrigny, Poincaré remembered the remark and Pétain paid for his outspokenness by being passed over when Joffre's replacement was being considered. "Poincaré feared for the Constitution," Serrigny recorded.[1]

Pétain believed that the army disorders were chiefly due to defeatist incitements tolerated by government weakness. But Ribot's government, along with Poincaré, seemed reluctant to take strong action in any direction. When Pétain told the War Cabinet that "we must make some examples in all the regiments that have mutinied and renounce any consideration of clemency in all cases of collective disobedience," Poincaré urged him to act as leniently as possible in order not to cause further discouragement.[2] Pétain

---

[8] B. Serrigny: *Trente Ans avec Pétain* (1959), pp. 63-4.
[9] Ibid., p. 82.
[1] Ibid.
[2] Poincaré: *Au Service,* Vol. IX, p. 161.

hardly needed this reminder: he had a high reputation for humanity in his dealings with the troops. Behind his frosty reserve lay a strong compassion for the ordinary soldier. He was noted for his efforts to spare unnecessary casualties. Early in the war he instilled confidence by his practice of personally checking the aiming points of all guns in his batteries before an attack. On his arrival at Verdun the cry went round: "Pétain's in charge. All will be well."

But it was clear that rigorous measures were needed in the dangerous situation he encountered immediately on taking over as Commander in Chief. Nevertheless, it was not the 412 death sentences (of which 356 were commuted) that chiefly marked Pétain's handling of the mutinies, but his constructive action in removing causes of grievance from an army that in its harsh discipline and lack of amenities, such as proper leave, decent rations, and adequate welfare services, to say nothing of miserable pay, was probably the worst-treated in Europe. And while he reduced military operations in the Chemin des Dames area to a minimum in order to rest and reorganize the troops, he made a point of close personal contact with individual soldiers. Almost daily from mid-June onwards his white-pennanted car left Compiègne on visits to formations, and in a few weeks he had covered ninety divisions, talking to the men, hearing their complaints, assuring them of improvements in conditions. For the first time in the war the *poilus* of the French Army were being made to feel that they mattered as human beings.

Pétain attempted to push his morale-raising campaign further by writing a series of articles for the *Bulletin des Armées* on "Why are we Fighting?" But after the first had appeared he was dissuaded from continuing by vague hints of official disapproval. Yet strong, straight, heartening propaganda was just what the troops had lacked all through the war. One of their biggest grievances was the distorted picture of the war, and their own part in it, put forth by a press that was at the mercy of both censorship and the propaganda machine. The millions who knew the realities of war were disgusted by the false romanticism and heroics with which it was invested in the papers. Pétain himself protested at the facile optimism of the press. "To brandish the seductive picture of peace prematurely before the eyes of men who daily face death and undergo the horrors of battle and the miseries of life in the trenches," he wrote in a report on the mutinies to the Minister of War, "is to seek to weaken deliberately all moral resources and high feelings that have up to now constituted the glory of the army in this long war."[3]

With Clemenceau and Pétain at the helm, France surmounted the gravest phase of the war. But at the end of 1917 the alternatives of "win or die" offered by General Messimy three years before were starker than ever. To the national war-weariness had been added the disaster of Russia's collapse as an ally, with all that this meant in increased German strength in the west. For France, even "winning" the war was no longer a matter of emerging as a triumphant victor, but of scraping through unbroken, still a fighting member of the Entente and contributing some of the "final battalions" that Joffre had prophesied would bring victory in this drawn-out struggle of attrition. Meanwhile the gloomy year was illumined by one of the war's most significant events: the intervention of America. Coming almost at the moment of the Russian Revolution and the breakdown of the French Army, it transformed a desperate situation into one in which there at least was hope, even though American troops could not be in the field until 1918. In the Chamber, Prime Minister Ribot paid tribute to the occasion with rolling Gallic eloquence. "The banner of the Stars and Stripes," he proclaimed, "is about to float beside the Tricolor. Our hands are about to join and our hearts to beat in unison. It will be for us, after so many sufferings heroically endured, so many bereavements and losses, a renewal as it were of the courage which has sustained us during this long ordeal. The mighty, decisive assistance of the United States will not be merely material; it will bring us especially moral succour and true comfort."[4] In mid-June General Pershing, American Commander in Chief, drove through Paris to the cheers of the crowds who welcomed him as the leader whose new armies from across the Atlantic could take the load from France's exhausted troops and turn the tide of the war.

---

[3] France—État-Major de l'Armée: *Les Armées Françaises dans la Grande Guerre* (1937), Tome V, Vol. II, p. 621.
[4] *The Times* (London), April 7, 1917, p. 8.

One year later, as the third great assault in what was to be the ultimate German bid for victory was held, and the whole front from the Channel to Verdun was on the move for the first time since 1914, Pershing's American divisions stood alongside the British and French, the forerunners of an American flood that would continue until the Armistice. But it was a Frenchman, General Foch, who commanded the Allied forces as Generalissimo in the last crucial battles from March onwards. The French Army, its morale recovered, was once more, under its restorer Pétain, playing its full part in the operations. Now, in Foch's Second Battle of the Marne, the counterstroke that started the final German rout in July, the French were in the forefront. But their dogged effort was nearly exhausted in the long ordeal of trench, barbed wire, and machine gun that had replaced the optimistic dream of a brisk, mobile war that would be over by Christmas 1914. When victory came in November, France's military contribution to the war could be measured by a total mobilization of nearly 8,000,000 (or 20 per cent of the population), and by a death roll of 1,385,000, figures proportionately higher than for any other belligerent. Existing theories of war had been found wanting, ancient ideas of gallantry had had to give place to new ones, grimmer and more demanding; but the shame of 1870 had been avenged, though at the cost of a whole generation of France's best men, and much else. The Third Republic, submitted to unexampled stresses, including internal treachery, had managed to stand firm. When Clemenceau and Foch (who did not always agree) embraced each other at the War Ministry on Armistice Day, the gesture seemed to reaffirm the unity of people and army, born out of the defeat of half a century before.

Above all, French troops had proved themselves in the most exacting test of their history. "Of what steel was forged this soldier of Verdun, whom France found at the appointed moment?"[5] Pétain was to ask at a ceremony on the Verdun battlefield nine years later. It was a matter for the future whether too much had not been demanded of that steel, and how dearly France would have to pay for the heavy calls made on the fighting spirit of her soldiers, let alone the actual casualties.

---

[5] Pétain: *Bataille de Verdun*, p. 138.

Chapter 3

$\ggg\!\ggg\!\ggg\bullet\lll\!\lll\!\lll$

THE WASTED TRUCE,
1918–1939

"It is not a peace treaty, it is a twenty-year armistice."

(Marshal Foch)

i

UNDERLYING ALL THE VICTORY celebrations of 1918–19 was a bitter sense of the sacrifice that France had suffered. It was to be seen in the proliferating war memorials of the postwar years, from the Tomb of the Unknown Soldier, with its Eternal Flame, beneath the Arc de Triomphe in Paris, to the lesser monuments in towns and villages all over France, unveiled to the accompaniment of speeches that invariably stressed the cost at which victory had been won. There was indeed irony in the fact that as a victorious nation in 1918 France was far more gravely injured than when defeated in 1870. There was sharper irony in the almost victorious bearing of the defeated German troops as they entered Berlin after the Armistice. Welcomed by enthusiastic crowds and brass bands playing "Deutschland über Alles," the Guards regiments marched past the Brandenburg Gate, to be greeted by their newly elected President Ebert. Amid these paradoxes of victory and defeat, France pledged herself to two main aims: to make Germany pay, and ensure that she would never threaten France again. Of the two, the paramount, all-embracing, long-term objective was, in a single word, Security.

Those who wondered at the French obsession with security had only to survey the ruined tracts of northern France, stretching almost from the Channel to the Vosges, across which the German armies had trampled and fought in four years' war. The total extent of the devastated area, ranging over ten departments, exceeded the size of Holland. This great zone, vital for its iron, coal, agriculture, and woolen and other manufactures, was one of France's most productive regions. Under the ravages of war and German occupation, with buildings, factories, mines, communications, and livestock destroyed, many small communes obliterated, and the trench-furrowed and shell-scarred soil made sterile, to say nothing of a population reduced to half its prewar figure, life in the region had come almost to a standstill.

In repairing the destruction, while at the same time weathering all the complex adjustments from war to peace, France faced a colossal task. Yet by a *tour de force* of energy and organization she virtually completed the operation by 1926. At an astronomical cost, the ten ravaged departments were restored and resettled to become once more a part of France's working economy. Signs of war had vanished from the rolling farmlands, the smoke of peacetime industries rose from the chimneys of rebuilt factories, new roads and railways were busy with traffic. For the five million Frenchmen of these revived territories, as indeed for all Frenchmen, as they looked east to the Rhine and the borders of Lorraine, the old lesson emerged with redoubled force: that the price of security was eternal vigilance.

But France's notions of ensuring security had been modified in the years since 1919. The Treaty of Versailles had reversed the shame of 1871, but it had not won all her demands for restitution, reparation, and security. She had recovered Alsace-Lorraine and been awarded a fifteen-year tenancy of the Saar coal field, but the reparations question was left unsettled and Foch's call for a permanent French occupation of the Rhineland was rejected in favor of a three-zone Allied occupation of the left bank lasting up to fifteen years, with permanent demilitarization. When Foch learned of the refusal of his plan, he exclaimed: "It is not a treaty of peace, it is a twenty-year armistice!"[1]

Further soured by the breakdown of the Anglo-American guarantee to aid her in the event of attack by Germany, and distrustful of the League of Nations, France began to make her own security alliances (with Belgium in the west, and Poland and later

---

[1] P. Reynaud: *Mémoires* (1960), Vol. I, p. 230.

the Little Entente in the east), while still implacably regarding Germany as an enemy that must be kept down by force. She became the more intransigent as she felt her Allies' attitude to a beaten but still dangerous Germany to be softening. "France, dripping with glory and with blood," declared Paul Reynaud, "was then the *chevalier de l'Europe.*"[2]

But in a Europe professedly dedicated to collective security, the role of chevalier was costly and difficult to sustain. The failure of France's bellicose Ruhr adventure in 1923, when 50,000 French troops marched in and unsuccessfully attempted to compel German compliance with reparation undertakings, proved the ineffectiveness of force. This, and a growing distaste among Frenchmen for the saber-rattling *revanchist* approach, induced a change of policy. It paved the way for the fall of the uncompromising Poincaré and the appointment to the Foreign Ministry of the internationalist and man of peace, Aristide Briand. With conciliation as his watchword, Briand stood for support of the League, cooperation with Britain and *rapprochement* with Germany. By 1926 the Locarno Pact (guaranteeing the frontiers of France and Germany) had been signed and Germany had entered the League of Nations. On the surface at least, the old hates and tensions were diminishing.

Yet whatever the pacts and promises of peace, there remained for France the problem of the hereditary enemy beyond the Rhine. Alike in victory and defeat, she seemed fated always to gaze uneasily eastward, aware, as the military historian Liddell Hart wrote in 1927, "that there lies the foe of tomorrow as of yesterday."[3] Germany might be beaten and disarmed and the Rhineland demilitarized, with the satisfaction which this gave France that in any new war the fighting would be on German, not French soil. But the hard fact was that after the evacuation of the Rhineland, fixed for 1935, France would confront, across a common border and a narrow ribbon of water, a historically hostile and warlike nation whose population was half again as great as hers.

She was still dogged by the old manpower inferiority for

---

[2] Ibid., p. 228.
[3] B. H. Liddell Hart: *The Remaking of Modern Armies* (1927), p. 241.

which no treaties could altogether compensate. Her postwar rate of 258,000 male births in 1919 was alarmingly lower than the figure of 400,000 in 1914. In 1919 Clemenceau warned that if France restricted herself to small families, victory would prove useless and the country would be doomed. France's governments heeded the caution; but the various measures taken to encourage a higher birth rate failed to halt the decline; and even though in the first postwar decade Germany's birth rate was falling even more steeply than France's, in 1931, in the vital age group up to nineteen years that would produce the future soldiers, France could number only 12 million against Germany's 21 million.

Setting aside the bitter experience of well over a million dead and ten devastated departments, it was thus the logic of numbers that committed the postwar General Staff once more to a strictly defensive policy. As in the decades after 1870, France now looked to her frontiers, reinforcing the doctrines of those years with the most significant lessons (as seen by her military chiefs) of World War I. The main difference between the 1870's and 1919 was that she now had to protect newly recovered Alsace-Lorraine. If this region, vital for its potash and coal, were to escape destruction in the event of an attack, it would have to be defended on the frontier itself. The best means of immediate defense, while troops in the rear were being moved forward, was a permanent fortified system. This was the military thinking that led to the building of the line named after André Maginot. A wounded war veteran, man of Lorraine, and postwar Minister of Pensions who basically mistrusted the idea of a pacific Germany, it was as Minister of War in 1922 that the forceful, energetic Maginot began his fight for the provision of northeastern defenses. Backed by his successor, Painlevé, he worked tirelessly throughout the 1920's to overcome financial and other obstacles and get his project realized. Meanwhile the experts of the General Staff brooded long and indecisively over the two fundamental questions: What kind of defenses should be built? And how far they should extend?

This uncertainty reflected a characteristic difference of view between France's two great war leaders, Joffre and Pétain. In the immediate postwar years both were closely studying France's defense problems, Joffre as President of the Commission for Fortified Areas, and Pétain—now a Marshal too—as Vice-President of the Army Council and Inspector-General of the Army (in all but name its peacetime commander in chief). Joffre proposed a string of separate fortified zones from the North Sea to the Swiss border, between which, he typically suggested, full-scale offensives could be launched. Pétain, on the other hand, advocated a continuous defensive system to cover the northeast frontier only. While the military committees and commissions deliberated these plans, it was not until 1928 that a fortification scheme was agreed upon, and then it was a compromise. Joffre's fortified regions were to be linked with Pétain's continuous defenses in a system covering the Rhine and northeast. With the "offensive" conception ruled out and the defenses—as far as they went—unbroken, Pétain's ideas had prevailed. The aging Marshal (four years younger, nevertheless, than seventy-six-year-old Joffre) was now supreme in French military affairs. France's destinies were in the hands of the soldier who believed in the static defensive and an impregnable front. The line that began to arise in the Metz and Lauter Fortified Regions and along the Rhine in 1929—and was never to extend westwards to cover the Franco-Belgian frontier—bore Maginot's name but carried on it the indelible imprint of Pétain's thinking.

ii

The completion of France's fortification system had been geared to the year 1935, the first of the *"années creuses"* when, owing to the low wartime birth rate, the annual intake of army recruits would begin to fall sharply from an average 240,000 to 170,000. The defense problem was accentuated by the Allies' final evacuation of the Rhineland in 1930, instead of 1935 as originally decreed. But even after the belated start of the Maginot Line in 1929, progress was slow (due partly to inadequacy of financial credits), being matched by the unreadiness of the army itself. "In default of a screen of concrete and barbed wire," asked Clemenceau, then nearly ninety but still fiercely watchful of France's security interests, "have we at least a living screen that can be put in a position instantaneously in the frontier zone? Nothing of the kind."[4] This was not altogether the fault of the

---

[4] G. Clemenceau: *Grandeur and Misery of Victory* (1930), p. 337.

General Staff. In response to the mood of a war-weary nation, military service had been reduced to eighteen months in 1923 and to one year in 1928. The whole military situation revealed an old paradox. The nation which could so successfully restore its 13,000 square miles of devastated territories within some six years of peace, was, a decade after the war, and despite the dangers of a renascent Germany, unable effectively to protect its most vulnerable frontier. While Germany was illicitly building up the *Reichswehr*, under General von Seeckt, into an army that had its eyes upon the future, the French Army was barely keeping up with the needs of the present.

In the twenties the patriotic devotion and military zeal that had marked the early days of the Third Republic were notably absent. With the war won and Alsace-Lorraine recovered, the much-depleted professional cadres of the French Army suddenly found themselves deprived of the sense of purpose that had inspired them in the prewar years. Not only were there no more worlds to conquer, but in the horror of the trenches war had lost its last vestiges of glory and glamour.

And, after the victory cheers had died, the army itself was the victim of a national mood that sought forgetfulness of war and the beguiling "normalcy" of peace. Almost like Kipling's "Tommy," courted in war but spurned in peacetime, it was respectfully relegated to a secondary place in popular esteem. It had nobly played its part and its sacrifice was commemorated in the endless rows of graves, the war memorials, and the disabled servicemen who were an ever-present reminder of the recent ordeal. Frenchmen were ready to honor their army for its wartime achievements but no longer to look on it as the supreme embodiment of *La Patrie*. The army, and its trade of war, could never be quite the same again for a people of whom André Siegfried declared in 1930: "Yesterday, today and tomorrow, they want peace and nothing but peace."[5]

The army was still further affected by the ferment of change stirring in postwar France. Along with the political swings between Right and Left (Bloc National, Cartel des Gauches, Union Nationale), France was experiencing several quiet revolutions. A

---

[5] A. Siegfried: *France: A Study in Nationality* (1930), p. 54.

steady drift from the land, growing industrialization and urbanization, a strengthening labor movement, the emancipation of women, a *bourgeoisie* impoverished by the fall of the franc, all helped to transform French life as the country shakily adjusted itself to peace. Fresh values were replacing old ones, notably in Paris, which was losing some of its traditional character and charm to become a booming, money-conscious tourist center. In the postwar flowering of European ideas the younger generation was taking up new cults like Dadaism and surrealism, and the theories of Einstein, Freud, Marx, and other revolutionary thinkers, which threatened the old disciplines. Liberalism of thought and action was the order of the day. Established notions of nationalism, patriotism, and militarism were challenged by the revulsion from war, mistrust of force and belief in collective security and the League of Nations. The ideals of peace and universal brotherhood were strongest among the millions of disillusioned ex-soldiers. "We give voice to the same cry: 'War upon war'!" called Henri Barbusse, expressing his passionate pacifist convictions at an International Congress of Ex-Servicemen at Geneva.[6]

Deprived of its old respect, without an inspiring goal, and subject to damaging cuts and economies, the army was falling into a vague *"malaise militaire."* The postwar inflation and high cost of living put officers and N.C.O.'s at a disadvantage financially. This, together with poor promotion prospects, was causing promising officers to leave the army for more attractive civilian employment and discouraging potential entrants from traditionally military families, thus cutting off a source of recruitment that France could ill afford to lose. General Gamelin, the army's future Commander in Chief, told the story of a general who, in trying to persuade the son of a friend to enter Saint-Cyr, stressed the sound prospects for junior officers. "General," replied the young man, "it is not the pay of a *sous-lieutenant* that worries me, it is yours."[7]

Nevertheless, the generals were staying on, perpetuating the blockage at the top that was so discouraging to ambitious colonels and majors. Their retirement age, which during the war had been fixed at sixty, rose in the twenties to sixty-two, sixty-five, and finally

---

[6] H. Barbusse: *Paroles d'un Combattant* (1920), p. 222.
[7] M. Gamelin: *Servir* (1946), Vol. II, p. 15.

seventy. The army, headed by the septuagenarian Pétain, was increasingly dominated by age. The General Staff and École were unduly influenced by the rigid military thinking of elderly wartime commanders whose minds were unreceptive to new ideas. Pétain's dicta, pronounced in his *Provisional Instructions for the Conduct of Large Units* (1921) that "a continuous front cannot be broken by the attacker," and "tanks can only be simple auxiliaries for the infantry," still held sway.[8] Among France's senior generals the trench-bound Western Front had created its dangerously persistent myth of stasis, impregnability, and defensive supremacy. It was a myth that enshrined not the final success of 1918—when defense lines had cracked and concentrations of tanks, used independently, had contributed to the breakthrough—but the long exhausting years of attrition that had gone before. Now, behind the passive concept of the Maginot Line, strategy was being neglected: warfare was being reduced to meticulously worked-out but unimaginative tactics that continued to give the infantry pride of place and subordinate movement to firepower—producing an army that Captain Liddell Hart described in 1927 as a "slow-moving steam-roller of fire"[9] of doubtful value against a mobile, thrusting attacker. Amid the cold logistical calculations of Pétain and his colleagues, the vigorous *volonté* of Foch and the broad offensive sweep of Joffre were lacking. The postwar French Army seemed to miss its old moral force. The loss of 80,000 of its officers, dead or disabled in the war, was beginning to make itself felt.

But the spirits of Foch and Joffre (who themselves died in 1929 and 1931 respectively) lived on in two of their closest wartime associates, Generals Maxime Weygand and Maurice Gamelin, who now moved into the topmost army posts. In 1931 Weygand, aged sixty-four, succeeded Pétain as Vice-President of the Army Council and Inspector-General of the Army, being himself succeeded as Army Chief of Staff by fifty-eight-year-old Gamelin. Weygand, sharp, dynamic, and aggressive-minded like Foch, had an almost exaggerated reverence for his old chief, in whom he saw "a conception always just, a thought always lofty, moral courage, resource in difficulty, modesty in success, greatness of spirit and

---

[8] Reynaud: *Mémoires,* p. 232.
[9] Liddell Hart: *Modern Armies,* p. 249.

serenity under ordeal."[1] Gamelin shared Joffre's strategic and offensive thinking, but was less sturdily realistic and more apt to indulge in abstruse intellectual flights. On taking over as Chief of Staff, he was told by Prime Minister Tardieu: "On the military level you and Weygand complement each other happily. If you're both men of action, he is impulsive and you are reflective."[2] It was these two middle-aged commanders who were to have the task of heading the French Army in the next fateful decade, as France moved uneasily and unreadily into World War II.

But the advent of Weygand heralded no basic change in military policy. The army continued to be dominated by the towering shadow of Pétain, who remained on the Army Council, to become War Minister in 1934. And even without Pétain, the army was still condemned to its negative and unenterprising role by public indifference and financial stringency. Apart from the popular desire to forget war and all its works, the heavy reductions in national expenditure dictated by the economic crisis of 1929 and its aftermath left the army ever more restricted. Meanwhile the European situation was deteriorating ominously. Whatever hopes Versailles had raised for peace were rapidly fading. In a Germany vigorously and violently emerging from its postwar prostration and still in the throes of slump and vast unemployment, Adolf Hitler was coming to power. In 1933 disarmament prospects were shattered by the failure of the Lausanne Conference, from which Hitler withdrew the German delegates, announcing at the same time Germany's retirement from the League. The proclamation of German rearmament which followed sounded a note of warning throughout Europe. For Frenchmen able to read the signs, the old fears and dangers were revived and security suddenly assumed a more urgent meaning.

Nevertheless, the army continued to be starved of men and resources. By 1930 its peacetime strength had been cut to twenty divisions, less than half the 1914 figure. In January 1933 it suffered a budget reduction of one billion francs, soon followed by other heavy cuts, including a measure to scale down the officer strength by 5,000. That same year the General Staff learned with

---

[1] M. Weygand: *Mémoires* (1957), Vol. II, p. 203.
[2] Gamelin: *Servir*, p. xxxi.

alarm that the German Army possessed twenty-one active divisions, with between thirty and fifty in reserve. The protests of Weygand and the military members of the Army Council went unheeded. In February 1934 Weygand sent a report to Pétain at the War Ministry stating that "the army today has sunk to the lowest level that the security of France can permit in the present state of Europe."[3] In May the fifteen military members of the Army Council, including Weygand and Marshals Lyautey and Frenchet d'Esperey, warned the government of the dangers of the European situation. "In its present state, the French Army will be in no position to face such a threat without grave risks."[4] General Weygand was reduced to angry frustration at the government's lack of response. "My feeling of impotence at getting the Government to see the military situation in its reality," he recorded on retiring from the army in January 1935, "made my last years of active service particularly painful."[5]

But the most far-reaching military misjudgment of these "painful" years was not immediately obvious to Weygand or anyone else. It lay in a pronouncement by Marshal Pétain at a meeting of the Army Commission of the Senate in March 1934 on the matter of frontier defense. He was dealing with the zone west of Montmédy, the point at which the Maginot Line was planned to end. "Starting from Montmédy are the Ardennes forests," he said. "They are impenetrable if we make some special dispositions there. . . . Since this front would have no depth, the enemy could not take action it it; and if he should, we will pinch him off as he comes out of the forest. Hence this sector is not dangerous—*donc ce secteur n'est pas dangereux*."[6] France's greatest expert on defense was prescribing the precise invasion route through which the German panzers would pour six years later.

iii

In 1934 France was also shown the path to military salvation. That December a tall, ungainly lieutenant-colonel of chasseurs, Charles de Gaulle, called at the office of Paul Reynaud, Minister

---

[3] Weygand: *Mémoires*, pp. 411–2.
[4] Ibid., p. 422.
[5] Ibid., p. 435.
[6] Gamelin: *Servir*, p. 128.

of Finance in Flandin's government. The busy Reynaud was at first reluctant to see him, but finally agreed when De Gaulle said: "It will be you or no one."[7] The colonel then proceeded to tell Reynaud, with calm self-assurance, that France did not possess the right army for her needs. There were over 200 miles extending west of the Maginot Line to the North Sea, through which Germany could penetrate France, by way of Belgium, on the classic invasion route: the armored corps that Germany was creating would break the French front and the main force would follow. De Gaulle maintained that French military doctrine was ignoring the revolution produced on warfare by the internal-combustion engine, and urged the formation of an armored corps on the German pattern, a shock force of 100,000 regulars, possessing overwhelming speed and a firepower double that of the whole French Army in 1914. It would be, declared De Gaulle, "a passing hurricane."[8] He spoke with "such power and clarity," Reynaud recorded, "that I was captured by the man and his plan."[9]

Politically as well as militarily, De Gaulle's project was pure heresy. To Left-wingers and Republicans who believed in universal military service and a national army, the idea of a specialized regular force struck at traditions rooted in the birth of the Third Republic and raised sinister visions of a professional army clique. Even the title of the book De Gaulle had already published outlining the scheme—*Vers l'Armée de Métier*—was enough to damn it. Consequently, when Reynaud proposed the formation of an armored corps in the Chamber in March 1935, he met powerful opposition and the motion was rejected. While he was speaking, General Maurin, Minister of War, whispered indignantly to Georges Mandel, a fellow minister: "So M. Paul Reynaud is busying himself with military matters now. What would he say if I concerned myself with financial questions?"[1] After the debate Reynaud asked Mandel: "What does Flandin say about it?" "He says your speech was 'idiotic,' " replied Mandel.[2]

Next day General Maurin enlarged on his objections with

---

[7] Reynaud: *Mémoires*, p. 423.
[8] Ibid., p. 422.
[9] Ibid., p. 423.
[1] Ibid., p. 430.
[2] Ibid.

arguments that revealed the whole basis of official military thinking. "How can anyone believe," he asked, "that we are still contemplating offensive measures when we have spent millions of francs to build a fortified barrier? Would we be mad enough to sally forth from this barrier on I don't know what risky adventure?"[3]

The General Staff gave De Gaulle's proposals equally short shrift, even though the Ministry of War was aware that Germany already possessed three panzer divisions and was creating three more. They were condemned as running counter to the whole Pétainist conception of defense. Tanks had left a bad memory from the days of World War I when, unwieldy and unreliable, they earned the name of *cerceuils roulants* (coffins on wheels). General Colson, Vice-Chief of Staff, refusing De Gaulle's request to publish an article on his ideas, blandly informed him: "We are gleaning something from them, be sure of that."[4] But the army Establishment made no secret of its antimechanization views. "Dangerous Utopias," "useless and undesirable" were the epithets of senior generals.[5] General Debeney, noted World War I commander and Army Chief of Staff in the twenties, held that armored corps would be useless for an attack in the Rhineland. General Weygand himself, whatever he thought of the technical merits of De Gaulle's plan, saw in it a threat to the army's unity. He also feared that the creation of a small regular elite would weaken the arguments for an extension of the conscription period, which he had been vigorously urging.

It required the jolt of Hitler's introduction of two-year military service in 1935 to extend French conscription likewise. But while the politicians and generals—too often tardy, prejudiced, and shortsighted—ordained the ways and means of defense against the growing German danger, France herself showed little of the solidarity and firmness of purpose that the situation demanded. Beneath the surface of her teeming Gallic energy she was a nation at odds with herself, the victim of a moral lassitude that had been with her since the guns had ceased in 1918. "We don't give the impression of a victorious people, nor do the Germans look like

3 Ibid., p. 434.
4 Ibid., p. 423.
5 P.-M. de la Gorce: *The French Army: A Military Political History* (1963), p. 272.

a defeated one," Henry Bordeaux had observed at the time of Versailles.[6] Thirteen years later he was ruefully commenting: "We have returned, after victory, to the same point as before the war, but with the aggravation of greater fatigue and weariness."[7]

At the start of 1934 the fruits of victory and benefits of peace were proving disappointingly illusory for France. The world economic crisis was affecting the value of the franc and bringing rising unemployment. With the continual run of ministerial crises that had begun with the resignation of Poincaré in 1929, government was subject to a chronic instability. More insidious, there was a network of intrigue and corruption in high places that explosively revealed itself in the Stavisky Affair.[8] France seemed destined to have her periodic scandals which struck at the national integrity. Fighting for her life during the war, she had been assailed by internal treachery; now the Stavisky sensation brought the whole system of Republican government into disrepute and led to an outbreak of civil disturbance, in which the Fascist Croix de Feu and the Communists rioted and demonstrated in the streets of Paris, momentarily threatening France with anarchy.

But for Frenchmen, bewildered and disillusioned by domestic troubles, there was a still graver preoccupation in the threat from Hitler's Germany. A peace-hungry people that for sixteen years had sought desperately to banish the thought of war saw with alarm the ominously aggressive gestures from the old enemy across the Rhine—the growing intransigence of Hitler, Germany's withdrawal from the League of Nations, and announcement of rearmament. The famous war correspondent Philip Gibbs, sampling the mood of France early in 1934, found in Paris and the provinces a widespread fear of war. "If a vote were taken," a Paris waiter told him, "the whole of the French working class would be against war,

---

[6] H. C. Bordeaux: *Histoire d'une Vie* (1962), Vol. VIII, p. 6.

[7] Ibid., p. 363.

[8] Serge Alexander Stavisky was a shady financier who committed suicide in January 1934 following the discovery of a large-scale fraud. It was widely thought that his death had been "arranged" by the police, at the behest of Chautemps, the Prime Minister, to cover up a far-reaching scandal involving eminent public figures.

for any reason."[9] A Russian refugee in Paris asserted: "France is obsessed by fear. They are afraid of a new war. The thought fills them with terror."[1] In the quiet cathedral town of Sens a sacristan observed that everybody in France was against another war, adding, "we are the greatest pacifists in the world, because of our losses twenty years ago."[2] A young Lyons businessman declared that the French people loathed the idea of war, making the point—as others had—that "one never sees military shows in France except for some special ceremony."[3]

Frenchmen had never gloried in war, but this passivity in the face of possible national danger was a new thing, and contrasted ill with the buoyant, united spirit observable in Germany. After Hitler's accession to the Chancellorship early in 1933, a politician telephoned General Gamelin and asked: "What do you think of it—Bonaparte or Boulanger?" "Neither," Gamelin answered. "The whole of Germany."[4] Regimented though they might be, there was a fearsome note of unanimity in the vast Nuremberg rallies, with their bands, banners, and massed phalanxes of cheering Nazi youth. Confident in his own people's support and shrewdly assessing French reactions, Hitler was soon ready to venture on his next and most daring step. On Saturday, March 7, 1936, in violation of the Versailles and Locarno treaties, German forces occupied the Rhineland.

In Paris that morning a council of ministers and generals hastily met at the Ministry of the Interior to consider the situation. The German forces involved amounted to no more than about one division, with a mere three battalions moved across the Rhine; but this was a direct challenge to France that might demand general mobilization and, in the last resort, war. At first the council, led by Prime Minister Sarraut, and Flandin, the Foreign Minister, favored military action. "I would like to see you at Mayence as soon as possible," Paul-Boncour, Minister for Geneva Affairs, told Gamelin. Gamelin was cautious. "I ask for nothing better," he replied, "but I must be given the means."[5] General Maurin, how-

---

[9] P. Gibbs: *European Journey* (1934), p. 30.
[1] Ibid., p. 41.
[2] Ibid., p. 66.
[3] Ibid., p. 126.
[4] Gamelin: *Servir*, p. 94.
[5] Ibid., p. 201.

ever, had other views. To Gamelin's demand for total mobilization as a preliminary to any action, Maurin exclaimed: "Mobilise the army? You know very well that you won't be going to war! All you'll do is injure the army's morale."[6] French military plans provided for the mobilization of 540,000 troops by the sixth day, while Germany had with the colors one million partly trained men and no trained reserves, though she was much the stronger in armored forces. The immediate military advantage was with France, outweighing the greater manpower and industrial resources eventually available to Germany.

The issue for France was clear: either to resist—preferably with British support, to which she appeared entitled under the Locarno Treaty—or to acquiesce in Hitler's seizure, and thereby suffer a resounding defeat whose consequences could not be foreseen. In the event, Britain disowned any obligation to back France; but there was little in France's recent record to suggest that she herself would be prepared to confront Hitler, even now that her vital interests were threatened by the presence of German troops west of the Rhine. Her whole military planning had ruled out offensive measures and left her unready for the kind of action that would now be necessary. And Frenchmen were showing such an aversion to war that they could hardly contemplate the thought of having to fight on any pretext. On the day after the German move, the government's resolve to resist was already cooling. Ministers began to feel that with general elections imminent, neither Parliament nor the public would agree to general mobilization. But to put the matter beyond the possibility of misunderstanding, Gamelin told them next day: "If Germany fights, we cannot hold back. It will be total war. And the Government should envisage this with a cool head."[7] The government needed little persuasion: Hitler's bluff—for on his own admission it was no more than this—was not called, and he registered his first victory against France without the firing of a shot.

Few French protests were raised against the climbdown. "The Government and our army leaders set the example," Reynaud wrote later, "and the country followed it."[8] Almost every section

---

[6] Reynaud: *Mémoires*, p. 476.
[7] Gamelin: *Servir*, p. 206.
[8] Reynaud: *Mémoires*, p. 476.

of the press supported the German action. Opinion in the École de Guerre was revealed in 1938 in a book—prefaced with a eulogistic foreword from Pétain by General Chauvineau, an École professor, in which he dismissed the German action as militarily unimportant for the French Army. Amid the chorus of evasion, excuse, and self-justification, one dissentient voice was Paul Reynaud's. In February 1937, with France's lack of armored forces in mind, he told the Chamber scathingly: "Just for want of an arm suitable for carrying out this mission, a great power has shown itself unable to advance twenty kilometres from its frontier . . . without calling up its reserves."[9]

Ordinary Frenchmen, spared the necessity of confronting Hitler at the Rhine, had breathed a sigh of relief. But any hope that Hitler would stop there was shattered by the succession of *coups* that followed—Austria, Czechoslovakia, Memel; and Hitler's example was imitated by his lesser partner, Mussolini. Still France seemed not fully awake to the peril of the situation. From 1936 to 1938 the Left-wing Front Populaire, with Léon Blum as France's first Socialist prime minister, had concentrated mainly on social reform, introducing measures that were hardly helpful to the rearmament drive now being belatedly undertaken. For instance, while German laborers worked a forty-eight-hour week producing Hitler's war material, French production suffered from the new forty-hour week. But at least efforts were made to close the gap between French and German military readiness by increasing the munitions output, nationalizing the arms industry, and even some move toward mechanization. However, in its basic military conceptions, the government remained firmly wedded to the *status quo*.

Despite the lesson of the Rhineland, which pointed the need of an offensive striking force (on the lines of De Gaulle's proposal) in certain circumstances, Left-wing antifascist thinking, with its belief in the "Nation in Arms" and distrust of a small professional army, solidly supported the defensive as exemplified by the Maginot Line. Édouard Daladier, now War Minister for the fifth time, reaffirmed his earlier views by opposing the formation of an armored division, though General Gamelin himself had recently in-

---

9 Ibid.

dicated to the Army Council the necessity of an offensive instrument to counter the German panzers. A blow seemed to be struck at the defensive doctrine by the *Instruction on the Tactical Utilization of Larger Units* for 1936, which stated that the offensive was the superior form of warfare, but this won little acceptance; and like the government, the General Staff as a whole continued to subscribe to the orthodoxy expressed in the Law of 1927, which laid down that the French Army's purpose was to protect France's frontiers and defend her overseas territories. France was still dominated by the spirit of Marshal Pétain.

Eighty years old in 1936, Pétain had left public life two years earlier, after nine months as War Minister in Gaston Doumergue's government. With his prestige undimmed, he remained a kind of father figure, wooed by the Left partly for his military conservatism which tallied with the Left's own defensive thinking, and partly for the qualities of elder statesman which would lend luster to any government. Though unbendingly authoritarian, he was seen as a man above party and seeking no personal power, the Savior of Verdun who might, at a moment when the black-uniformed Croix de Feu was introducing a new and ugly threat into French politics, become the Savior of France from fascism and the protector of her democracy.

Léon Blum had published a glowing eulogy of Pétain in *Le Populaire* on his election to the French Academy in 1931. The antimilitarist-turned-ardent-patriot, Gustave Hervé, proclaimed in the columns of his paper, *La Victoire,* that the nation needed Pétain. The deputy Pierre Cot, shortly to be Air Minister in Blum's government, echoed the cry for Pétain as a man of unquestioned loyalty, revered by all old soldiers. But Pétain, thinking now of his retirement, was unmoved by these appeals. (He was, however, to reappear in public life once more before World War II, as Ambassador to Spain.) Instead, he preferred to sun himself in his modest Mediterranean property at Villeneuve-Loubet, an upright soldierly figure still with the flowing *moustache de la revanche* of his cadet days, seeking his monument not in the shifting sands of politics but in the impregnability of the Maginot Line and the whole theory of defense that went with it.

Unfortunately for France, events were already proving how

vulnerable these were. The Maginot Line, a great fortified steel-and-concrete right angle protecting (in varying depth, strength, and continuity) France's entire eastern and northeastern frontiers from Basel to Montmédy, was belatedly completed in 1938. It was never intended to take it farther west than Montmédy because the Franco-Belgian frontier was judged to be too near such vital centers as Lille, and the subsoil seemed unsuitable for massive concrete structures. There was also a political consideration: the desire not to offend Belgium by the building of fortifications which might imply that France would not come to Belgium's help in the event of German attack. It was therefore planned that in this area French forces should advance, as necessary, into Belgium. At that same Army Commission meeting of 1934 at which Pétain had written off the dangers of the Ardennes sector, he pointed out: "We must move into Belgium. . . . We shall protect Lille, but not by fortifications in France."[1] But this strategy was nullified late in 1936 when Belgium, noting the growing danger from Germany, prudently declared her neutrality.

The fundamental weakness of the Maginot Line was then revealed: it was no longer a barrier secured in the west (beyond Pétain's "safe" Ardennes) by a cushion of Belgian territory, but a line that could be turned, a perilous open-ended commitment. Moreover, a basic inconsistency in the Pétainist defensive strategy was now apparent. It had produced a hybrid defense line, depending, along one part of its length, on static fortifications, and, along another part, on a troop mobility that would be effective only if it were spearheaded by the very armored formations that Parliament and the General Staff had rejected. However badly Hitler's panzers might blunt their teeth against the guns and concrete of the Maginot Line, they would make short work of the old-fashioned marching and lightly mechanized infantry that was Pétain's appointed defense line west of Montmédy.

It was now clear that in the very zone over which the German invading forces had swept in 1914—and might well do so again, if war came—the primarily defensive French Army was committed to a war of movement for which it was totally unequipped. Half-hearted attempts to fortify the Franco-Belgian frontier after 1936

---

[1] Gamelin: *Servir*, p. 129.

could not rectify the situation. The thinking of the politicians and generals who, under Pétain's spell, had put their faith in a partial wall of concrete and at the same time opted against tanks and airplanes, was exposed in all its weakness.

iv

But the Maginot Line had a more insidious danger. In failing to give their people an inviolable wall, France's leaders gave them instead a myth. To Frenchmen avid for security the impregnability of the Maginot Line was like the deity of whom the skeptic said: "If God did not exist, it would be necessary to invent Him." Despite its weaknesses and shortcomings (of which the public knew nothing) it massively fulfilled the hopes and lulled the fears of the most peace-dedicated nation in Europe, offering, it seemed, the complete answer to the German threat. In the thirties the story grew up that the Line extended from Basel to Dunkirk, and even down to the Mediterranean. This legend was assisted by the ambiguity of politicians and actively fostered by the French and foreign press, which published farfetched accounts of huge fortifications girdling the frontiers of France in an unbroken wall. The Line became synonymous with safety: every mention of it contributed to the comfort of a barrier behind which France could withstand all onslaughts. Above all, Frenchmen believed that if war should come again, the Maginot Line would preserve the nation's manpower from a repetition of the slaughter of 1914–18.

This wastage of a generation on the battlefields of the Western Front was the unhealed wound that ate into the spirit of France as war once more threatened Europe. There were other factors that left her unready to meet the challenge when it came in 1939: the failure of her political and military leaders to provide the right means of national defense, which was itself influenced by the popular reluctance to face the realities of the worsening situation; the political instability and corruption that brought government into disrepute and left the nation disunited, uninspired, and without a clear sense of direction; the breakdown of old disciplines and ideas of patriotism; a lessening respect for the army and the lack of drive within the army itself; the quest for peace and "normalcy" at all costs. But underlying them all was the trauma of World War I, not only the bitter memory of invasion and prolonged suffering and privation, but also the actual impoverishment of the sturdiest part of the male population through war casualties (one man in six of those called up). To the immediate loss in national vigor and leadership, both in the army and in civilian life, could be added the future and potential loss—measured by the unborn French males (approximately one million) who would have been twenty or more in 1939. No nation as essentially unwarlike as the French could suffer this tax on its vital resources without dire effects. Reduced to seeking security with a minimum of accompanying effort, France committed herself to the leader who seemed to offer this, Marshal Pétain, and to the magical though illusory panacea of the Maginot Line.

Two years before the outbreak of World War II, one of France's senior soldiers, General Debeney, pinpointed the issue for France. He wrote:

> Among a people which wishes to live and is bent on justifying its right to live, the firm decision to maintain its independence is the foremost of virtues. The means of creating and maintaining the strength which is the guarantee of this independence have long been studied; but these would be useless if they were not served by a virile *volonté*. More than anything else the war of material is also a war of wills, and only the moral preparation of a nation can give strength to the material means in the face of a possible war. This moral preparation calls for a government that governs and a people ready for the effort. Can one believe indeed that a nation educated in a reasoned patriotism, having a quiet pride in the victory of yesterday, accustomed to effort in peacetime, and the service of a State fully aware of its own authority—can one believe that this nation would tempt an aggressor? Never shall the peace which we all desire have a better guarantee.[2]

Though General Debeney's implication about the efficacy of French security measures was misleading, in other respects he precisely outlined what was necessary for France's survival. His words also contained a veiled warning. The tragedy was that the picture he drew of a dedicated, determined nation was almost the exact reverse of that which described France as the war clouds gathered in the late thirties.

---

[2] M. E. Debeney: *La Guerre et les Hommes* (1937), p. 378.

PART
TWO

BATTLE
AND
DEFEAT

Chapter 1

PLAN D AND PLAN YELLOW

"Courage, energy, confidence."
(General Gamelin to his troops)

A T HIS SUPREME HEADQUARTERS in the gloomy casemates of
the Château of Vincennes, General Gamelin, Allied Commander in Chief, was speaking on the telephone with General
Georges, Commander in Chief, Northeast. "So, general," Georges
said, "it is the Dyle manoevre." "Since the Belgians are appealing
to us, do you see what else we can do?" asked Gamelin. "Obviously not," Georges replied.[1] Soon after, from his own headquarters at La Ferté-sous-Jouarre, 30 miles northeast of Vincennes,
Georges telephoned General Billotte, commanding the Allied First
Army Group. "Holland-Belgium, manoeuvre Dyle," he ordered
tersely.[2] Down through the formations went the order, launching
the great forward move of the Allied armies to their Dutch and
Belgian battle stations.

Two hours before, in the fine and tranquil dawn of Friday,
May 10, 1940, the armed truce that had hung uneasily over Western Europe for eight months had been finally shattered.[3] With
formidable speed and power, Hitler's air and land forces had
irrupted across the frontiers of Holland, Belgium, and Luxembourg
in a concerted assault from the North Sea to the Moselle. Simultaneously German bombers attacked targets in France as far south

---

[1] M. Gamelin: *Servir* (1947), Vol. III, p. 389.
[2] G. Roton: *Années Cruciales* (1947), p. 141.
[3] Denmark and Norway were invaded on April 9.

as Lyons. Again after twenty-six years, the West was challenged
by the military might of Germany.

Throughout the Western capitals it was a tense and anxious
night. Reports of German troop movements on the Netherlands
frontiers had been steadily accumulating, and now invasion seemed
imminent. In Brussels the Cabinet remained in emergency session
from 1 a.m. onward. At The Hague the Dutch Foreign Minister,
Dr. van Kleffens, sat up in his office with colleagues until the small
hours, after the Defense Minister's warning of a dawn assault. At
2:30 Van Kleffens went home to snatch a brief rest, and woke at
4 o'clock to the sound of German bombers. Soon after, he received
a telephone report from the Dutch Minister in Brussels that the
Belgian capital had been bombed. He consulted his Prime Minister,
then telephoned to the Dutch ministers in Paris and London a vital
code word—the signal for them to request the aid of France and
Britain. Simultaneously, in Paris, Prime Minister Paul Reynaud
received a telephone call from the Belgian Ambassador informing
him that Belgium was attacked and appealing for France's help.

Only after the first attacks on the Low Countries did the
German ultimatums arrive. The German Minister at The Hague
and the Ambassador in Brussels called on the respective foreign
ministers with almost identical notes. These stated that the Germans
had long known of a Franco-British plan to invade Germany by
way of the Low Countries, and that they understood the invasion
was about to be launched: consequently, in order to forestall it
and ensure Dutch and Belgian neutrality, German troops had been
ordered to move into these countries. Both ministers promptly
rejected the notes and made it clear that their countries would resist
Germany's aggression to the utmost. In Holland, Queen Wilhelmina
issued a stirring proclamation. In Belgium, general mobilization was
ordered and King Leopold assumed command of the Belgian
Army.

As the wires and ether of Allied Europe resounded to a welter
of pleas, protests, pledges, across the Rhine the voice of Germany
spoke. At 7 a.m. Goebbels broadcast to the nation, using the same
theme as in the German notes to Holland and Belgium. Ninety
minutes later Foreign Minister von Ribbentrop issued a memorandum to the press repeating the argument. And Hitler, leaving
for his Western Front headquarters, published an order to his

troops declaring that the hour had come for the great battle that would decide the destiny of the German people for the next thousand years.

The French Army, in its positions from the Channel to the Swiss border, had been alerted for action on the evening of the ninth. Almost everywhere its first intimation of the German offensive had been the widespread air attacks that were synchronized with the assault on the Low Countries. Bombs roused the sleeping staff at the main French GHQ, Montry, and likewise the men of the 7th Colonial Infantry Regiment, 200 miles eastward near Vittel, in the Vosges. The French 9th Army, in the Meuse sector, was surprised by heavy dawn attacks on its airfields. At Vincennes itself, five miles east of Paris, the wailing sirens rang through Supreme Headquarters just after 5 a.m.

Gamelin's staff was first alerted four hours earlier, by a telephone call from a duty officer at the Ministry of National Defense in Paris, reporting suspected German troop movements along the German-Luxembourg frontier. Almost simultaneously, reports arrived of unspecified activity on the Dutch and Belgian borders. Then followed a long silence, in which officers, recalling false alarms of the previous November and January, began to think that the German moves might be a feint. But the detailed reports that started flowing in from the French Minister at Luxembourg, via the Foreign Ministry, from 3:15 on virtually settled all doubts. Final certainty came in a report from General Georges's Northeast Headquarters at 5 a.m. stating that French army airfields had been bombed. Through the night General Gamelin had been kept informed of events by his Chief of Staff, Colonel Petibon. When the German offensive was confirmed he moved into his office to take control.

General Maurice Gamelin, aged sixty-seven, devoted lieutenant of Joffre in World War I and French Commander in Chief since 1935, was known for his bland imperturbability. Now he appeared calm and unflurried, even buoyant. A staff officer arriving from Montry GHQ just after Gamelin had given Georges the "Dyle Maneuver" order had never seen him so self-satisfied. A small stocky figure, his short legs canvas-gaitered, he was pacing the headquarters corridor, "quietly humming a martial air."[4] "He

---

[4] A. Beaufre: *Le Drame de 1940* (1965), p. 230.

was awaiting the battle," explained another officer. "Now it has arrived, [he feels] it is everyone's duty to conduct it with confidence."[5]

In fact, only a few days before, Gamelin seemed to have been skeptical of the battle materializing so soon. According to Paul Reynaud, he had restored army leave on May 7, despite two warnings, on April 30 and May 3, from the Military Attaché in Berne that the Germans would attack between May 8 and 10—with Sedan as the main objective.[6] But Gamelin had complete faith in his strategic counterplan. He believed his troops were ready. And he was convinced that the German offensive would be broken. Now, around 7 a.m., as the leading Allied units swung northward into Belgium and Luxembourg, from Supreme Headquarters he issued his first Order of the Day: "The attack which we have foreseen since October has been launched this morning. Germany is opening against us a struggle to the death. The watchword for France and all her Allies is: 'Courage, energy, confidence.' As Marshal Pétain said twenty-four years ago: '*Nous les aurons.*' "[7]

At this moment the morale of the French Army was probably higher than at any time since the start of the war. "All hearts are full of enthusiasm, certain of final victory," declared an officer of the 2nd Dragoons, 3rd Cavalry Division, whose regiment entered Luxembourg around breakfast time.[8] Keenness and fighting spirit obviously varied from unit to unit: but for every French soldier moving into battle—seasoned regular or older-class reservist— there was a sense of release from the long months of inactivity that had passed since September 1939. The boredom, frustration and waiting were over. What there was of "courage, energy, confidence" would now come into its own. But other things were needed too: plans, preparations, weapons adequate to confront a powerful enemy waging a kind of war totally different from that of 1914–18. This applied particularly to the French, whose army comprised the bulk of the forces ranged against Germany and would bear the brunt of the coming struggle.

---

[5] J. Minart: *P. C. Vincennes, Secteur 4* (1945), p. 101.
[6] P. Reynaud: *In the Thick of the Fight*, trans. J. D. Lambert (1955), p. 394.
[7] Gamelin: *Servir*, Vol. III, p. 390.
[8] C. A. de Gontaut-Biron: *Les Dragons de Combat* (1945), p. 50.

The French High Command had started planning to counter a German offensive in September 1939. Relying on the existing protection of the Maginot Line and the Ardennes, it assumed from the outset that Germany would again invade Belgium, in a repetition of the modified Schlieffen Plan of 1914. At the end of September General Georges, commanding in the Northeast, produced a plan —the Escaut hypothesis—for two Allied armies, one French, one British, to advance into Belgium in the event of attack (provided Belgium agreed) and form a defense line along the Escaut, or Schelde, River from the French frontier at Conde to Ghent. The Belgians, it was calculated, would extend the line from Ghent to Antwerp. But early in November, following intelligence reports that German offensive plans included Holland, the plan was amended to allow for a possible Allied move into Holland. The High Command soon realized, however, that the Escaut Line was not far enough eastward to permit an adequate coverage of Dutch territory. Consequently, in mid-November the Escaut hypothesis was abandoned. In its place was adopted the Dyle hypotheses, by which the Allies would occupy a line based on Belgium's more easterly Dyle River. Approved by the Allied Supreme Council in London on November 17, the Dyle Plan (Plan D) became the official Allied scheme for meeting a German advance into the Low Countries.

The High Command was handicapped by the strictly neutral attitude of the Dutch and Belgians. In their anxiety not to offend Germany, the two governments steadfastly declined to join in Allied defense consultations. But both Holland and Belgium had a useful chain of water obstacles on which they were relying to resist, initially at least, any German attack. In Holland there were the Yssel and Maas (the Dutch Meuse) rivers, running roughly north to south with a small gap in between. Behind these were tracts of land capable of flooding, notably the Grebbe Waterline. There was also a belt of concrete pillboxes, extending south to the Maastricht fortress, just outside the Belgian border. In Belgium there was the Albert Canal, running southeast from Antwerp to the Meuse at Liège. North of the canal, the land was floodable. Secondly, there was the Belgian Meuse itself, which ran southwestward from Liège to Namur, and then south from Namur toward Givet, in France. East of this southerly part of the Meuse lay the allegedly impenetrable Ardennes.

Nevertheless, General Gamelin had to make his plans on the assumption that the Low Countries would, on invasion, admit Allied troops. Thus in March 1940 he extended Plan D to include part of Holland, where a French army would occupy the Breda–Saint-Léonard Line. The Franco-British-Belgian armies would now hold a line, running roughly south to north, from Mézières in France, right across the center of Belgium, to a point within the frontier of southern Holland. From south to north, the plan would involve five armies: the French 9th Army, the French 1st Army, the B.E.F., the Belgian Army, the French 7th Army. Of these, the French 9th and 1st Armies, the B.E.F., and the French 7th Army were currently stationed along the Franco-Belgian frontier from Mézières eastward to the Channel. If and when Germany invaded the Low Countries, they would wheel northeast into Belgium, pivoting on Mézières, with the French 7th Army on the left moving straight through Belgium to straddle the Belgian-Dutch border. Together with the Belgian Army, they would then cover the following sectors from south to north: French 9th Army, Mézières-Namur; French 1st Army, Namur-Wavre; B.E.F., Wavre-Louvain; Belgian Army, Louvain-Antwerp; French 7th Army, Turnhout-Breda. North of the 7th Army, the eight divisions of the Netherlands Army would cover Holland.

In working out Plan D, Gamelin and the High Command were conscious of that old menace, the German right wing, which had carved its way through Belgium into France in August 1914. They believed that once more, as in 1914, the main assault would come in the Belgian plains north of Namur. The region south of Namur—the wooded, hilly territory of the Ardennes, and the steep-banked Meuse—they discounted as presenting no serious threat. ("Hence this sector is not dangerous," Pétain had told the Army Commission of the Senate six years before.) For this reason they made the fateful decision to place their two strongest armies —the 7th and the 1st—north of Namur, and their weakest to the south.

Pétain himself had foreshadowed Plan D when he said in 1934 that France must move into Belgium to protect Lille. Nonetheless, the plan was a radical departure from everything the French High Command had previously stood for. The French Army was abandoning a continuous fortified line within its own borders for a discontinuous, doubtfully fortified line in the middle of Belgium. Yet it was still committed to a strategy of static linear defense, despite the fact that it would have to be highly mobile to reach its distant positions, and that the German operations in Poland had shown that only a defense in depth could counter the enemy's swift and powerful armored penetrations.

The four Franco-British armies assigned to execute Plan D were to be formed into First Army Group under General Billotte.[9] This group also included, on its right flank, the French 2nd Army, holding the Sedan sector and the western end of the Maginot Line. Unlike the rest of the group, the 2nd Army would not move forward into Belgium, though it would send light cavalry forces into Belgian Luxembourg. On the right of First Army Group were Second and Third Army Groups, holding the rest of the Maginot Line and the Rhine defenses as far as Switzerland. From the Channel to the Swiss border were to be stationed, at the beginning of May 1940, a total of 102 divisions (92 French and 10 British). Behind these was ranged Gamelin's general reserve of 11 infantry (including one motorized) and 3 armored divisions.

The High Command's attitude to armored warfare was illustrated by the history of these armored divisions. When war broke out, none of them existed. Not until mid-January 1940 were the 1st and 2nd Divisions formed, and the 3rd even later; and of these only the 1st was, in General Georges's view, ready to fight on May 10. At that time the 2nd and 3rd were still below strength and not fully trained and equipped. Throughout the early spring they were assembling, exercising, and maneuvering in the training camps of Champagne—a highly tentative and experimental arm of the French Army. The 4th Armored Division had not yet come into being. This was to be hastily created after Hitler had attacked.

On the map, Plan D had a certain bold simplicity. Along with the Belgian Army, one British and three French armies would face the Germans on a 100-mile barrier of rivers and fortifications down the length of Belgium. But, in relation to the needs of Plan D, there were strange anomalies in what was allotted to Billotte's First

---

[9] A unified command was achieved only after May 12. Before this, the French 7th Army and the B.E.F. were under General Georges's orders.

Army Group out of the total of 102 divisions posted from the Channel to the Swiss border. While Billotte disposed 40 divisions, Second and Third Army Groups, guarding their permanent defenses, comprised 62. And of the total of 31 French "active" divisions (those which were reinforced with young reservists), Billotte was allocated only 10. Moreover, the most weakly manned part of the whole front was not behind the steel and concrete of the Maginot Line but in the central sector occupied by First Army Group's 9th and 2nd Armies. Here, along a poorly fortified 95-mile frontage, would stand 16 mediocre divisions, half of them reservist. This was the zone, south of Namur and facing the Ardennes, on which, as the French High Command calculated, there would be no major German attack.

In the New Year, Gamelin's ideas about the main direction of German attack seemed confirmed by the Germans themselves. On January 10, a German plane carrying two officers made a forced landing in Limburg, northeast Belgium. One of the officers had in his possession a set of operational instructions for an imminent invasion of Belgium. These included orders for a general air-supported attack toward the North Sea, through the Belgium-Luxembourg zone, and an assault in army strength west of Maastricht (into northeast Belgium). The offensive was apparently fixed for dawn on the fourteenth. The Belgian and French High Commands took the threat seriously. In both countries the troops stood ready to move to battle stations. The Belgian frontier barriers were opened to admit the Franco-British armies. But on the fourteenth nothing happened, and after a few hours the state of alert was relaxed. Whatever the Germans' real intentions, at least they learned that in the event of invasion the Allied forces would advance into Belgium with the agreement of the hitherto neutral Belgians.

The captured orders also prescribed an airborne attack in south Belgium, between the Meuse and Sambre rivers. And they particularly mentioned the Meuse sector, extending south from Namur to the French frontier, noting the lack of permanent fortifications and troop concentrations in the area. This was the allotted front of the weak 9th Army. But the French High Command was more interested in the disclosure of the enemy plan to launch the main attack through the Belgian plains, as in 1914. In any case, it saw no reason for altering Plan D. "The information gathered from the German fliers did not, as far as I was concerned," Gamelin wrote later, "have any influence on our decisions."[1]

Up to now the official German invasion plan had in fact been for an orthodox outflanking movement in Belgium, on the lines of the Schlieffen Plan. This was laid down in the first version of Plan Yellow, produced by the General Staff on October 19, 1939. After the fall of Warsaw, Hitler had quickly turned his attention westward. Plan Yellow was the result of his directive of early October, ordering preparations for an offensive in the west. Version One specified an attack through Holland, Belgium, and Luxembourg with the primary aim of seizing central Belgium and defeating as much as possible of the Allied armies. Three army groups were involved in it, operating respectively in Holland, central Belgium and the Ardennes. The strongest was the middle one, General Fedor von Bock's Army Group B, which was to thrust across Belgium to the coast. Thus the main weight of the German attack would come, as the French Staff was anticipating, north of Namur.

But one German general, Fritz von Manstein, was not happy about the plan. Von Manstein was Chief of Staff to General von Rundstedt, commander of Army Group A, the group detailed for the Ardennes operation. As he saw it, Von Bock's group, in central Belgium, would clash with the strongest Allied forces and achieve nothing decisive. Von Manstein's own idea was for the principal attack to be made by Army Group A in the less heavily defended Meuse-Ardennes sector. The question was whether the German panzer divisions could negotiate the notoriously difficult Ardennes terrain. Von Manstein consulted the tank expert General Heinz Guderian, who, after closely studying the problem, concluded that the operation was practicable. By now Von Manstein's chief, Von Rundstedt, was equally interested in the proposal; and at the end of October he sent a memorandum to the OKH (the German Army High Command) in Berlin, putting the case for the Ardennes concept.

This was the start of a long tussle between OKH on the one hand and Von Manstein and Von Rundstedt on the other. OKH

---

[1] Gamelin: *Servir*, Vol. III, p. 163.

refused to consider the amendment, despite a stream of further memoranda from Army Group A. Finally, at the end of January, the too-persistent Von Manstein was posted off to command an army corps at Stettin. His plan seemed fated to founder. But he had support in an unexpected quarter. Hitler himself was unconvinced about Plan Yellow: he feared that his panzers in Belgium might be stopped by the Allies blowing up a number of essential bridges. From the beginning of November the Führer began to consider other possibilities, notably a stronger effort in the south. He even provisionally ordered that Army Group A should take over Army Group B's panzers, if these should be halted in Belgium. As yet he did not visualize the main assault being switched to his left or southern wing. But in mid-February Von Manstein happened to dine with him on his way to Stettin, and took the opportunity of explaining Army Group A's views to him.

The Allied seizure of the German orders in January had already jeopardized the existing Plan Yellow. Von Manstein's meeting with Hitler sealed its doom. Hitler was sufficiently impressed with the Ardennes concept to adopt it at once. On February 18, he embodied it in his War Directive No. 10, which said: "Forces operating south of the line Liège-Charleroi will force a passage of the Meuse between Dinant and Sedan (both inclusive) and will advance through the French frontier defences towards the Somme estuary."[2] General von Brauchitsch, Commander in Chief, who had conceived the original plan and stubbornly defended it ever since, finally had to give in. A week later, Plan Yellow was issued in its fifth and definitive form. This, at last, gave Von Rundstedt's Army Group A the main—and enormously preponderant—role in the coming offensive. Built up from 2 to 3 armies —44 divisions, of which 7 were armored—it was to make a rapid crossing of the Ardennes and Meuse between Sedan and Dinant, and establish bridgeheads with a view to advancing toward the Channel. By a fateful play of circumstance, directly in its path would stand the weakest formations of the whole Allied line, the French 2nd and 9th Armies.

---

[2] H. R. Trevor-Roper, ed.: *Hitler's War Directives, 1939–1945* (1964), p. 22.

Chapter 2

➤➤➤➤➤➤➤➤➤●◄◄◄◄◄◄◄◄◄◄

LULL IN THE WEST

"There shouldn't be any bombing until May, 1941."
(A French General)

ABOUT 2 A.M. ON MAY 8, 1940, a French bombing squadron was returning from a leaflet-dropping raid on Düsseldorf. Suddenly its commander, Colonel François, spotted below him a long lighted transport column. Flying down to take a closer look, he saw that it was a 60-mile convoy of German armored vehicles moving toward the French frontier. Back at base, François tried to make an urgent report to his commanding general, but could not get the duty officer on the telephone as the N.C.O. in charge had orders not to disturb anyone until 7 o'clock. On François's insistence, an officer finally came on the line to take his report. Nothing more happened until midday, when an air force general visited François's camp. François repeated his story to the general, who coolly replied: "Don't worry, colonel, there shouldn't be any bombing before May, 1941."[1]

In the weeks and months before Hitler struck in the West, too many Frenchmen in and out of uniform thought like this. Although France was physically mobilized for war, in a more total sense she was unready. The long truce had bred a complacency and overconfidence, produced a slackening of the urgent mood that had alerted the nation the previous autumn. The feeling was abroad that—as in the words of British Prime Minister Neville Chamberlain—Hitler had "missed the bus." Frenchmen were convincing themselves that Germany could be beaten without any actual shooting; or that, even if there was shooting, there would be no

---

[1] M. Ribet: *Le Procés de Riom* (1945), p. 496.

repetition of the slaughter of the last war. But beneath the easy thinking lay a deeper motivation—a strong aversion to war itself. Renewed confrontation with Germany was the historic challenge that had hung over France since her defeat in the Franco-Prussian War of 1870. She had met and overcome the challenge in the years 1914–18, but at a nearly crippling cost. Now it had recurred with greater menace; and it found France less than fully committed as a nation, lacking the iron determination and unanimous driving force needed to prosecute all-out war.

France had entered the war with none of the idealism that had fired her in 1914. As the mobilization posters went up in the first days of September 1939, there were no flowers, no cries of *"À Berlin!"* The soldiers had responded with a dour fatalism, aware of the realities of war—as their fathers had not been, twenty-five years before. They were "resolute and determined," noted Louis Lévy, correspondent of the Left-wing *Le Populaire,* "ready for heroism, though not for bravado."

Unhappily for the morale of the French Army, the long ensuing months of virtual idleness and almost peacetime routine offered no chance for heroism. While in 1914 the troops were plunged straight into battle, now they stagnated in the inertia of France's *"drôle de guerre."*

On mobilization, France's Field Army numbered 2,776,000, and her Army of the Interior, 2,224,000. From the first, the High Command was confronted with the problem of how to employ these vast forces. Apart from the minor early operations in Alsace-Lorraine, there was no way for them to gain battle experience. (And even here the High Command, for reasons of its own, discouraged fighting, giving orders that German working parties, when observed, must not be fired on.) All that could be done was to take advantage of the respite with training and work on improving the defenses on the Franco-Belgian and Franco-Luxembourg borders. But as the months passed with no move from Hitler, discipline and keenness suffered. Installed behind the Maginot Line and protected by the Belgian frontier, the Meuse, and the dense curtain of the Ardennes, troops began to believe that, with Germany supposedly being starved into defeat by blockade, they would never actually have to fight.

Many of the older reservists, married and family men, wondered why they had been called up at all. They resented being dragged from civilian life to waste their time aimlessly soldiering when they might have been better employed at home. This mood was encouraged by peace propaganda that came from both front and rear. In the Maginot Line the troops were bombarded by a constant barrage of German antiwar propaganda in the form of leaflets, loudspeaker exhortations, and messages displayed on billboards. Now that the fighting in the east was finished and the Danzig and Polish questions settled, the French were told, there was no point in France continuing the war. Away from the line, in the crowded back areas, the men were subjected to the pacifist views of the French Communists.

To make matters worse, late in 1939 winter set in hard and bitter. This slowed down what training there was and in many places stopped work on the defenses. Training was one of the major difficulties of the High Command during these months. Four fifths of the French Army was composed of reservists: likewise 100,000 of its 128,000 officers were from the reserve. In a number of inferior reservist or "Series B" divisions, the men's average age was as high as thirty-five. These troops were in poor physical shape and badly in need of toughening up, let alone training. Moreover, the officers and N.C.O.'s in charge of them had had only short peacetime instruction courses and were inexperienced in up-to-date arms and equipment, as well as lacking in training expertise. This was in contrast to the cadres of the German Army, formed during the immediate prewar years and trained in units that were on a war footing and had the most modern equipment. The French High Command tried to give as many men as possible battle training by sending units for a spell in the more active parts of the Maginot Line. Here, in the advance posts, they were in contact with the Germans and could take part in patrols, ward off surprise attacks, live under fighting conditions. But these active interludes, not more than seven days in duration, were too short to be of much value.

When troops were not undergoing a semblance of training, they were put to defense work. From the Channel to the Maginot Line there was an extensive defense program—barbed-wire laying, building of tank traps, pillboxes, and strong points. In the Maginot Line itself there was constant reinforcement. Vital as this work was, often it was carried out at the expense of training. In March

1940, a British observer behind the Maginot Line noted men who should have been training digging fieldworks to extend the depth of the Maginot defenses. In some units, active troops were so used to working as pioneers that when the Germans attacked in May 1940 they were surprised at being ordered to fight. But despite the French Army's concern with defense, much of the work executed in these months was uncoordinated and inadequate. In certain key sectors like the Meuse, it was not even completed by the beginning of May.

But there were other things wrong with the French Army too. It seemed to lack the drive and energy necessary to make it an effective fighting instrument. Not all the apathy apparent among units was due to the prolonged inaction of the *"drôle de guerre."* Too many men had brought with them a malaise from civilian life— a nationwide malaise stemming from the ordeals of World War I and the troubles and disillusionments of the peace years. While the crack regular formations were as good as ever, reservist divisions— especially in the rear areas—were poorly disciplined, slack, un-soldierly. Likewise, the reservist officers and N.C.O.'s failed to exert the authority that was vital for their troops' efficiency. The old officer-soldier relationship of World War I was being replaced by a new "democratic" attitude. "We no longer dare to command, and our men no longer know how to obey," a lieutenant told General Charles Menu at the beginning of May 1940.[2] The tough, experienced General Touchon, who was to command in the May operations, diagnosed the trouble as a failure of officers and N.C.O.'s to reassume, upon call-up, the old habits of authority which they had lost during civilian life. The effects of this were to be seen in the coming battles. At the end of May an officer declared to General Gamelin: "My reserve officers? Many of them don't command any more. They discuss things with the *syndicat*."[3]

The faults were equally evident in the army's top echelons. From the High Command downward, many senior officers showed little sense of urgency. General Alan Brooke, commanding the British 2nd Army Corps in France, found most of those he met "excellent company, amusing conversationalists, familiar with all the latest gossip from Paris, and thoroughly unreliable."[4] André

---

[2] C. L. Menu: *Lumière sur les Ruines* (1953), p. 48.
[3] Gamelin: *Servir* (1946), Vol. I, p. 357.
[4] A. Bryant: *The Turn of the Tide* (1957), p. 70.

Maurois, on a preinvasion tour of areas just behind the front, wondered how the "amiable old men" recalled as colonels and generals would cope in the event of attack.[5] Often commanders were not in close enough touch with their formations. In the headquarters messes they wined and dined in peacetime luxury. At one mess Brooke had to sit down to a two-hour banquet that left him unfit for work for the rest of the day. A few energetic generals like Huntziger tried to combat the inertia and instill their men with a fighting spirit. But the leadership defects reached right up to Supreme Headquarters itself. By his own admission General Gamelin was unaware of any morale weakness in the army. On his frequent tours of higher headquarters, he later recalled, no general had ever mentioned to him a lack of confidence in his troops. "Living exclusively in contact with army commands," he confessed, "I recognise that I had not sufficiently realised the state of mind that was tending to spread through the whole country and army."[6]

The reverses of May 1940 were to shock Gamelin into a sudden sweeping condemnation of the troops whose shortcomings he had failed to detect before. Reporting to the government on the Meuse operations, he wrote on May 18: "The French soldier, the citizen of yesterday, did not believe in the war. His interest did not extend beyond the group in his factory, office or field. Prone to constant criticism of anyone wielding authority, encouraged . . . to enjoy an easy day-to-day life, in the inter-war years today's call-up man did not receive the moral and patriotic education that would have prepared him for the drama in which the fate of the country was to be enacted."[7] Gamelin seemed to forget that the High Command had had eight months in which to reindoctrinate these defaulting troops.

The truth was that the *"drôle de guerre"* had induced what General Laffargue called a "doctrine of minimum effort"[8] on both the army and home fronts. Laffargue saw the High Command and the government as equally responsible: neither the military nor civil leaders were giving the country any moral preparation for the

---

[5] A. Maurois: *Why France Fell*, trans. Denver Lindley (1941), p. 91.

[6] Gamelin: *Servir* (1947), Vol. III, pp. 386–7.

[7] Ibid., p. 425.

[8] A. Laffargue: *Justice pour Ceux de 1940* (1952), p. 117.

trials to come. Apart from the disappearance of most able-bodied males, civilian France retained an almost peacetime atmosphere in these waiting months. Troops returning home on leave saw nothing to inspire them with the zeal that was wanting in the Zone of the Armies. The stern early mood of *"Il faut en finir"* was swiftly fading and many Frenchmen felt that since Germany had achieved her aims in the east, there was small point in continuing to oppose her. But if the war had to go on they had little doubt about the result. The press, fed with official propaganda, optimistically assumed victory as a foregone conclusion: Germany, it was implied, would eventually be beaten by the Allied blockade; and in any case there was the impregnable Maginot Line. In Paris life proceeded almost normally. At night the city was dimmed by an ineffective blackout, and there were sandbags at the Arc de Triomphe and round the Obelisk in the Place de la Concorde. Places of entertainment, reopened in November after a brief closing, did their usual business. There was no food rationing, and Parisians celebrated Christmas with a gay disregard for the war. As for the front, this was becoming increasingly remote from people's thoughts. After four months of eventless war, Paris—and with it, France—seemed lulled into a comfortable oblivion of danger.

But beneath the carefree civilian surface, France was slowly gearing herself for war. In setting up a Ministry of Munitions and mobilizing industry for war production, the government had first to overcome the difficulties caused by the call-up of one man in eight for the forces. Initially, the mobilization of some 135,000 key industrial specialists had adversely affected production, and these men later had to be recalled to industry. With all the wartime dislocation of manpower, and the reorganization necessary for turning the country over to arms production, not until April 1940 were the guns, planes, and tanks rolling from the arsenals and factories in full volume. But the late start meant that output of some weapons would be insufficient; and, equally serious, owing to the High Command's faulty assessment of military needs, certain vital armament was of unsuitable design or lacking altogether.

All the evidence suggested that, on the ground, the coming battles in the west would be dominated by the tank. Ranging swift, wide and deep, as in Poland, it was the new master of the battlefield. But in framing its arms program, the French High Command was committed to the logic of Plan D. This, with its basis of static linear defense, allotted the tank only a secondary role, as supporting arm to the infantry. Consequently, though production was to reach about 3,000 by May—approximately equaling the German figure—the French tanks were ill-fitted for modern mobile warfare. Compared with the German tanks—lightly armored, lightly gunned, and built primarily for speed and range—they were slow, heavy and unwieldy. The largest, of 35 tons, had armor up to 70 millimeters thick, and mounted two guns, a 47mm. and a 75mm. These could withstand all German tank or antitank fire and pierce all German armor. Firepower and strength were the chief assets of all French tanks, but for these they sacrificed precious mobility and cruising range and speed.[9]

The High Command was likewise ignoring the other main lesson of Poland: the key offensive role of aircraft. While Germany would have available by May something over 3,000 planes, including up to 400 Stukas, France would have no more than about 1,200—with no dive bombers. This gave a German superiority of almost 3 to 1, though the opposing fighter strength (if the 130 British fighter planes to be based in France in May 1940 were added in) would be roughly equal—an Allied total of 800-odd compared with a German total of 1,000 at most. In speed, however, the Germans would have the advantage: their Messerschmitts (Me 109's and Me 110's) were capable of about 360 miles an hour, as against the 306 miles an hour of the French Curtiss, the 300 miles an hour of the Potez and Morane, and the 356 miles an hour of the French-based Hurricanes. (The Spitfires were faster, but were based in Britain.) As to heavy and medium bomber strength, France would be enormously inferior in May 1940: against Germany's 1,470, she would dispose about 150.[1]

Similarly with antiaircraft artillery: compared with the German total of 9,300, the French were to turn out less than 3,000. French antitank gun production, 8,000 at the highest estimate, was to be well below the army's needs. Only in field artillery was

---

[9] The main types of French tanks were the light-medium R 35 and H 35, the fast-medium Somua 36, and the heavy B 1 and B 2. Other types were the H 39 and R 40. The main German types were the panzer Kw I, Kw II, Kw III, and Kw IV. (A. Goutard: *The Battle of France, 1940*, trans. A. R. P. Burgess (1958), p. 29.

[1] Goutard: *Battle of France*, pp. 32–4.

France to exceed Germany. In this arm for which she was always famous she would, by May, possess over 11,000 guns of all calibers from 75mm. to 280mm., as against Germany's 7,700-odd. But even here France was at a disadvantage, for her artillery was mainly horse-drawn and therefore unsuited to mobile operations.

With the coming of spring, the long respite of the *"drôle de guerre"* was ending. Early in April, German forces occupied Norway and Denmark; and it was clear that Hitler was soon to launch his full-scale offensive in the west. How far France had taken advantage of the eight-month lull to gird herself for war—morally and militarily—would now be seen.

Calmly contemplating the position in the stony isolation of Vincennes, Gamelin had no qualms about the outcome of the approaching struggle. Unfortunately, his own confidence in the army's readiness was not matched by the government's confidence in him. Within less than twenty-four hours of the German attack, a major Cabinet crisis arose, which involved Gamelin's leadership. The Prime Minister, Paul Reynaud, who had succeeded Éduoard Daladier in March, was profoundly dissatisfied with Gamelin's handling of the French part in the recent Allied expedition to Norway; and now he decided to relieve him of his command. Early on May 9 he informed President Lebrun of his intention, and then put the proposal to the Cabinet Council. Though the majority was in favor, the move was opposed by Daladier, the National Defense and War Minister and Gamelin's faithful supporter. Confronted with this situation, Reynaud resolved to resign as soon as a new government could be formed.

That night the Germans invaded. In the face of the national emergency, Reynaud rescinded his own resignation and withdrew his objections to Gamelin. On the tenth he wrote to the Commander in Chief at Vincennes: "General. The battle has begun. One thing only counts: to win the victory. We shall all work in unison to this end." Gamelin replied: *"Monsieur le President. There is only one answer to your letter of today. France alone is of importance."*[2]

---

[2] P. Reynaud: *In the Thick of the Fight*, trans. J. D. Lambert (1955), p. 287.

Chapter 3

➤➤➤➤➤➤➤➤➤ ● ◄◄◄◄◄◄◄◄◄

[81]

THE CONFRONTATION

"Now Gamelin has the battle he waited for."

(Paul Reynaud)

THE DAWN SILENCE was broken by the drone of aircraft flying out of the east. The steady thrum woke sleeping Dutchmen in the broad heathlands of North Brabant and beyond the Maas as far as Rotterdam and The Hague. Farther south, it echoed over the Belgian countryside, the towns and villages of Limburg, the rooftops of Antwerp and Brussels. As the sound passed overhead, people wondered uneasily what it meant. Some Dutchmen thought that German planes were heading to attack England. But for thousands of Dutch and Belgians the answer came in the thunder of exploding bombs. At approximately 4:30 a.m. Western European time, Hitler was opening his offensive on the Low Countries.

All over Holland and Belgium the bombs struck devastatingly at the vitals of national defense—airfields, hangars, barracks, and antiaircraft gun sites. Swiftly on top of the bombs came the swarms of paratroops, dropped from Junkers 52 transports. Then followed the glider-borne forces, armed with grenades, machine guns, and flame throwers. Supporting the paratroops, these men raced to seize strategic bridges, airfields, fortress defenses. Although Dutch and Belgium troops had been alerted overnight, at scores of points they were overwhelmed by the violence and suddenness of the attack. To add to the confusion, the Germans were dropping dummy paratroops, and in Holland large numbers of fifth-columnists were appearing. Before the sun was well up on this morning of May 10, havoc had been created throughout the Dutch and Bel-

gian rear areas by what was, relatively, no more than a handful
of determined, highly trained airborne assault troops.

Meanwhile, across some 170 miles of Dutch, Belgian, and
Luxembourg frontier rolled the leading units of two German army
groups—the great invasion force of Plan Yellow. For his western
offensive Hitler had massed about 117 divisions, including an
OKH reserve of some 42. He was thus committing about 75 divisions to the attack on the Low Countries and Luxembourg. In
the north, the 18th Army (General von Küchler) and the 6th
Army (General von Reichenau)—comprising General Fedor
von Bock's Army Group B—were sweeping into Holland, and
Belgium north of Liège. Their task was to subdue Holland and
contain the maximum body of Allied troops in Belgium. South of
these, the 4th Army (General von Kluge), supported by the 12th
Army (General List) and the 16th Army (General Busch)—
General von Rundstedt's Army Group A—were surging over the
borders of central Belgium and Luxembourg. Theirs was the cru-
cial role: to push through the Ardennes, cross the Belgian and
French Meuse, and advance westward through northern France.
For this they were allotted 45 divisions as against Army Group
B's 28.

Rumbling forward into Luxembourg, in the vanguard of
Army Group A, was a formidable array of panzers. This was the
armored spearhead—no less than 7 out of the German Army's entire total of 10 panzer divisions—that was to crash its way west
between Dinant and Sedan and onward to the Channel. Now it
was concentrated in two formations, General von Kleist's group of
5 divisions and Hoth's group of 2, attached to Von Kluge's 4th
Army command. The 3 remaining armored divisions were with
Army Group B in the north, but even of these, 2 were already
earmarked to supplement the 4th Army striking force as operations
developed. In all, Von Kluge's army was to have at its disposal
some 2,500 tanks.

As the first battles flared along the invaded borders, one sector of the German front remained tensely quiet. Away to the east
of Luxembourg, General Ritter von Leeb's Army Group C stood
facing the Maginot Line. With the 17 divisions of his two armies,
the 1st (General von Witzleben) and the 7th (General Dollmann),
Von Leeb was performing an undramatic but vital task. He was
securing the German left flank and immobilizing something like

three times the number of French divisions stationed behind the
Maginot defenses from Luxembourg to the Swiss border—those
in the four armies of Second and Third Army Groups, commanded
respectively by Generals Prétalat and Besson.

But west of the silent Maginot Line, along the Franco-Belgian
border, there was intense activity. At 6:30 a.m. General Georges
had passed the "Plan D" order to First Army Group. Now, soon
after seven, on a 150-mile line from Mézières to the English Channel, the Allied armies were on the move.

Preparing to head past the frontier barriers into Belgium were
First Army Group's advanced formations—the 1st Light Mechanized Division of the French 7th Army, the 2nd and 3rd Light
Mechanized Divisions (General Prioux's famous Cavalry Corps)
of the French 1st Army, the vanguard divisions of the B.E.F.'s
1st and 2nd Corps. These were the troops that would cover the
Plan D positions until the main forces arrived. Behind them the
bulk of the Franco-British armies were forming up to follow. That
day they would begin the great northeastward wheel through Belgium that would bring them to their planned defense sectors. In
the Allied lines this was a tonic moment. Now at last there was
a fighting role for all those units that had soldiered through the
long months in their camps and barracks behind the French frontier: the French, the British, and the men from overseas serving
under the Allied flags; the French 7th Army's 9th and 25th Motorized Infantry Divisions and 21st, 4th, 60th, and 68th Infantry
Divisions; Lord Gort's nine B.E.F. divisions; the French 1st
Army's 2nd and 5th North African Infantry Divisions, 1st Moroccan Infantry Division, and 101st Infantry Division; and the divisions of the French 9th and 2nd Armies that were to guard the
Belgian and French Meuse.

These divisions had widely varying distances to go. To reach
the Dutch-Belgian border beyond Antwerp and form a link with
General Winkelman's Dutch Army the French 7th Army, commanded by General Giraud, had to cover well over 100 miles.
The B.E.F., assigned the 17-mile Louvain-Wavre sector, had
70-odd miles to travel. The French 1st Army, commanded by
General Blanchard, below the B.E.F. on the 25-mile Wavre-
Namur front, had about fifty. Committed to the shortest advance
of all was the French 9th Army, led by General Corap. The 9th
had merely to pivot on a point somewhere north of Mézières and

cover a 50-mile front behind the French and Belgian Meuse extending north to Namur.

There remained one gap to fill: the Antwerp-Louvain Line, between the French 7th Army and B.E.F. sectors. This was assigned to the Belgians. But the Belgian Army had a more vital part than this to play in Plan D. It was to be the whole backbone of the preliminary defense of central Belgium. Fighting on its own soil and with its flanks covered by the advance Franco-British formations, it would take the main initial weight of the German attack. Of its total of twenty-four infantry divisions, ten would hold the key defensive positions on the Albert Canal, the Meuse, and the fortified bases of Antwerp, Liège, and Namur. Two forward divisions would stand on the frontier canals, and two would operate in Belgian Luxembourg. One division would remain on the permanent Antwerp-Louvain defense line, protecting Brussels; and other divisions would be in reserve. On the staying power of the Albert Canal and Liège divisions depended, it could be said, the success or failure of Plan D. To enable the main Franco-British forces to reach and occupy their lines, the Belgians would have to hold for up to five days. Only then could they safely fall back to the Antwerp-Louvain Line.

This five-day time factor was the crux of Gamelin's Plan D. Could the Belgians withstand for so long what might well be a Poland-style *blitzkrieg*? When the Franco-British armies were finally in place, the Allied forces strung across Belgium would comprise a total of some fifty-three divisions. Banking on his conviction that the chief German assault would come in the Belgian plains, Gamelin was sending his best formations right into Belgium. Of the three French armies, the strongest was Blanchard's 1st (comprising the two light mechanized divisions of the Cavalry Corps, three "active"[1] and one "Series A"[2] infantry divisions). Almost as strong was Giraud's 7th Army (with one light mechanized division, two motorized infantry divisions, one "active," one "Series A" and two "Series B"[3] infantry divisions). By far the weakest of the three was Corap's 9th Army (with one motorized

---

[1] "Active" divisions: existing before the war, these were of top fighting quality.

[2] "Series A" divisions: superior or first reserve divisions.

[3] "Series B" divisions: inferior or second reserve divisions.

infantry division, one "active" infantry division, two cavalry divisions—consisting of one horse brigade and one light motorized brigade—two "Series A" and two "Series B" infantry divisions, one fortress[4] infantry division and one Spahi brigade). On a par with the 9th was General Huntziger's 2nd Army, which was guarding the Sedan sector at right angles to the 9th Army. (Huntziger's army comprised two "active" divisions, two cavalry divisions similar to those of Corap, one "Series A" and two "Series B" infantry divisions and one Spahi cavalry brigade.)

Under the early sun, the Allied advance columns roared up the flat Belgian roads. In the townships of West Flanders and Hainaut, welcoming Belgians hailed them as they passed—the forerunners of the massive Franco-British aid to come. But crucial hours and days would elapse before that aid could be fully deployed. Already, in the frontier battle grounds to the northeast, the fighting was going badly for both Dutch and Belgians.

Shocked and disrupted by the dawn attacks, they were now under heavy pressure at various points in front and rear. In Holland, General Winkelman's troops were falling back to the Maas and Upper Yssel. More serious, in a forced retreat in the Maastricht Peninsula (the tongue of Dutch territory separating Belgian Kimburg from Germany) they had failed to destroy certain vital Maas (Meuse) bridges. It was here in the Maastricht Peninsula that the Germans were concentrating the main weight of their assault. Against this 30-mile front were being hurled four corps and one armored corps of General von Reichenau's 6th Army, supported by massed dive bombers. The seizure of the bridges was disastrous for the Belgians. It enabled the Germans to turn the eastern end of the Albert Canal and cross the canal itself as well as the Maas near Maastricht. Meanwhile, the great Belgian fort of Eben Emael, a few miles south toward Liège, was in danger of falling to a violent airborne attack. Its capture would lose the Belgians the use of its powerful guns commanding the Albert Canal.

Farther to the rear, other hazards were appearing. During the morning a French advance party reached the French 1st Army

---

[4] Fortress divisions: static divisions, used for manning fortifications.

line between Wavre and Namur, to find defenses virtually non-existent. This sector, linking the Dyle and Meuse River lines, included the difficult "Gembloux gap," a tract of bare and open country particularly favorable for tanks. Late in 1939 the Belgians were supposed to have started building antitank obstacles here, but had changed their minds and constructed them more forward, at Perwez. Now, surveying the ground between Wavre and Namur, the French were amazed to discover a terrain almost devoid of obstacles, trenches, and strong points. Immediately to the north, the B.E.F.'s Dyle position was in much the same state. For both armies this meant an expenditure of precious time digging themselves in on their arrival.

It was the B.E.F. and French 1st Army sectors that were chiefly menaced by the swift German crossing of the Meuse and Albert Canal. The Cavalry Corps of General Prioux (the 2nd and 3rd Light Motorized Divisions, which were the 1st Army's advance formations) found itself in a dangerous situation when it reached its forward covering positions on the line Tirlemont-Hannut-Huy in the afternoon. With no main force behind it and the Belgians being hard-pressed by Von Reichenau's troops less than 30 miles in front, it was perilously exposed. To the north, the 7th Army's recently arrived 1st Light Mechanized Division was in similar trouble. This division, ordered to establish liaison between the Dutch and Belgians, was in danger of being isolated when the Belgians, under their commander General Bogaert, withdrew to the west of the Albert Canal in the face of a German panzer advance over the canal bridges. The Belgians had been expected to hold along the canal line for up to five days, while the Franco-British armies got into position behind them. Now their early reverses threatened to upset the whole Allied defense scheme before it was even operating.

Down on the southern flank of First Army Group, General Corap's 9th Army was moving into action. The 9th had an important initial role: to send its advance formations—the 1st and 4th Light Cavalry Divisions and the 3rd Brigade of Spahis—across the Meuse into the Belgian Ardennes to reconnoiter the strength of approaching enemy forces. If necessary the troops were to fight a delaying action while the main body took up position along the French and Belgian Meuse. But the 9th got off to a slow start.

Though it had the shortest distance to travel of any of the armies, not until the afternoon did its motorized elements reach the Meuse. Then General Corap took the questionable decision to hold them back from crossing until morning. Communicated to GHQ, Northeast, at La Ferté, at 5 p.m., this order was countermanded by General Georges, who instructed Corap to push his formations forward at once. But vital time was already lost for probing the armored threat steadily moving west through the Ardennes.

In the Sedan sector to the right of the 9th Army, the motorized elements of General Huntziger's 2nd Army swung into movement more quickly than Corap's. (At least part of the 2nd Army had been poorly served by Intelligence. The first that a signals officer in a reserve division, the 71st, knew of the German attack was when he picked up an appeal by the King of the Belgians at 7:30 a.m. on his radio set.) Huntziger managed to send his leading mobile units over the Meuse soon after 7 a.m. on receipt of final orders from First Army Group. While the main body of the 2nd Army was to remain statically guarding the Sedan front, these formations—the 2nd and 5th Light Cavalry Divisions and 1st Cavalry Brigade—had a similar role to those of the 9th. They were to advance to a line Bastogne-Arlon, in the Ardennes, facing the Luxembourg border, slightly south and east of the 9th Army's line.

The 2nd Army front had thus far escaped with no more than a dawn visit of enemy reconnaissance planes. War still seemed remote from this border zone where the Meuse flowed gently against the wooded background of the Ardennes. Most of the civilian population was still there. General Huntziger had not encouraged a rush of evacuation. "I prefer risk to catastrophe,"[5] he said. In the small holiday town of Bouillon, just over the Belgian frontier, the citizens seemed unable to grasp that the Germans had attacked. As the French troops clattered through the streets en route for the Ardennes, they stood at their doors gazing blankly at them. Even the mayor failed to realize the gravity of the situation. That afternoon Huntziger called on him to arrange for one of the town's hotels to be converted into a military hospital. The mayor was also a doctor, and Huntziger had to wait until he returned

---

[5] P. Allard: *La Vérité sur l'Affaire Corap* (1941), p. 32.

from his rounds. When he appeared he was amazed at Huntziger's request. "But, *mon general*," he stammered, "Bouillon is a summer resort. Our hotels are reserved for tourists! Do you really think we are in any danger?"[6] Historic, picturesque Bouillon, dominated by its eighth-century castle and almost encircled by the curving Semois River, had many attractions for visitors. It possessed other properties too—as the Bouillonnais would soon discover. With the protection of France in mind, the famous French fortification expert Sébastien de Vauban called it "the key of the Ardennes."

Forty miles east, the wooded tracks of the Ardennes already echoed to the din of General von Kleist's panzers. They had entered Luxembourg at 5:35 a.m. between Vlanden and Echternach, and pushed on unresisted except for roadblocks. Three hours later the leading units had reached the border of Belgian Luxembourg at Martelange, where a blown-up bridge had temporarily delayed them. Now, in the early afternoon, the panzer forces were forging west in three great columns.

Von Kleist's five-division group was headed on the left by General Heinz Guderian's XIX Armored Corps of three divisions, moving in arrowhead formation—the 1st Panzer Division preceding in the center, the 10th on the left, and the 2nd on the right. These were making for Sedan. Slightly behind them and to the right were the two panzer divisions—the 6th and 8th—and the motorized division of General Reinhardt's XLI Armored Corps, aiming toward Mézières. To the north again was General Hoth's corps of the 5th and 7th Armored Divisions and the 20th Motorized Division, whose direction was Dinant on the Belgian Meuse. With 276 combat tanks and 32 command tanks to a division, this made a total of over 1,500 tanks. Supporting them were the thirty-seven infantry divisions of General von Rundstedt's Army Group A; and behind these stood the forty-two divisions of the German General Reserve—the base of a huge steel-tipped wedge pointed at a 60-mile sector of the Franco-Belgian front.

For the German panzers, the approach march through the Ardennes of Belgian Luxembourg was a feat no less outstanding than the subsequent Meuse breakthrough. In the past, armies had

---

[6] E. Ruby: *Sedan, Terre d'Epreuve* (1948), p. 81.

always preferred to avoid this "wild and ancient forest."[7] Tradition said that in its wooded depths the four sons of Duke Aymon held out for eight winters against Charlemagne. A rugged region of heights and ridges, plateaux, and valleys, the forest's steep, rocky ravines and plunging torrents alternated with heath, bog, narrow winding trails, and trackless woodland. The frequent gorges running parallel with the roads gave small scope for lateral maneuver. While infantry troops might not find the forest insuperable, long columns of motorized vehicles might easily get immobilized if one of them broke down. They were also open to air attack in the many clearings, and to hold up from ambushes and roadblocks

This Ardennes operation of May 1940 would later be acclaimed for its supreme element of surprise. In fact, the German Army had come this way before, in August 1914. As part of the Schlieffen Plan, the 4th and 5th Armies—the center pivot of the German line sweeping down on France—were assigned to advance through the northern and southern Ardennes toward the French 4th and 3rd Army positions. These armies were ordered to counterattack in a bold move to break the German center. One French commander, General Lanrezac, who knew the Ardennes well, viewed the project with dismay. As General Langle de Cary's 4th Army was preparing its flanking attack on the German 4th Army, Lanrezac warned an officer of Langle de Cary's staff: "You meet in turn narrow gorges, with steep and wooded banks, dense forests and swampy plateaux. All this country is eminently suitable for the defensive and for ambushes. And it's there you're going to fight a battle! You won't enter this region, and if you do you won't get out."[8] The warning proved well founded. The Ardennes actions resulted in a resounding French defeat, with the 4th Army pushed back on Stenay and Sedan, and the 3rd on Verdun. Thenceforth the French had reason to remember the Ardennes for the bloody reverses they suffered in its glades and wooded depths— at Virton, Tintigny, Rossignol, and Neufchâteau.

Despite the German penetration and French defeat, the French High Command continued to see the Ardennes as a prime defen-

---

[7] H. Bidou: *La Bataille de France* (1941), p. 100.
[8] Ruby: *Sedan*, p. 16.

sive asset, the safest zone around France's borders from the English Channel to Switzerland. At the same time it disregarded the only possible means by which the forest might be used to French advantage—the positioning in it of a powerful attacking force that would be more than a mere protective or delaying screen and could disrupt and scatter, by ambush and every form of destructive tactics, advancing German formations. During the interwar years the concept of the Ardennes security gained strength. Pétain's pronouncement in 1934 that the southern exit from the forest was a sector "not dangerous" set the seal of high authority on the notion. So effective a barrier was the Ardennes considered that for some 90 miles along its fringe—between the western end of the Maginot Line at Montmédy and Mauberge—no substantial fixed fortifications were built.

Now, as the massed panzer columns spearheaded their way toward this gap, the German Army was embarked on a daring gamble. Into the hazardous terrain of the Ardennes, with its added risk of enemy opposition, was being committed no less than seven tenths of Germany's total armored strength. But the advancing tank formations had one major advantage: a number of serviceable east-west roads, especially in the directions converging on Rocroi and Sedan. They also benefited from the care with which the enterprise was prepared. Once convinced that this was feasible, the shrewd and experienced Heinz Guderian—called in initially to advise by Von Manstein—set himself to its planning with minute care. For weeks he intensively trained his panzer units over a stretch of German territory similar to the Ardennes—the hilly Eifel region between the Rhine and Moselle rivers and the Luxembourg frontier. So thoroughly did he rehearse the XIX Armored Corps that he issued orders to it covering operations up to Day 5 of the offensive (May 14). Guderian later commented that he had to make only minor changes to these orders which, in the main, were carried out entirely according to plan.

Belgian resistance in the Ardennes borderland had not been severe. Sporadic opposition from strong points of Chasseurs Ardennais, and holdups from mine fields, barbed-wire obstacles, and roadblocks were soon overcome. What could have been a danger to the close-packed moving columns—attack from the air —did not materialize. During the day not one Allied plane appeared in the sky. The Germans' first real clash came with General Huntziger's cavalry forces. In the late afternoon, the French 2nd Cavalry Division, pushing on through comparatively open country toward its southern objective, Arlon, ran into a leading body of panzers. Fighting flared up in a 30-mile zone between Arlon and Florenville, almost on the French frontier. After a battle lasting until dusk the French withdrew, badly mauled at some points, to a line extending from Étalle on the Semois River up to Neufchâteau, 15 miles northwest—well back from the Bastogne-Arlon Line they had been ordered to reach. Farther north, Huntziger's 5th Cavalry Division had arrived at Libramont without meeting the enemy.

But the 5th Cavalry's left flank was now being threatened by the failure of General Corap's 9th Army formations to cross the Meuse to their forward positions north of Saint-Hubert. At GHQ, Northeast, General Georges realized the threat, and late that evening ordered Corap to hurry his cavalry to the line Marche-Rochefort to cover the Libramont flank. On the tactical scale, Georges was attempting to rectify the faults of the Ardennes situation—the lack of cooperation between Corap's and Huntziger's advance formations. But at this moment neither he nor the 9th and 2nd Army commanders realized the formidable strategic menace that was looming through the forest barrier to the east.

Supreme Headquarters seemed unaware of the Ardennes threat. For General Gamelin the picture was dominated by Von Reichenau's concentrated assault against central Belgium. After a brief early visit to GHQ, Northeast, he had left General Georges to carry on with the Plan D deployment, satisfied at the way operations were going. At Vincennes later that morning, he told the Controller-General of the Army, M. Jacomet, that the Germans were giving him just the chance he was waiting for. Jacomet was entirely won over by Gamelin's confident manner. But among those who already knew about Plan D or now realized its implications for the first time, there were many who doubted its soundness. One skeptic was Yves Bouthillier, a senior official in the Finance Ministry, who was astonished that Gamelin should risk leaving well-fortified lines to move the bulk of the Allied forces into Belgium. Meeting Bouthillier soon after leaving Gamelin,

Jacomet said to him: "If you had seen, as I did, Gamelin's broad smile as he explained to me the direction of the enemy's attack, you would have no misgivings."[9] Bouthillier was unconvinced. His doubts were reinforced when, a little later, he ran into Lieutenant Colonel de Villelume, liaison officer between Gamelin's headquarters and the Foreign Ministry, on the steps of the Quai d' Orsay. This senseless move, De Villelume declared, would end up in a fortnight between the Oise and the Channel. In higher quarters still, Reynaud himself—strongly influenced by De Villelume—was unhappy about the Plan D maneuver. While dressing early that morning in his rooms at 5, Place du Palais Bourbon, he said drily to Paul Baudouin, Secretary of the War Cabinet: "Gamelin is saved. Now he has the battle he waited for. . . . I am disturbed," he added. "We shall see what Gamelin is worth."[1]

By evening the Vincennes staff's general impression of the situation was favorable. But Supreme Headquarters was not the best place from which to judge the battle. Under its massive stone pile it was cloistered, remote—more like a monastic retreat than a great military nerve center.

The archaic atmosphere of Vincennes seemed to set it apart from the struggle developing 150 miles to the northeast. In turn a royal residence and state prison, with a fort added, the ancient castle embraced nine centuries of French history. Its ponderous walls and dark dungeons gave it a gloomy, forbidding air. "To me Vincennes seemed to drip with blood,"[2] General Spears noted, recalling the castle's turbulent background on a visit there in November 1939. For the philosophic Gamelin, these surroundings had a strange appeal. He sensed keenly their crowded associations —"sometimes glorious, rarely happy, occasionally sad, even grim."[3] In his austere, cell-like quarters—their only comfort a radiator and a bath—he spent, as he recorded, "hours of meditation" through the eight months of the *"drôle de guerre."*[4]

---

[9] Y. Bouthillier: *Le Drame de Vichy* (1950), Vol. I, p. 19.
[1] P. Baudouin: *The Private Diaries,* trans. Sir Charles Petrie (1948), p. 27.
[2] E. L. Spears: *Assignment to Castastrophe* (1954), Vol. I, p. 53.
[3] Gamelin: *Servir* (1947), Vol. III, p. 435.
[4] Ibid.

Vincennes' casemates, housing Supreme Headquarters offices, looked out on the moat where the Duc d'Enghien was executed in 1804 and the major World War I traitors in 1917. Into these offices the sun never reached. May 10 was, as one officer noted, "a splendid day with brilliant sun which can only be guessed at from the depths of the fort where no light penetrates."[5] The overall effect was depressing, and not conducive to a feeling of immediate contact with events. More serious, it was plain on this Friday that Supreme Headquarters was out of touch operationally. Not only was it failing to receive a prompt and up-to-date flow of information, but in some cases—in respect of top-priority messages —it was actually being bypassed. This was a reflection of Gamelin's real status as Generalissimo.

In the matter of command Gamelin filled an anomalous role. As well as being Allied Commander in Chief he was France's Commander in Chief and National Defense Chief of Staff. But despite his titular supremacy, once hostilities started he had virtually no say in the direction of operations. At Vincennes he presided over a cumbersome three-tiered command structure which incorporated GHQ, Land Forces, at Montry, and GHQ, Northeast, at La Ferté-sous-Jouarre. He himself had created this edifice the previous January. Originally, the entire GHQ was concentrated at Vincennes, with General Georges, commanding in the Northeast as Gamelin's deputy, under the same roof as Gamelin. Then, in a radical reorganization, Gamelin promoted Georges to Commander in Chief, Northeast, with a GHQ of his own, 35 miles away at La Ferté. He likewise shifted his Chief of Staff, General Doumenc, to a new GHQ, Land Forces, at Montry, midway between La Ferté and Vincennes. The result was that now, on May 10, the real power of command lay with General Georges, while Doumenc became a kind of intermediary between Georges and Gamelin. Although Gamelin remained in closest liaison with them, he saw himself as exercising an advisory and supervisory function. This meant that in the fast-moving situation of war he was little more than a figurehead.

He was thus—as some Vincennes officers uneasily noted during the day—being accorded a low priority in the circulation of

---

[5] J. C. Minart: *P. C. Vincennes, Secteur 4* (1945), p. 108.

information or even short-circuited. On vital operational matters General Vuillemin's Air Force HQ and the Admiralty were communicating straight with GHQ, Montry, or GHQ, Northeast, rather than Vincennes. The position was similar in the nonoperational sphere. Signals that Vincennes was receiving from overseas diplomatic and military attachés had been transmitted first to the Quai d'Orsay or the War Ministry in the rue Saint-Dominique. And the Zone of the Interior, as distinct from the Zone of the Armies, depended on orders not from Gamelin as National Defense Chief of Staff but from the Minister of National Defense and War. In every channel Gamelin and Supreme Headquarters seemed insulated from direct intervention in events. To crown all, Vincennes did not possess a radio post. The Supreme Commander was entirely cut off from wireless communication with the front or any headquarters.

Chapter 4

➤➤➤➤➤➤➤➤➤●◀◀◀◀◀◀◀◀◀

SETBACK IN BELGIUM

"I have confidence in the Cavalry Corps."
(General Billotte)

AT LAST France faced the actuality of war. As the Allied vanguard rolled forward into Belgium, a surge of optimism swept the country. Saturday's newspapers reflected and encouraged the popular mood. Referring to the eight-month delay before the German attack, *Le Petit Parisien* declared that this had fortunately been taken advantage of by the French and British. "We dispose of a magnificent army which, for the last six months," boasted *L'Epoque,* "has had ready the most marvellous system of fortifications that has ever existed."[1] *La France Militaire* foreshadowed an Allied victory by force of arms and spoke of Germany's "exemplary punishment."[2] At the huge, ornate Hotel Continentale in the rue Castiglione, Paris, the Ministry of Information moved into action on a war basis. From now on, its bland official handouts would echo this complacent tone. As in World War I, all military news and opinion was under the control of the French censorship. One British journalist in Paris, Alexander Werth, saw the dangers of this policy for the French public. Never had any question been allowed in the press about the impregnability of the Maginot Line or the certainty of victory, Werth was to note next day. "The censorship had caused dreadful harm to France," he added. "It has cultivated a smug complacent frame of mind. And I doubt whether, after all this soft soap, French morale will be able to stand up to a terrific blitzkrieg."[3]

---

[1] W. Picht: *La Fin des Illusions: l'An 1940* (1940), p. 19.
[2] Ibid., p. 20.
[3] A. Werth: *The Last Days of Paris* (1940), p. 29.

Even while Frenchmen read the brave phrases in Saturday's papers, the first flotsam of war was surging across the French frontiers. From Luxembourg and Belgium, cluttering the border routes, came the streams of refugees. The night before, in the small Luxembourg town of Esch (just east of Longwy in France) a patrolling cavalry formation of General Condé's French 3rd Army was nearly swamped by a mob of panicking civilians. An estimated 25,000 men, women, and children poured through Esch's main street toward the French customs post. A German bombardment of the factories and exits of the town increased the terror of these Luxembourgers. Farther west, around Sedan, the frontier zone was packed with French and Belgian fugitives. The evacuation of the Sedan sector was precipitated by German bombing at 4 p.m. on the previous afternoon. And by dawn on this Saturday all southbound routes were a mêlée of people, assorted vehicles, livestock. Mingled with the trekking Frenchmen were queues of Belgian cars. All along the frontier to the English Channel swelled this same traffic—a foretaste of the flood that would soon choke the roads of northern France.

Before a large war map in Reynaud's office in the Quai d'Orsay, Colonel de Villelume was explaining the situation to Reynaud and a few colleagues. De Villelume was concerned that the Allies were advancing into Belgium unmolested by enemy air attacks. "Are they letting us walk into a trap?" he asked.[4] Reynaud himself was worried at what he considered the dangerous speed of the Allied progress, and the lack of precise intelligence about the Belgian forces. But above all he was distrustful of the whole Plan D operation. Soon after, in the presence of Baudouin, the War Cabinet Secretary, he voiced his doubts in a telephone call to Daladier. "We are laying aside our armour," he said, "by which I mean that we are leaving the fortified positions along our frontier and exposing ourselves when we suffer from an inferiority both in men and in material. We are offering our naked bodies to the blows of the German Army." "What do you want to do?" Daladier answered. "Gamelin is in command and he is putting his plans into execution."[5]

---

[4] P. Baudouin: *The Private Diaries (March 1940 to January 1941)*, (1942), p. 28.
[5] Ibid.

In Holland the Dutch forces had never recovered from the effects of yesterday's assault. Now they were steadily giving way under Von Küchler's pressure. The Yssel defenses had been breached and, farther south, General Winkelman's troops were retreating westward beyond Tilburg toward Breda—thus forcing the French 7th Army's advance formations to fall back likewise on Breda. Holland's cities were taking heavy punishment from the air. Rotterdam and Amsterdam were on fire from repeated bombing. On the airfields defenders were being overwhelmed and the small Dutch air force immobilized by the thousands of parachutists and airborne troops who had been landing since dawn on the tenth. Invaders were even arriving by water, brought down the Rhine in barges. And in the rear confusion was being spread by Dutch fifth-columnists. Within hardly more than twenty-four hours, organized Dutch resistance was breaking before this deadly combination of speed, violence, and surprise.

To the south the Belgians were faring little better. Here German tactics were broadly the same, except that more armor and fewer parachutists and airborne troops were being used. But already the linchpin of the Belgian defense was cracking. As a panzer division of the 16th Armored Corps thundered across the unbroken Meuse bridges at Maastricht, the Belgian Army began to abandon its Albert Canal positions to avoid being outflanked. And at Liège the fort of Eben Emael, besieged since yesterday, fell, reinforcing the German grip on the junction of the Meuse and the canal.

The worst ordeal came from the air—where the *Luftwaffe* was deploying its Stukas in a sky bare of Allied planes. Over the Maastricht and Liège areas flew the dive bombers in mass formation, heading to bomb the Meuse defenses. Watchers near Liège saw them line up and take aim with complete immunity above the town and dive into the Meuse Valley toward their targets. Some almost shaved the water, fired at point-blank by demoralized Belgians who cursed at the absence of Allied fighters. This was the new weapon, which would pin good soldiers to the ground in helpless terror. Now, before it, and before the German tanks and guns and advancing troops, moved the growing procession of Belgian refugees. Burdened, slow-moving, clogging the roads, they added to the worries of the Belgian High Command.

For the French advance formations, the unexpected Belgian

reverses were creating a problem. To General Prioux in particular, it was plain that the abandonment of the Albert Canal positions endangered the forward line his own Cavalry Corps was ordered to occupy. He was further concerned at the undefended state in which he had found the Gembloux Gap sector—the 1st Army's prearranged line. Prioux was one of France's ablest generals—"a magnificent man," in the words of Major Archdale, the British Liaison Officer with First Army Group: "He inspired confidence."[6] But in view of the immediate situation Prioux was feeling far from confident himself. By early afternoon on the 11th he concluded that, without support, his corps would be unable to carry out its assignment—that is, make a stand on its covering line for as long as five days.

Prioux came to an even graver conclusion. In default of adequate Gembloux defenses and of Belgian ability to hold the enemy he now saw Plan D itself—as it affected the 1st Army—too risky to execute. The only alternative, he believed, was to revert to the old Escaut Plan as first mooted by the French High Command, which prescribed holding a line on the more westerly Escaut River. His Chief of Staff agreed with him. At 3 p.m., from his Command Post at Aisches, he notified GHQ, Northeast, and other HQ's of his views. At La Ferté, General Georges turned down the proposal (which would have necessitated not only the 1st Army but the entire 1st Army Group radically altering its strategic dispositions at a moment's notice). Georges promised, however, to expedite the 1st Army's arrival by ordering it to move by day as well as by night, and to place the Cavalry Corps in reserve when its covering task was completed.

At 8 p.m. Prioux received a visit from General Billotte, commanding First Army Group. Billotte was an old friend, and they discussed the matter at length. He acknowledged Prioux's predicament, but stressed that he must hold on while Blanchard's divisions hurried forward to their Gembloux positions. "I know that from tomorrow you're going to experience some very tough moments," Billotte said on leaving. "But I know too what I can expect from you and your men. I have confidence in the Cavalry Corps."[7]

---

[6] E. L. Spears: *Assignment to Catastrophe* (1954), Vol. I, p. 229.
[7] R. Prioux: *Souvenirs de Guerre* (1947), p. 69.

In the next three days this trust was going to be needed. It was on General Prioux's corps that fell the brunt of a full-scale panzer assault as part of the German 16th Armored Corps hammered its way toward the Gembloux Gap.

Following the breakdown of the Belgian front north of Liège, the Belgian Army was ordered to pull back during the night of the eleventh-twelfth to its Dyle line north of Louvain. This left Prioux's two divisions—their combined armored strength was only some two thirds of that of one panzer division—as the sole barrier to the next advance by the panzers that had breached the Albert Canal–Meuse positions. Deploying along the 24 miles of the Tirlemont-Hannut-Huy Line, in good tank country, they awaited attack. It opened in the afternoon with a heavy Stuka raid. Then the panzers followed, probing at the center of the line near Hannut. The fighting lasted until evening and ended inconclusively. But the French tanks—the light Hotchkiss types, the twenty-ton Somuas and thirty-one-ton B types—showed that, properly commanded, they were a match for the lighter, more maneuverable German machine.

As the tanks clashed and the guns blazed around the village of Hannut, some 20 miles westward the long convoys of Blanchard's 1st Army were rolling into their positions on the Wavre-Namur Line. They had speeded their movements to some purpose. By nightfall some two thirds of the army had arrived. But Prioux's covering task was not finished. At 11 a.m. on the thirteenth the battle was resumed on the Tirlemont-Huy Line. Preceding his tank attacks with a violent 90-minute Stuka and artillery bombardment, the enemy now made furious efforts to break through. Under ceaseless pressure the French stood firm until 4 p.m. Then Prioux decided to retire behind the Perwez-Marchevolette Line—the 10-mile-wide Belgian antitank obstacle less than 9 miles in advance of 1st Army's Wavre-Namur positions. Early next morning, in a renewed assault, the Germans blasted a gap in the obstacle but, in the face of bitter French resistance, failed to get through in strength. The Cavalry Corps had held up the enemy advance long enough for the 1st Army to move into place, but at a heavy cost—two thirds of its light tanks, one third of its mediums, hundreds of its men. Now, late in the afternoon of the fourteenth, it was withdrawn behind the 1st Army lines.

. . .

By that evening, the Plan D line between Antwerp and Namur was established. Three Allied armies—the Belgians between Antwerp and Louvain, the B.E.F. on the Dyle between Louvain and Wavre, the French 1st Army between Wavre and Namur—were in place across the heart of Belgium. But nothing on this front had quite gone according to schedule, as was being uncomfortably realized at Supreme Headquarters.

A Vincennes staff officer, Colonel Minart, summed up the situation after three days' fighting (up to the end of the twelfth). Minart stressed these points: 1. the continuing inadequacy of information being received at Supreme Headquarters about the conduct of the battle and the movements of the Allied armies; 2. the Belgian Army's inability to hold its defense positions, notably the Albert Canal Line; 3. the air battle, in which German superiority was almost overwhelming, despite determined Franco-British efforts. Without bombers, Minart commented, it was impossible to help Holland, whose cause now seemed hopeless; 4. Gamelin's determination to fight on the Dyle-Meuse Line, notwithstanding the foregoing factors—lack of information from the front, the Belgian failure, Allied air inferiority.

Gamelin was still leaving Georges to conduct operations "in the fulness of his prerogatives."[8] But Minart noted that he was beginning to intervene informally in matters he had intended to leave to his subordinates. The colonel cited the withdrawal of General Prioux's Cavalry Corps behind the 1st Army, which he claimed resulted from a "suggestion" from Gamelin to General Georges. The inconsistencies of the command relationship were, in fact, starting to be apparent. On the morning of the thirteenth Gamelin returned from a visit to GHQ, Northeast, "concerned" to find that no substantial reserves had been moved near the front.[9] But seemingly he issued no orders to correct the omission.

From the liaison angle, the tripartite splitting of the army's top command was already proving awkward. A dozen miles from Vincennes, in the spacious late-nineteenth-century Rothschild mansion of Montry, worked the Army Chief of Staff, General Doumenc,

---

[8] M. Gamelin: *Servir* (1964), Vol. I, p. 335.
[9] Ibid., p. 336.

and his entourage. Some 20 miles beyond, dotted among the holiday villas and chalets of rural La Ferté-sous-Jouarre, on the banks of the Marne, was General Georges's GHQ. A dozen miles east of this was Georges's command post, the elegant, park-surrounded property of Les Bondons, once the residence of the French writer Georges Ohnet. Les Bondons was over an hour from Vincennes by road, and between these two and Montry there was a constant traffic of pennanted staff cars as Gamelin and Doumenc visited Georges and each other, often twice a day. In the matter of interheadquarters communication there was one glaring deficiency: Montry possessed no teleprinters. Thus every hour dispatch riders sped from there to Vincennes with routine summaries collated from the armies' Intelligence reports.

La Ferté itself, set up the previous January, was signally unfitted as a wartime GHQ. With its original 1,000-strong staff now pruned, it was still a rambling, scattered complex with an unwieldy communications network. Even General Georges's own office had grave drawbacks. According to Colonel Minart, Les Bondons "could not have been less suited for a command post at a moment of crisis."[1] Three of its four ground-floor rooms—the railway transport officers' department, the office of Georges's Chief of Staff, General Roton, and a small anteroom—were in continual turmoil as staff and messengers came and went, visitors waited, telephones and typewriters shrilled and clattered. In the fourth, a large salon behind General Roton's room, sat General Georges, barely insulated from the prevailing chaos.

Square-built, tanned from long African service, Claudel Georges was one of France's ablest and most highly rated generals. His mind was alert and forceful, and there was a firm soldierly look about his rugged, trim-mustached features. But unhappily Georges still suffered from the effects of the bullet wounds he had received at Marseilles in 1934, when he was present at the assassination of Alexander of Yugoslavia and French Foreign Minister Jean Barthou. Since then he had been forbidden to fly and he permanently wore a woolen glove on one hand. How much his injuries had seriously undermined his health it was hard to judge: only the test of battle would tell. Meeting him the previous August, his

---

[1] J. Minart: *P. C. Vincennes, Secteur 4* (1945), p. 185.

old friend Edward Spears thought perhaps he had aged as a result
of them but was struck by his vigor. Georges was in fact named as
the most likely successor to Gamelin. For this reason—and possibly
because Georges belonged to the Reynaud "clan" while Gamelin
was a Daladier man—the two were said to be not entirely com-
patible. But there was no evidence of this disturbing their military
relations. The sole potential cause of difficulty between them now
was the peculiar mechanism of the command structure.

If he lacked clear-cut direction from Gamelin, Georges had
an invaluable colleague in General Alphonse Doumenc. Daily the
thin, agile Doumenc strode into Les Bondons to remain hours in
conference with the Commander in Chief, Northeast. In the quickening tempo of the first days' fighting he was spending most of
his time with Georges, often accompanied by his Chief of Staff
(Operations), General Koeltz. Brisk, precise, quick-tempered,
Doumenc was known for his work as a transport specialist in World
War I, when he had organized the famous *Voie Sacrée* at Verdun.
This had earned him a glowing citation for his "intellectual activity,
courage and endurance."[2] Now he was injecting his practical optimism into the somewhat gloomy atmosphere of Les Bondons.

The Germans' early seizure of the Maastricht bridges and
Fort Eban Emael had brought dismay to Georges's staff. It was
only the Cavalry Corps' covering defense of the 1st Army front that
had redeemed the situation and saved Plan D from foundering at
the start. But elsewhere in the Low Countries there was little room
for complacency. As Prioux's cavalry fought their bitter three-day
battle with the panzers of General Hoepner's 16th Armored Corps,
Holland was moving toward imminent defeat.

By the twelfth more French 7th Army advance units had
completed their 100-mile dash to the Dutch frontier zone. But no
French intervention could now be effective: the whole Dutch front
was crumbling. In the north the provinces of Groningen and Fries-
land fell, while farther south Von Küchler's forces crossed the Maas
and Yssel and a panzer division pressed on to reach the outskirts
of Rotterdam. Winkelman's forces withdrew to a line based on
Amsterdam and Utrecht, and in the rear fifth-columnists were
busy sabotaging the water defenses and Amsterdam's entire public

---

2 Ibid., p. 195.

utility services. By the thirteenth, Holland was split in two. Everywhere the Dutch were being forced back with heavy losses. On the Maas estuary airborne troops seized the vital Moerdijk Bridge just south of Rotterdam and 30 miles from The Hague. With Queen Wilhelmina leaving the Netherlands aboard a British warship and the government preparing to follow, Dutch capitulation was now a matter of hours. Late next day, Tuesday, May 14, General Henri Winkelman, the Dutch Commander in Chief, issued an order that fighting was to cease. Holland's resistance had lasted just under six days.

For the Allies the immediate effect of this was that Von Küchler's 18th Army was released to fight elsewhere. The French High Command faced the unpleasant fact that one of France's best armies had been wasted on a futile mission. Its commander, that "veritable tiger," the ardent, impetuous General Henri Giraud, had, in the dubious interests of Plan D, been required to lead his divisions right across Belgium and diametrically away from the front where they might most be needed.[3] And the 7th had a rough time in executing its far-flung assignment. On the eleventh one of its advance motorized units suffered a devastating four-hour air attack on the Antwerp-Breda road. When the main forces engaged on the fourteenth south of Bergen op Zoom (near the Dutch-Belgian border), they were pressed back into Belgium, where they encamped at Antwerp.

But this was the least of Gamelin's worries on May 14. Holland—small, militarily weak, and not easily defensible—was never expected to withstand the massive weight of German invasion for more than a few days. As for the 7th Army, this could be moved south and regrouped. Even the struggle developing in central Belgium—the battle according to Plan D—was no longer of paramount importance. For the French High Command a much larger crisis now loomed. In the last twenty-four hours it had been clear that the real German offensive was being staged not in the Belgian plains west of Liège but on the forgotten sector of the Meuse front between Namur and Sedan.

---

[3] Spears: *Assignment*, Vol. I, p. 78.

Chapter 5

➤➤➤➤➤➤➤➤●≪≪≪≪≪≪≪

THREAT FROM THE ARDENNES

"The struggle is now going to start."
(General Huntziger to his 2nd Army troops)

THE MOVING PANZER COLUMNS stretched half across the forest. To a depth of miles, every road to the west was a dense mass of grinding vehicles—tanks, armored cars, gun carriers, staff cars, ancillary transport, motorcycles. In the rear, fanned out on all available routes, plodded division after division of the helmeted, field-gray infantrymen of Von Kluge's and List's 4th and 12th Armies. Before them, as Day 2 dawned over the Ardennes, stood the thin screen of Huntziger's and Corap's cavalry. And beyond, barred only by the Meuse and a few ill-equipped formations, was the way into France.

The first clash came at mid-morning when German tanks attacked the 9th's 3rd Spahi Brigade and the 2nd's 5th Cavalry Division at Libramont and Neufchâteau. Aided by Stukas taking advantage of the forest clearings, the panzers threw back the French with heavy losses. By late afternoon of the eleventh, Huntziger's cavalry had retired southward behind the Semois River, almost on the French border. Corap's cavalry, its right flank exposed by this withdrawal, had to retreat likewise. Rolling forward in the vanguard of the Germans' southern wing was Guderian's XIX Armored Corps, still in the arrowhead formation with the 1st Panzer Division leading in the center and the 10th and 2nd following on the left and right. By nightfall the 1st Panzers were at the outskirts of Bouillon on the southern edge of Belgian Luxembourg and within sight of Sedan, 10 miles to the south. Away northward, in the middle of the forest beyond Saint-Hubert, Corap's 1st and 4th Cavalry Divisions were now left isolated by Belgian and French withdrawals on left and right. At 10 p.m. Corap ordered these back across the Meuse—a move that was started at 2 a.m. on the twelfth and completed twelve hours later, after some losses caused by German tank attacks at the northern end of the French line.

On the eleventh the Sedan sector suddenly woke to an atmosphere of war. All day German bombers roared in to attack, and the roads southward streamed with lengthening columns of refugees. Wounded or evacuated cavalry troops began to filter back from the Ardennes. That night the heavy battery at Torcy, near Sedan, opened up. Its flashes lit the sky as it rained shells on the German positions round Bouillon. To the men of the 2nd Army, standing along the Sedan defenses, came the realization that the battle was swiftly approaching this zone which had never expected to see any fighting.

At their command posts at Senuc and Vervins, both Huntziger and Corap now began to recognize the extent of the Ardennes threat. During the night Corap sent General Billotte, at First Army Group headquarters, a request for reinforcements. The appeal at last alerted the French High Command. While its General Order No. 12, dated May 11, confirmed the Allied intention to adhere to Plan D, orders were given to dispatch toward the Sedan-Mézières hinge one armored and three infantry divisions as from May 12, to arrive between the fourteenth and seventeenth.

But even the fourteenth would be too late. On the evening of the twelfth, while the French army chiefs were still concentrating mainly on the successful development of the Dyle Plan, the 1st Panzer Division of Guderian's XIX Armored Corps crossed the French frontier north of Sedan.

As in central and north Belgium, the advance French formations in Belgian Luxembourg were supposed to delay the enemy for up to five days. In fact, on this third day the cavalry of both the 9th and 2nd Armies was already back on the left bank of the Meuse, leaving the way clear for the advancing panzers. Although some French units offered stiff resistance, all were thrown back in more or less disorder. After a day-long assault, withstood by local defense outposts as well as long-range artillery from across the Meuse, Bouillon fell that evening. Pressing forward across the

twisting Semois River, German tanks of the 1st Panzer Division
seized their first French positions—Fleigneux and Saint-Menges.
As dusk fell, the enemy stood within a stone's throw of the
Meuse.

Forty miles north, another German breakthrough menaced
the Belgian Meuse. Roughly parallel with Guderian's group, General Hoth's panzer corps—the northern prong of the three-pointed
armored spearhead—had been heading toward Dinant. Now the
leading units of the 7th Armored Division, commanded by Erwin
Rommel, raced forward in the afternoon to within a few miles of
Houx, slightly north of Dinant. Thus, by the end of Day 3, the
Germans covered the Meuse at both ends of the 9th and 2nd Army
sectors. And as more enemy tanks and motorcycle troops debouched from the green depths of the Ardennes, nowhere on the
river's left bank were Corap's or Huntziger's forces yet fully deployed. Corap's artillery and infantry were still arriving, and
Huntziger's divisions were in process of making a last-minute
switch in position.

On the eleventh Corap had left his headquarters at Vervins in
order to direct the northward movement of his troops personally.
But Corap was unfortunate. He spent both the eleventh and twelfth
in his staff car on roads so jammed with traffic that he was immobilized and unable to give any orders. Corap—soon to be the
chief scapegoat for the Meuse disaster—was already, as implied by
Prime Minister Reynaud, failing to react promptly enough to the
situation. According to instructions, he should by now have
shifted his headquarters to the more forward position of Chimay,
over the Belgian border. Instead he was still based at Vervins,
some 40 miles behind his front.

On Huntziger's forces at Sedan, the arrival of the enemy
made a sudden and startling impact. Around 6 p.m., as the last
of the cavalry and supporting infantry limped back battered and
exhausted, German detachments appeared without warning on the
wooded heights beyond the Meuse. Simultaneously the Sedan area
was subjected to a violent bombing attack. The battle for the river
crossings seemed imminent. Huntziger had been assessing the
strengths and weaknesses of his defense line and speculating on
the points where the Germans might strike. "I am worried about
my left," he noted uneasily. "Are not the Germans going to at-

tempt a major blow at the hinge?"¹ Huntziger was indicating the weakest spot on the whole Meuse front—the junction between the 2nd and 9th Armies, at the Bar River, near Mézières. Yet that same day, the twelfth, a high-level decision was being taken that would accentuate the weakness. In a reorganization of General Billotte's sphere of command, General Georges was removing the 2nd Army from the First Army Group and bringing it under his own personal control, while leaving the 9th Army with General Billotte. The two armies, which it might be vitally necessary to direct as a unified force, would thus be subject to the orders of two different headquarters.

Wherever else the Germans attacked, Huntziger knew that the 2nd Army would soon be in the thick of the battle. And he was in no doubt of the ordeal facing his troops. To the officers, N.C.O.'s and men of the 2nd Army he issued an Order of the Day dated May 12:

> In the course of three days of hard fighting with the utmost self-sacrifice, the cavalry units of the 2nd Army have made contact with the enemy in Belgian Luxembourg and, in accordance with their mission, delayed the moment at which its forces attack our defence positions. The struggle is now going to start on these positions. I enjoin that on them no retirement whatever be permitted. Every piece of ground on which the enemy sets foot must be retaken. The honour of commanders of all ranks is involved in holding on without regard to losses. No *defaillance* will be tolerated. We shall all of us defend the sacred soil of our country. I am certain of the 2nd Army. Huntziger.²

For the French, the three-day Ardennes operation was a costly failure; they suffered heavy casualties while causing little delay or inconvenience to Hoth's and Von Kleist's panzers. But one thing the rear-guard units managed to do before being jostled back across the river. All along the Meuse and its tributary, the Chiers, they left the bridges blown. In the Sedan sector, the demolition was planned with meticulous care. The X Corps commander, General Grandsard, delegated part of the task to his divisional generals, and retained for himself the responsibility for the actual Sedan bridges. Teams were appointed to prepare each bridge, with

---

¹ E. Ruby: *Sedan, Terre d'Epreuve* (1948), p. 117.
² Ibid., p. 120.

orders not to detonate except when the enemy was immediately approaching. In fact nearly all the bridges were blown as soon as the cavalry had passed, with the result that no bridges were taken by surprise. And in cases where the first detonation failed, there was time to repair the fault before the Germans arrived. Aerial photographs taken next day proved the success of the destructions—so nailing the sorry story, put out by Reynaud in a speech to the Senate on the twenty-first, that the enemy captured the bridges unbroken. German evidence itself discounted Reynaud's charge. "It is thus untrue," said a German report, quoted later by Grandsard, "that the bridges of the Meuse and Sedan fell intact into our hands . . . and that one must seek there the reason for our breakthrough."[3]

Destruction was equally thorough in the 9th Army zone. At the bridges on the Belgian Meuse, teams of French sappers had doubled up with the Belgian teams on the eleventh. Their efficiency was to be confirmed by the report of General Duffieux, president of the Commission of Inquiry set up by Gamelin's successor, General Weygand, on May 20 to establish responsibility for the Meuse defeat. In the dossier submitted by Duffieux was incontrovertible photographic evidence showing that all bridges were wrecked except that at Mézières, which was left to give the French defenders last-minute access to the river's left bank.

That evening of May 12, two signals went from GHQ, Northeast, to Vincennes. One reported the blowing of all Meuse and Chiers bridges except for two or three which would go up after the last units had crossed. The other stated laconically: "The defense now seems well assured on the whole Meuse front."[4]

---

[3] C. Grandsard: *Le 10 e Corps d'Armée dans la Bataille, 1939–1940* (1949), p. 118.

[4] M. Gamelin: *Servir* (1946), Vol. I, p. 336.

Chapter 6

THE NEGLECTED FRONT

*"The defences in the Sedan region
are rudimentary."*
(Report by Deputies Frammond and Taittinger)

THE MEUSE is one of the great rivers of western Europe. Rising near Langres, in the Haute-Marne, it follows a meandering 560-mile course through France, Belgium, and Holland, where it becomes the Maas and splits into two branches, one of which enters the Rhine above Rotterdam, and the other the Hollandsch Diep. In France, it runs roughly north as far as Stenay, where it turns more sharply northwest, passing Sedan and Mézières and then switching north again, with increasing twists, to Givet on the Franco-Belgian border. Thence it proceeds north to Namur and then northeast to Liège. Roughly northward again, it passes Maastricht on the Dutch-Belgian border, finally to flow through Holland in a broad westerly arc toward the sea.

Called by the French a "sleepy" river, the Meuse courses quietly past historic places and picturesque, romantic scenes. But its associations are far from pacific. For though, unlike the Marne, the Aisne, the Somme, no great battles are named after it, its key position as a waterline defense against attack from the east has constantly brought it into the fighting zone. As memorials to the struggles that have taken place along its banks stand the war-scarred towns of Verdun, Saint-Mihiel, Sedan, Namur, Liège. In particular, the river becomes militarily important in the region of Stenay (south of the western end of the Maginot Line), where it approaches and begins to run parallel to the Franco-Belgian frontier south of the Ardennes. It continues to skirt the frontier after turning north at Mézières, until it reaches Givet at the top of the small appendix that juts into the Belgian province of Namur. But though it here leaves the frontier to flow well inside Belgium, past Dinant, Namur, and Liège, it retains its importance as a barrier flanking the western fringe of the Ardennes. Now, entering Holland, it becomes a vital frontier river once more as it edges up the narrow Maastricht Peninsula and then hugs the Dutch-German border, past Venlo and almost as far as Nijmegen. After that it turns sharply west, curving above Holland's North Brabant.

The portion of the Meuse entrusted to the French Army in May 1940 ran from somewhere east of Sedan to Namur, in Belgium—about 90 miles in all. Almost every place name on this stretch of placid, winding river recalled past battles in which French had clashed with Germans, in World War I or earlier.

Sedan had been a battle ground in two wars. Lying at the foot of the wooded hills which rise beyond the right bank of the Meuse, this small clothworking and garrison town with its dismantled fortress was the scene of the defeat that made its name a byword for French military disaster. Just north of it, in September 1870, Marshal MacMahon's army of some 90,000 men was surrounded by the Prussians and forced to surrender. Sedan's environs teemed with reminders of the battle—Bazeilles, Balan, La Moncelle, Givonne, Daigny, Illy; the hill of Frenois, from which King William of Prussia watched the battle; Floing, where a monument was raised to the French cavalry, the "*brave gens*" who inspired William's admiration. In the first onrush of the German offensive in August 1914, Sedan fell once more—to be partially retaken by Americans just before the Armistice. To the west and north, the other Meuse outposts fell equally quickly: ancient Mézières, with its Vauban citadel; the small, drab industrial center of Givet; Dinant, surmounted by its rocky cliffs; Namur, whose ring of powerful forts, expected to hold out for six months, was captured within four days. For France, in 1914, this was a clear and brutal demonstration that neither the strongholds and other defenses of the Meuse, nor the riverline of the Meuse itself, were sufficient barrier against German armies debouching swiftly and unexpectedly out of the Ardennes.

The Meuse varies considerably between Sedan and Namur. In the Sedan area (where it is about 60 yards wide) it is less enclosed than farther downriver toward the Belgian frontier. But

in places its south bank rises sharply enough to expose defenders
to attacking forces on the north-bank slopes and prevent defending
infantry from deploying in suitable depth. Moreover, German
troops moving toward the river would find good protection in
north-bank villages like Donchery and Bazeilles and the outskirts
of Sedan itself. On the other hand, from the dominating heights of
Marfée Wood, south of Sedan, French artillery could command
the whole forward zone as far as the Ardennes Forest some six
miles to the north, and cover the roads used by advancing enemy
tanks. But the Sedan sector included another river besides the
Meuse—the Chiers, which joins the Meuse from an easterly direction, at a point just east of Sedan. In Gamelin's view the line of
the Chiers was the least easily defendable part of the whole sector,
for here the wooded heights of the north or right bank descended
almost directly to the river, allowing the enemy to approach unseen.
In addition, the north-bank slopes were higher than on the south
bank and provided good artillery sites.

This was the sector assigned to General Huntziger's 2nd
Army. Very different was General Corap's sector. Turning north
from Mézières, the Meuse Valley quickly becomes narrower,
deeper, and more winding. On each side steep wooded banks and
craggy cliffs fall almost sheer to the river's edge. But the army
chiefs differed about the defensive advantages of this stretch.
Gamelin saw the terrain as favoring the French. "The Meuse
there is very compressed between rocky perpendicular cliffs,
absolutely unscaleable to tanks," he noted, "and often very difficult for infantry."[1] But the practical-minded Doumenc thought it
suited the attackers, "because its wooded banks lend themselves to
infiltrations, its windings increase the area of ground to be fought
over, and the defending force lacks a wide view and good fields
of fire."[2]

From Givet northward to Namur, the Meuse widens here and
there but generally remains enclosed. Givet and Dinant, being both
on the right bank, provided the French with useful bridgeheads;
and on the northern flank of Corap's sector, the guns of Namur's

---

[1] M. Gamelin: *Servir* (1946), Vol. I, p. 325.
[2] A. Doumenc: *Histoire de la Neuvième Armée* (1945),
p. 75.

southerly forts could sweep the river. One clear advantage to attackers from the east lay in the generally greater height of the right
bank.

To be effective, the natural defenses of the whole Namur-
Sedan stretch needed strong reinforcement. But the Sedan sector
had its special problems. The difficulty of holding the Chiers Line,
and the lack of depth north of the Meuse (which at Sedan was five
miles from the frontier) endangered Sedan itself. In the interwar
years worried local deputies made requests for proper defensive
arrangements to be made here; but the French High Command,
accepting that the ground north of the Meuse was untenable and
that Sedan would quickly fall in the event of attack, could only
adopt a compromise. It ordered the building of a number of advanced posts consisting of strong points connected by barbed
wire which, along with road-mining, would do no more than
delay an enemy attack. Seven such posts were built. The Sedan
defenses were put to the test in 1938 in an exercise directed by
General Prételat, then commander-designate of the 2nd Army.
The aim of the exercise was to study the possibility of an enemy assault by armored and motorized forces from the direction of Belgian Luxembourg.

Seven divisions, of which four were motorized, and four
tank brigades made a mock attack on the Sedan positions. The
results were conclusive: the defenses were so decisively overwhelmed that the general commanding the defending force asked
that the findings on the exercise not be officially made known, so
that his troops would not be demoralized. At the final discussion
on the operation held in the citadel at Verdun, General Gamelin
was present. Addressing the conference, he gave his assurance
that the Sedan defenses would be reinforced in good time to meet
any attack.

But in the next months these peaceful reaches of the Meuse
showed few signs of increased defense work. Even by the beginning
of December 1939, almost the only obstacle along the river's south
bank was a continuous line of barbed wire. Not until this time did
the High Command inaugurate a large-scale defense program—
whose provisions included three types of blockhouses, concrete
shelters, and antitank obstacles—for sectors like Sedan. For a
start, Sedan was to have some sixty casemates, twenty-five on the

principal line, fifteen on the stop line, and twenty on the *position de résistance*. But actual work did not begin until January, to be held up then by icy weather in which canals froze, roads were unusable for trucks, and concrete became too set to flow. It was April before progress was fully resumed. Meanwhile General Huntziger, like Corap on his left flank, was repeatedly asking GHQ for defense equipment as well as armament, but with little result. Of the ten thousand land mines he demanded, he received two hundred.[3]

Sedan's defense weaknesses were startlingly revealed in March by two deputies, M. Frammond, member for Le Lozère, and M. Taittinger, a Paris member. In a report to the Commision de l'Armée, the government, and the High Command, made after an inspection tour of the 2nd and 9th Army sectors, Frammond and Taittinger commented on the 2nd Army defenses as follows:

> The defensive organisation in the Montmedy (Maginot Line) region appeared formidable. These consist of old works—1935— strengthened by recent works, an extension in fact of the Maginot Line. But the satisfactory impression ceased on arrival at Sedan. In this region there is great dependence on the forest of Ardennes and the Meuse to protect Sedan, which perhaps gives these natural obstacles an exaggerated importance. The defensive organisations in this region are rudimentary, not to say embryonic. On the road from Bouillon (in Belgium) to Sedan, as on other access routes, the defense consists of *"maisons fortes"* whose powers of resistance could be only of short duration. The barbed wire entanglements, the demolitions provided for, and the resistance of the *"maison fortes"* cannot give more than an hour's delay. . . . The Meuse constitutes a marvellous anti-tank ditch, but it is not very wide; it is fairly shallow, and its current is quite slow for much of the year. The troops appointed for the defence of this sector (the cavalry formations) have a high morale. . . . But one feels that they are destined to be sacrificed on the spot, and that the real resistance will take place on this side of the Meuse. This intention of the High Command is not very sound, but even so it is essential for the works on the resistance line to be finished, provided with armament, and put into a state to fulfill their role. In some of these works only the scaffolding is completed and the concrete not yet poured. Others are without firing-apertures, anti-gas material and some of their armament. For a proper defence to be made on the south bank, there remains much to be done. Little is lacking in the

---

[3] P. Allard: *La Vérité sur l'Affaire Corap* (1941), p. 19.

XVIII Corps sector (east of Sedan), but in General Grandsard's
X Corps sector the work must be pressed on energetically and
with all the necessary resources. It should be noted that most
of the troops we visited are of "series B" regiments; that
DCA (Air Defence) is almost non-existent, and that the 2nd
Army's aviation is reduced to one observation plane and a few
fighters. German planes move freely over this sector, photograph
every movement on the ground and then fly off at the first sight
of our fighters.[4]

Frammond and Taittinger were no more encouraging about
the 9th Army's defenses.

This army [they reported] holds a region which seems to lend
itself even more to the defensive than the 2nd: difficult ground
and steep slopes whose protection can easily be organised. There
are admittedly traditional invasion routes in this sector, but a
number of small works are built or on the way to completion,
which cover these points. Certain "infantry-type" works have
been built near Charleville (Mézières). These, mined against infiltration, would give no real protection. . . . The artillery works
have been better planned. But we should mention that the steel
apertures are lacking, that the *portes de clôture* are of wood and
that the anti-gas material is wanting. The *"section technique du
génie"* type of works is used in this region. We have seen several
in construction; some had their scaffolding finished; in others,
concrete was still being poured. This region will not be ready
for two months. But a certain number of small works are finished,
which will allow quite a stout resistance. . . . Aircraft (which
are not under army command) are no doubt at the disposal of
Army Group or GHQ. The result, from the psychological point
of view, is bad. The DCA, non-existent in the 2nd and 9th
Armies, is up to now ineffective. The few fighters have been unable to intercept the fast and well-armed German planes. In most
minds, this produces a deep anxiety. It seems, in fact, to all well-
informed people that so long as we French and British do not
establish an overwhelming air superiority, our troops, even if
fired by a magnificent offensive spirit, will not have the indispen-
sible accompaniment to success.[5]

Despite the Frammond-Taittinger disclosures, little action was
taken. By May 10 the 2nd Army's defenses were still woefully de-
fective. On the main resistance line, casemates were uncompleted,

---

[4] J. Bardoux: *Journal d'un Témoin de la Troisième . . . 1940*
(1957), pp. 425–7.
[5] Ibid.

with only one 75mm.-gun casemate ready, at the Bellevue cross-roads just south of Sedan. On the stop line, the casemates had hardly risen above ground level. And in the rear, work remained in a primitive state. Even on the central part of the front, a 25-mile sector, to be manned in May by the three divisions of X Corps, the defenses were not impressive. North of the Meuse at the fringe of the Ardennes, there was an advanced line of pillboxes; along the principal line behind the river were trenches, barbed wire, and pillboxes averaging eight to the mile (many of them unfinished); and behind this, at the foot of the slopes looking down on the river, there was only a barbed-wire line. The vital antitank obstacle running for about a mile from Bellevue to Wadelincourt, across the southern exit from Sedan, stood half-completed.

The 9th Army's defenses were equally unready as May approached. Along the Belgian Meuse, north of Givet, there was no defensive system at all. The only work the Belgians had done in the previous months was to prepare the bridges for destruction. On the French Meuse, from Givet southward by way of Revin, Monthermé, and Mézières to the 9th Army's junction line with the 2nd Army at the Bar River, the organization was similar to that on Huntziger's front. A barbed-wire barrier ran along the south or left bank, reinforced with trenches and pillboxes (not all completed). More barbed wire covered the stop line. At Mézières a bridgehead was established, and across the river from Mézières and Monthermé were advanced strong points, protecting the routes to these objectives. But, as with the 2nd Army, many installations were unfinished when the German offensive broke. Notably, a number of antitank ditches were without stakes or mines. According to a 9th Army officer, delays in the concreting work were due to the employment of civilians, who worked a forty-hour week, with Saturdays and Sundays free.[6]

Early in November 1939 General Alan Brooke, commanding the British II Corps, attended a ceremonial review of French troops at their base in northern France. The occasion was the anniversary of the arrival of the German armistice delegates in the Allied line in 1918. Dominating the scene was a monument bearing the inscription: *"Ici triomphe par sa ténacité le Poilu!"*

---

6 Ibid., p. 18.

This should have been a stirring, solemn moment. But as he stood at the saluting point beside the French general, Brooke was shocked at the slovenly turnout of the passing columns. "Men unshaven, horses ungroomed, clothes and saddlery that did not fit, vehicles dirty, and complete lack of pride in themselves or their units," he recorded.[7] Brooke was still more dismayed at the men's sullen, "insubordinate" expressions, and their almost total failure to obey the order "Eyes left." He was invited afterwards to inspect some of the nearby French defenses. Noting an unfinished antitank ditch, he asked whether this would be provided with covering fire. "Ah bah!" replied the French general, "that'll be done later. Come on, we'll go to lunch now!"[8]

Brooke's host was General Corap, and the troops he saw on this November day were the men of the French 9th Army.

This was the army that was to hold 60 miles of the Meuse Line. After the Meuse disaster of mid-May, much was to be made of the *défaillance* of the luckless 9th. But, basically, the spirit of Corap's troops—stolid Bretons, Normans from Rouen, men of the Loire—was little different from that of most of the French Army. Few of the reservist thousands who rejoined the colors in September 1939 were particularly keen to fight, and the older they were, the less eager were they. It happened that the 9th Army contained the highest quota of older reservists and static troops of any army stationed outside the Maginot Line. Of its seven infantry divisions, only two were "active" or of first-rate quality. Four were reservist divisions, of which two—the 53rd and 61st Infantry— were "Series B" (classed as "definitely inferior, badly armed, over-aged and under-trained").[9] Finally, the 102nd Infantry was an equally low-grade fortress division, with a role confined to fixed defenses. This was difficult material to work on while the army languished in the long inaction of the "*drôle de guerre*," especially as most of the officers were themselves reservists and subject to the same limitations.

For sixty-two-year-old General André-Georges Corap, the command of the 9th was a thankless task. Fate and the mistakes of

[7] A. Bryant: *The Turn of the Tide, Based on the War Diaries of F.-M. Viscount Alanbrooke* (1957), p. 71.

[8] Ibid., p. 72.

[9] T. Draper: *The Six Weeks' War: France, May 10–June 25, 1940* (1946), p. 28n.

others—together with his own—were to make him France's most
controversial general of World War II. Stocky, steel-blue-eyed,
Norman-born, he was seen by one admirer as the "perfect type of
Viking."[1] On the other hand, André Maurois, visiting the 9th Army
just before Hitler's attack, summed him up as "a reserved man,
held in high esteem by his superiors, unmilitary in appearance,
and running to fat around the middle. He had trouble getting into
a car. His conversation was very interesting, but one felt his attention was directed wholly toward the past."[2] "The trouble is that
old Corap," Maurois's lieutenant guide told him, "though he's a
good enough man and has had a fine career, isn't fond enough of
banging the drum. . . . An Army needs to bang its drums, needs
reviews and music—a bit of polish in fact. . . . You'll see it for
yourself: the dust is beginning to settle on us here."[3] Maurois was
struck by the atmosphere of sleepy Vervins, site of Corap's headquarters, "whose rough cobblestones resounded to the unhurried
tread of military men walking to their offices with the peaceful
punctuality of civil servants."[4]

Corap had served on the staffs of Foch, Pétain, and Weygand, and fought in North African campaigns, finishing as Commander in Chief in Morocco in 1936. Now he was in charge of an
army that seemed dogged by neglect from the start. General
Georges conceded later that the 9th was always treated as a "poor
relation."[5] It began the war as a mere army detachment, and only
after repeated requests from Corap was it raised to army status.
According to Gamelin, War Minister Daladier was not enthusiastic about Corap's appointment to an army command. He thought
he had aged and become mentally slow. But Gamelin himself,
while admitting that the general's appearance was against him,
held that he had always shown good leadership qualities and knew
his job, with the added advantage that he was thoroughly familiar
with the 9th Army's terrain.

Corap was constantly asking GHQ for more artillery. Only

[1] Allard: *L'Affaire Corap*, p. 24.
[2] A. Maurois: *Why France Fell*, trans. Denver Lindley
(1941), pp. 88–9.
[3] A. Maurois: *The Battle of France*, trans. F. R. Ludman
(1940), p. 171.
[4] Maurois: *Why France Fell*, p. 88.
[5] Reynaud: *In the Thick of the Fight* (1955), p. 308.

his two "active" divisions, the 5th Motorized and the 4th North African, had antitank guns, and these were mostly the old 37's. The new, highly efficient 47's did not begin to be issued until the moment of the attack on May 10. The 5th Motorized Division alone possessed antiaircraft guns. In a report dated March 1940, Corap requested from Gamelin forty-five batteries of twenty-five, and received three.[6] Field artillery was equally scarce. The 9th disposed only three groups of 73's and three batteries of 25's. As for tanks, the army's total complement was two hundred, of which a third were last-war types. Of aircraft, it had one weak fighter group and one reconnaissance group. To defend his river line, Corap, like Huntziger, kept demanding deliveries of antitank mines, but was told that, of the two thousand being produced per month, most had to go to the operational front in Lorraine.

Yet it was in doubt as to who was mainly responsible for these defects. Gamelin later recorded that when he inspected the 9th Army front with Billotte at the beginning of March, Corap expressed himself full of confidence in the execution of his mission under Plan D. Asked by Gamelin if he had anything to notify in connection with the forthcoming operation, Corap "made no mention of any deficiencies."[7] But a slightly different picture emerged from later testimony produced by General Georges. Georges was to place on the file of the Riom Court (set up in July 1940 to try leaders alleged to have contributed to France's defeat) a note from his staff detailing certain demands that Corap sent to the High Command as a result of this (or possibly another) inspection by Gamelin.

Away to the right of the 9th Army, Huntziger's 2nd Army was facing the same problems. Like the 9th, it was predominantly a reservist army, with two "Series B" divisions, the 55th and 71st —as mediocre as Corap's 53rd and 61st. The story of the 55th was typical of almost any of the low-grade reservist divisions standing on the Meuse Line.

Hailing from the Bourges area and the Loire Valley regions of Beauce, Nivernais, Sologne, the average age of the men of the 55th Infantry Division was over thirty. Mostly married and fathers

---

[6] Allard: *L'Affaire Corap,* p. 19.
[7] M. Ribet: *Le Procés de Riom* (1945), p. 499.

of families, they were the army's "*crocos*," the recalled old-timers who had forgotten much of the soldiering they had learned in their one-year service. Many were out of training and overweight, but their spirit on rejoining was passable if not enthusiastic. Unhappily, they arrived at their depots to find almost no uniforms available, and for weeks had to parade, drill, and march in a motley array of civilian clothes. This lowered morale from the start, for the aggrieved "*crocos*" felt that the High Command was either inefficient or was not taking them or the war seriously. But the real weakness of the 55th—as of all similar divisions—lay in its dearth of regular officers. Of its total officer strength of 450, only 20 were "active"—with the colonel the sole regular officer in each regiment of 3,000 men. Even at divisional headquarters, 40 of the 47 officers were reservists. The general picture was the same in the 71st Division (then in reserve behind the 2nd Army's front line), made up of Parisians; but here the regimental commanders had all reached the age limit and had been recalled from retirement.

Without an adequate regular cadre, everything suffered—administration, discipline, training. Many reservist officers, and likewise N.C.O.'s, were reluctant to give orders and use their authority; and because their own knowledge was rusty and out-of-date, they made poor instructors. Moreover, in the New Year existing training programs had to be severely cut to allow for the intensified defense work that now belatedly started. "Infantrymen became navvies, and the officers, directors and inspectors of works," recorded a French general.[8] Henceforth battle preparations took second place. In February a First Army Group instruction prescribed three weeks' training in the rear for each infantry regiment, but in practice no unit managed to fit in more than a two-week spell.

Even when officers were keen and competent, they tended to think in terms of the last war. "They were too old," said a junior officer of the 71st Division. "For modern war you need officers to be young, alert, *sportifs*."[9] In these conditions it was impossible to weld the "*crocos*" of the 55th or 71st into a cohesive military force. Their fighting morale was further affected by too-

---

[8] C. L. Menu: *Lumière sur les Ruines* (1953), p. 189.
[9] Allard: *L'Affaire Corap*, p. 34.

close contact with civilians in the billeting areas, enemy radio propaganda clandestinely listened to, the optimistic tone of the press, and the deadening lull of the *"drôle de guerre"* itself—which fostered the comfortable belief that they would never have to go into action.

At General Huntziger's headquarters in the wooded Argonne village of Senuc, there was no apathy. Life at Senuc, 25 miles south of Sedan, was austere and strenuous—its tone set by Huntziger himself. The general had what a colleague called a "dedicated daily routine."[1] He rose early, took a short, vigorous constitutional, lunched with spartan plainness, spent the afternoon visiting and inspecting units, returned at night to work, and rounded off the day with "simple relaxation."[2] Slim, erect, distinguished-looking, of mixed Alsatian-Breton parentage, Huntziger was one of France's more intellectual generals. His rather aloof manner hid a natural affability. Officers admired his wide culture, sharp incisive mind, infallible memory, and the powers of leadership he had gained in service in the Near and Far East, Brazil, and Madagascar. Appointed to the Conseil Supérieur de Guerre, he was considered as a possible future Supreme Commander. But most of Huntziger's experience lay in the staff and diplomatic spheres; and command of the 2nd Army was the first senior operational post he had held. Like Corap, he knew nothing about mechanized warfare.

According to his aide, Captain Vernes, Huntziger was "not only a soldier, but . . . a psychologist."[3] In his efforts to combat his troops' inertia and stiffen morale, Huntziger tried psychological methods. Helped by one of his staff officers, Captain Henri Massis, head of the army press section, he started a fortnightly bulletin, the *Documents du Combattant,* published at Senuc, whose aim was to explain why they should be prepared to fight, why it was essential for them to be standing guard along the Meuse. But apathy and skepticism were too strong for Huntziger's propaganda to be effective. His bulletin was discontinued after ten issues. The 2nd

---

[1] E. Ruby: *Sedan, Terre d'Epreuve* (1948), p. 42.
[2] Ibid.
[3] Allard: *L'Affaire Corap,* p. 31.

Army's morale might have been better if it had not, like the 9th, been starved of weapons and defense installations. After continually indenting for more armaments and defense materials, Huntziger finally received (according to the writer Paul Allard) half his defensive and one tenth of his arms requirements. Not until April did the 55th Division get its company antitank guns, and then there was little time left for training in their use. The 71st Division had no modern antiaircraft artillery and likewise almost no antitank guns. When the offensive broke, at least one company had only three 25mm. pieces, of which one was for instruction and unusable. It was alleged that during the whole war period to May 1940, most of the 55th and 71st Divisions never heard a shot fired. One 71st Division officer told Allard that he was refused an issue of cartridges even when he offered to pay for them. Finally he bought a supply himself, while on leave.

In the matter of defense deficiencies, blame was later to fall on Huntziger himself. At the Riom hearing of 1942 a 2nd Army artillery officer, Major Cahier, accused him of serious delays in authorizing fortifications and, in one case, of causing vital defenses to be removed. Cahier stated that, in view of Huntziger's dilatoriness, he had gone ahead with building certain antitank obstacles himself, after getting the approval of his immediate superior. The obstacles were situated at the foot of the two steep narrow routes that debouched from the Ardennes Forest toward Sedan, and they greatly facilitated the defense of these routes. Soon after they were finished in early May, claimed Cahier, Huntziger ordered them to be demolished.

Huntziger had resented the recent Frammond-Taittinger criticisms of the Sedan defenses. In a reply that Reynaud thought "supercilious and peremptory" he wrote on April 8: "The remarks of M. Taittinger (who seems, moreover, to be somewhat badly informed, at least on certain points) could have been of great importance if we had awaited them before undertaking the organisation of this position."[4] He seemed, in fact, skeptical about the likelihood of the Germans attacking at all. Three weeks before the offensive M. Jacomet, Controller-General of the army, asked Huntziger during a visit to Senuc: "In your opinion, are the Germans

---

4 Reynaud: *Fight,* p. 89n.

going to attack?" "Certainly not," Huntziger answered. "On the contrary, they are frightened that we are going to do so! Come back in a fortnight. You will see the sector in more detail; you will thus be able to note for yourself how uneasy they are."[5]

Whoever was chiefly answerable for the weakness of the Meuse front—and responsibility was widespread and rooted deep in the past—on May 10, 1940, the way stood open to the invader right from Sedan to Namur. Underequipped, undertrained, underindoctrinated, behind their frail defenses Huntziger's and Corap's second-rate divisions would meet the full shock of Germany's armored assault.

---

[5] Ibid., p. 294n.

Chapter 7

BREAKTHROUGH ON THE MEUSE

"The air bombing is not harming the troops."
(General Georges)

IN GENERAL DOUMENC'S OFFICE at GHQ, Montry, Captain André Beaufre was marking up the war map with the latest battle information. Studying the map, he came to a stark conclusion. The main axis of the German effort was no longer in Belgium above Liège, but along a line Luxembourg-Mézières. With a charcoal arrow Beaufre swiftly scored the new axis for colleagues to see. This was the moment—early on the morning of Mo..day, May 13—when the German grand strategy became finally and inescapably plain to the French High Command.

The situation was also being noted at GHQ, Northeast. Colonel Baril, head of the 2nd (Intelligence) Bureau, recalled that his office possessed a German operations plan covering the Ardennes, and forthwith went to look for it. But the bureau's files contained as many as seven or eight varying plans, and at this stage Baril found it hard to tell which one applied. In any case, even now Georges's staff was not unduly concerned at the German move. Such a maneuver, in limited strength, had always been foreseen as a possibility. And the official view still was that the deeper the enemy committed himself to the Ardennes "trap" the better.

But at Supreme Headquarters, Vincennes, the high confidence felt on Day 1 of the offensive was beginning to wane. Surveying the German push toward the Belgian plains and the developing threat against the Meuse, Gamelin judged it time to

appeal to his troops. At 1 a.m. on the thirteenth he issued this
General Order: "We must now stand up to the onslaught of the
enemy's mechanised and motorised forces. The hour has come
to fight all-out on the positions fixed by the High Command. We
no longer have any right to retreat. If the enemy makes fresh
local breaches we must not only plug them, but counter-attack and
retake them."

The Supreme Commander's words carried somber undertones. On the tenth he had sent the Allied armies forward with
the call: "*Nous les aurons!*" Now, only three days later, he was
urging them to hold fast at all costs. Between the lines of the Order
something else could be read: Gamelin was implying that what
was at stake was nothing less than the whole French strategic conception—the continuous defense line. If this went, the French
Army—and with it the British—might crumble; for nowhere on
the Allied front was there any defense in depth; and France's
strategic reserve, to plug the breaches and counterattack, was almost
nonexistent.

The twelfth had ended ominously for the French 2nd and 9th
Armies. Hustled out of Belgian Luxembourg, all their cavalry units
were back across the Meuse at least two days before schedule; and
almost everywhere from Namur to Sedan, German forces were
pushing west and south out of the Ardennes toward the river. Only
the air force had shone that day. The 2nd Army's fighter group had
intercepted *Luftwaffe* bomber squadrons as they attacked the Sedan
area, destroying some thirty planes for no French losses.

Now it was a question when the Germans would attempt
the crossing. Anxious to press on with speed, General von Kleist
wanted his panzers to force a passage at once, without waiting for
the infantry to go ahead of him. This he signified to Hitler's ADC,
General Schmundt, who flew from the Führer's headquarters on
the twelfth expressly to ask him his intentions. Then, calling General Guderian to his command post, Von Kleist ordered him to be
ready to launch his XIX Armored Corps across the Meuse at
4 p.m. next day, the thirteenth. Back at his headquarters in the
Hôtel du Panorama at Bouillon (where, as townspeople tell, a
stuffed boar's head fell on him as he pored over his maps),
Guderian planned the forthcoming assault: with Sedan as the

center of attack, the 2nd, 1st, and 10th Panzer Divisions, deployed from west to east, were to storm the river in a tight, three-pronged thrust.

At one point in Belgium, the Germans were already across the Meuse. On the afternoon of the twelfth a motorcycle reconnaissance patrol of Rommel's 7th Panzer Division found a weir linking both banks at Houx, just north of Dinant. Repulsed at first, the patrol succeeded in crossing the weir after dark, unseen by the French defending battalion that remained on the heights of the west bank instead of descending—as Corap had ordered—to the river's edge. By the time artillery was contacted and had dropped over 1,000 rounds onto the weir, the German patrol was installed on the left bank.

This had been a day of crucial contest—a race between French and Germans to reach the Meuse in strength. Though the French had fewer handicaps than the Germans—with clear roads and a shorter distance to travel—it was a race they were losing. As the long columns of sweating, straining panzer crews, motorcyclists and infantrymen neared the clearings of the Meuse throughout the hours of the twelfth, many of the 9th Army positions on the west bank were yet unmanned. And Corap's troops were still plodding north, heading for rendezvous that were nowhere much more than 50 miles from their French bases.

On the northernmost part of the 9th Army's front, south of Namur, the 5th Motorized Division (General Boucher) of General Bouffet's II Corps was already in place. So, too, were the 61st Infantry Division (General Vauthier) and 102nd Garrison Division (General Portzert) of General Libaud's XLI Corps, which guarded the southernmost sector from Vireux, south of Givet, to Pont-à-Bar, and had not had to move at all. But the coverage of the central sector, from Dinant to Vireux, remained hazardously thin. Due to hold this winding 20-mile stretch were the reservists of General Martin's XI Corps—the 18th Infantry Division (General Duffet) and 22nd Infantry Division (General Hassler).[1] By the end of the twelfth, no more than five battalions of the 18th had arrived, and almost none of the 22nd.

---

[1] In General Hassler's absence on leave, the 22nd was temporarily commanded by a deputy.

In the adjoining 2nd Army sector, not even the nominally static formations of General Huntziger were in position. Among General Grandsard's X Corps confusion reigned, caused by a belated shuffle of divisions. Up to May 10, the X Corps consisted of the 55th Infantry Division (General Lafontaine) on the left, and the 3rd North African Division (General Chapouilly), on the right. But that day General Huntziger decided to enlarge the corps by bringing up the reserve 71st Infantry Division (General Baudet) from Vouziers, some 30 miles in the rear. Not until late on the twelfth did the 71st arrive, with orders to interpose itself between the 55th and 3rd North African—just to the right of Sedan. As it moved into its new and unfamiliar positions it spread disorder on the whole corps front, forcing the two displaced divisions on left and right to take up partially fresh stations.

East of Sedan, toward the Maginot Line, the 2nd Army's other corps—the XVIII (General Rochard)—remained undisturbed. Rochard's corps, holding the line of the Chiers, was fortunate: it was outside the immediate sphere of attack. Ironically, it comprised two of Huntziger's best divisions, the "active" 3rd Colonial (General Faloy) and the "Series A" reservist 41st (General Bridoux). But there was sharper irony in the layout of the formations west of XVIII Corps. Here, across the vulnerable junction point of the 9th and 2nd Armies—from Sedan to Mézières —Corap and Huntziger had placed four of their weakest divisions. In one continuous line stood Corap's 61st Infantry and 102nd Garrison Divisions, and Huntziger's 55th and 71st Infantry Divisions—the "*crocos*," the static fortress troops, the least battleworthy soldiers of two mediocre armies.

Against this frail line were massing, through the brief night of the 12th–13th, five panzer divisions—Guderian's three opposite Sedan (although part of the 2nd Division had not yet reached the Meuse from the Semois River), and Reinhardt's 6th and 8th opposite Monthermé, in the center of Libaud's XLI Corps (9th Army) sector. Farther north, against the almost equally shaky XI Corps sector around Dinant, the 5th and 7th Panzers of Hoth's XV Corps were marshaling their forces. Behind the German armor and assault troops on the forest's edge, the long motorized columns rolled westwards from as far back as Bastogne, their undimmed lights blazing through the trees.

For the Germans committed to the Ardennes operation, these

were hard, exacting hours. All, from top commanders down, were extended in grim purposeful effort to keep moving, to maintain the tightly scheduled Plan Yellow timetable. Officers and men were exhausted, red-eyed from lack of sleep. But weary as they were, they were fired with hope, confidence, and stern resolve as they prepared, before the dawn of the thirteenth, for the next step —the great breakthrough.

Only a few hours before, GHQ, Northeast, had signaled Vincennes that the Meuse defenses were "well assured." In fact, in two of the Germans' three chosen target areas, Sedan and Dinant, by daybreak on the thirteenth the French were not even properly in position. Behind Sedan, Huntziger's X Corps had not got over the disruption caused by the arrival of the 71st Division; and along the Dinant-Houx sector of the Belgian Meuse, Corap's XI Corps troops were still marching in.

At Houx, like the first trickle through a dam, began the penetration that would soon breach the Meuse like a flood. Here, at 3 a.m. on the thirteenth, the motorcycle battalion that was already over the river reached the nearby heights and broke up a defending unit of the 18th Infantry Division. In the next hours, despite intervention by the 5th Motorized Division (stationed immediately to the north), it advanced farther inland. Meanwhile, around 10 a.m. the Germans made another crossing: after stiff resistance a rifle regiment of Rommel's division forced its way over the river at Bouvignes, south of Houx.

On boats, rubber canoes, straw rafts, even by swimming, more men gained the west bank. By noon the Germans held a bridgehead around Houx two miles deep and three miles wide.

At Supreme Headquarters the news of the Houx crossing caused a shock of dismay. Suddenly Vincennes awoke to the fact that the Meuse—let alone the Ardennes—was not the impassable barrier it had been imagined to be. Since the tenth, Gamelin's staff had hardly given a thought to the Meuse front south of Namur— the river line seemingly so safely protected by its wooded, rocky slopes. Now "all attention is going to concentrate on what happens on the Meuse," noted Colonel Minart.[2] For the next ninety minutes the staff waited tensely for reports of the counterattack promised

---

[2] J. Minart: *P. C. Vincennes, Secteur 4* (1945), p. 136.

by GHQ, Northeast. When nothing was heard by 2 p.m., even Gamelin was impatient. Twice in fifteen minutes he telephoned 9th Army headquarters. On his second call, General Thierry d'Argenlieu, Corap's Chief of Staff, replied calmly: "The Houx incident is *en cours.*"[3]

The Houx invaders never amounted to more than a small force, without tanks or heavy guns. Yet—predictably—their success in gaining a foothold sent alarm through the French Command. As they ranged over the heights behind Houx, every higher headquarters rang with urgent orders to counterattack. Corap pressed his XI Corps commander, General Martin; Billotte, by both telephone and a personal visit in the afternoon, pressed Corap; finally, that evening, Georges pressed Billotte, with categorical instructions to see that the enemy was thrown back over the Meuse on the fourteenth. For this purpose, Georges told Billotte, he was allocating a strong assault group including the 1st Armored Division (from the reserve), then assembling at Charleroi, on the Sambre, some 20 miles northeast of Dinant.

The grim fact was that on the thirteenth no counterattack was launched at Houx. Though one was ordered by the commander of the 5th Motorized Division for 1 p.m., it never materialized. The regiment was an hour late starting, and when it finally got moving it was at once attacked and scattered. Then II Corps commander, General Bouffet, ordered the 14th Regiment of Motorized Dragoons (5th Motorized Division) into action. But the dragoons could not be in place until late evening, and the operation had to be deferred to next day. Likewise, the tired reservists of XI Corps failed to produce any sort of counterblow. Night fell with Rommel's men firmly lodged on the left bank. Into the bridgehead that they had forced, more troops would swiftly and inevitably follow—then guns, tanks, the whole strength of Hoth's panzer corps. For Corap's Dinant forces, outfought in this limited initial clash, the prospects of rectifying the situation on the morrow looked bleak.

But at its very baptism of fire the 9th Army faced a double crisis. On the thirteenth, its Meuse Line was being broken in not one but two places. Forty miles south, around hill-flanked Monthermé, where the Meuse met the twisting Semois, General Port-

---

[3] Ibid.

zert's 102nd Garrison Division was under furious assault from advance units of Reinhardt's XLI Armored Corps—the center prong of the great three-spiked panzer thrust launched against the Meuse that day.

Like the 18th Division of Martin's XI Corps, the men of the 102nd Garrison Division were pitched into battle almost before they realized that war had come their way at all. Only from 9 a.m. that day, when enemy movements were spotted across the Meuse opposite Monthermé, were they alerted to the prospect of imminent action. In their pillboxes and behind their barbed-wire lines, these untrained, unseasoned troops took post and waited. Ninth Army headquarters, already engaged in trying to handle the breakthrough farther north, uneasily took note of this second threat to its front. "We are watching the Monthermé region," General d'Argenlieu assured Gamelin, when reporting on the Houx situation at 2:15 p.m.[4]

Forty-five minutes later the assault started. Under a thickening valley mist, two battalions of the 6th Panzer Division rushed the river's approaches opposite Monthermé. Breaking the stubborn initial resistance from the 102nd's concrete bunkers and artillery, the enemy stormed over the river. For some reason the preliminary Stuka attack, which had been planned, failed to take place; and the Germans had to rely mainly on point-blank tank fire from across the river—a devastating bombardment, which wrecked half the town. After a tough fight, the Germans gained the heights beyond Monthermé; and in the late afternoon more boatloads crossed the river to strengthen the enemy bridgehead. By nightfall Reinhardt's men were digging in before the French second defense line. They had virtually cut off the vulnerable Givet Peninsula, to their north. And behind them gleamed the French Meuse.

As the fighting flared at Monthermé, 30 miles southeastward a fiercer battle was raging. Guderian's forces were moving against Sedan in an assault that included a massive and sustained air strafe. What the 102nd Garrison Division troops were luckily being spared in the way of air attack, their 2nd Army comrades were receiving

---

[4] Ibid.

in full measure. For six hours the X Corps reservists cowered under the bombs of the diving Stukas that—more effectively than any gunfire—opened the way for the Sedan landings and produced the widest breach in the Meuse Line that day.

At dawn on the thirteenth X Corps was still maneuvering into its new positions; Lafontaine's 55th Division on the left, Baudet's weary 71st in the center, and Chapouilly's 3rd North African on the right. In some irritation, Lafontaine was having to reorganize his sector to make room for the 71st. His only benefit from the reshuffle was a relatively dense artillery coverage. All told, the 55th now mustered on its narrow five-mile front 140 guns of varied caliber. This advantage was somewhat offset by the order to conserve ammunition for counterfire instead of using it unrestrictedly against tank concentrations across the Meuse.

If any X Corps division was looking for targets that morning, rarely can there have been such a massed display. From first light the enemy was assembling on the opposite bank. In plain sight of the 55th's lookouts, serried columns of tanks and motor vehicles emerged from the forest cover, making for Saint-Menges, Floing, Bazeilles, the outskirts of Sedan. Down the field paths filed long lines of infantry. The build-up continued steadily through the morning. By noon, observers estimated, there were some 400 vehicles in the Saint-Menges and Sedan areas, and perhaps as many more to the north of Bazeilles. One French commander, General Menu, later speculated that if the artillery had mounted a full-scale, concerted blow at this assemblage, Guderian's panzers might have been broken up before they even attempted the Meuse crossing. "What a chance," Menu lamented, "to acquire imperishable glory, by smothering at birth the German offensive and transforming all these mechanized and armored units into scraps of burnt and twisted metal."[5]

Equally, bombers could have been called in; but 2nd Army headquarters informed the Zone of Air Operations that these were not needed as artillery was, in fact, engaging. But though 55th Division's artillery did open up on the concentrations, its fire was too slight to cause substantial damage. Apart from the continued dislocation of the X Corps divisions and the necessity to save am-

---

[5] C. L. Menu: *Lumière sur les Ruines* (1953), p. 213.

munition, Menu attributed the artillery failure basically to lack of liaison throughout the chain of artillery command—itself due to training deficiencies among the reservist gunner units.

But the French guns stayed almost silent that morning for a more compelling reason. The whole area was paralyzed by a massed bombing attack—staged by General Sperrle's Third Air Force in response to a request by Guderian, whose artillery had not yet arrived. The planes, mostly Stukas, began coming over around 9 a.m., stepping up their assault two hours later. From then on, they subjected the Sedan positions to a continuous onslaught lasting until midafternoon. Wave after wave flew in, seeming to awe-struck observers to follow the same precise tactics. From one group of about forty, circling at 600 feet, two or three would peel off simultaneously, descending nearly to ground level as they bombed—their main targets being the forward blockhouses and pillboxes. Meanwhile another forty Stukas would circle at 1,200 feet, waiting to replace the lower group after they had all released their bombs. Farther back a third and independent group picked out battery sites and similar objectives.

No less than twelve dive-bomber squadrons operated over Sedan that day—with explicit orders from Guderian to obliterate the French defenses. Weaving around them were his own protective fighter squadrons. These, and German reconnaissance planes, were the only aircraft seen over Sedan on the thirteenth. Anguished Frenchmen looked up in vain for a sight of Allied fighters amid the swarming Stukas. The previous day they had made a brave show against Sperrle's bombers, but now they were conspicuously absent. The *Luftwaffe* dominated the skies.

The fathers of these Sedan defenders had experienced the bombardments of Verdun and the Somme—shellfire far deadlier than the bombs of the Stukas. But on the troops huddling near the Meuse the effect of the bombing was, in the words of General Ruby, "incomparably more terrifying."[6] Each man felt that the Stuka screaming down was coming straight at him. It seemed impossible that he could escape its bombs. The din shattered the nerves and stupefied the mind. Aside from this, the superficial destruction was formidable: under the rein of explosions the

---

[6] E. Ruby: *Sedan, Terre d'Epreuve* (1948), p. 126.

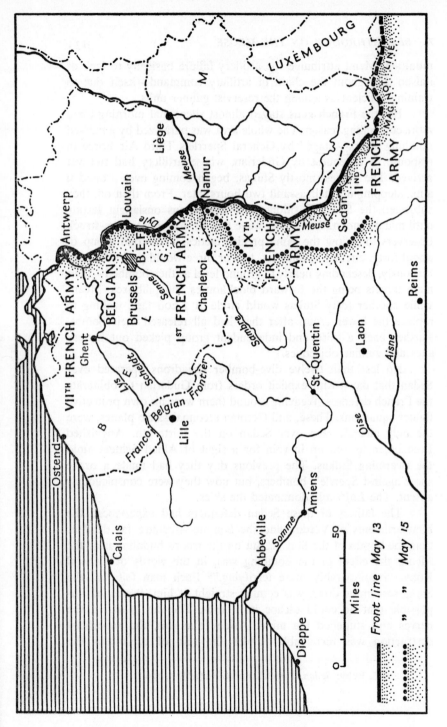

1. Belgium and France: the Allied positions on (a) May 13, 1940,

forward defense lines were reduced to a shambles. Guns were blown askew and overturned, concrete installations dislodged or half-buried, their apertures gaping crazily skyward or rammed into the earth. And over the blockhouses rose a curtain of fume-laden dust. In addition to bombs, the advance posts were raked by withering fire from tank, antitank, and even flak guns that had been brought up close on the opposite bank. The flat-trajectory shells slammed devastatingly into the loopholes of pillboxes.

For the French gunners, this was a fearsome initiation. Until that day many of them had never fired a single round. Even so, initially some batteries managed to go into action; but as the assault grew in fury during the morning, the opposition tailed off. From 3 p.m., the guns still firing faced a new menace—bombardment by Guderian's newly arrived artillery: four groups of 105mm. and four groups of 150mm. pieces positioned on a one-and-a-half-mile front.

In the 55th Division's sector behind Sedan, chaos prevailed from the start of the attack. As early as 9 a.m. the divisional communications officer, at the 55th's command post at Fond-Dagot (near Bulson), reported that he was out of telephone contact with the front, and that repairs were impossible during the bombing. Shortly after, the radio posts were destroyed, and General Lafontaine found himself cut off from all communication with his troops. He had no means of knowing whether any of his batteries were still firing—and if so, what their targets were. Around 1 p.m. the assault intensified, apparently concentrating on the narrow Wadelincourt-Donchery front, south of Sedan itself.

On the right of the 55th, General Baudet's 71st Division was in similar plight. When the first bombs hurtled down, the troops were still digging in on their new terrain. Concerned at the likelihood of imminent attack, at 11 a.m. Baudet got in touch with his corps commander, Grandsard, at his command post at La Berlière. Surprisingly, even now Grandsard was discounting the chances of the enemy making a full-scale crossing attempt that day; and he reassured Baudet to this effect. But soon Grandsard changed his mind. At 2 p.m. he ordered forward two reserve infantry regiments and a reserve tank battalion to a prepared line south of Sedan.

At Fond-Dagot, Lafontaine himself was convinced by early afternoon that the *Luftwaffe*'s attack heralded a German cross-river operation within the next hours—right against his own sector, which covered Sedan. At 3 p.m. he too telephoned Grandsard to express his fears and urgently request Allied air support. Grandsard immediately telephoned the army commander at Senuc. In Huntziger's absence, he spoke to his Chief of Staff, Colonel Lacaille, and passed on Lafontaine's plea. From Lacaille he got a somewhat inconclusive reply—with no promise of support. Meanwhile, as the Stukas wheeled and dived and the bombardment moved to its climax, the assault troops of Guderian's three panzer divisions stood poised on the river's north bank, abreast of Sedan.

On the French side, few guns were still firing. Either they had been knocked out or their demoralized crews had gone to ground. Bomb-shocked defenders still in the forward blockhouses peered helplessly through the smoke pall that blanketed the river —without fire directions from the rear and, in any case, unable to see what targets to aim at. By its sheer weight and duration, the attack had neutralized nearly all resistance in the narrow Sedan hinterland. Crouched in their foxholes and bunkers, Baudet's and Lafontaine's men waited numbly for the ordeal to end.

To cover his crossing, Guderian had ordered a final thirty-minute bombing of maximum intensity, starting at 3:30 p.m. As soon as the last bomb debris had scattered, the 1st Panzer assault troops hit the shore near Gaulier, west of Sedan—elements of a motorcycle battalion, a lorried infantry brigade, and the crack Gross Deutschland infantry regiment. Leaping from their five-man rubber rafts, they ran for the French forward casemates. Their immediate mission was to seize the small river loop forming the Iges Peninsula, including Glaire and Torcy. This they achieved with comparative ease, despite having to negotiate large stretches of open ground. Everywhere the stunned, smoke-blinded French were quickly overwhelmed; and almost unopposed, the Germans raced on toward Frenois, Bellevue, the Marfée Wood—cutting off Sedan from behind.

Simultaneously, the 10th Panzer assault troops—the 69th and 86th Rifle Battalions—came ashore near Wadelincourt, just south-east of Sedan. These did not have such an easy progress. Caught by enfilading fire from undestroyed bunkers, they found themselves bottled up in a narrow zone around Wadelincourt. West of Sedan, the 2nd Panzer Division, with part of its forces still waiting at the

Semois River, did not manage to put over its assault group at all. But any setbacks to the 2nd and 10th were outweighed by the quick success of the 1st Panzer Division. Guderian was later to note that its attack—enormously aided by the German air and artillery preparation—went ahead as smoothly as a training exercise. By sunset the men of the 1st Panzers had cut through the French defense line at the base of Marfée Wood, two miles inland from Sedan. And by the day's end there was a German bridgehead four miles wide and four deep around Sedan.

As at Houx and Monthermé, in these first hours there was nothing irreparable in the Sedan breakthrough. Only small forces were across the Meuse, with no tanks or heavy guns. In all three places the Germans, in precarious possession of limited footholds, were vulnerable to a determined counterattack. Visiting X Corps headquarters at La Berlière between 5 and 6 p.m., General Huntziger saw the Sedan position as still within control. He ordered Grandsard to plug the gap and then counterattack, then soon left for his Senuc headquarters. Here there was even more optimism. When news was received of the Wadelincourt crossing—initially by some fifty men, according to reports—Huntziger's staff dismissed the threat. "There will be as many prisoners," it was confidently asserted.[7] At La Ferté, General Georges too was viewing the breakthrough without undue alarm. His report, dispatched to Supreme Headquarters between 4 and 5 p.m., spoke of "enemy infiltrations" north of Sedan and in the Iges Peninsula, and mentioned other German troop movements and concentrations, together with artillery fire. "The air bombing," the report added, "is continuous, but is not causing harm to the troops."[8]

General Georges was reckoning without the moral effect of the bombing on the unseasoned X Corps units. Even as Supreme Headquarters was assessing the implications of his report, the situation at Sedan was sliding out of control.

---

[7] Ibid., p. 144.
[8] Minart: *P. C. Vincennes*, p. 138.

Chapter 8

STAMPEDE AT SEDAN

"The tanks are at Bulson!"
(Retreating French troops)

PANIC WAS SWEEPING the ranks of the 55th and 71st Divisions. Suddenly these ordinary Bretons, Normans, men of the Loire, working-class Parisians, had cracked under the stress of battle. Along with X Corps troops, they were everywhere retreating in wild disorder—artillerymen, infantry, even officers. Around 6 p.m., word flashed through the 55th's sector that enemy tanks were across the Meuse. The rumor seemed to start at several points simultaneously. One tank scare—possibly the first—originated from a X Corps battery commander at Chaumont (east of Marfée Wood), who noted heavy firing, together with "departure lights," near Marfée Wood. He immediately reported the suspected presence of German tanks to the corps artillery command post at Flaba. Shortly after, another unit sighted more "tanks" moving south from the Wadelincourt area. Within minutes, groups of men were bolting from their posts with cries of "Enemy tanks." Others joined them as they ran; and soon every road from Sedan was packed with men, horses, and vehicles herding out of the battle zone.

In fact, no German tanks crossed the Meuse on the thirteenth. The Sedan defenders were being stampeded by a handful of their own tanks, moving in support toward Bulson. Those who had not seen "German" tanks blindly believed those who thought they had. Others were retiring in obedience to nonexistent "orders." "One is in the presence of a phenomenon of collective hallucination," wrote General Ruby.[1] To aggravate the situation, the prolonged bombing had wrecked communications, isolated command posts and individual units, and left the various formation headquarters ignorant of what was happening in the forward zones, and unable to check information and exercise any control. Once started, the mass hysteria was not only unstoppable but so swiftly contagious that it invaded divisional and corps headquarters.

The panic was worst in the rear areas. At his command post at Fond-Dagot on the Bulson-Maisoncelle road, General Lafontaine was surprised shortly after six by a mob of troops careering southward from Bulson—men of two infantry and two artillery regiments. "The tanks are at Bulson!" they yelled.[2] Some were firing blindly into the air. The spirited, energetic Lafontaine was astounded. Dashing into the road with his staff, he tried to reason with them and restore some sort of order. In an effort to stop the rush, he had trucks placed across the road. Most infantrymen had jettisoned their rifles, and the gunners—mainly from the heavy batteries near Bulson, Noyers, and Chaumont—had abandoned their guns. These artillerymen claimed to have seen the mysterious departure signals from the southern fringe of Marfée Wood, along with German tanks at Chaumont and Bulson.

Officers, too, were joining in the rout. When challenged, they insisted that they had been ordered to retire, but could produce no confirmation, or say who had issued the order. Their example incited more troops to quit. Quickly, the rearward artillery command posts emptied; telephones to the front went dead; forward gunners—still manning their guns against the advancing Germans in the Sedan pocket—found themselves stranded. Without communication or firing instructions, these also decamped. The panic spread in widening circles, striking deepest among the corps and divisional heavy artillery. Around Chaumont, thickly sewn with command posts and batteries, almost the only post not abandoned was that of Lieutenant Colonel Pinaud, commanding the 147th Infantry Regiment. Pinaud stood firm while neighboring artillery teams scuttled. Behind these gunners, the corps heavy artillery command itself was in total disarray. The commander at Bulson

---

[1] E. Ruby: *Sedan, Terre d'Epreuve* (1948), p. 133.
[2] Ibid., p. 132.

(controlling Group B artillery) suddenly reported to his superior at Flaba (controlling Group A) that there was fighting 500 yards from Bulson and that he was about to be surrounded by German machine gunners, and asked permission to retire. This was granted, and both commanders ordered their entire groups to withdraw and left their command posts. (Later, on orders from the general commanding corps artillery, they returned to their posts, but their personnel had vanished in the stampede. That night the Group A commander at Flaba committed suicide.)

Even General Lafontaine was caught up in the flight. About 6:30, the commander of the 110th Artillery Regiment, whose command post was near Fond-Dagot, doubled to 55th Division headquarters with alarming news of a German advance. Without waiting to check, Lafontaine's staff reported to Grandsard, who authorized the general to move his command post south to Chemery. The Fond-Dagot headquarters was evacuated in such haste that Colonel Chaligne, divisional infantry commander, whose command post was likewise at Fond-Dagot, was not warned of it. And (possibly to deny it to the enemy) the headquarters signals unit partly wrecked the telephone exchange. Black smoke rose into the evening air as the headquarters files were hurriedly burned. By car and on foot the staff headed precipitately out of Fond-Dagot —leaving a deserted headquarters, to which liaison officers were to return from the front that night, amazed to find everybody gone without explanation.

At Chemery pandemonium reigned. Lafontaine's party arrived there amid scenes of "unimaginable panic" as runaway troops surged through the village and long transport columns from nearby divisional depots rolled southwards.[3] Military police barriers were swept aside in the press. Along with X Corps gunners, much of the 55th Division seemed on the move. Lafontaine was now in a desperate predicament. Grandsard had telephoned him at Fond-Dagot ordering a counterattack for dawn on the fourteenth, to be made by all available X Corps reserves. This entailed moving up to the line Connage-Bulson-Haraucourt two groups consisting of the 213th Infantry Regiment supported by the 7th Tank Battalion, and the 205th Regiment supported by the 4th Tank Battalion. In

---

[3] Ibid., p. 135.

the turmoil of his makeshift command post, with hardly any communications or headquarters facilities, the harassed Lafontaine sat down to plan the attack. There he was joined by Colonel Chaligne from Fond-Dagot, impatient for information on the coming action. Outside, in the darkness, the fugitives still swarmed past—gunners and men of three identifiable infantry regiments, along with tracked vehicles, *voiturettes,* 25mm. guns. Lafontaine's staff tried vainly to barricade the street and hold back the fighting units to form them up to take part in the counterattack.

Lafontaine had completely lost touch with what was happening in his sector. He had no idea which units were still in place and which had joined the retreat. Toward midnight he sent out three officers to different points to check and report back. One failed to return, the second could not even get through, and the third—ordered to rendezvous with the 7th Tank Battalion—found the tanks submerged by fleeing troops. In the confusion it was virtually impossible for Lafontaine to go ahead with the counterattack without further briefing from General Grandsard. So around 1 a.m. he decided to see Grandsard at La Berlière. His car, too, was halted on the choked roads. Having reached no farther than Stonne after an hour, he gave up and returned to Chemery. Behind him, a X Corps staff officer was fighting his way from La Berlière to Chemery with an order confirming the dawn counterattack. The order was issued at 1:30 a.m., but the officer did not reach Chemery until four o'clock.

Sharing Lafontaine's command post at Chemery was Lieutenant Colonel Labarthe, commanding the 213th Infantry—a unit detailed for the counterattack. The 213th was due to move off in the small hours for a position on the forward Chéhéry (not to be confused with Chemery) Bulson Line. But Labarthe had strong misgivings about his troops going into action. In fact, he was opposed to the whole operation. "Whatever happens, no counterattack!" he kept repeating.[4] Not only was he apprehensive about the morale of the 213th in this dire situation, but he doubted whether they would ever reach their position in the chaotic state of the roads. Labarthe appealed personally to Lafontaine to modify the order. Lafontaine consulted Lieutenant Colonel Cachou, X

---

[4] Ibid.

Corps Deputy Chief of Staff, who just then was at his command post. Cachou agreed that the 213th should halt on the nearer Chemery-Maisoncelle Line. At 6:20 a.m. the regiment moved off —one unit, at least, that was heading toward and not away from the battle front. But Labarthe was still worried. As he left, he told Lafontaine: "General, you're sending my regiment on a mission of sacrifice."[5]

Colonel Cachou himself was trapped in the retreating flood. On his way back to La Berlière he had to abandon his car and make a long trek on foot before being picked up by a patrolling police car. It took him two and a half hours to regain X Corps headquarters. The mass exodus of the Sedan troops was paralyzing the entire sector. As well as halting vital traffic en route to the front, it was rendering the command impotent by impeding transmission of orders and information. Staff officers, dispatched to clear essential routes, gave up in despair. The onrush of men and vehicles carried all before it.

From the 55th Division, the panic had swiftly spread to the 71st. Here, too, it was the back areas that were worst affected. Around 6:30, an excited motorcyclist dashed up to a signals unit sheltering in the stone quarries near Raucourt and shouted: "The Germans are at Bulson!"[6] Elsewhere the cry rang through command posts, bunkers, gun sites, to cause a headlong exodus. General Baudet's divisional command post at Raucourt was thrown into a furor by an alarm allegedly emanating from X Corps itself. According to General Ruby, about 6:30 Raucourt received an urgent telephone call from Colonel Badel, X Corps Chief of Staff, announcing that enemy tanks had reached Chaumont. Badel instructed Baudet to form a defensive loop, facing west, and bring up an infantry regiment and a tank battalion to a prescribed line, in readiness to launch a counterattack. Ten minutes later Badel called again, to report that the tanks were at Bulson and Lafontaine was evacuating his command post. (Ruby's account was later contested by Badel, though substantiated by officers of the 71st.) In the mounting crisis, the tough and forthright Baudet, "a man of duty," had to make a quick decision.[7] Immediately he ordered

[5] Ibid., p. 149.
[6] P. Allard: *La Vérité sur l'Affaire Corap* (1941), p. 37.
[7] Ibid., p. 39.

abandonment of his headquarters. With his divisional artillery commander, Colonel Dieuleveult, he sped off for La Bagnolle, at the extreme left limit of the 71st's sector.

As with the 55th, the evacuation of senior artillery command posts contributed to the *débâcle*. Distracted corps and divisional gunners tried vainly to contact rear headquarters staffs which had taken off in the stampede—like the officer whose battery was under pressure near Haraucourt. Unable to get a reply from the deserted Group A artillery post at Flaba, at 10 p.m., in desperation, he destroyed his guns and withdrew. But against the great current of retreat, some units stood fast and even pressed forward under the leadership of cool-headed and courageous commanders. Captain Benedetti, an artillery officer, himself went to X Corps headquarters for orders and then took his men through a horde of fugitives to their counterattack position. Another unit, Lieutenant Colonel Montvignier-Monnet's 205th Infantry Regiment—one of those which Colonel Badel had instructed Baudet to move up for a counterattack—set out at short notice from La Besace to Maisoncelle, though tired after a long night march. It had to battle its way among an oncoming procession of trucks, filled with runaways shouting: "Don't go on! The Germans are here!"[8] But before it reached its rendezvous the 205th was intercepted by a motorcyclist, who brought orders canceling the attack.

Amid the confusion of that day, there was some mystery about the source of such orders. In several cases retirement orders seem to have been given by individuals who purported to be officers but were unknown to the troops. There were also instances of unidentified telephone orders that seemed deliberately aimed at increasing the chaos. For example, Major Piquetti, commanding the 38th Artillery Regiment (71st Division), was ordered to withdraw his *avant-trains*—with the result that his guns were put out of action. And in the rear, allegedly false orders drew civilians into the stampede. It was even claimed that telephone cables were found cut. If the reports were genuine, it may well be that fifth-columnists were at work, having infiltrated across the frontier in the guise of refugees.

Spread by the vanguard of deserters, the panic was biting deep into the rear. That night it infected 2nd Army units as far

---

[8] Ruby: *Sedan*, p. 140.

back as Grandpré, Buzancy, and Vouziers, 30 miles south of Sedan. To head off the growing stream of fugitives, Colonel Serin, 2nd Army Provost Marshal, hurriedly called in a reinforcement of two companies of *gardes mobiles* from Châlons and Vitry. Echoes of the panic even reached 2nd Army headquarters. About 9 p.m. two agitated engineer officers arrived at Senuc, demanding to see Huntziger. To the general they excitedly reported that they had seen German tanks at Vendresse, 10 miles south of Sedan. In scathing terms Huntziger castigated them as liars. What they had taken to be German panzers, he told them, was the 2nd Army's 7th Tank Battalion.

News of the Sedan breakdown was slow to reach beyond 2nd Army headquarters. Neither La Ferté nor Montry—and certainly not Vincennes—knew of it before midnight. But at Supreme Headquarters this was a day of shocks. As the successive reports of the Meuse crossings arrived, anxiety mounted in the somber, subterranean casemates. For Gamelin and his staff the whole strategic picture was drastically changed for the worse. No longer could the German moves south of Namur be dismissed as a secondary supporting action for a main operation across the Belgian plains. It was now clear that they were on a scale that jeopardized the success of the whole Plan D conception. Following General Georges's first message reporting "enemy infiltrations" at Sedan, came another—apparently very delayed—at 9:25 p.m.[9] This stated that at 5 o'clock there had been "quite serious trouble" south of Sedan and that the 3rd Armored Division had been called. At 11:45 Vincennes received another message—a situation report ending with the reassuring words: "We are calm—*Nous sommes calmes.*" But this hardly allayed the misgivings at Supreme Headquarters. As officers not on night duty drifted uneasily to bed around midnight, in Gamelin's office the light burned on into the early hours.

Elsewhere the *débâcle* was causing consternation and even unrestrained grief. Soon after midnight a top-level emergency conference was held at a senior French headquarters—attended by

---

[9] J. Minart: *P. C. Vincennes, Secteur 4* (1945), p. 138.

Air Marshal Barratt (British Air Officer Commanding in Chief), General d'Astier de la Vigerie, General Billotte, the liaison officers to General Georges and General Vuillemin (French Air Officer Commanding in Chief), and others—to discuss it. This, as described by an anonymous British Air Intelligence Officer, was "a tragic affair. Most of the French officers were in tears, some quite openly sobbing . . ."[1]

Around 2 a.m. the telephone rang in Captain Beaufre's quarters at GHQ, Montry. General Georges was calling from his command post at Les Bondons. "Ask General Doumenc to come immediately," he said.[2] Within an hour Doumenc and Beaufre arrived at Les Bondons—to find in Georges's office an atmosphere, as Beaufre put it, "like that of a family in which one is watching over the dead." Beaufre describes vividly what followed. The room was in half-darkness, and silent except for the quiet voice of a staff officer, Major Navereau, who was speaking on the telephone. General Roton, Georges's Chief of Staff, was slumped dejectedly in a chair. As they entered, Georges came quickly up to Doumenc. His face was white. "Our Sedan front is broken!" he exclaimed. "There's been a collapse—*il y a eu des défaillances.*" He fell back into a chair, stifling a sob.

Doumenc was flabbergasted. But he reacted quickly. "General, it is war," he said. "In war there are always incidents like these." Georges went on to explain that the 55th and 71st Divisions had "given ground" after a terrible bombing: that X Corps headquarters had reported that the position was breached and German tanks had reached Bulson toward midnight. He broke into more sobs. For a moment everyone was too overcome to speak. Then Doumenc took command of the situation. "Come, general," he said briskly to Georges, "every war has seen its routs. Come over to the map. We'll see what can be done."

Standing in front of the big wallchart, the tall, lean Doumenc sketched out a plan. It was essential, he emphasized, to plug the gap—"*colmater,*" as one said in 1918. How could this be done? The army possessed three armored divisions—its whole armored

---

[1] *The Diary of a Staff Officer at Advanced Headquarters North, B.A.F.F., 1940* (1941), p. 10.
[2] A. Beaufre: *Le Drame de 1940* (1965), pp. 232–4.

reserve. The 1st Division was in Belgium, in the process of unloading in the Charleroi region preparatory to taking part in the Dyle operation: it could counterattack from north to south (on General Corap's front). The 3rd, just south of Sedan, could counterattack from south to north. The 2nd, en route to the Dyle, could be unloaded in the Vervins area and directed to counterattack from west to east. These three divisions, comprising six hundred tanks, could engage concentrically against the pocket to hurl the Germans back to the east bank of the Meuse. The 3rd, at Sedan, could attack next morning. It would be a hot fight, but the front should be capable of being restored.

Doumenc's forceful handling of the crisis had a tonic effect on the shattered staff. Tension was relaxed and the gloom lifted. After quick consideration, Georges ratified all the proposals, and consequent orders were issued forthwith. Beaufre turned up the lights and roused the mess cook to make coffee. Soon after, he returned with Doumenc to Montry, feeling that the night's "evil spell" was banished from Les Bondons.

Chapter 9

THE WIDENING BREACH

"We felt that the situation had suddenly become tragic."

(Paul Baudouin)

FOUR DAYS HAD PASSED, days of mounting German pressure all along the western battle front. As Day 5 dawned, nowhere was the struggle going well for the Allies. In the north, the Dutch front was disintegrating under the onslaught of Von Küchler's 18th Army; in the center, the Belgians had been forced back from their forward defense positions and Prioux's Cavalry Corps was desperately warding off the attacks of Von Reichenau's 6th Army in the direction of the Gembloux Gap; and in the south, the Meuse Line was breached in three places by Hoth's and Von Kleist's assault troops. But no long resistance had been anticipated from the small Dutch forces, battling heroically though they were; and behind the hard-pressed Cavalry Corps stood the divisions of the French 1st Army, flanked on the north by the B.E.F. Incomparably the gravest threat was on the Meuse.

At Houx, Monthermé, Sedan, everything depended, on Tuesday, May 14, on the French ability to launch effective counterattacks.

As this was being uneasily realized by the French High Command, Germany's military chiefs at OKW (High Command of the Armed Forces) and OKH (High Command of the Army) were reviewing the situation with great satisfaction. Except that Holland was taking longer to defeat them expected, Offensive Yellow was proceeding according to plan. The Allied armies were deployed in precisely the positions on which Hitler had counted when framing his grand strategy for the Ardennes breakthrough. In his Directive No. 10 of the previous February, he had prescribed that "forces operating south of the line Liège-Charleroi will force a passage of the Meuse between Dinant and Sedan and will advance through the French frontier defenses towards the Somme estuary."[1] Now Von Rundstedt's army group was presented with its chance to achieve this. On the crucial fifth day of the Battle of the West, Hitler issued his Directive No. 11—the instruction for an all-out assault across the Meuse.

The Directive ran as follows:

1. The progress of the offensive to date shows that the enemy has failed to appreciate in time the basic idea of our operations. He continues to throw strong forces against the line Namur-Antwerp and appears to be neglecting the sector facing Army Group A.

2. This fact and the swift forcing of the Meuse crossing in the sector of Army Group A have established the first essentials for a thrust in all possible strength north of the Aisne and in a north-westerly direction, as laid down in Directive No. 10. Such a thrust might produce a major success. It is the task of forces engaged north of the line Liège-Namur to deceive and hold down the greatest number of enemy forces by attacking them with their own resources.

3. On the northern flank the Dutch Army has shown itself capable of a stronger resistance than had been supposed. . . . It is the task of the Army . . . to bring about the speedy fall of Fortress Holland.

4. All available motorised divisions will be transferred to the optional area of Army Group A as soon as possible. Armoured and motorised divisions of Army Group B will also be switched to the left flank as soon as there are no further prospects of effective operations in their own sector and as the situation allows.

5. The task of the Air Force is to concentrate strong offensive and defensive forces for action, with the focal point at Army Group A, in order to prevent the transfer of enemy reinforcements to the front and to give direct support to our own forces. . . . *signed*: Adolf Hitler.[2]

In the 9th Army's sector there was still a semblance of control and coordination. The command was functioning, and there had been no major breakdown, as at Sedan. But Corap's troops

---

[1]H. R. Trevor-Roper, ed.: *Hitler's War Directives, 1939–1945* (1964), p. 22.
[2] Ibid., pp. 25–6.

were hardly in a state to hold their existing line, let alone counter-attack. The main body of Martin's XI Corps had arrived only the previous day and found no prepared positions. Moreover, the advance guards made the initial error of installing themselves on the heights above the Meuse and not on the riverbanks. Now tired, ill-trained, and ill-equipped, Martin's troops were committed to defend a stretch of unfamiliar front, one point of which was already breached. During the night Corap had issued orders for the containment of the enemy bridgehead within an arc based on the Meuse, from Anhée to Anseremme. This was backed by a more aggressive order from Billotte to push the enemy back to the Meuse. The first and most immediate operation—postponed from the afternoon of the thirteenth—was allotted to the 14th Regiment of Motorized Dragoons and the 1st Divisional Reconnaissance Group (II Corps, 5th Motorized Division). At dawn they were to recapture the plateau village of Haut-le-Wastia, behind Houx.

The attack went in at 4:45 a.m. The French surprised the German motorcycle battalion holding the village and took forty prisoners—only to be forced back soon afterward to Corap's prescribed containment line. Meanwhile, the Meuse Line was caving in at two new points, north and south of Houx. At Yvoir, to the north (in II Corps sector), a German infantry division got a foothold on the west bank; and to the south, near Dinant (in XI Corps sector), the tanks of Rommel's 7th Panzer Division rolled across the river at Bouvignes, on pontoons built by German pioneers who had worked feverishly through the night. The daring Rommel planned to race straight on through the Philippeville "Gap," 20 miles west, after his riflemen and motorcyclists had cleared the heights dominating the left bank. Facing the Germans here were the scattered and weakish units of General Duffet's 18th Infantry Division. By midmorning the French positions were falling wholesale to the German assault: Surinvaux, Rostenne, Hontoire, Flavion.

Beyond this thin defensive crust there was little to protect the Belgian hinterland from the onward thrust of Rommel's panzers. To pave the way for his main advance, he sent forward tanks and riflemen toward Onhaye, which barred the passage through the Philippeville Gap. Stoutly defended, Onhaye finally fell in late afternoon. Then the 7th Panzers surged westward, though slowed by fierce opposition from elements of the reserve 4th North African

Division (ordered into action by Corap), the 1st Light Cavalry Division, and some units of the 18th Division. When night fell the 18th's defense lines existed no more.

On the 18th's right, the other XI Corps division, the 22nd, was also in trouble. In the morning a German infantry division forced a crossing of the Meuse north of Givet, partially overrunning the 22nd. The acting commander (Hassler was still on leave) ordered the division back to a position six miles from the river. By evening the 22nd Division was in contact with the Meuse only south of Vireux, and was retreating in disorder. In an effort to save the situation, Martin decided to redeploy the corps, together with the bulk of the 4th North African Division, along a line linking it with Libaud's XLI Corps on the right. But events were moving too fast for him. Before the realignment could be carried out, orders came for a general retirement of the 9th Army.

General Corap spent an anxious morning hurrying between his formation headquarters, trying vainly to stem the growing disintegration with orders to commanders to plug the gaps and strengthen the wavering lines. He was concerned to note his troops' poor morale—largely due to the incessant air attacks. Everywhere he went he heard the same distracted cry: "Why aren't our planes hitting back?" Corap was even more disturbed at the lack of steadiness of some senior officers. Sensing the first ominous signs of breakdown, he put out a stern order: ". . . At the moment when the fate of France is in jeopardy, no weakness will be tolerated. It is incumbent on staffs to give an example to all ranks and, if necessary, compel obedience. Commanders who fail will be punished without mercy."[3]

But no order could stiffen the faltering divisions of XI and XLI Corps. As the day passed they lost all cohesion as a fighting force. Only the left flank of the 102nd Garrison Division (XLI Corps)—the 42nd and 52nd half-brigades of colonial machine gunners—stood fast, on a line to the right of Monthermé. For two days they were to hold Reinhardt's assault troops, thus preventing his 6th and 8th Panzers from joining in the main German breakthrough on May 15. Otherwise, with the collapse of the 18th, 22nd, and 61st Divisions, the center of the 9th Army's Meuse Line was crumbling from Dinant to Monthermé.

---

[3] P. Allard: *La Vérité sur l'Affaire Corap* (1941), p. 42.

This was a victory for German surprise, violence, and—above all—the internal-combustion engine. In the north, Rommel's tanks and motorized vehicles paralyzed the defense by sheer speed and mobility. Bypassing the French forward positions, they raced inland to wreak havoc in the rear. They overwhelmed command posts, strangled communications, stopped the transmission of orders, and immobilized the whole command system. While the Germans were using the radio in "clear" to save time, the French were reduced to sending runners, many of whom never reached their destination —or, if they did, arrived too late. Hence, junior commanders were left to their own initiative, forced to issue orders without regard to the overall situation. As headquarters control snapped, the front became fragmented and units found themselves isolated. The XI and XLI Corps sectors were already in chaos as a result of the widespread low-level bombing attacks that preceded the ground assault. Unopposed by a single Allied plane, the bombers fanned out over the battlefield and spread terror among Martin's and Libaud's unblooded reservists. Few units withstood the effect of the double onslaught.

At various points retirement became a rout. "Panic gripped some troops in the course of withdrawal," admitted General Doumenc. "Numerical inferiority and dispersal contributed to the *défaillances*. On top of this there was the demoralizing and destructive impact of the bombing."[4] In the rear, there were scenes akin to those at Sedan on the previous day. The roads were filled with truckloads of bewildered front-line troops, and men from rear echelons who had lost contact with command and were moving back in search of a rallying point from which to reorganize. But here the confusion was increased by swarms of civilian refugees. To add a touch of horror, German armored patrols were suddenly appearing among the slow-moving refugee columns and machine-gunning them. The German spearheads surprised rear-based service units that never expected to see the enemy. Away from the roads, the woods were full of troops of all arms, on the run from the ubiquitous tanks. Among them were gunners whose horse-drawn guns had been stranded when German planes had machine-gunned the horses.

---

[4] A. Doumenc: *Histoire de la Neuvième Armée* (1945), p. 133.

By evening the great exodus had gathered volume. The best part of three 9th Army divisions were disengaging from the Meuse in defeat and disorder. The columns straggled westward along the roads of Belgian Namur, and southwestwards into France's Aisne Department—still harried by German planes. "We pass through Couvin (in Belgium, 10 miles west of the Meuse)," recorded a 22nd Division battery commander, "where columns of all sorts are tangled up together—gunners, troop convoys, tracked vehicles, motorised reconnaissance groups, along with bands of terrified civilians. The chaos grows, and our men, in the last stages of exhaustion, clamber on to any vehicle they see, despite their officers' efforts to stop them. Leaving Couvin, we are machine-gunned by enemy planes. Women and children lie at the side of the road. Our men fall too. Swarms of planes come over, machine-gunning and bombing . . ."[5]

Many of these retreating troops were in a bitter mood. They saw themselves as victims of events beyond their control, hopelessly handicapped by lack of proper equipment, beaten through no fault of their own. This was the spirit of a 61st Division infantry regiment—the 332nd—ordered to move back on Maubert-Fontaine, on the French frontier, a dozen miles southwest of Couvin. It was "the result of the cruel reversal of the situation, of their having to abandon their positions without fighting, the absence of French artillery and aircraft, the shock of the bombings, and the overwhelming flood of refugees."[6] These men were also angry at their inadequate armament, which consisted of no more than portable arms and very little ammunition.

During the fourteenth there remained one reasonable hope of saving Corap's northern flank—the rapid intervention of General Bruneau's 1st Armored Division. But a disastrous chapter of delays prevented the division reaching the front in these vital hours. The 1st Armored Division was originally dispatched to Charleroi, in Belgium, on the eleventh, to be at the disposal of Blanchard's 1st Army in the Gembloux Gap. Late on the evening of the thirteenth, following the Houx breakthrough, Georges informed Billotte that he was sending Bruneau's division forward to counter-

---

[5] Ibid., pp. 158–9.
[6] Ibid., p. 165.

attack at Houx. But seemingly the division received no orders that
night; and meanwhile it remained at Charleroi, 20 miles back from
the Meuse. Not until after Doumenc's swift decision at GHQ,
Northeast, in the early hours of the fourteenth was it finally alerted
for action. Some time in the morning Billotte assigned it to Martin,
XI Corps commander, to clear the Dinant pocket forthwith. But it
was 1:30 p.m. before Bruneau was called to Martin's command
post at Florennes for briefing, and five o'clock when he actually
arrived there. He was then instructed to form his division in a
specified rectangle and attack as soon as possible in the Dinant
direction. In early evening—when XI Corps was fast disintegrating
—Bruneau's force headed east from Charleroi. Slowed up by the
congested roads, only part of the corps arrived at its rendezvous
that night; and the attack was postponed until next day.

In General Georges's dim-lit office at Les Bondons, Doumenc
had sketched out a similar plan to salvage the Sedan front—a
northward thrust by the 3rd Armored Division. But, frustrated by
holdups and countermanded orders, this too failed to materialize.
By nightfall, as the 2nd Army's center and left-flank positions
almost totally disintegrated under renewed German assaults, the
opportunity for armored counterattack had passed.

After yesterday's rout, Grandsard's shattered X Corps was
virtually out of the battle. A new 2nd Army Order had assigned
the defense of the Sedan sector to General Flavigny's XXI Corps,
comprising the 3rd Armored Division and the 3rd Mechanized and
5th Light Cavalry Divisions. An officer of "sang-froid, authority
and sense of command," Flavigny was highly thought of by Huntziger.[7] He knew the 2nd Army terrain well, having organized the
defenses of the more easterly Longwy sector early in the war. Originally a cavalryman, he fought in the infantry during World War I
and was an expert on tank warfare. His 3rd Armored Division,
commanded by General Brocard, contained two battalions of B
tanks and two of H tanks, a towed-artillery regiment and truck-
borne infantry. But the strength of the 3rd was mostly on paper.
Although the military writer Captain Goutard described it as "fully
capable of holding its own against the 10th Panzers," General

---

[7] E. Ruby: *Sedan, Terre d'Epreuve* (1948), p. 160.

Georges considered that when the German offensive broke it was still undertrained and underequipped.[8] On May 10 the division was dispersed around the Rheims area, and its own Chief of Staff, General Devaux, later testified that it had begun its training as a complete formation only on May 1, was not up to strength, lacked essential equipment, and was notably without any "unit of command, of petrol supply and breakdown services." In short, according to Devaux, it was not ready to take on the role now assigned to it.[9]

At about dawn, with the 3rd Mechanized Division, the 3rd Armored arrived at Chesne, nine miles from the battle zone. Ahead of them, in the strengthening light, lay the panorama of villages and wooded hills sloping to the Meuse—the Sedan pocket, scene of yesterday's *débâcle*. Whatever the division's technical state of readiness, the troops' morale was good. They rolled toward the battlefield eager to get to grips with the enemy—the more so as they had seen something of the 55th's panic retreat while moving up. Brocard planned to attack at noon in the Chemery-Maisoncelle direction, in a massed sortie from the north edge of Maison-Dieu Wood. But the delays now began. It was actually one o'clock before the division was ready to move off to the start line, and 4 p.m. when it was finally deployed for the attack. But by now the operation had been called off. At 3:30, Flavigny, at his command post at Senuc, changed his mind and ordered the division to spread out in defensive positions right across the 2nd Army sector from Omont to Stonne. The counterassault was deferred until next afternoon.

Brocard's belated arrival was apparently due to slow passing of orders and valuable time spent refueling. In any case, it was enough to throw out the whole attack plan by leaving the 3rd Mechanized Division unsupported. Huntziger, impatiently awaiting news of the operation, was furious to hear it had been put off. He at once radioed to Flavigny: "I learn with indignation that my orders have not been carried out, that the counter-attack from which we might have expected great results has not taken place

---

[8] A. Goutard: *The Battle of France, 1940*, trans. A. R. P. Goutard (1958), p. 143.

[9] P. Reynaud: *In the Thick of the Fight*, trans. J. D. Lambert (1955), p. 311.

because the commander of the 3rd Armoured Division has not given the general commanding the 3rd Mechanised Division sufficient support. I would like you to make a personal inquiry immediately into these sorry facts."[1]

Ironically, even while XXI Corps was heading toward Sedan soon after dawn, the first of Guderian's panzers were crossing the Meuse. Fanning almost unopposed over the battlefield, at no time on this crucial day were they confronted by the French armor. It fell to the improvised X Corps assault force, laboriously assembled by Lafontaine in the confusion of the 55th Division's rear the night before, to face the German tanks.

Here again, there were fatal delays. Lafontaine's mixed tank-and-infantry force was supposed to attack at dawn, advancing in three successive phases, its final objective being the line of the Meuse. But, struggling against the chaos on the roads, not until 7 a.m. did the first group manage to move. Ninety minutes later, at a point midway between Chemery and Chéhéry, it ran into a strong panzer column. Its light tanks were severely battered and its infantry dispersed and driven back to Mont-Dieu Wood. Lafontaine thereupon canceled the advance of the second group, ordering it to deploy on the north edge of Raucourt Wood. This was the end of the 55th Division's counterattack. It was also the end of the 55th Division as a fighting force.

The 55th's breakup signaled the collapse of the 71st Division, on its right. With its west flank exposed, the 71st pulled eastward to the Ennemane River. This sudden withdrawal started another wave of disorder among the already demoralized troops. Gunners and infantry abandoned their Ennemane positions in a repetition of yesterday's stampede; and during the day the command increasingly lost its grip on units whose one thought was to get out of the way of the Germans. By nightfall the 71st Division had faded away from the battle front.

There was a grim inevitability about the disintegration of the 71st. From a safe rear position these troops were thrown into action without warning and at a moment's notice. They had hardly arrived when they were in the thick of a pulverizing air attack.

---

[1] Ibid., p. 314.

Most of them were surprised to find themselves in the fighting line at all, one officer recalled. As older-class reservists with poor equipment and no battle training, "they thought they would find active trops in front of them."[2] Above all they were shattered by the massive, unopposed bombing. During the raids of the thirteenth, they quickly adopted a rough but all-too-accurate method of aircraft identification. "When there are three planes, they're French" was the cynical cry of men in their foxholes scanning the skies over Sedan. "When there are forty, they're Germans. You can't go wrong!"[3] Without any reserves of morale and unable to hit back, the troops felt they were against hopeless odds. Retreating units angrily refused to obey officers' appeals to stand fast. "Look, men, here are some guns. There's plenty of ammunition. Carry on fighting!" called one artillery colonel to a crowd of gunners. "Colonel, we want to get home and carry on with our jobs," they shouted back. "There's nothing to be done. We're finished, betrayed!"[4]

By noon the German panzers were masters of the Sedan front. The 1st and 2nd Armored Divisions were across the Meuse in strength and ranging well inland, and the 10th—partly delayed the day before—was still assembling its forces along the left bank, just southeast of Sedan. Guderian now had one overriding aim: to forge on westward with all speed, cutting through the plains of northern France to the sea. That afternoon the two leading divisions of XIX Armored Corps wheeled west in two great columns, Veiel's 2nd Panzers on a northerly line toward Flize and Sapogne, and Küchner's 1st Panzers on a southerly line toward Vendresse, leaving their southern flank guarded by the Gross Deutschland infantry division. Meanwhile the main body of the 10th would shortly advance south from the Meuse toward Bulson (to follow on westward in its turn, as soon as a division of the 14th Motorized Corps had crossed the Meuse to take its place in the Sedan sector). But until it did, for a few vital hours on the afternoon of the fourteenth there was a vulnerable gap in Guderian's armor— between the 10th, still in the Meuse Valley, and the 1st and 2nd,

---

[2] Allard: *L'Affaire Corap,* p. 38.
[3] Ibid.
[4] Ibid., p. 39.

speeding away westward. For Flavigny's XXI Corps, belatedly marshaling a few miles off for its counterattack, this was the opportunity to drive a wedge between the German panzers and perhaps throw the 10th Armored Division back across the Meuse. But on that day of lost chances the opportunity was never taken.

The one determined effort to counter the Sedan breakthrough on the fourteenth came from the air. From noon to 2 p.m., waves of Allied bombers—French Potezes and Moranes, British Fairey Battles and Blenheims from Air Marshal Barratt's Advanced Air Striking Force—flew in to bomb the bridges being hastily run up— at Gaulier and elsewhere, or blast the enemy columns moving south from the Meuse. In the face of the intense flak that defended the bridges, they pressed home repeated low-level attacks, suffering heavy losses—40 French and 67 British planes. Despite the gallant attempt, the bridges remained intact.

This might have been a much stronger effort. In the early afternoon, what an anonymous British Air Intelligence officer called a "most momentous decision" was taken. Air Marshal Barratt secured the agreement of Lord Gort and Generals Gamelin and Georges to a request being put to the British War Cabinet for the use of the British home-based Bomber Force in the Sedan sector within the next two hours. While B.A.F.F. (British Air Forces in France) headquarters at Tergnier, near Laon, anxiously awaited confirmation of this move, General Swayne, Liaison Officer to General Georges, telephoned to say that Georges would be satisfied with 100 bombers only, from the French-based Bomber Command. At Tergnier, hopes of a massive air blow against Guderian's forces were shattered. "Caution, safety first, and too late, the usual sequence," noted the British Intelligence officer in exasperation. "All the dash and drive is left to the Germans."[5]

At 2nd Army headquarters, some optimists still clung to fantastic hopes. Arriving there with two press colleagues that morning to report on the Meuse battle, the Reuters correspondent Gordon Waterfield found officers "confident of success."[6] Captain Massis, head of the Army press section, told Waterfield a German offensive

---

[5] *The Diary of a Staff Officer at Advanced Headquarters North, B.A.F.F., 1940* (1941), p. 12.
[6] G. Waterfield: *What Happened to France* (1940), p. 34.

at Sedan was expected that evening or next day. "We are withdrawing our advance posts, as has always been our intention,"
Massis said, "but we will hold the Germans on our main defense
line."[7] Massis's information was hours out of date. At that moment,
the main defense line no longer existed, the Sedan divisions were
crumbling, and the roads round Senuc were being raked by German
bombers. The correspondents had arranged a two-day visit and
were installed in a comfortable office with no hint of impending
emergency. They were even promised an interview with Huntziger. The first sign of trouble came when this was canceled. The
general, they were informed, was too busy to see them: instead they
were given his latest Order of the Day to read. Then it was suddenly announced that 2nd Army headquarters was pulling back
to Verdun, 35 miles southeast. That afternoon Waterfield and his
colleagues were driven off to nearby Vouziers, escorted by a lieutenant who complained he would have to cancel a stage perform-
ance billed for the Sedan troops on the fifteenth.

By evening, Huntziger's headquarters convoy was heading
for Verdun. Older officers might recall a sobering coincidence: it
was a French 2nd Army that defended Verdun in World War I,
when Verdun symbolized stubborn, last-ditch resistance. Now, from
Verdun's gloomy Landrecourt Fort, Huntziger would command the
remnants of a 2nd Army that had broken under German assault
in less than twenty-four hours. Landrecourt had been prepared
earlier as an alternative command post to Senuc, in case of need.
Compared with Senuc, it was a change for the worse on all counts.
Senuc had been austere, but Landrecourt Fort was, as General
Ruby recorded, *"sinistre."*[8] Its dark underground casemates (now
to house Huntziger, his personal staff, and 2nd and 3rd Bureaus,
while other staff occupied neighboring Dugny Fort) were permanently lamp-lit, and the old stone walls were so dank that constant
heating was required, even in this abnormally warm May. Huntziger's quarters comprised a single small cell, serving as office and
bedroom: his dining room was next door, in an officers' dormitory.
Moving in to this cramped, forbidding headquarters, Huntziger
at last felt the full impact of defeat. That night he remarked rue-

---

[7] Ibid.
[8] Ruby: *Sedan*, p. 210.

fully to one of his staff: "I shall always be the *vaincu* of Sedan."[9]
For him, one horrific incident stood out among the day's
reverses. During the morning he received a report that French
soldiers had been seen from the heights above the Meuse, emerging
from their bunkers with their hands up in surrender. Steeling himself, he gave the order for his artillery to fire on them.

As the Meuse front collapsed, Huntziger had not had much
help from the overburdened Georges, at GHQ, Northeast. Earlier
he had urgently telephoned Georges for guidance. "My left has
been broken on the Meuse," he said. "To keep my army together,
I ought to pull it back, but in which direction? Should I cover the
Maginot Line or Paris?" "Give me details of your situation,"
Georges answered. Huntziger explained the position, and Georges
said: "I'll give you an answer in an hour." Not hearing from him,
Huntziger later called him again. "Do what seems best (*Faites
au mieux*)," Georges replied briefly.[1]

On General Claudel Georges the strain was visibly telling.
Only Doumenc's intervention at Les Bondons had averted his collapse the night before; and now this valiant commander no longer
seemed able to bear the heavy burden of directing the huge and
complex battle. It was obvious that his nerve had partially gone
—the result of the injuries he had received at Marseilles in 1934.
During his routine morning visit to Les Bondons on the thirteenth,
Gamelin was struck by the almost defeatist atmosphere in Georges's
office. On the fourteenth he spent both morning and afternoon
there, "judging," he recorded, "that my presence was necessary
from the point of view of morale."[2] Georges's appearance gave
him cause for concern. "The general seemed to me at this moment
truly exhausted," he noted. And he added: "I hoped that the depression I noticed—and I was not the only one to perceive it—
would be temporary, and was the result of his physical fatigue."[3]
Gamelin's Chief of Staff, Petibon, even urged him to accept
Georges's invitation to dine at Les Bondons henceforth. "Georges
would be happy," he told Gamelin, "to feel himself in constant

[9] Ibid., p. 177.
[1] R. de Bardies: *La Campagne 39–40* (1947), p. 133.
[2] M. Gamelin: *Servir* (1946), Vol. I, p. 349.
[3] Ibid., Vol. I, pp. 15–21.

touch with you and assured of your support."[4] Gamelin was with
Georges when Georges was called to the telephone to hear Huntziger's personal report of the order he had given for the surrendering Sedan troops to be fired on. The Supreme Commander
remarked Georges's deep emotion as he put down the receiver and
passed on Huntziger's message to him.

Meanwhile, only muted echoes of the battle were reaching
Gamelin's own headquarters. Vincennes still suffered both from
lack of information and toned-down or overoptimistic versions of
what was really happening. At 7 a.m., GHQ, Montry, had radioed:
"The operation which had been mounted at Houx has failed and
been started again."[5] In fact, no further concerted attack was made
at Houx. Thirty minutes later, GHQ, Northeast, sent a situation
report—"so long wanted on our armies,"[6] wrote Captain Minart—
which announced of the 2nd Army: "The breach at Sedan is
plugged on the stop-line. . . . Counter-attack with strong forces
launched this morning at 4.30 a.m."[7] No such assault was ever
made. At 10:50 a.m., Montry sent another report on the 2nd
Army as at 10 a.m.: "General impression is that army is in hand
and that troops are holding."[8] Such distortions were less the fault
of Montry or Les Bondons than symptoms of the growing disruption of communications lower down and absence of clear-cut intelligence from the front itself. But, in default of full and accurate
battle news, Vincennes was occupied with other war questions that
day. There was concern as to whether the Germans were going to
invade Switzerland, and so turn the flank of the French eastern
armies. Here, too, Supreme Headquarters was handicapped. It had
no information on the overall distribution of enemy forces, and in
particular of the number and quality of the main formations stationed across the Rhine. "To know quickly," complained Minart,
"it would need a 2nd Bureau installed at Vincennes."[9]

At GHQ, Montry, this was a day of tense waiting and fading
hopes. During the morning Doumenc's staff stood anxiously by
for news of the 3rd Armored Division's counterattack at Sedan.

---

[4] Ibid., Vol. I, p. 349.
[5] J. Minart: *P. C. Vincennes, Secteur 4* (1945), p. 23.
[6] Ibid., p. 24.
[7] Ibid., p. 25.
[8] Ibid., p. 26.
[9] Ibid., p. 146.

Then came the report that this was deferred to 4 p.m.—although no reason was given. "The nightmare started again," recorded Captain Beaufre.[1] With the message that the operation was postponed once more, pessimism grew. Meanwhile news was arriving of the 9th Army's setbacks along the whole sector from Givet to Namur. "The hours pass," Beaufre wrote, "and one feels the situation is getting worse every minute."[2] Whatever the precise situation was, the war map in Doumenc's office now showed a huge German clearance of the Meuse, right across Corap's and Huntziger's fronts. As the staff surveyed the picture, the implication was clear. "One can no longer deny a catastrophe," said Beaufre. "The French armies are breached in their centre."[3]

Along with everything else, the vulnerable Bar River Line— junction of the 9th and 2nd Armies—had gone. Forces hastily thrown in by Corap and Huntziger to defend the line were swept aside in the westward drive of Guderian's panzers. Corap's weak 53rd Division (hurried up from the reserve) and Huntziger's cavalry group fell back to west and south respectively, leaving a perilous gap between the right and left flanks of the two Meuse armies. As Corap and Huntziger strove to direct operations from their widely separated Vervins and Senuc command posts, the price was being paid for lack of united command at this vital point. And not only were the formations defending the Bar Line subject to two different army commanders, but by Georges's order, effective as from that day, the 2nd Army was removed from Billotte's First Army Group and placed directly under Georges himself. Georges now made a desperate effort to plug the widening gap. From 200 miles away in eastern France, he called in General Touchon, commander of the reserve 6th Army. Touchon was to report immediately to Huntziger at Senuc, with instructions to take over all units in the area and re-form the broken defense line. But in the crucial remaining hours of the fourteenth, Touchon could do nothing. It was 4 p.m. before he arrived at Senuc, and three hours later when he reached his new command post at Rethel, on the Aisne.

---

[1] A. Beaufre: *Le Drame de 1940* (1965), p. 236.
[2] Ibid.
[3] Ibid.

Only one new formation was available to attempt to block the gap on the fourteenth, and, of this, not all units had arrived by nightfall. Summoned from the distant Army of Alsace (Bourret's 5th Army), General de Lattre de Tassigny's 14th Division was hastening north from the Reims area. With advance elements, Tassigny reported to Corap at Vervins and heard from him of the Sedan breakthrough—although Corap was apparently unaware that Huntziger's troops were in full retreat. "Very anxious but by no means distraught," Corap ordered Tassigny to join up with the 53rd Division on the 9th Army's right, and there re-establish liaison between the 9th and 2nd.[4] Tassigny led forward his forces—only about one quarter of the division's total strength—through stampeding 9th Army troops, only to find that the 53rd Division had disappeared, leaving a gulf through which the Germans were pouring. Reporting back to Corap, he was told to occupy the second defense position—a 25-mile line for which he had only his 152nd Regiment together with a Spahi brigade of Corap's and a light cavalry division of Huntziger's. By the time he had moved to this line, the German tanks were there. Then, to his relief, he learned that Touchon's army was taking over.

In Paris, the government was watching the situation with mounting alarm. Reynaud and his colleagues had found no comfort in any of the events of the last four days. The Prime Minister had always perceived the possible dangers to which Plan D exposed the Allied armies in Belgium; and now had come news of the Meuse breakthrough. Early that afternoon De Villelume had returned from Vincennes with a report of the 2nd Army's collapse at Sedan. Reynaud asked him whether the forces in Belgium had been ordered to retire. Telephoning Supreme Headquarters, De Villelume discovered that they had not. "We felt that the situation had suddenly become tragic," noted Baudouin.[5] As Reynaud saw it, with German tanks free to drive south and west through the broken Meuse Line, one of two things might now happen. The Germans would either make a feint attack toward the North Sea, or move directly

---

[4] L. Lévy: *The Truth About France*, trans. W. Pickles (1941), p. 23.
[5] P. Baudouin: *The Private Diaries (March 1940 to January 1941)*, trans. Sir Charles Petrie (1948), p. 29.

on Paris. According to him, the High Command thought Paris the more likely objective.

At three o'clock the War Committee[6] met to consider the position. Immediately afterwards, at 5:45 p.m., Reynaud telephoned the following message to Winston Churchill (British Prime Minister since May 10):

> Having just left the War Committee, I am sending you, in the name of the French Government, the following statement:
> "The situation is indeed very serious. Germany is trying to deal us a fatal blow in the direction of Paris. The German Army has broken through our fortified lines south of Sedan. Should it succeed, it will be due to our inability to resist the combined attack of heavy tanks and bombers. To stop the German drive, so long as there is still time, and to allow our counter-attack to succeed, the German tanks must be isolated from their supporting Stukas. This is only possible through a considerable force of fighter aircraft.
> "You have already willingly sent us four squadrons, which represents more than you promised.
> "To win this battle, which could well be of decisive importance for the whole war, it is essential that you send immediately ten additional squadrons. Without such a contribution, we cannot be certain that we shall be able to stem the German advance.
> "Between Sedan and Paris, there are no defences comparable with those in the line which we must restore at almost any cost.
> "I have confidence that, at this critical hour, British aid will not fail us."[7]

Two hours later, at No. 10 Downing Street, Churchill read Reynaud's message to the War Cabinet; and at 8:30 p.m. he replied to Reynaud as follows:

> The British War Cabinet and General Staff have given the most careful consideration to the request which you addressed to me this afternoon, and we are losing no time in studying the means of meeting the situation.
> We have called in Staff Officers who are in position to give us details of the last-minute state of affairs, so that we can be sure that all available resources are employed to the utmost in the common cause.[8]

---

6 The War Committee consisted normally of certain ministers, the Supreme Commander, the Admiral of the Fleet, and, as president, the President of the Republic.

7 Reynaud: *Fight*, pp. 319-20.

8 Ibid., p. 320.

Chapter 10

THE FATEFUL FIFTEENTH

"Yes, it's the destruction of the French Army."
(General Gamelin)

CHURCHILL'S MESSAGE did little to reassure Reynaud. So worried was the French Premier that he telephoned Downing Street again at 7:30 the next morning, rousing Churchill from sleep. He repeated his plea for British fighter aid and, when Churchill seemed "surprised," exclaimed dramatically: "We are beaten. We have lost the battle."

Churchill was skeptical. "Impossible," he replied. "Experience shows that, at the end of a certain time, all offensives peter out by themselves. In five or six days, they will be compelled to stop in order to get supplies."

"All is changed," cried the excited Reynaud. "A torrent of tanks is bursting through."

"Will you let me telephone Georges?" Churchill asked. Reynaud readily agreed.[1]

"I rang up General Georges, who seemed quite cool, and reported that the breach at Sedan was being plugged," recorded Churchill. "A telegram from General Gamelin also stated," he added, "that although the position between Namur and Sedan was serious he viewed the situation with calm."[2]

The doughty fighter Winston Churchill was more likely to

---

[1] P. Reynaud: *In the Thick of the Fight,* trans. J. D. Lambert (1955), p. 320.

[2] W. S. Churchill: *The Second World War* (1949), Vol. II, pp. 39–40.

accept Georges's and Gamelin's versions of the situation than the alarmist picture presented by Reynaud. But Reynaud's was nearer the truth. On this morning of Wednesday, May 15, as the Meuse front crumbled beyond recovery and the German spearheads drove forward into France, the Battle of the West took on a new and graver aspect. With the collapse of the French Army's continuous defense line, not only were cherished military theories swept away; now France herself was in jeopardy. And suddenly danger menaced Paris.

In World War I it was a month before Paris was imperiled by the marching German armies. This time Hitler's mechanized columns were threatening the capital after only five days. At Supreme Headquarters Gamelin—however he professed to view the Meuse situation—took the Paris threat seriously enough to start considering the city's defense and the evacuation of a key ministry. Early on the fifteenth he contacted Vincennes General Hering, Military Governor of Paris, and General Colson, Chief of Staff at the Ministry of War. With Hering he discussed the "eventual defence of Paris," for which he proposed to arrange with Georges for the dispatch of several divisions; and with Colson he went over the previously agreed government plans for the removal of the War Ministry to the Tours area, 145 miles southwest of Paris.[3]

Hering was struck by Gamelin's frank and confident manner. "He revealed the situation to us without hiding anything of its gravity," Hering recalled later.[4] "Then he gave us his instructions with a self-command and clarity of mind that impressed me. So much so that on returning to my headquarters at Les Invalides, I said to my officers: 'The situation is not good; it's even extremely serious. But happily General Gamelin is holding the reins of command with a firm hand.' "[5]

In the bright May sunshine, Parisians went about their business unaware of the hovering threat. Official censorship still banned all mention of the Meuse breakthrough. At most, there were hints that the war might go on for some time and that the Allies would hold as long as needed. Two days before, Minister

---

[3] M. Gamelin: *Servir* (1949), Vol. III, p. 398.

[4] Hering was testifying in Gamelin's defense at the Riom trial.

[5] Gamelin: *Servir* (1946), Vol. I, p. xvii.

of Information Frossard complacently declared in a broadcast that Verdun and the Somme had lasted six months. This provoked a British correspondent in Paris to ask wrathfully: "Haven't the French Ministers realised yet that this type of war is different?"[6] The newspapers were quietly confident on the fifteenth. "The advantage which we had in 1914 with our admirable 75mm. gun," commented *L'Epoque.* "we are rediscovering this time in our *char de combat.* In all the hand-to-hand fighting it is proving itself superior. It is an immense trump card."[7] *Le Journal* was guardedly encouraging. "We have adopted a defensive attitude," it said. "This means that we are awaiting the enemy on a position chosen by us. . . . Little by little, we are approaching the line on which we must hold. Our armies will hold."[8]

At that moment, the only sector on the Allied front where the armies were holding was in the center. The B.E.F., its morale high, was standing firm on the Louvain-Wavre Line, despite the shaky state of the Belgians on its left. To the B.E.F.'s right, the French 1st Army was fighting hard to repel the violent panzer and infantry assault of Von Reichenau's forces. Working in close cooperation with the well-armed German tanks were the massed Stukas of Kesselring's and Sperrle's Air Fleets—unopposed by Allied planes. The main shock of attack was being borne by the 1st Moroccan Division on the Gembloux Plateau. Here, before evening, the line would be dented; and despite a counterattack, the Germans would hold a pocket of some four square miles near Namur; but finally the Germans would be halted: no enemy armor would break the main French line.

While Lord Gort's and Blanchard's troops held fast, everywhere else the Allied front was in various stages of foundering. In the north, the Dutch Army was laying down its arms, crushed by the overwhelming weight of Von Küchler's 18th Army. And in the south the dissolution of Corap's and Huntziger's armies was proceeding apace.

At 2 a.m. Corap informed Billotte that his troops were retiring on the whole front and that he intended to halt them at a

---

[6] A. Werth: *The Last Days of Paris* (1940), p. 34.
[7] W. Picht: *La Fin des Illusions: l'An 1940* (1940), p. 33.
[8] Ibid.

defense line on the French frontier. Billotte agreed but ordered Corap to establish an intermediate line, Walcourt–Signy-l'Abbaye, running northwest to southeast and then north to south from Belgium into France. This was roughly at right angles to Corap's projected line; and in front of it General Martin (XI Corps) had drawn up yet another defense line, Oret–Matagne-la-Grande, running approximately north to south. As the harassed troops surged back in the darkness of the May night, units lost contact with each other. Amid a confusion of orders, some made for one line and some for another. Some even headed on into France without stopping anywhere.

At First Army Group headquarters, Billotte had been watching Corap's handling of the situation with growing dissatisfaction. Corap, he now decided, was no longer able to exercise effective control and must be removed. At 4 a.m. he telephoned a situation report to Georges at Les Bondons and proposed Corap's replacement by Giraud—who now, with the 7th Army's withdrawal from Holland, was available for a more active command. George agreed, and orders were sent forthwith to Giraud at Antwerp to report to 9th Army headquarters, Vervins, and take over from Corap as of 4 p.m. that day. In exchange, Corap would assume command of the 7th Army.

Hour by hour, the 9th Army was breaking up. Only in the north, where the 5th Motorized Division of II Corps held its position, covering the 1st Army's right flank, were there any signs of stasis. In the center, the remnants of Martin's XI Corps filtered away southwestward—the 18th Division to a point well behind Martin's stop line, the 22nd as far as Chimay, 10 miles from the French frontier. That evening a First Army Group liaison officer was to return to Billotte's headquarters with the report that he had seen General Duffet (18th Division) and General d'Arras (1st Light Cavalry Division) at Rance, and "they don't know where their troops are."[9] Martin himself—like Corap, he too was to be relieved of his command that day—was trying desperately to keep a grip on his scattered units. Early in the morning Corap had telephoned him at Froidchapelle, asking him to hold at all costs. But around noon, troops that were still on his defense line retreated

---

[9] A. Doumenc: *Histoire de la Neuvième Armée* (1945), p. 177.

upon the appearance of Rommel's tanks, which were thrusting west toward Philippeville. Martin spent the afternoon attempting to communicate with Corap by telephone. He finally reached him at Wignehies, and was ordered by Corap to make every effort to stop the Germans on the frontier line. But Martin was to find this line (south of the Maubeuge fortifications) "a complete vacuum." "There were no troops to receive us," he added. "Our first task was to get the blockhouse doors opened by the engineers."[1]

To the south of the XI Corps, the two XLI Corps Divisions— the 61st Infantry and 102nd Garrison Divisions—were likewise disintegrating. General Vauthier, commanding the 61st, reported in the afternoon to his Corps commander, Libaud, that all communications with Vervins were being cut and that he was finding it difficult to regroup elements of his division owing to the flood of refugees.

Thousands of fleeing civilians were cumbering the roads out of the 9th Army battle zone. As word spread of the German advance, panic had seized whole districts. Gendarmes passed through the villages shouting: "You must leave!" At a moment's notice people were abandoning their farms and dwellings, grabbing whatever possessions they could. Driving their livestock before them, pushing bicycles and wheelbarrows, crowding onto overloaded cars and farm carts, they joined the great southwestward trek— uncertain where they were going but all heading away from the enemy who had ravaged these lands once before. Amid the shuffling mass were mothers carrying crying babies, old folk hobbling on sticks. "An entire province is emptying," wrote an observer.[2] The refugees kept looking fearfully up to the sky for signs of German planes. Despair marked their faces as columns of retreating troops forced their way through the shambling lines: if their own soldiers were moving back, it was obvious the battle was lost.

The same traffic was pouring back behind the 2nd Army front. At Vouziers-on-Aisne, 25 miles southwest of Sedan, refugees had packed the streets and main square all night; and during the morning growing numbers of troops straggled through. To Reuters correspondent Waterfield and his colleagues, lodging here over-

---

[1] Ibid., p. 179.
[2] R. de Bardies: *La Campagne 39–40* (1947), p. 154.

night after leaving Senuc, these men told of the devastating effects of the German dive-bombing—something they had never been trained to expect. German Dorniers were now ranging over Vouziers itself, bombing and machine-gunning. The hospital was full of refugees who had been wounded while on the roads. Waterfield was struck by the total lack of direction given to these frightened people, who would have done better to stay where they were. Hungry for hard news of the Meuse battle, the correspondents could glean only rumors from the refugee crowds. Even the army press lieutenant who met them at Vouziers in the morning could tell them little except that German armor had crossed the Meuse and was advancing rapidly. "I do not believe that the GHQ of the 2nd Army itself had a very clear knowledge of what was happening," Waterfield noted.[3]

At remote Landrecourt Fort, Huntziger and his staff could only guess at the true position. Landrecourt was 40 miles from the front, communications were tenuous, and the battle situation bewilderingly fluid. For them the only certainty was that the Germans were not being stopped, let alone pushed back. Once more the plans for an armored counterattack were falling through; and with them, on this May 15, was vanishing the French Army's last chance of plugging the massive German penetration through the Sedan bridgehead.

In a widening sweep, Guderian's leading panzer units were forging south and west from the Meuse. The previous night, the 10th Division had halted beyond Maisoncelles; the 1st Division, splitting into two spearheads, had—after stalwart resistance from Chanoine's cavalry group and the 3rd Spahi Brigade respectively —been stopped near Vendresse, and at Singly in the 9th Army sector; and the 2nd, dividing likewise, had headed toward Boulzicourt and Poix-Terron, thereby rolling up the 9th Army's 102nd Garrison Division. Now, on the broken 2nd Army front, one intact formation stood immediately available between Sedan and the French hinterland—Flavigny's XXI Corps.

GHQ, Northeast, estimated that the XXI Corps might yet retrieve the Sedan situation, despite its abortive effort the previous

---

[3] G. Waterfield: *What Happened to France* (1940), p. 40.

day. Georges's Chief of Staff, Roton, envisaged an operation which, "though it will be engaged in conditions much less favorable than yesterday's, could still pay."[4] During the night Georges had ordered Huntziger to remount the assault by sending Brocard's 3rd Armored Division as far as possible toward the Meuse. Soon after dawn Huntziger passed the order to Flavigny for a strong tank-based operation on the axis Bulson-Sedan. Here was an opportunity to break up elements of the 10th Panzers, whose command post was at Bulson. But in midmorning Flavigny modified the plan with orders to Brocard and Bertin-Boussu (commanding the 3rd Motorized Division) for a mixed tank-and-infantry operation, and put the infantryman Bertin-Boussu in command. Moreover, he reduced the offensive scope of the plan by prescribing a staggered three-stage advance, the last line of which—restricted to Marfée Wood—was well short of the Meuse. The whole scheme was in fact amended to a cautious, semi-defensive operation, with Brocard's armored forces diluted among Bertin-Boussu's infantry. But with zero hour set for 3 p.m., Brocard found he could not bring up his tanks—dispersed along the extended line on which they had been halted the day before—in time. The advance was rescheduled for 5:30, but it was soon clear that all Brocard's tanks would not be in place by then. Flavigny nevertheless ordered Bertin-Boussu to move at a time of his own choosing, with whatever tanks were available. Then, at five o'clock, he canceled the attack.

For Flavigny's tough, eager troops this was the second frustration in two days. Morale could suffer as badly in such circumstances as by outright defeat. Yet even this fiasco was relieved by a fine example of fighting spirit. The cancellation order reached the start line after some tanks had already moved off to the attack. One tank commander, World War I veteran Captain Aulois, led his company on in the face of intense fire. His own tank was immediately hit and its driver killed; but the remaining tanks continued to advance the best part of a mile until radioed to retire. Aulois himself, badly wounded, was dragged from his tank and ordered the survivors of his crew back to their lines. All night he lay on the ground, to be picked up next day by a German patrol.

---

[4] E. Ruby: *Sedan, Terre d'Epreuve* (1948), p. 185.

He was taken before an officer, who asked him: "Captain, was it you who commanded the tanks that attacked us?" When Aulois admitted this, the German said simply: "I congratulate you."[5]

Yet Guderian's Sedan position was not as impregnable as it seemed. At one point on his southern flank—the village of Stonne, between the Raucourt and Dieulet woods—a massive blow by Flavigny might have changed the situation drastically. Stonne had been captured overnight by men of the Gross Deutschland regiment, and early on the fifteenth was retaken by French tanks. Tired, overstrained, anxiously awaiting reinforcement by the 14th Motorized Corps, the Gross Deutschlanders made unsuccessful efforts to regain the village. On a morning visit to the 10th Panzers' command post at Bulson, Guderian judged the position to be "delicate." And at Army Group A headquarters, General Von Rundstedt took uneasy note of the Stonne setback. Already dubious about the wisdom of Guderian's spectacular advance, he now ordered him not to proceed beyond the Sedan bridgehead. Guderian was furious. He protested aginst this order which, as he saw it, threatened to wreck his whole assault plan. Reluctantly Von Rundstedt gave in and allowed the advance to continue, although he impressed on Guderian the need for caution. By evening, as the leading units of the 14th Motorized Corps moved in, the risk to the 10th Panzers' shaky southern front had passed.

Nowhere during the tense hours of the fifteenth did French armor fulfill the hopes of the French High Command. "The order is to hold on," commented Captain Beaufre at GHQ, Montry. "We're awaiting the decisive action of the three armoured divisions." But at the end of the day he had to admit: "No news of the divisions. It seems they've done nothing or their action has been ineffective. The Germans are advancing inexorably."[6]

While the 3rd Armored Division procrastinated at Sedan, on the woodlands of Belgian Namur the 1st was being cut to pieces. General Bruneau's 1st Armored Division, belatedly ordered forward on the fourteenth to aid the faltering divisions of the XI Corps, found itself right in the path of Hoth's panzer group. For

---

[5] Ibid., pp. 185–6.
[6] A. Beaufre: *Le Drame de 1940* (1965), p. 237.

most of the day it was involved in bloody fighting. The panzers had resumed their westward advance at dawn, and around 9 a.m. Rommel's 7th Division attacked the 1st Half-brigade as it was refueling. The battle continued intermittently until late afternoon; and when the 28th Battalion received the order to retire on the Florennes-Mettet Line, only seven of its tanks remained. The 37th Battalion, doggedly resisting in the Flavion-Ermeton zone, lost almost its entire tank force. And by evening the 25th and 26th Battalions could muster no more than twenty tanks apiece. Meanwhile Rommel's leading panzers, outflanking the 2nd Half-brigade, reached Philippeville at noon. Toward evening Bruneau made an attempt to regroup the battered division in the Solre-le-Château region, across the French border, but had to abandon the idea owing to the dispersal of his units. Finally he ordered a general withdrawal to Beaumont, 15 miles west of Philippeville.

On this retreat the 1st Armored Division suffered its *coup de grâce*. Attacked by panzers that had raced ahead as far as Beaumont, it lost twenty-eight more tanks. By the end of the day, Bruneau's force no longer existed. "It fought bravely, one against two," said Colonel de Bardies. "It was sacrificed in order to stop a rout—sacrificed entirely in vain, for the rout goes on."[7] At sunset the elated General Rommel surveyed the situation from a hill near Philippeville. "Looking back eastwards," he noted, "'I was able to contemplate, in the gathering dusk, innumerable dust columns ascending as far as the eye could see—heartening signs which showed that our armoured advance into conquered territory had begun."[8]

In the central sector, the 2nd Armored Division (General Bruché) never even got into action. Delayed by a grotesque confusion of orders and failure of transport organization, it was being swallowed up in the general chaos as its units detrained at Hirson en route for the front. The 2nd was urgently needed for General Touchon's new army detachment, assigned to plug the gap that was developing southwest of Sedan. Without this armor Touchon was powerless to resist Guderian's and Reinhardt's panzers—for

---

[7] De Bardies: *La Campagne*, p. 147.
[8] E. Rommel: *The Rommel Papers*, ed. B. H. Liddell Hart (1953), p. 16.

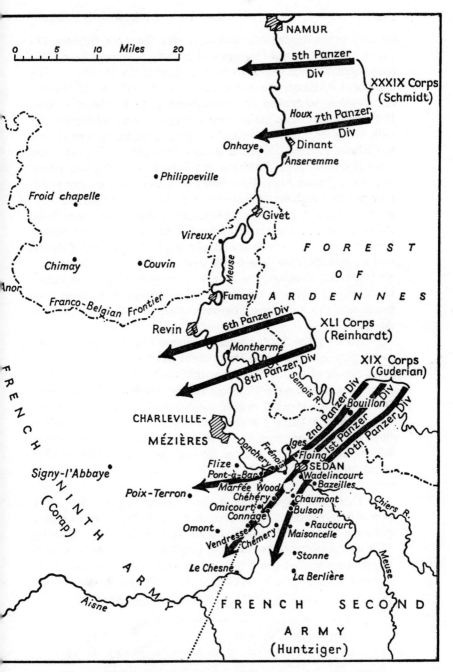

2. *The vital breakthrough: progress of the seven armored divisions across the Meuse, May 13–15, 1940.*

his only other dependable formation was the 14th Infantry Division (Tassigny), and this was still arriving piecemeal from Château-Porcien, some miles back near Rethel on the Aisne. His additional divisions, the 53rd, 61st, and 102nd—all of the 9th Army—were so broken and battle-worn as to be almost useless. But Touchon's immediate concern was to set up a containment line with whatever forces he had. At 2 p.m. from his command post at Château-Porcien, he issued an order to hold at all costs a line from Rocroi to Signy-l'Abbaye and Poix-Terron. But this operation was a forlorn hope. Four hours later General Tassigny grimly reported to Touchon: "All elements of the 53rd Division between Poix-Terron and Launois have been annihilated. The enemy holds Poix-Terron. . . . The 14th Division infantry has been very delayed by bombing and the units are all mixed up. . . . Between Faissault and La Bascule there is a 5-mile void. . . . Short of ammunition, the 53rd is retreating in a state of demoralisation."[9] On receipt of this report Touchon decided there was only one thing to do— retire south to the Aisne, between Attigny and Neufchâtel-sur-Aisne.

Through Touchon's breached defense lines the German tanks raced deep into the Aisne Department. As they edged toward the great massif of the Île-de-France that traditionally guarded Paris, new place names were featuring on the headquarters war maps. By 8 p.m. a vanguard panzer column had reached Montcornet, 22 miles from Laon. "With what anguish," wrote Henri Bidou, "one begins to see appearing in the dispatches the names of rivers which flow in the very heart of France, the names of towns which stand for France herself."[1]

There was anguish too in the rapid writing off of the three armored divisions. At the crucial moment of the German breakout from the Meuse bridgeheads, France's armored force—two thirds of it uncommitted to battle—had failed conspicuously to stop the panzer onrush. But one hope—a somewhat desperate one at that —remained for French armor that day, and even it was still only on paper. Four days before, command of a newly projected 4th

[9] De Bardies: *La Campagne*, p. 165.
[1] H. Bidou: *La Bataille de France, 10 mai–25 juin 1940* (1941), p. 110.

Armored Division had been assigned to the commander of the 5th Army tanks in Alsace, fifty-year-old Colonel Charles de Gaulle, the single-minded professional soldier who for years had campaigned vainly for a French armored force. Now, from his headquarters at Le Vésinet, De Gaulle was called to GHQ, Northeast, to receive instructions for the immediate formation and employment of the new division. At Les Bondons he met General Doumenc, who told him that the High Command was forming a defensive front on the Aisne and Ailette rivers to bar the way to Paris, and that Touchon's army would deploy there. "With your division, operating alone in the region of Laon," Doumenc added, "you are to gain the time necessary for the taking-up of positions."[2] De Gaulle then saw General Georges. The irony of the situation was not wasted on Georges. "There, de Gaulle," he said. "For you have so long held the ideas which the enemy is putting into practice, here is the chance to act."[3]

De Gaulle left Les Bondons with an ominous impression of the atmosphere at GHQ. Georges appeared to him "calm, cordial, but visibly overwhelmed." The staff, he noted, was making valiant efforts to cope with the ever-mounting burden of work caused by the reverses of "these terrible days." "But," De Gaulle added, "one could feel that hope was departing and that the spring was broken."[4]

A sense of catastrophe was seeping through the High Command. Officers at GHQ, Montry, were glum and pessimistic. "Nothing covers Paris any more," recorded Beaufre, "and there's no reserve anywhere at hand. The battle appears irretrievably lost."[5] From Supreme Headquarters, Vincennes, all pretense of confidence had vanished. The staff passed what Minart called "a gloomy, endless day, with a deathlike feeling about it. . . . The immense drama of the frontiers has no echo in the tainted air of this submarine without a periscope, which is Vincennes."[6] Although no notably disastrous news was coming in, the whole staff was

---

[2] C. de Gaulle: *War Memoirs*, Vol. I: *The Call to Honour,* 1940–42, trans. J. Griffin (1955), p. 42.

[3] Ibid., p. 43.

[4] Ibid.

[5] Beaufre: *Le Drame*, p. 237.

[6] J. Minart: *P. C. Vincennes, Secteur 4* (1945), p. 147.

edgy and nervous. At messtime, officers ate their meals hastily, avoiding the topic that occupied everyone's mind. Some tried to relieve the tension by playing puerile games in their offices. "At all costs," stated Minart, "it was necessary to fight against the haunting vision of defeat."[7]

Gamelin himself was still outwardly unruffled—though Minart professed to detect a "hidden and growing fear" beneath his calm exterior.[8] Now he was shutting himself up more and more with his Chief of Staff and aides. On his morning visit to Georges at Les Bondons, he had been startled to learn of orders for the withdrawal of the 61st and 102nd Divisions (XLI Corps) "despite the fact that the front was not broken."[9] He thereupon decided to intercede directly with Winston Churchill.[1] At 9:10 a.m. Gamelin sent this telegram to his representative in London, General Lelong:

> Urgent. Go and see Mr. Churchill and General Ironside. Tell them:— Situation serious following clearance of the Meuse by the Germans between Namur and Sedan region. (Eastwards) from Chiers-Meuse confluence, position intact. Counter-attacks are in progress. The French Command is facing the situation calmly. It requests all possible help from British aviation which, in any case, has up to now rendered the greatest service and for which we are warmly grateful. Gamelin.[2]

While at Les Bondons, Gamelin was told by Georges of Billotte's request for the replacement of Corap. At that moment Daladier arrived at Georges's command post. As National Defense Minister, it was Daladier's prerogative to approve the appointment of army commanders. He listened to Georges's report and gave his consent to the mutual transfer of Corap and Giraud between the 9th and 7th Armies.

Earlier, Gamelin had sent a member of his personal staff, Lieutenant Colonel Guillaut, to the 9th Army sector to study the situation personally. (This was the first time he had ever dispatched a liaison officer to one of his armies.) Guillaut returned to Vincennes that evening with an alarming story. He had found the 9th's position "truly critical."[3] Corap's staff no longer knew

---

[7] Ibid., p. 148.
[8] Ibid.
[9] Gamelin: *Servir,* Vol. I, p. 339.
[1] See above, page 162.
[2] Gamelin: *Servir,* Vol. III, p. 399.
[3] Ibid., Vol. III, p. 407.

where its divisions were. Everywhere on the roads Guillaut met fleeing troops: whole bodies of men were retreating at the sight of German motorcyclists or a few armored vehicles. Gamelin was so shocked by Guillaut's report that he decided forthwith not to give Corap command of the 7th Army but to post him to the officers' reserve. He telephoned his decision to Georges, who approved, though reluctantly, for he had a strong liking for Corap. Gamelin also felt regret. "It was hard for me to take this measure against an old companion in arms," he wrote later. "But sentiment must not stand in the way of duty. I have always since declared that, if General Corap did not fulfil the hopes we placed in him, he committed no offence affecting his honour. And in the last analysis, it must be recorded that he did not have at his disposal all the resources that should have been made available to him."[4]

Guillaut was at Vervins when General Giraud arrived during the afternoon to take over command of the 9th from Corap. Encouragingly, he reported that Giraud's presence had immediately raised the spirits of the demoralized staff. Giraud was a robust, self-confident general who had the gift of inspiring officers and men. Typical of his fighting approach were his words to an officer of the 2nd Armored Division: "From now on we've got to hold at all costs. I'll give the example myself. I won't leave my command-post till a German colonel appears at the entrance."[5] Giraud spent the rest of the day reviewing the situation with Corap. For the weary, dejected Corap this was a painful experience. Whatever his shortcomings as a commander, he had been saddled with an assignment that a far superior general would have found impossible. Events had moved too fast for him from the first—and, apparently, he still failed to realize the extent of his army's collapse. "As I leave the 9th Army," he wrote on quitting Vervins, "my heart is full of sadness because, harassed and broken as it is, I fear it may not be able to hold."[6]

In Paris uneasy rumors were beginning to circulate. Newspapermen especially, starved of hard facts, were speculating darkly about what was happening on the Meuse front. That evening their

---

[4] Ibid., Vol. I, p. 340.
[5] De Bardies: *La Campagne*, p. 155.
[6] A. Doumenc: *Histoire de la Neuvième Armée* (1945), p. 178.

suspicions were confirmed by a statement from Colonel Thomas, the War Ministry's official spokesman. In the large, trophy-hung conference room at the Ministry, Colonel Thomas announced to a gloomy gathering of press correspondents the news of the Sedan crossing. (Even this was twenty-four hours out of date.) The Germans, said Thomas, had adopted against France the methods they had already used against Poland. Now it was a war of movement. "The situation is serious," he added, " but it is neither critical nor desperate."[7]

At his office in the Quai d'Orsay, Paul Reynaud indulged in no such soothing view. He faced what was now, undisguisedly, a crisis of the first magnitude. And while he grappled with the threat to France, he was also conducting a sharp internal feud—with his own National Defense Minister and Supreme Commander. At ten that morning Colonel de Villelume, liaison officer between GHQ and the Quai d'Orsay, had reported the collapse of the Meuse armies, with some nine divisions in full retreat. "The position is the more serious in that our armies in the north have not yet begun to fall back," commented Paul Baudouin, who was present.[8] At once Reynaud telephoned Daladier to ask what countermeasures Gamelin proposed. "He has none," Daladier answered. In Baudouin's hearing, the flabbergasted Reynaud repeated the words aloud. Reynaud was constantly complaining that he could never get information from the High Command, or exert any influence over it. By the "High Command" he chiefly meant Gamelin, in whom he had no confidence as Generalissimo. Now he gave vent to his exasperation. "Ah! If Marshal Pétain were only here," he exclaimed, "he would be able to influence Gamelin. His wisdom and equanimity would be a great help."

Through the rest of that day, Reynaud waited anxiously for news. Back at Supreme Headquarters, De Villelume was trying with small success to extract information from Colonel Petibon. Gamelin's Chief of Staff vigorously objected to what he considered De Villelume's curiosity. "If this goes on," he declared, "I will not give any information at all." At about 7 p.m. De Villelume reported to Reynaud what meager details he had gleaned, and mentioned

---

[7] Werth: *Last Days*, p. 42.
[8] P. Baudouin, *The Private Diaries (March 1940 to January 1941)* (1948), p. 30.

Petibon's poor attitude. Reynaud flared up in anger. "It is time to put an end to this comedy," he burst out. "I must be Minister of National Defense. Daladier will have to go to the Ministry of Foreign Affairs or resign."[9]

For Reynaud and his War Cabinet, one fear had been steadily crystallizing all day—the fear for Paris. The Cabinet had become increasingly anxious about the threat to Paris since the start of the German breakout the previous evening. In the last twenty-four hours nothing had stopped the German advance; and now—although enemy intentions could as yet only be guessed at—Paris seemed to them the obvious target for the panzer columns speeding unopposed through the widening 40-mile gap southwest of Sedan. As the late afternoon sun of May 15 stretched its long shadows over the busy boulevards and crowded café terraces of Paris, Guderian's and Reinhardt's leading tanks were little more than 120 miles away from the French capital. Responsible for the fate of Paris, Reynaud was handicapped by the lack of firm news from Vincennes and the difficulty of sifting fact from rumor. At 6:15 he was alerted by a "telephoned S.O.S." from Daladier. On the strength of this, fifty-five minutes later he dispatched a dramatic plea—the third in twenty-four hours—to Winston Churchill in London: "We lost the battle last night. The road to Paris is open. Send us all aircraft and troops you can."[1]

For a few tense hours that night, France's leaders contemplated the imminent fall of Paris. While Parisians peacefully dined and slept, a bizarre drama played itself out over the telephone lines between Paris and Vincennes. At 8:30, from Supreme Headquarters, Gamelin urgently called Daladier at the War Office in the rue Saint-Dominique to inform him of the reported passage of a German armored column between Rethel and Laon. Daladier was incredulous. He had recently returned from a War Committee meeting at which Gamelin, who was present, had reassured him about the battle situation. "No! It's impossible!" he declared. "You must be wrong! It's impossible!" Then he gasped: "You must attack at once!" "Attack? What with?" answered Gamelin. "I've no more reserves." After further talk he went on: "Between Laon

---

[9] Ibid., pp. 30–1.
[1] Reynaud: *Fight*, p. 321.

and Paris, I've not got a single body of troops."[2] At this revelation Daladier seemed to shrink visibly. "So, it means the destruction of the French Army?" he asked finally. "Yes, it's the destruction of the French Army," Gamelin replied. A startled witness of this conversation was William C. Bullitt, U.S. Ambassador to France, who just then was visiting Daladier. At 9:05 Bullitt hurried back to his embassy to cable a report of it to Cordell Hull in Washington. "It seems clear," he added, "that, failing a miracle like that of Marne, the French Army will be totally destroyed."[3]

Some time later, Gamelin called Daladier's office again. General Decamp, a member of the Minister's cabinet, answered. Gamelin told him that he did not wish to disturb Daladier, and left Decamp to decide whether this was necessary. Then, briefly outlining the latest situation, he added that the government should be prepared to leave Paris as soon as the battle approached the capital. The Prime Minister and the Minister of National Defense and War, he proposed, should remain, but all the others should be ready to leave immediately the decision was taken. Shortly after, Gamelin was called to the telephone by Reynaud himself. "So, the situation is as bad as that?" asked Reynaud. "You're demanding that the Government should leave Paris without delay? That's what General Decamp tells me." "I didn't exactly say that," replied Gamelin. And he repeated what he had explained to Decamp. "I'm simply asking that the Ministers hold themselves ready to leave, so as not to make a disorderly withdrawal if the Germans advance on Paris." "Ah! I prefer that," said Reynaud.[4]

Gamelin then telephoned Daladier to report his conversation with Reynaud. Daladier seemed calm and self-possessed. "I'm not leaving Paris," he said, "and you aren't either, I hope?" "No," answered Gamelin, "you'll find me always at your side whenever necessary. We must continue to direct the war so long as we're responsible. So I'll have plans made for the eventual removal of GHQ." "Obviously," answered Daladier.[5]

---

[2] Pertinax (pseudo): *Les Fossoyeurs* (1943), Vol. I, pp. 91–2.

[3] J. G. P. M. Benoist-Méchin: *60 Jours qui Ebranlèrent l'Occident*, (1956), Vol. I, p. 162.

[4] Gamelin: *Servir*, Vol. III, p. 408.

[5] Ibid.

At the height of the alarm, the telephone rang in the office of Paris Prefect of Police, Roger Langeron. A Supreme Headquarters officer was on the line, wanting to know how many *gardes mobiles* and trucks Langeron had. The road to Paris was open, the officer declared, and it must be barred by all possible means. The astonished Langeron replied that only a few hundred *gardes* remained in Paris: all the rest were mobilized. Those available, he assured the officer, were at the army's disposal, but he did not see how they could delay the advance of German armored forces. When his caller hung up, Langeron immediately telephoned the Minister of the Interior, Henri Roy, to report the incident. Roy thereupon summoned Langeron to a meeting at the Ministry in the Place Beauveau. Present in the Minister's room were Reynaud, Daladier, Generals Hering and Decamp, and Gamelin's staff officer, Lieutenant Colonel Guillaut. They discussed the crisis at a tense conference that lasted until the early hours of the morning. But by 3 a.m., Langeron noted, the situation as regards Paris had become less threatening. One of the main decisions of the meeting was that the military government of Paris would henceforth be attached to the Zone of the Armies.

In bed and asleep, the Secretary of the War Cabinet, Paul Baudouin, was roused by the telephone at 2:30 a.m. German armored divisions were near Laon, he was told, "the road to Paris was open . . . and Paris might well fall during the course of the day."[6] Baudouin was instructed to dress, pack his belongings and wait for orders. At 5 a.m. Reynaud telephoned him. He had returned from the meeting and asked Baudouin to come and see him. According to Reynaud's version of the conference, related to Baudouin a few hours later, "Daladier was broken down, and General Hering, in a state of collapse, had advised the Government to leave Paris without delay." Furthermore, said Reynaud, Gamelin had announced categorically: "As for Paris, I disclaim all responsibility from now, Thursday evening." "Which," as Reynaud remarked to Baudouin, "is a polite way of washing his hands."[7]

On that night of the fifteenth, the first breath of defeat

---

6 Baudoin: *Private Diaries*, p. 31.
7 Ibid.

seemed to blow through the casemates of Vincennes and the corridors of the Quai d'Orsay. But amid the confusion and disarray that threatened to paralyze French leadership, Reynaud was sustained by a heartening thought. Speeding south on the Sud Express was his special envoy, General Pujo, on a vital mission. Pujo was bound for Madrid, to bring back to Paris the aged and respected soldier who had been the Savior of Verdun and was now French Ambassador to Spain—Marshal Philippe Pétain.

Chapter 11

➤➤➤➤➤➤➤➤➤●◄◄◄◄◄◄◄◄◄

PLAN D ABANDONED

"We shall have to change methods, and men."
(Paul Reynaud)

ALONG THE DUSTY BELGIAN ROADS west of Liège moved a
seven-mile column of French troops—a mixed force of
1,500 ambulancemen, engineers, pioneers, and infantry from the
2nd North African Division of Blanchard's 1st Army. Doggedly
they fought off German air attacks, loosing thousands of machine-
gun bullets against the diving Stukas. These tough North Africans
were in good heart but mystified. "The men want to know where
I am leading them," noted their commander, Captain Barlone, in
his diary for that day, Thursday, May 16. "But I conceal the fact
that we are returning to France. They feel that things are not
going too well, but do not suspect defeat."[1] Defeat was a strong
word, but now its shadow loomed right across the Allied front in
Belgium. Blanchard's army was withdrawing, and, to the north of
it, the B.E.F. and Belgian formations would soon follow. Full
of fight, the stalwart French and British divisions that had swung
north to battle less than a week ago were pulling out before their
main forces had even had the chance to confront the enemy in
a major clash. Seven days after the start of the German offensive
the Dyle Plan was abandoned.

The withdrawal had been inevitable since the previous day,
when the 9th Army's II Corps—the last of Corap's formations to
hold its positions—had finally retreated to the line Fosses-Mettet,

---

[1] D. Barlone: *A French Officer's Diary 23 August 1939–1
October 1940*, trans. L. V. Cass (1942), p. 50.

and left Blanchard's right flank perilously exposed. During the night of May 15–16, Billotte had thus ordered Blanchard to move back his right on Charleroi, while he temporarily maintained the B.E.F. and the Belgian Army on their existing lines. In this he was influenced by King Leopold's insistence on covering Brussels, even if his forces had to stand alone. But on the sixteenth, after further pressure from Billotte, Leopold gave way; and the general retirement was ordered for the night of the sixteenth–seventeenth. General Gamelin now faced the collapse of his whole grand strategy; and to the menace overhanging Paris and northern France was now added the threat to Lord Gort's, Blanchard's and Leopold's armies—a threat incalculable in its consequences.

But as May 16 dawned, the fighting zone was steadily approaching Vincennes itself. With the German panzer columns racing for the Aisne, the old fort seemed to Colonel Minart suddenly plunged in the "very atmosphere of battle."[2] Such was the emergency on the front covering Paris that at 6:30 a.m. Gamelin flashed this message to his commanders: "Have everybody notified that, even when encircled, they must hold on and form kernels of resistance. As soon as the waves of tanks . . . have passed, they must strive to destroy the succeeding infantry or light armored vehicles, and act in the enemy rear to cut his communications and food supplies."[3] "Kernels of resistance" was a revolutionary tactic for the orthodox-minded Gamelin to order—and a measure of the critical situation he now judged his southern armies to be in. But amid all other cares Gamelin's immediate concern was for the safety of Paris. Despite the crucial shortage of troops to man the broken front, during the night he had directed forty squads of *gardes mobiles* to be withdrawn from the army and put at the disposal of the Military Governor, and he was about to instruct General Georges to allocate Hering a further three divisions.

In Paris alarm was still running high. Ministers and officials— if they had slept at all—were waking to what Baudouin called a "distracted day."[4] Through the tense hours of that Thursday they would be in a flurry of fear and indecision as the fate of Paris

---

[2] J. Minart: *P. C. Vincennes, Secteur 4* (1945), p. 151.
[3] Ibid., p. 153.
[4] P. Baudouin: *The Private Diaries (March 1940 to January 1941)* (1948), p. 31.

seemed to hang in the balance. Supreme Headquarters was partly to blame for this attitude. At 4 a.m. Édouard Herriot, President of the Chamber, had been roused by an officer from Vincennes who announced that Paris was in imminent danger and advised him to prepare immediately for the evacuation of the Chamber of Deputies. "Is the situation as desperate as that?" asked the bewildered Herriot. "Yes," said the officer. "The Army is riddled with Communism and is no longer holding anywhere."[5] Two hours later, Pertinax, the political commentator, was telephoned by a friend who reported that Mme de Portes, the confidante of Paul Reynaud, had just told him a German armored column was approaching Laon. At nine o'clock Georges Mandel, Minister for the Colonies, arrived at his office to be greeted by the same story. Reynaud even learned that an armistice was being talked about at Supreme Headquarters. On this his terse comment was: "Armistice means *capitulation*."[6]

Reynaud himself was in an acute dilemma. In the light of Gamelin's disclaimer of responsibility for the safety of Paris after midnight on the sixteenth, should he or should he not order the evacuation of the government and ministries? One man who had no doubts was the Military Governor. Hering, an ex-Commandant of the École de Guerre with unconventional military views and a reputed dislike of politicians, wanted immediate evacuation. Now, from his office in Les Invalides, he addressed an urgent letter to Reynaud:

> Mr. President—In the present circumstances I deem it wise, for the purpose of preventing any disorder, to suggest that you order the evacuation of the Government—except the National Defence Department, or at least, their senior grades—the Chamber of Deputies and the Senate to the pre-arranged evacuation areas. I should be obliged if you would inform me of your decision as soon as possible. Hering.[7]

This apparently decided Reynaud. He scrawled his countersignature across the letter, and by 11 a.m. orders were being issued to the ministries to evacuate their archives, while the govern-

---

[5] A. Kammerer: *La Vérité sur l'Armistice* (1944), p. 24.
[6] P. Reynaud: *In the Thick of the Fight* (1955), p. 323.
[7] Ibid., p. 322.

ment was to be ready to quit Paris at short notice. But somewhere at this point Reynaud telephoned Gamelin at Vincennes and got a gleam of hope. "As to the withdrawal of the Ministries, we have until midnight to make a decision?" he asked Gamelin. "Certainly," Gamelin replied. "On our latest information," he added, "it doesn't seem that the Germans are heading for Paris."[8]

At noon, in his office at the Quai d'Orsay, Reynaud called an emergency meeting of the presidents of the Senate and Chamber and various ministers, the Military Governor, the Prefect of Police, and other officials, to make a final decision on evacuation. After an agitated discussion—in which one speaker even suggested bringing shallow-draft gunboats up the Seine to defend Paris—it was decided to withdraw the departure orders. But it was agreed that the Minister of Public Works should inform the presidents and ministers at two o'clock of the number of lorries which each could count upon in the event of evacuation. "I stated that, so far as the Government was concerned, it ought to remain in Paris," recorded Reynaud, "no matter how intense the bombing might be, but that it should, however, take care not to fall into the enemy's hands: it ought to leave the capital only if a threat of this nature should materialise, and, in that event, at the last moment."[9]

Meanwhile, a fantastic scene was taking place in the courtyard of the Ministry of Foreign Affairs on the Quai d'Orsay. Smoke and flames were rising upward from a huge pyre fed by Foreign Ministry documents that were being thrown out wholesale from the Ministry windows. This drastic measure was allegedly ordered by Alexis Léger, Secretary-General of the Foreign Ministry, in anticipation of the Ministry's imminent departure. He had called in sailors from the Ministry of the Marine to perform the task. From every floor the files and archives showered down, some packages bursting open as they hit the ground. In the courtyard, doorkeepers and clerks heaped them onto the growing bonfire. As one observer later told Edward Spears, the fire was tended "by hurrying, flustered officials, young, sallow, under-developed diplomats, men with beards, others whose glasses trembled on their noses . . . some with great piles of dossiers, others with a few

---

[8] M. Gamelin: *Servir* (1947), Vol. III, p. 409.
[9] Reynaud: *Fight,* p. 322.

sheets of paper."[1] It was noted that the biggest contribution was coming from the third-story offices, which housed the most important documents. As the flames took hold, clouds of charred fragments shot into the air, to fall on astonished passers-by. The burning was to continue through the day, its smoke clearly visible from the Esplanade des Invalides and Chamber of Deputies. At one point Reynaud and Georges Mandel were seen watching pale-faced from the steps of the Ministry garden as workmen sprayed the massed papers with gasoline. So impatient were those directing the holocaust that they even considered, it was said, having some of the files thrown straight into the Seine.

The crisis atmosphere was swiftly spreading through Paris. As wild rumors flew, the streets were transformed by ominous signs. The change occurred literally within the space of the morning. To Senator Jean Bardoux, walking on the boulevards at 10:30, the Paris scene appeared "normal." Just after midday "the impression was quite different."[2] Buses and taxis were vanishing, requisitioned to transport troops and bring refugees from Rheims, and there were more private cars on the roads, taking people out of the city. This was the day when fear first gripped Paris. Consistently misled by optimistic communiqués and press reports, Parisians now learned the truth of the situation with a surge of shock. "There is panic in the air," commented Alexander Werth, assessing their reactions.[3] Those who could look back quarter of a century were reminded of Paris at the time of the Battle of the Marne.

In the Palais-Bourbon, the Chamber of Deputies buzzed with alarmist stories. Frightened members were saying that the Germans had entered Laon and Rheims, were advancing in a motorized column flanked by two armored divisions, and would be in Paris that evening. Another report had it that two French divisions— the 71st and 55th were named—had stampeded after being attacked by flame-throwing tanks and were nearing Valenciennes. These divisions, it was claimed, were composed of Parisians who

---

[1] E. L. Spears: *Assignment to Catastrophe* (1954), Vol. I, p. 147.
[2] J. Bardoux: *Journal d'un Témoin de la Troisième . . . 1940* (1957), p. 308.
[3] A. Werth: *The Last Days of Paris* (1940), p. 43.

were being worked on by Communist agitators. They were even said to be marching on Paris to proclaim revolution in the capital. It was common talk that the government and Parliament were leaving Paris immediately. Amid this hysteria Reynaud arrived to address the House at 3:30 p.m. Pale and grave, he outlined the military situation and declared categorically that the government would remain in Paris. And he added—significantly—"The times we are about to experience will perhaps have nothing in common with those we have recently seen. We shall be called on to take measures which yesterday would have seemed revolutionary. Perhaps we shall have to change methods, and men. . . . We are full of hope. Our lives count for nothing. One thing alone counts: to preserve France!"[4]

The House rose and gave Reynaud a standing ovation. Édouard Herriot, presiding, ended the meeting on a stirring patriotic note: "France feels the greatness and tragedy of this trial. She will remain equal to her past and to her destiny."[5]

For miles behind the front, the great rout was continuing.

Early that morning a tank unit moving north to the Belgian frontier approached the village of Dizy-le-Gros, 15 miles north of Neufchâtel on the Aisne. The bomb-scarred village lay silent and seemingly empty. Suddenly members of the unit saw small groups of soldiers emerging from it in the Neufchâtel direction. They had no arms, helmets, or packs. They shuffled along, some on sticks, some with their boots off and tied round their necks. Their belts and tunics were undone and they were dusty and sweating. But what chiefly struck the tank unit's medical officer, André Soubiran, was the faces of these men. They were "hopeless, gaunt, dazed with fatigue."[6] These were the troops of Sedan. Among a party of gunners was an exhausted 2nd Army captain who asked Soubiran for transport to Sissonne, for his wounded. Soubiran asked where the Germans were. "There, very close. Everywhere!" cried the distraught officer. "We haven't run," he said. "You can't imagine what happened at Sedan. We did our best, and our artillery fire

---

[4] Benoist-Méchin: *60 Jours,* Vol. I, p. 177.
[5] Ibid.
[6] A. Soubiran: *J'Etais Médecin avec les Chars* (1943), p. 106.

killed plenty of men on the other bank. Then they sent bombers over. They came for two days in endless waves, at a height of 60 feet. One by one our guns were destroyed. Finally there was no battery left, nothing but these 15 men and myself. In front of us and behind us, no more men, no more equipment, no more tanks, and no planes in the sky—nothing, nothing to put up any resistance."[7] The long procession straggled on southward. Soubiran noticed that some men were drunk, the necks of bottles sticking out of their haversacks. A few pedaled by on bicycles.

Farther west, large numbers of disorganized troops were converging on Compiègne—80 miles back from the Meuse. By midmorning some 20,000 9th Army men and elements of an army headquarters from Vervins (presumably the 9th) were reported there, and part of a corps headquarters at Beauvais. Soon after, the figure had reached 30,000 and was still growing. According to the Chief of Staff, 2nd Region (in the Aisne Department), reporting to Vincennes from his headquarters at Marle, near Vervins, all these men were withdrawing to Compiègne on specific orders. Some carried instructions issued by a XLI Corps staff captain. This news produced a wave of anger at Supreme Headquarters. Wrathful officers demanded to know on what authority the captain had acted. More consternation was caused by the arrival of a chasseurs lieutenant with a group of men at the north gate of Vincennes at 2:30 p.m. Exhausted and hungry, they had come straight from the front. In his dust-covered uniform, the lieutenant was escorted to the casemates for questioning. He claimed that the day before his battalion, part of 1st Armored Corps, had been dispersed after a clash wih enemy tanks outside Montcornet. Unable to contact his commander, he had taken a car and driven with some of his men to Saint-Quentin, 35 miles northwest of Montcornet. Here, to his amazement, he was ordered to rejoin a reserve depot well south of the Seine. Everywhere, he said, the rapid appearance of German tanks had led to indescribable panic. "In 1814 the cry was *'Voilà les cosaques,'*" commented Minart sardonically. "In 1870, *'Voilà les Uhlans';* in 1940, *'Voilà les blindés.'*"[8]

---

[7] Ibid., pp. 107–9.
[8] Minart: *P. C. Vincennes*, p. 161.

The great tide of uniform was even nearing Paris. Bars and cafés on the city outskirts were suddenly full of men of all arms who had lost their units and officers and were just drifting away from the front. And reinforcing them, came the refugees—a vast, pitiful population herding south from the Pas-de-Calais, Nord, and Ardennes departments. In that day's intensified staff traffic between Vincennes, Montry, and Les Bondons, exasperated officers found themselves delayed on the cluttered routes and in villages where defenses were being hurriedly thrown up. Surveying this work, Minart was not impressed. "None of these places seems capable of filling the 'kernel of resistance' role which Gamelin ordered," he concluded. "And there are no road barriers which would effectively stop the enemy."[9]

Supreme Headquarters was complaining about the paucity of information arriving from GHQ, Northeast. Apart from an early report direct from the 2nd Army, the most reliable source of intelligence that day was the Chief of Staff, 2nd Region—answerable not to the army at all, but to the Ministry of the Interior. While Vincennes officers—immured in their "submarine without a periscope"—chafed impotently at the lack of news, Georges's headquarters itself was little better informed. Its staff was being overwhelmed by the quickening tempo of what the official French communiqué of the sixteenth at last admitted to be "a war of movement." Almost the whole front, from central Belgium to the reaches of the Aisne, was shifting back in anything from orderly withdrawal to headlong flight. In some areas, a front hardly existed at all. The most total confusion reigned over what was still nominally the 9th Army sector. From Philippeville southward, communications and liaison had collapsed, formation headquarters had lost touch with their decimated units, isolated commanders were trying frantically to marshal motley groups of men on improvised defense lines inside France.

The 9th Army was virtually defunct. Not even the energetic Giraud, its new commander, could save it. All that could be done was to attempt to assemble its remnants on the French frontier defenses. Of the II Corps, General Bouchet's hard-pressed 5th Division was trying to regroup behind the fortified line at Mau-

---

[9] Ibid.

beuge. The reserve 4th North African Division, scattered by Hoth's panzers after a stubborn defense on the Anhée-Morville Line, was straggling back to the French frontier. Of the XI Corps, the remains of Duffct's 18th Division were retreating to the frontier from Beaumont, with orders to regroup at Claire-Fontaine. A few hundred survivors of Hassler's 22nd Division were being thrown into the defenses at Anor and the forest of Saint-Michel. But some of these defenses were completely inoperative. One infuriated battalion commander, with fifty exhausted and hungry men, found his blockhouses unequipped and without doors, their automatic weapons unusable and apparently sabotaged. The 61st and 102nd Divisions of Libaud's XLI Corps, attacked and overrun by Reinhardt's panzers as they erupted from the Monthermé zone, had evaporated.

To officers working to hold their men together, one of the day's orders brought a sour taste of irony. It seemed to enjoin the impossible. Emanating from Gamelin himself as General Order No. 17, it was especially directed at the 9th Army. "It is recalled," ran the order, "that by the terms of para 18 of the Instruction on Service in the Field, commanders must devote all their energies to maintaining discipline, encouraging flagging spirits and keeping men of all ranks at their posts. *If necessary, commanders must ensure obedience by force.* All commanders who do not comply with these instructions are failing in their duty."[1]

Often the orders of GHQ, Northeast, were out-of-date when they reached the formations concerned, sometimes even at the moment they were issued. On the morning of the sixteenth, Georges's General Order No. 14 detailed Touchon's Army Detachment to hold the line from Anor to Omont. But already late on the fifteenth, the enemy had reached Omont and other points on the line. A further instruction ordered Touchon to regain control of the heights at Signy-l'Abbaye and Omont, but he had no forces available for this. His 14th Division was installed on the Aisne between Attigny and Château-Porcien. The huge pocket opened up by Reinhardt's and Guderian's panzers was almost devoid of French troops. And by that evening Reinhardt's leading tanks had raced through Vervins and Guise to reach the Oise.

As for French armor, the 1st Armored Division had been

---

[1] Gamelin: *Servir* (1946), Vol. I, p. 352.

almost destroyed yesterday. And now the 2nd—after an inexplicable cancellation of its latest orders to counterattack at Montcornet—was assigned the purely defensive mission of holding the crossings of the Oise and the Sambre Canal. All that could be immediately mustered was some fifty tanks, which were to contain the advance of Guderian's panzers between Guise and La Fère, northwest of Laon. The 3rd Division was likewise standing in a strung-out defensive role south of Sedan. General de Gaulle, charged with the formation of the 4th Armored Division, spent the day reconnoitering with a skeleton staff in the Sissonne Canal area. "The impression I gained," he noted, "was that large German forces which had debouched from the Ardennes . . . were marching, not southwards, but westwards, to reach Saint-Quentin."[2] De Gaulle watched as streams of refugees and routed troops poured southward. Some soldiers had been overtaken by German tanks and ordered to jettison their arms and head south so as not to choke the roads. The Germans told them they had no time to take them prisoner. As De Gaulle records, his experiences that day roused him to "limitless fury."[3] They also inspired in him a heroic resolve. "If I live," he told himself, "I will fight, wherever I must, as long as I must, until the enemy is defeated and the national stain washed clean."[4]

Soon after four o'clock a British Flamingo aircraft touched down at Le Bourget Airport. From it emerged the short sturdy figure of Winston Churchill, followed by General Sir John Dill, Vice-Chief of the Imperial General Staff, and General Ismay, Assistant Secretary to the War Cabinet. In trying to assess the battle situation, Churchill and his War Cabinet colleagues were finding it increasingly difficult to get a clear picture of events. As seen from Downing Street the position was grave, but just how grave they could not determine. Even the War Office, Churchill commented, was not receiving the full information on which to base judgment. There had been a note of growing desperation in

---

[2] C. de Gaulle: *War Memoirs*, Vol. I: *The Call to Honour, 1940–42*, trans. J. Griffin (1955), p. 43.
[3] Ibid.
[4] Ibid.

Reynaud's three appeals to Churchill for immediate aid, especially fighter planes. Gamelin, too, had been urgently asking for fighters—his latest request had been sent that day. During the morning Churchill decided there was only one thing to do. "I felt it imperative to go to Paris that afternoon," he recorded.[5] Now, after a short stop at the British Embassy, he drove to the Quai d'Orsay for the first of the vital Anglo-French meetings that were to mark the coming weeks.

The conference began at 5:30 in the Prime Minister's office. In addition to Churchill, Dill, and Ismay, the British group included Air Marshal Joubert de la Ferté, assistant to Air Chief Marshal Cyril Newall. The French party consisted of Reynaud, Daladier, two Cabinet colleagues, Gamelin, Darlan, and General Bergeret, Deputy Chief of Staff of the French Air Force. An air of gloom pervaded. To emphasize it, from the long windows of Reynaud's room were visible the bonfires of the Foreign Office files, still burning in the courtyard below. Seated or standing round an easel that held a large map showing the Allied line marked in black, members listened to an opening statement by Gamelin. The Supreme Commander described the Sedan breakthrough, the destruction of the Meuse armies, the enemy's rapid armored advance westward with the aim of either reaching the coast or turning on Paris. Behind the panzers, Gamelin continued, some ten motorized divisions were following—cutting between the Allied forces to the north and south. For the first time, Churchill and his colleagues were appreciating the full extent of the disaster. Before leaving London they had not considered the Sedan breakthrough irremediable. Now they saw that the French High Command was already thinking in terms of defeat. Churchill's biggest shock came when he asked Gamelin: "Where is the strategic reserve—*Ou est la masse de manoeuvre?*" and Gamelin answered with a shake of the head: "*Aucune.*" "I was dumbfounded," recorded Churchill.[6] He walked to the window to watch the smoke still wreathing up from the burning archives.

In the ensuing discussion Churchill fought to persuade the

---

[5] W. S. Churchill: *The Second World War,* Vol. II: *Their Finest Hour* (1949), p. 40.
[6] Ibid., p. 42.

dejected French leaders not to give up hope. He questioned the wisdom of withdrawing the northern armies from their Belgian positions, refused to treat the enemy panzer advance as a total disaster, and pressed for a counterstroke against the "Bulge." He asked Gamelin when and where he planned to counterattack the flanks of the German salient. Gamelin gave a shrug and answered: "Inferiority of numbers, inferiority of equipment, inferiority of method . . ."[7] Then the question of aircraft arose. It was to help close the gap that was endangering Paris, said Gamelin, that the French had requested British air support. Churchill explained that Britain had thirty-nine home-based fighter squadrons, which were essential for the defense of the British war industry against German bombing. For this reason it was difficult to afford fighter aid to France, although Britain had provided four squadrons for the Sedan operations and had just dispatched four more.

The meeting broke up. Churchill was no longer in doubt about the gravity of the crisis. When he returned to the British Embassy, he decided, and Dill concurred, to ask the War Cabinet to authorize the transfer to France of six more fighter squadrons. At 9 p.m. Ismay dispatched a telegram—worded, for security, in Hindustani—outlining the position and requesting sanction for the six squadrons. "Situation grave in the last degree . . ." the telegram ran. "I consider the next two, three or four days decisive for Paris and probably for the French Army. . . . I must have the answer by midnight in order to encourage the French Army . . ."[8] The reply arrived about 11:30. The Cabinet had agreed. At once Churchill drove with Ismay to Reynaud's private apartment in the Place du Palais Bourbon. Reynaud had retired and the apartment was in semi-darkness. At length he appeared in his dressing gown and Churchill announced the Cabinet's decision. Then he asked the delighted Reynaud to call Daladier to his apartment to hear the news. Upon the Defense Minister's arrival, Churchill reread the Cabinet message. Daladier rose from his chair and shook Churchill's hand in silent thanks. For some time afterward, Churchill paced the room brandishing his cigar and delivering a "forthright harangue" on the theme of continuing the fight and

---

[7] Ibid., p. 44.
[8] Ibid., p. 45.

striking the Germans hard.[9] Reynaud listened attentively, head erect. Across the table, Daladier, according to an observer, sat hunched and despondent.

Amid the defeatism sweeping the Zone of the Armies, some hope and optimism persisted. That evening, at Coulommiers, an R.A.F. staff officer watched a great procession of vehicles moving to collect troops and transport them to the front. "The townspeople still seemed cheerful," he noted. "There was a good deal of shouting and cheering and an exchange of the usual signs of thumbs up. For an hour or two one thought that the spirit of France was reviving."[1]

At Supreme Headquarters morale was at a low ebb. Colonel Minart remarked on the "panic" mood invading the offices by the end of the day.[2] In a quixotic gesture of defiance, Colonel Petibon had a 75mm. gun installed at the north entrance to the fort. The staff began to prepare for flight, clearing cupboards, packing files, removing maps from the walls. One officer brought his canteen down to his office in readiness for departure. The work continued through the night, while exhausted officers slumped down in chairs for a brief sleep. Even Gamelin showed signs of unease. He moved restlessly about, alternately seeking the company of his Chief of Staff and his aides. "No one dares to approach him," said Minart. "It is indeed a lost battle."[3]

---

[9] Reynaud: *Fight*, p. 326.
[1] *The Diary of a Staff Officer at Advanced Headquarters North, B. A. F. F., 1940* (1941), p. 20.
[2] Minart: *P. C. Vincennes*, p. 163.
[3] Ibid.

Chapter 12

➤➤➤➤➤➤➤➤➤●◀◀◀◀◀◀◀◀◀◀

[194]

THE ECLIPSE OF GAMELIN

*"The old stones of Vincennes have just witnessed a
new execution."*

(Colonel Minart)

ALMOST UNCHECKED, the seven panzer divisions were sweeping
on. There was an awesome precision about their advance.
They had cleared the Forest of Ardennes, crossed the Meuse,
surged across the Belgian Namur and the French Ardennes and
Aisne departments—still in the broad line-abreast formation in
which they had entered Luxembourg a week ago. Now, on May
17, the German columns were cutting into the heart of northern
France. In the south the 1st Panzers of Guderian's XIX Armored
Corps—with the 2nd on their right and the 10th on their left and
to the rear—were approaching the Oise in two groups, one north
of Saint-Quentin, the other to the south. In the center the 6th
and 8th Armored Divisions of Reinhardt's XLI Corps, on left and
right respectively, were advancing on the Oise via Rumigny and
Vervins. Behind these two corps moved the three divisions of the
14th Motorized Corps. In the north were the 5th and 7th Armored
Divisions of Hoth's Army Group, charged with the key role of
outflanking the northern Allied armies by reaching the line Mau-
beuge-Cambrai-Arras. Assigned to reinforce these next day were
the 3rd and 4th Panzer Divisions and 20th Motorized Division of
the XVI Armored Corps, shifted—much to his dismay—from
Bock's Army Group B. Within twenty-four hours nine German
armored divisions would be heading through the huge corridor
left exposed by France's broken armies.

Yet the sheer speed of the panzer drive was bringing its own
troubles. At OKH headquarters Hitler himself considered that the

rapid advance was leaving the southern flank of the German front dangerously open to a French counterattack. That morning he visited Army Group A headquarters at Charleville and warned Von Rundstedt to pay close attention to his left flank. Likewise, in order to slow down the armored advance, he instructed Von Kleist's group not to proceed beyond the Oise until further orders. Meanwhile General List's 12th Army was to pivot southwestward and take up defensive positions. Hitler wished to avoid, at all costs, the chance of a German setback, which might dangerously restore French morale. The orders were passed along to the various German headquarters, causing repercussions. In a towering temper Von Kleist rushed off to see Guderian. As Guderian records, they met at Guderian's airfield, where Von Kleist violently rated him for disobeying orders by advancing so precipitately. When Von Kleist finished, with equal heat Guderian burst out that it was clear he was not trusted by his superiors, and asked to be relieved of his command. He returned to corps headquarters, warned General Veiel to be ready to take over from him, and radioed a report to Von Rundstedt. From Von Rundstedt the order came back to take no action until he had seen General List, who was on his way to visit him. List arrived early in the afternoon, heard Guderian's story, and then passed on a categorical instruction from Von Rundstedt that Guderian not resign his command: explicit orders to halt the advance had come from OKH and must be obeyed. Guardian accepted the explanation and expressed his gratitude to List for clearing up the misunderstanding.

But as the panzer columns rolled forward on Friday the seventeenth, one thing was becoming clear: Paris was reprieved, at least for the moment. Veering away from the capital, Guderian's and Reinhardt's tanks streamed west and northwest—toward the sea. The first phase of the great battle was over. In seven days the Germans had dispersed or annihilated two French armies, gained a massive foothold in France, and nullified the Allied strategic plan. From now on, the tempo of disaster would accelerate. In five more days the enemy would reach the Channel coast, isolate the Franco-British forces in Belgium and thereby cut the Allied armies in half. And within that time momentous things would have happened in France. Reynaud would have replaced Daladier as Minister of National Defense and War, the octogenarian Pétain

would be installed as Deputy Prime Minister and the Allied armies
would have a new Commander in Chief.

From the start of the offensive on the tenth, Gamelin's continued tenure of command had, as far as Reynaud was concerned,
been little more than a respite. Only the overriding national crisis
had induced the Prime Minister, prepared as he was to resign
unless Gamelin were replaced, to retain office himself with Gamelin as Supreme Commander. Reynaud had never believed in
Gamelin's Plan D, with its committing of two French armies—
to say nothing of the B.E.F.—deep into Belgian territory. His
fears seemed justified when these armies were endangered by the
German breakout from the Meuse bridgeheads on the fifteenth.
And his speech to the Chamber on the afternoon of the sixteenth
clearly implied his intention to remove Gamelin. "Perhaps we shall
have to change methods, and men," he had said. The general he
had in mind to succeed Gamelin was Maxime Weygand. Aged
seventy-three but young for his years, Weygand had been recalled
from retirement at the beginning of the war and appointed Commander in Chief in the Near East. In 1935 he had completed a
four-year term as French Commander in Chief. To Reynaud, impressed with his "fighting spirit," he seemed "surrounded with
the halo of Foch's glory."[1] Weygand, if anyone, was the commander to restore the position and revive the faltering French
Army. So on the morning of the seventeenth Reynaud telegraphed
Weygand at Beirut: "The gravity of the situation on the Western
Front is increasing. Please come to Paris without delay. Make
suitable arrangements to transfer your functions to the high authority you may choose. Secrecy of your departure is desirable."[2]
Unlike Gamelin, Weygand had never held a field command.
Although he had reorganized the Polish Army and launched a
successful offensive against the Bolsheviks in 1920, he was essentially a staff officer—in De Gaulle's view "a brilliant second," as
he had shown while serving under Foch in World War I.[3] He was

---

[1] P. Reynaud: *In the Thick of the Fight*, trans. J. D. Lambert (1955), p. 342.
[2] M. Weygand: *Recalled to Service*, trans. E. W. Dickes
(1952), p. 45.
[3] C. de Gaulle: *War Memoirs*, Vol. I: *The Call to Honour,
1940–42*, trans. J. Griffin (1955), p. 57.

the career soldier par excellence—even down to his spruce, impeccable turnout. Tradition-loving, authoritarian, and somewhat contemptuous of politicians, during his spell as Commander in Chief he had fought hard against government measures to whittle down the army's strength. But since then he had publicly testified to its high fighting capabilities. In a speech at Lille in July 1939, he declared: ". . . I believe that the French Army is a more effective force than at any time in its history. Its material is first-rate, its fortifications are first class, its morale is excellent, its High Command remarkable. No one amongst us wants war, but I affirm that if we are compelled to win victory, we will win it."[4] Nonetheless, privately he seemed less optimistic about its invincibility—especially without himself at his head. About the same time, discussing with General André Laffargue the chances of war in Europe and his own possible role as the army's Commander in Chief, he remarked: "I fear only one thing—that they'll call me when it's too late!"[5] Now, as the summons went out to him in distant Beirut, it seemed that he was being proved right. In a new Order of the Day, issued that evening, Gamelin was enjoining the French Army to conquer or die:

> The fate of the country, that of our allies, and the destinies of the world hang upon the battle now in progress.
> British, Belgian, Polish soldiers, and foreign volunteers, are fighting at our side.
> The British Air Force is fully engaged along with ours.
> Every man who cannot advance should be killed at his post rather than abandon the piece of ground that has been entrusted to him.
> As always in the gravest hours of our history, today the watchword is:—
> *Conquer or die. We must conquer.*[6]

The stark appeal recalled the Orders of Joffre in the darkest moments of World War I. But it was no sterner than the situation demanded. The Allied positions in Belgium were crumbling. Pressed by Reichenau's forces—which that day took Brussels, Louvain, and Malines—the French 1st Army and the B.E.F. were making their fighting retreat to the Escaut. The roads of Belgium and

---

[4] E. L. Spears: *Assignment to Catastrophe* (1954), Vol. I, p. 190n.
[5] A. Laffargue: *Justice pour Ceux de 1940* (1952), p. 158.
[6] M. Gamelin: *Servir* (1947), Vol. III, p. 412.

northern France were choked by hordes of refugees who blocked the path of troops and guns bound for the front. South of the French border, the High Command now realized that the panzer advance was directed to Amiens and perhaps to the Channel. At the same time, Georges was trying to throw a screen of divisions along the Somme and the Aisne. And Gamelin, thinking beyond immediate defense, was planning a counterattack to enable the Somme armies to join up with those in the north while there was still time. To this end he was forming a new 7th Army, to be led by General Frère, a corps commander in the 5th Army. Calling Frère to Les Bondons, he told him his intentions. Gamelin noticed the general's eyes light up at the news. "He has the spirit of a great commander," he wrote.[7] But at his First Army Group Headquarters at Douai, General Billotte was pessimistic. When General Prioux reported to him—after a hazardous journey along bomb-wrecked roads—to ask how he could employ his Cavalry Corps, Billotte replied despondently: "We are heading towards a fresh Sedan, worse than that of 1870. Stay with the 1st Army, it needs you!"[8]

General Frère's mission had an inauspicious start. Late that night he was at Amiens with his Chief of Staff and aide— his entire staff—and the prefect of the Department and the region's commander, when General Vauthier, commanding the remnants of the 61st Division, telephoned him. Vauthier was at Vermandovillers, 25 miles away, trying to locate his superiors. "Come at once," he was ordered.[9] It took Vauthier six hours to reach Amiens, along roads cluttered with thousands of newly evacuated civilians. "The tanks have just reached Saint-Quentin," Frère's Chief of Staff told him. "Deploy your division on the Somme from Ham to Peronne." "My division consists of 300 men, a battalion commander and three automatic rifles," answered Vauthier. "Then do your best to hold the Brie bridge on the Saint-Quentin–Amiens road."[1] Vauthier returned to Vermandovillers and sent his three automatic rifles off to the Brie Bridge. Fortunately for this tiny force, it was not called into action: the Germans advanced along another route.

Operating just to the northeast of Frère's front was the 7th

---

[7] Ibid., Vol. III, p. 411.
[8] R. Prioux: *Souvenirs de Guerre* (1947), p. 86.
[9] C. L. Menu: *Lumière sur les Ruines* (1953), p. 337.
[1] Ibid.

Army's old leader, General Giraud. For the audacious Giraud, directing the relics of the 9th Army (with a few formations hurriedly added) in the Cambrai–Le Cateau–Saint-Quentin area, his new command was to be unhappily brief. Late on the eighteenth, accompanied by two officers, Giraud found himself in enemy-held country near the village of Le Catelet. After abandoning their car, the trio were fired on by a German patrol and took shelter in a wood. Giraud ordered his two companions to make their own escape while he himself, troubled by an old wound, spent the night under cover of a hedge on the Le Catelet–Cambrai road. At dawn a column of French lorries, headed by a gun carriage, came up the road. Giraud mounted the gun carriage and the convoy proceeded north toward Cambrai. Almost at once it ran into German tanks of the 1st Panzer Division. The carriage knocked out the first tank and was then stopped by three more. Giraud and the others ran for a nearby farm building, which was quickly surrounded by tanks. "I judged it was useless to get the men who were there killed," recorded Giraud, "and I ordered them not to fire."[2] The party was rounded up and marched off. It was 6 a.m. on the nineteenth. Within less than four days of taking over from Corap, General Giraud was a German prisoner.

Accustomed to the austere calm of Vincennes, Gamelin had never understood how Georges could work in the turmoil of Les Bondons. The thin-partitioned offices resounded to the din of telephones and typewriters and perpetual traffic of officers and orderlies. In the main anteroom every piece of furniture, including the cretonne-covered chaise longue, was littered with files, pads and notebooks. Officers' *képis* cluttered the grand piano. Events had moved so fast that maps of Finland and Norway still hung on the walls. Visiting Georges on the morning of the eighteenth, Gamelin was dismayed afresh at the chaos and, in particular, at Georges's lack of privacy. Callers were continually disturbing him and he was constantly emerging to talk to various officers. Now, Gamelin observed, the general was showing unmistakable signs of exhaustion. "How can he keep a grip on affairs in such sur-

---

[2] A. Doumenc: *Histoire de la Neuvième Armée* (1945), p. 272.

roundings, without anywhere to withdraw and think?" he asked
himself. He mentioned the matter to Doumenc, who was equally
worried. "I can tell you sincerely, *mon general*," said Doumenc,
"that Georges shows me every trust and understanding, and I'm
grateful to him for that. But you will have to take over effective
direction of affairs yourself. It would be to everybody's interest,
though, to avoid any sort of clash." "I quite understand," replied
Gamelin. "Just warn me of the right moment."[3]

Gamelin was still unaware that he was under the shadow of
dismissal. But, in Paris, Reynaud's moves to "change methods
and men" were already taking effect. Marshal Pétain had answered
his appeal to return to France. Arriving from Madrid early that
morning, he had accepted the Premier's invitation to join the
government. Ambassador to Spain since March 1939, Pétain had
declined to join Daladier's government at the beginning of the war;
but now the eighty-four-year-old marshal had placed himself un-
reservedly at Reynaud's service. "The French like old men," wrote
Reynaud later, "and . . . they love the glorious soldier."[4] Most of
all they revered their greatest living military hero, the veteran
patriot who symbolized steadfastness in battle and wise leadership.
That night Reynaud was to announce Pétain's appointment in a
radio broadcast. After outlining the situation and declaring that
it was "grave" but not "desperate," he said: "What the country
expects from the Government is not words. For years it has heard
too many of these. It is deeds that the nation wants. Here is the
first decision that I have just taken. The victor of Verdun—the
man thanks to whom the attackers did not pass in 1916, and to
whom the spirit of the French Army was restored in 1917 in
preparation for victory, Marshal Pétain—has returned this morning from Madrid, where he has rendered so many services to
France. Henceforth he will be at my side as Minister of State
and Vice-President of the Council. . . . He will remain there until
victory."[5]

Reynaud had hastened to induct Pétain into the war situation.
During the afternoon he escorted him to both Georges's and

[3] Gamelin: *Servir*, Vol. III, p. 415.
[4] Reynaud: *Fight*, p. 340.
[5] J. G. P. M. Benoist-Méchin: *60 Jours qui Ebranlèrent
l'Occident* (1956), Vol. I, pp. 204–5.

Gamelin's command posts. In his office at Les Bondons, Georges rolled down a large map and demonstrated the Allied and German positions to the tall, impassive marshal. Several times he paused to remark sorrowfully: "It is a difficult situation."[6] Driving on to Vincennes, Pétain then received a briefing from Gamelin, who had been waiting in his office with Daladier. With the aid of an array of maps displayed in his operations room, Gamelin went into a long and detailed exposition. "Affected but always elegant and fluent," he described the course of the battle and causes of the French defeat[7] and was—according to his account—at pains to support Georges, and stress his own determination to assume personal direction of the battle as and when he thought necessary.[8] He also entered a strong plea for Corap. "A commander can be unlucky without being blameworthy," he commented later, in reference to what he told Pétain.[9] At the end, Reynaud and Daladier walked out together, leaving Pétain momentarily alone with Gamelin. Pétain extended an affectionate hand to him. "I pity you with all my heart," he said. Gamelin replied: "I'm thinking only of France." He accompanied the marshal to his car, and as it moved off Pétain gave him a friendly wave. "It was the last time I was to see him," recorded Gamelin.[1]

At 5 a.m. on Sunday the nineteenth, Gamelin was roused by a telephone call from Doumenc. "I got back from La Ferté at one o'clock," Doumenc said. "I have the clear impression that the moment has come for you to intervene. I can't go into it at length on the telephone." "Alright," answered Gamelin, "send Koeltz to me to bring me up to date, and I'll meet you at Les Bondons at 8 o'clock."[2] At 6:30 Koeltz arrived at Vincennes and confirmed what Doumenc had said. The staff at GHQ, Northeast, was aware of what ought to be done, but nobody was taking de-

---

[6] Reynaud: *Fight*, p. 344.

[7] Gamelin's verbal appreciation was virtually the same as the written report he submitted to Daladier that day, the eighteenth, following a request from the Minister of National Defense and War, dated May 16.

[8] Ibid.

[9] Gamelin: *Servir*, Vol. III, p. 417.

[1] Ibid., p. 418.

[2] Ibid., p. 428.

cisive action. A series of partial counterattacks had been ordered in which the various reserves were being used piecemeal. The time had come for a concerted operation.

Just before eight, Colonel Minart, acting as Gamelin's liaison officer, arrived at Les Bondons. As his car stopped under the great trees of the park, General Doumenc came forward to meet him. "General Gamelin must take over command," he told Minart tersely.[3] Almost at once Gamelin's pennanted car drew up and he got out, accompanied by his aide, Lieutenant Colonel Simon. Short, stocky, his legs sheathed in the invariable canvas gaiters, Gamelin strode into the house. A group of silent officers made way for them as they moved to Georges's office. After a brief talk with General Vuillemin, whom he had asked to meet him at Les Bondons, Gamelin conferred privately with Georges. The Commander in Chief, Northeast, was showing signs of deep depression and fatigue. Gamelin informed him that he thought it necessary, as Supreme Commander, to draw up the general plan of the maneuver that was now indicated, and asked to be shown to some place where he could work undisturbed. He was taken to a room on the first floor. There, in his rather crabbed hand, he carefully set down his "Personal and Secret Instruction No. 12":

19th May.

General Gamelin to:—
General Vuillemin, Commander-in-Chief of the Air Force,
General Georges, Commander-in-Chief, North-East.

Without wishing to intervene in the conduct of the battle in progress, which depends on the authority of the Commander-in-Chief, North-East, and while approving all the dispositions that he has taken, I judge that at present:—
1. There is reason to continue to extend westwards the front of our eastern armies and the coverage of Paris, and to maintain the link with First Army Group;
2. That, as concerns First Army Group, rather than allow it to be encircled, it is necessary to act with extreme boldness: on the one hand by opening up for itself, if needs be, *la route de la Somme*; on the other by throwing specially mobile forces in the rear of the German Panzer divisions and motorised infantry divisions that are following them up. It seems that there is at present a vacuum behind this first echelon;

---

[3] J. Minart: *P. C. Vincennes, Secteur 4* (1945), p. 187.

3. To prepare, with all available means, an offensive in the direction of the Mézières bridges;

4. All French and British air resources should now have as their aim participation in the battle:

From the fighter angle, to retain, as a priority, the command of the air on First Army Group's front, and protect our movements along strategic routes by all possible means;

From the bomber angle, to act against the German columns moving west by taking them in the rear and *remontant* their routes to the west;

Subsequently and at the right moment, hold themselves ready to support the action of the 2nd Army;

In the interval, take action by means of bombing and river mines against the Meuse bridges;

5. *Everything is a matter of hours—Le tout est une question d'heures.*

Signed: Gamelin.[4]

Gamelin showed the text to Doumenc and Koeltz and signed it, after certain amendments, at 9:45 a.m., giving orders for copies to be sent to Reynaud, Daladier, and Pétain. Then, in the large downstairs salon, he read it to Georges and Vuillemin and a few other officers. The listeners stood attentively as he recited the directive in calm, measured tones. Quietly Georges and Vuillemin signified their approval. Alone with these two, he told them that if the plan did not succeed, he thought it would be difficult to defend metropolitan France. "But," Vuillemin interjected, "shouldn't the Government be warned?" "It will be time enough if the operations turn out badly," answered Gamelin. "If we raise this possibility now, they'll call us pessimists and say we have given up in advance."[5] As Georges went off to issue instructions, Gamelin took a stroll in the garden with Vuillemin, whom he admired as "a magnificent soldier."[6] He was interrupted by a message informing him—for the first time—that Weygand was due to arrive in Paris that morning. Apparently unruffled, he replied with an invitation to the general to come and meet him at Les Bondons.[7] Over the years Gamelin had achieved a remarkable self-control. Now, though obviously guessing what his own fate was to be, he

---

[4] Gamelin: *Servir* (1946), Vol. I, pp. 3–4.
[5] Ibid., Vol. III, p. 431.
[6] Ibid.
[7] Later, he changed the rendezvous to Vincennes.

gave no hint of his feelings. Lunching as Georges's guest soon
after, he seemed the most carefree person at table. While Georges
sat pale and dejected, surrounded by worn-out, anxious colleagues,
Gamelin managed to keep up a show of small talk and even muster
a joke. For Captain André Beaufre, who was present with his
chief, Doumenc, there was a ghastly air of pantomime about that
lunch. The chef, he recorded, had made brave efforts to produce
a banquet worthy of a "wedding feast." Instead, it turned out more
like a "burial repast."[8] The *pièce de résistance* was the sweet—a
huge raised confection, Beaufre recalls, covered with angels' hair
(*cheveux d'ange*). Gamelin ate it with relish and drank his coffee,
imperturbable as ever.

Gamelin's one piece of comfort that day came from the
British. After lunch General Dill called at Les Bondons to assure
him on behalf of General Ironside, C.I.G.S., that his orders, what-
ever they might be, would be carried out by the British forces.
Fully aware of the gravity of the situation, Ironside proposed a
meeting somewhere in the north. But undue hopes were promptly
dashed by a telephone call to Georges from Billotte at First Army
Group. Georges returned from the telephone to tell Gamelin:
"Billotte claims that the British are considering withdrawing on
Calais and Dunkirk."[9] Gamelin could only repeat to Georges what
Dill had just said, and on this uncertain note he hurried back to
Vincennes.

In Paris, at the great Cathedral of Notre Dame, a solemn ceremony was in progress. The government had come in a body to
attend a service of prayer for the granting of victory to France.
Among the procession of dark-clad ministers and other notables
the crowd picked out the small figure of Reynaud, his features
calm and resolute; Daladier, limping as a result of a recent fall
from a horse; Mandel, in a long black cloak; Bullitt, the United
States ambassador, sporting a white gardenia. Onlookers were
surprised to note so many French personalities known for their
agnostic views interceding with the Almighty. Many Parisians
concluded that things must be going badly indeed for such men
to be seen in church.

---

[8] A. Beaufre: *Le Drame de 1940* (1965), p. 238.
[9] Gamelin: *Servir*, Vol. III, p. 432.

From Notre Dame Reynaud drove not to the Quai d'Orsay but to the Ministry of War in the rue Saint-Dominique. That morning he had taken over from Daladier as War Minister—implementing the third of his decisions to stiffen the French war effort, and removing from Gamelin his strongest prop and closest political ally. The change had been made the day before, and Daladier was now Minister of Foreign Affairs, while Mandel had been transferred to the Ministry of the Interior. Daladier had told Gamelin of the moves while waiting with him at Vincennes for Reynaud and Pétain. "I wondered if I ought to stay in the Government," he said. "But I thought that, at this critical moment, I ought not to desert and create difficulties."[1] As Reynaud admitted, he knew nothing about the Ministry of War, and deeply regretted not having taken it on two months before. Now, at his unfamiliar desk in the spacious Empire-style apartment looking out on the tree-shaded courtyard of the Ministry, Reynaud awaited his most important interview that day—with General Maxime Weygand.

Weygand landed at Étampes airfield, 35 miles southwest of Paris, soon after midday on the nineteenth. During the early hours of the eighteenth, he had left Beirut with his aide, Captain Gasser, and had stopped overnight at Tunis. There was an ill omen about his arrival on French soil. As the Glenn Martin plane touched down, its undercarriage broke and it pancaked on its belly right across the airfield. Weygand clambered out of the twisted fuselage, shaken but unhurt, and drove on to Paris. By early afternoon, alert and dapper in his khaki tunic and riding breeches, he was in conference with Reynaud at the rue Saint-Dominique. "I offered him the succession to Gamelin," wrote Reynaud, "who seemed to all of us responsible for the disaster."[2] He added that he intended to allot Weygand the broadest powers by appointing him Commander in Chief in all theaters, ground, sea, and air. Weygand did not consent immediately. He wanted time to consider and examine the situation for himself. Asking permission to visit Gamelin's and Georges's command posts, he left for Vincennes with Gasser at about three o'clock.

---

[1] Ibid., Vol. III, p. 416.
[2] Reynaud: *Fight,* p. 344.

He arrived to find Gamelin not yet back from Les Bondons. While awaiting his return, Weygand discussed the position with staff officers around a map in the operations room. Then Gamelin returned and, after a few words of greeting, ushered him to his office. For both men this was a tense and painful moment. They were old associates and to some extent rivals—Gamelin had been Chief of Staff when Weygand was Commander in Chief; and Gamelin, Weygand's successor, had recommended him for the Near East command in 1939. Each drew his different military ideas from a great World War I leader—Weygand from Foch, and Gamelin from Joffre. In his quick nervous energy, Weygand was even reminiscent of Foch. Gamelin, though he lacked the heavy stolidity of Joffre, possessed Joffre's unflurried calm. Under the stress of the last ten days—and notably the last hours—that calm had been sorely tried. Now it was wearing thin. As the two generals faced each other in Gamelin's office, Weygand was struck by the change in Gamelin, whose "face showed traces of fatigue and anxiety."[3] Weygand told him briefly that he had been called to Paris and was putting himself in touch with the situation. Gamelin then expounded at length his Personal and Secret Instruction No. 12 of that morning, which, as he explained, involved breaking the encirclement of the northern armies, restoring their contact with the southern forces, and creating a new continuous line along the Somme and the Aisne. Weygand was "entirely in agreement with this conception," Gamelin recorded. Weygand mentioned that he was proposing to visit Georges at Les Bondons. "Since you're going to see him," Gamelin replied, "do get him to organise himself and his staff better. You like him and he'll listen to you. He works in an atmosphere of total confusion. He attends to far too many details himself and he's wearing himself out." As he left, Weygand said suddenly: "You know that Paul Reynaud doesn't like you?" "I know that," answered Gamelin.[4]

At Les Bondons Weygand was shocked by the altered appearance of Georges, who came out into the garden to meet him and Gasser. The Commander in Chief looked exhausted and told Weygand that he had not been sleeping. Moving to Georges's

---

[3] Weygand: *Recalled,* p. 48.
[4] Gamelin: *Servir,* Vol. III, pp. 432–3.

office, they passed members of his staff, who rose from their desks and "bowed mournfully."[5] After a forty-five minutes' talk with Georges, Weygand left late that afternoon for the rue Saint-Dominique. He had seen enough at Vincennes and Les Bondons to make him decide to accept the appointment.

When Weygand was shown into Reynaud's room at the War Ministry around 6:30, Pétain was with the Premier. Reynaud had asked the aged marshal to be present to meet Weygand and hear his decision. Weygand "told me that he would accept command," wrote Reynaud.[6] Paul Baudouin, who was in attendance as Secretary of the War Cabinet, was so certain of Weygand's acceptance that, according to his account, he prepared the decrees nominating him to succeed Gamelin without instructions from Reynaud. Re-entering the room after leaving the documents there, he heard Weygand telling Reynaud: "Very well, I accept the heavy responsibility you give me. You will not be surprised if I cannot answer for victory, nor even give you hope of victory."[7] Much moved, Reynaud shook Weygand's hand and thanked him "for his courageous decision, which France will know how to appreciate fully."[8] He then signed the decrees, one of which canceled the functions of the Commander in Chief, ground forces, and the other appointed Weygand Chief of Staff of National Defense and Commander in Chief of all theaters of operations, thus giving him greater powers than ever Gamelin had possessed. As the general left the room, he said ruefully to Baudouin: "You were right when you told me on the day I went away, that I would be recalled by aeroplane, and that I would arrive after a disaster." Baudouin asked him his first impression of events. "Bad," Weygand replied. "The position is grave, but one must not despair."[9]

Gamelin was to be notified of the changes at once. Reynaud stayed behind in his office to write him a covering letter—virtually a letter of dismissal—to accompany the copies of the decrees that were being sent to him. Waiting for the letter to be typed, he

[5] Weygand: *Recalled*, p. 48.
[6] Reynaud: *Fight*, p. 344.
[7] P. Baudouin: *The Private Diaries (March 1940 to January 1941)*, trans. Sir Charles Petrie (1948), p. 35.
[8] Benoist-Méchin: *60 Jours*, p. 214.
[9] Baudouin: *Private Diaries*, p. 35.

casually opened a drawer of his desk and discovered the file on Gamelin, left there by Daladier. Reynaud glanced through the notes on Gamelin's early career. As a young second lieutenant, Gamelin had been highly commended, he read, graduating from Saint-Cyr in top place. With a pang of compunction the Prime Minister realized he might have phrased his letter to him more warmly. He thereupon canceled his first draft and wrote another. "I have the honour," he said, "to bring to your notice two decrees which the President of the Republic has just signed. I am sending you the thanks of the Government for the services which you have given the country during a long and brilliant career."[1]

At Vincennes, Gamelin now knew beyond doubt that his hours of command were numbered: he awaited only the final notification. General Maurice Gamelin was paying the price of twofold failure. Not only had his Dyle Plan foundered disastrously, but he had mishandled, it was argued, his relations with Georges and neglected to exercise proper control of the battle. But, to the last, Gamelin was to maintain that he had acted entirely within his terms of reference as Supreme Commander. He would be strongly assailed for opening his Personal and Secret Instruction of that morning with the diffident phrase: "Without wishing to intervene in the conduct of the battle . . ."[2] Yet he insisted that "the battle is the affair of the North-East Command," that he did not wish to wound the susceptibilities of Georges, and that in any case Supreme Headquarters was concerned with the broader issues of relations with the air force and navy, the government, the British through General Ironside, and the Dutch. His military responsibility, as he saw it, was "to help those charged with carrying out operations, not to hinder or embarass them."[3] This was the general arrangement that Daladier had explained to Parliament, with Parliament's unanimous approval. Only when Gamelin was convinced that he ought to step in over the head of the Commander in Chief, Northeast, did he envisage going beyond these provisions. Such a moment had come that morning. His critics would say that he should have intervened much sooner, perhaps as early as the

---

[1] Reynaud: *Fight*, p. 345.
[2] Gamelin: *Servir* (1946), Vol. I, p. 3.
[3] Ibid., Vol. III, p. 428.

tenth—and in a more decisive way. Basically it was a matter of interpretation, stemming from the unwieldy and ambiguous structure of the High Command. A more ruthless and dynamic commander than Gamelin might have read his brief differently—or torn it up altogether when he saw that Georges was being overwhelmed by the tide of the German advance.

Meanwhile Gamelin continued to act out his role of Generalissimo with growing weariness. Among his callers that evening was General Corap. The indignant Corap wanted to know why he had been summarily removed from the 7th Army almost before he had been appointed to it. Gamelin went toward him with outstretched arms. "My poor friend," he said, "you've had a hard blow. But I told Paul Reynaud and Marshal Pétain yesterday that your honor as a soldier was not in question. Wait patiently. . . . For the moment you will be kept on the reserve. We shall examine calmly the events in which you have been involved."[4] "But the Somme is my country," declared Corap. "I was commanding it in peace time! I fortified it! I am just the man to command that region!" "Yes, perhaps you are," Gamelin admitted absently. Then the mask dropped for an instant. "Anyway, it's of no importance. We are all done for. Weygand is going to take over command. But what's the point? Everything's lost."[5]

As Gamelin brooded in his office, his staff (according to Colonel Minart) was being seized by something like panic. Back from a day-long visit to Montry and Les Bondons, Minart found the command post seemingly in the throes of removal, with officers hastily packing their baggage. Cupboards were almost cleared, and the 75mm. gun had been withdrawn from the north gate, after loud protests about its uselessness. For Minart, the sorry scene crowned what had been a day of discouragement. Observing the situation from Doumenc's and Georges's headquarters, he had concluded that Gamelin's Personal and Secret Instruction No. 12 was already a dead letter. "From hour to hour, events were overtaking the intentions of the High Command," he recorded.[6] Increasing enemy pressure and widespread disorder in and behind

---

4 Ibid., Vol. III, p. 433.
5 P. Allard: *La Vérité sur l'Affaire Corap* (1941), p. 49.
6 Minart: *P. C. Vincennes*, p. 194.

the French lines were rendering any sort of coherent plan unworkable. Amid the confusion reigning at Georges's command post, one figure stood out—the forceful, indomitable Doumenc. Whatever he thought of the real chances of Gamelin's plan succeeding, Doumenc was working with galvanic energy to get men, materials, and equipment to the front. "He stimulates, pushes, jostles," said Minart admiringly.[7]

Minart hurried to report to Gamelin. His chief was alone, seated at his desk facing the door, rubbing his soft, well-kept hands gently together in a characteristic motion. Minart described the disorganization at Les Bondons and then broached an idea he had been considering. "You have only one alternative, *mon general*," he said. "That is, to give the command of the French Army to Huntziger."[8] Since the Sedan rout, Huntziger's XXI and XVIII Corps had made a firm stand to the south and east of Sedan. He had inspired his troops by his coolness and determination. One battle-weary battalion commander, listening to him speak, exclaimed: "After that, I feel another man. What a pity my comrades weren't here."[9] Recently Huntziger had issued an army order, aimed at countering the spread of panic and restoring morale, of which he had 25,000 copies printed at Rheims and which had so impressed Reynaud that he had ordered it to be reproduced in the national press. Now Huntziger seemed to Minart pre-eminently the best commander to replace Georges. Exhausting every argument he could think of, Minart closed by urging: "He's the man we must appeal to. Let me take a car and escort you to him."[1] Gamelin had listened in silence. Finally he raised his hands in a hopeless gesture. Minart knew that he was speaking to a defeated man.

At about 9 p.m. a staff car drew up at the north gate of the fort. From it stepped a member of the War Minister's Military Cabinet, Captain Bonnet, carrying an important personal communication for Gamelin. Two or three officers watched as Bonnet, looking pale and strained, entered the casemates. In Gamelin's office he handed the general the two decrees and Reynaud's letter. "It is the end for me—*C'en est fini pour moi*," wrote Gamelin. He

---

[7] Ibid., p. 195.
[8] Ibid., p. 196.
[9] E. Ruby: *Sedan, Terre D'Epreuve* (1948), p. 215.
[1] Minart: *P. C. Vincennes*, p. 197.

telephoned Darlan, Vuillemin, and Georges to say good-bye. To his aides he remarked laconically: "I wish General Weygand greater success than I've had."[2]

By ten the next morning, after a brief meeting with Weygand and a cool final handshake, Gamelin had left Supreme Headquarters. His car headed west into Paris, bound for his modest ground-floor apartment in the avenue Foch, and obscurity. Only his immediate entourage saw him off. A few curious clerks looked out of office windows. The guard turned out to give a general's salute. Gamelin's quiet going recalled the departures of other French Commanders in Chief suddenly axed in the middle of war: the wry leave-taking of Joffre from GHQ, Chantilly, in December 1916; the silent disappearance of Nivelle from GHQ, Compiègne, in May 1917. "The old stones of Vincennes have just witnessed a new execution," wrote Minart, overstressing the melodrama.[3]

---

[2] Gamelin: *Servir*, Vol. III, p. 434.
[3] Minart: *P. C. Vincennes*, p. 198.

Chapter 13

WEYGAND TAKES OVER

"But men are made of flesh and blood."
(Captain Beaufre)

SMALLISH, WIRY, AND TRIM OF FIGURE, General Weygand was
vigorous for his seventy-three years. Emerging from his first
conference at GHQ, Montry, on the afternoon of the twentieth, he
astonished the staff by leaping down the garden steps and sprinting
100 yards across the grass. His bulky aide-de-camp, Captain
Gasser, trailed behind. The show of energy had a tonic effect on
Doumenc's officers: it seemed to promise a new strong grip on
affairs at that dark moment. Weygand himself gained "a heartening
impression" from his initial contact with Montry.[1] But he was less
satisfied with the Vincennes–Montry–La Ferté command organization as a whole. His complaint was not that Gamelin's staff
failed to intervene with Georges, but that it intervened without
going through General Doumenc, Army Chief of Staff. He held that
if Gamelin wished to be relieved of direct command of the north-
eastern armies, he should have afforded Georges the proper means
of exercising the command instead of only a modest staff at La
Ferté. If, on the other hand, he wished to exercise the command
himself, he should have had the necessary bureaus centralized at
Vincennes. In fact, he had done neither. Weygand's remedy was
to impose a much tighter personal control, "to do nothing in
future without Georges, to assume with him and over him every

---

[1] M. Weygand: *Recalled to Service*, trans. E. W. Dickes
(1952), p. 51.

responsibility."[2] Abandoning Vincennes as his main headquarters, he forthwith installed himself and his immediate staff in Doumenc's office at Montry, and arranged to eat in Doumenc's mess and sleep in a nearby villa.

From then on he was to observe an exacting daily routine. His first call was always at Montry, where he received reports, made decisions, issued instructions. Then he would drive out to see General Georges at Les Bondons, and sometimes follow with a visit to General Besson, commander of his new Third Army Group (formed by him on the twentieth to cover Paris) at Fer-rières-en-Brie. Here he might confer with Besson and Georges together. By eleven o'clock he was in Paris for the regular morning conference with Reynaud, Pétain, and later Darlan, at the Ministry of War. After lunch he would hurry off to an army command post, look in at Vincennes, or visit Georges again. Later he might make a second trip to Paris. For this extended round he had two sets of cars and two parties of motorcycle escorts.

The new Supreme Commander was now to be in personal contact with General Georges twice or even three times a day. He quickly noted the improvement in Georges' morale. He told Reynaud on the twentieth that when he had first met him the previous day, "Georges was like a man who had received a violent blow in the stomach and finds it difficult to pull himself together again." "But today," said Weygand, "he is better. He feels that he is being backed, and I am doing everything I can to put some energy into him. I have the impression he will be all right."[3] The next day he sent Georges a personal note urging that the army's defense be inspired with a "character of resolution, aggressiveness, ingenuity, and persistence which should render it implacable."[4] On the twenty-fourth he was to say to Baudouin: "General Georges feels that I am backing him, for I always tell him that I share his responsibilities to the full."[5]

Weygand's immediate plan—based on Gamelin's Personal and Secret Instruction—was to unite the northern and southern

[2] Ibid., p. 54.
[3] P. Baudouin: *The Private Diaries (March 1940 to January 1941)*, trans. Sir Charles Petrie (1948), p. 37.
[4] Weygand: *Recalled*, p. 119n.
[5] Baudouin: *Private Diaries*, p. 45.

forces by means of concerted attacks from north to south (Arras toward Amiens) and south to north (Amiens toward Arras). This would seal off the German armored spearheads and release the northern armies from the imminent threat of encirclement. That day he telephoned Billotte at Douai, ordering the First Army Group to strike southward. The troops must fight "*comme des chiens*," he urged Billotte.[6] But the despondent Billotte was fast losing hope of any recovery. The previous day, visiting General Prioux at his command post at Oppy, southwest of Douai, he had unburdened himself about what he considered the desperate position of the First Army Group and—with the Oise Valley lying open and undefended—the danger menacing Paris. "Neither I nor 1st Army can any longer give you the orders which the situation demands, in time for them to be effective," he told Prioux.[7] But even while Weygand was spurring on Billotte, the situation was worsening still further. On Monday, the twentieth, driving steadily west, Guderian's tanks took Amiens and reached Abbeville at the mouth of the Somme. The Germans had gained the Channel and separated the million-strong French, British, and Belgian forces in the north from the French armies in the south.

In a huge, snowballing mass behind the Allied front moved that other army—the refugees. To the enemy these fleeing northern populations were worth several divisions for the disruption they had already caused among 1st Army Group's communication lines. The British, at least, had foreseen the refugee problem that would arise if and when the Germans advanced in the thickly populated Lille-Roubaix-Tourcoing area. During the previous winter they prepared a large-scale evacuation plan, by which some 800,000 people would be shifted and dispersed, in case of need, to northwest France. This plan had been put into effect, and the zone was largely clear of civilians as the Allies began to retire. But on the afternoon of the twentieth General Alan Brooke, commanding the British II Corps, was astounded, on leaving his Wambrechies headquarters, to see thousands of fugitives surging not westward but from west to east—back to the evacuation zone. "They were all haggard-looking," he noted, "and many women were in the

---

[6] A. Beaufre: *Le Drame de 1940* (1965), p. 241.
[7] R. Prioux: *Souvenirs de Guerre* (1947), p. 93.

last stages of exhaustion, many of them with their feet tied up
with string and brown paper where their shoes had given out. They
were covered with mud from throwing themselves into the ditches
every time a plane flew over. There were old men trundling their
wives in wheelbarrows, women pushing prams piled high with all
their belongings, and all their faces distorted by fear . . ."[8] Brooke
immediately contacted the Prefect of the Nord Department, who
confirmed that these were the 800,000 evacuees from the Lille
region, returning to their homes. These luckless folk had been
caught in the rear by the panzers sweeping across northern France,
and were herding away from one danger toward another.

That day, in his first Order to the Allied armies, Weygand
strove to rally his troops to a maximum effort:

> Having been summoned by the confidence of the the Govern-
> ment to the post of Commander of the whole of the theatres of
> operations, I count upon everyone bringing fierce energy to the
> accomplishment of his duty in all circumstances.
> No failure, whatever its source, can or will be tolerated.
> It is well to resist, it is still better to return blow for blow,
> but victory will be secured only by the man who hits harder
> than he is hit.[9]

Now began the Battle of Flanders and Picardy. Under the
radiant sun of that May, the old battle grounds of World War I
would be fought over again, the old names figure once more in the
dispatches—Courtrai, Ypres, Menin, Douai, Lens, Arras. For nine
days the encircled Allied armies in the north would fight desperately
to ward off the growing German pressure. Rolled back from the
Escaut to the Lys and then to the coast around Dunkirk, the
British and part of the French forces would embark on their mass
evacuation. Meanwhile the Belgian Army would surrender unconditionally. Daily the process of defeat continued. On the
twenty-first, as Weygand confirmed his plan for a double Allied
counterblow from north to south, the Germans captured Arras;
and away in the southeast, Rethel fell. Next day Guderian's armored divisions raced up the French coast to attack Boulogne, and

---

[8] A. Bryant: *The Turn of the Tide,* (1957), Vol. I, p. 111.
[9] Weygand: *Recalled,* p. 72.

German bombers pounded Boulogne, Ostend, Calais, and Dieppe. On the twenty-third the British were forced to withdraw from Arras, recaptured the day before. On the twenty-fourth Boulogne fell, Calais was invested, the Germans took Tournai, and there was fighting in Ghent. On the twenty-fifth the Germans completed their encirclement of the northern armies, and the Belgians showed signs of breaking. Two days later the Allies had to abandon the pocket they held at Valenciennes and retire northward. On the twenty-eighth the Belgians surrendered; and by then the British would have started to evacuate the beaches of Dunkirk.

Throughout Monday, the twentieth, one question troubled Weygand: Would the twenty-four Belgian divisions, the nine British, and the twelve of Blanchard's army be able to avoid the German trap? Communications were so bad that he decided to go and investigate the situation for himself. This entailed a hazardous journey through or over the enemy lines. Reynaud, whom he saw that evening with Pétain, was so worried at the risks that he tried to dissuade him. "It would be a fatal blow to France," he told Weygand, "if you were taken prisoner or your plane shot down."[1] Backed by Pétain, Weygand declared that it was essential for him to go. He thereupon arranged a conference for next day, at a Belgian rendezvous to be decided on with Generals Billotte and Ironside and the King of the Belgians. The meeting finally took place at the Ypres Town Hall at 3 p.m. Weygand and his staff arrived there after a journey marked by mishaps and delays. At the Le Bourget airfield, their departure point, no plane was ready and their takeoff was held up for an hour. Heading north, Weygand's aircraft and escorts were attacked by a group of Messerschmitts. They landed, as planned, at an airfield near Bethune—to find it devastated by bombs and abandoned. Weygand's staff toured the countryside to find a telephone in order to contact General Billotte. It was then decided to fly on to Calais airfield—also wrecked by bombing. At Calais, Weygand met General Champon, French liaison officer with King Leopold, and managed to obtain a car to complete the journey to Ypres. For four hours those at the conference discussed the coordination of the Allied forces in Belgium, the carrying out of Weygand's counter-

---

[1] Baudouin: *Private Diaries,* p. 36.

attack plan, and an Allied withdrawal westward if the plan should fail. When Weygand left at 7 p.m., Lord Gort, who was supposed to attend the meeting, had not yet arrived. On his appearance an hour later, Billotte reported the proceedings to him.

Tragedy followed close on this conference. Driving back in the darkness, along traffic-congested roads, to his headquarters at Béthune, General Billotte met with a fatal accident. He was rushed to the hospital with a fractured skull, and died next day. He might have been saved if he had worn a tin helmet like his driver. "A general of great character," in Beaufre's view,[2] Billotte had carried a heavy burden of command over the past twelve days, and was becoming overwhelmed by the strain. Weygand, meeting him on the twenty-first after a long interval, noted that "the fatigues and anxieties of the past two weeks had left a deep mark on him."[3] General Ironside, reporting to the British War Cabinet late on the twenty-first, commented that for over a week he had "failed to carry out his duties of co-ordination and appeared to have no plans."[4] Billotte was to be replaced forthwith by Blanchard, from the 1st Army.

While Weygand sat in conclave at Ypres, in Paris Paul Reynaud was addressing a hushed and startled Senate. In frank, unvarnished terms he revealed for the first time the full extent of the Allied disaster. "The country is in danger," he solemnly told the House.[5] Explaining the strategy that had committed the French and British to leave their fortified lines and advance into Belgium, he described the German attack against the hinge of the French Army between Sedan and Namur. He candidly admitted the weakness of Corap's army, and stressed the difficulty of defending the Meuse—"mistakenly considered as a serious obstacle to the enemy."[6] "That is not all," he went on. "Through unbelievable faults, which will be punished, bridges over the Meuse were not

---

[2] A. Beaufre: *Drame de 1940* (1965), pp. 242-3.

[3] Weygand: *Recalled*, p. 64.

[4] W. S. Churchill: *The Second World War*, Vol. II: *Their Finest Hour* (1949), p. 55.

[5] H. F. Armstrong: *Chronology of Failure: The Last Days of the French Republic* (1940), p. 41.

[6] Ibid., p. 42.

destroyed. Across these bridges the Panzer divisions passed to the attack, preceded by fighter planes which attacked our scattered, badly organised, badly trained divisions." After further words he added what amounted to a weighty condemnation of French military policy: "The truth is that our classic conception of warfare has run counter to a new conception . . ."[7] Reynaud's indictment carried bitter undertones: it was he who, six years before, had tried—unsuccessfully—to get Parliament to adopt De Gaulle's proposal for a French armored corps.

Senators and deputies from the northern areas had been bringing back their own reports—of chaos and confusion on refugee-packed roads, panicking civilians abandoning their homes on the strength of unidentified telephone calls, deserters throwing down their arms and seizing any available transport, huge stores of military and industrial materials left undestroyed in the path of the German advance. At Saint-Quentin there was said to be enough flour to feed a German army for a week; the warehouses of Roubaix were loaded with vast stocks of wool. Anxious members were asking how France could carry on without the coal and chemical and metallurgical production of the Nord Department. Paris was now believed to have only one week's coal supply. In the corridors of the Chamber of Deputies, Deputy Pierre Laval was heard to declare: "France has been placed in a situation in which she has no alternative but death or dishonour."[8] Reynaud's own choice was clear. When M. Charles-Roux, the new Secretary-General of the Foreign Ministry, called on him during the twenty-first, he explained the situation to him with the aid of a large map pinned to the tapestry in his office, and announced bluntly: "Whatever happens, I shall not surrender."[9]

The mood of Paris was tense and uneasy. Technically the capital was now in the Zone of the Armies, and although it was reprieved from the threat of imminent attack, Parisians were under no illusions about the war situation. Day by day the trickle of evacuation was growing. Alexander Werth had observed a telltale sign among the shoppers at the popular Galeries Lafayette: increased

[7] Ibid., p. 43.

[8] J. Bardoux: *Journal d'un Témoin de la Troisième . . . 1940* (1957), p. 319.

[9] P. Reynaud: *In the Thick of the Fight* (1955), p. 362.

buying of shoes and suitcases. Alarming rumors were rife and the
press had taken on a gloomier tone. "Each day that passes without
a catastrophe," announced *L'Époque* on the nineteenth, "should
be considered as a day of victory."[1] On the twentieth the papers
were reduced from four pages to two. By a hundred indications,
Frenchmen were aware of the deepening crisis. The government had
already ordered a twelve-hour day for all workers in aircraft factories, and aircraft engineers had been "mobilized." Soon Mandel,
Minister of the Interior, would call on government officials to work
a fifty-two-hour week and keep their offices open twelve hours
daily. Meanwhile, the nation took what comfort it could from
Reynaud's effort to stiffen resistance by the appointment of Pétain
and Weygand.

As First Army Group struggled back across the plains of
Flanders, its cohesion was weakening. Only a strong, decisive grip
from Army Group headquarters could keep the tired divisions of
three national armies operating as a unified force against Von
Reichenau's massive drive. For days this had been lacking. Now
Lord Gort, impatient at the absence of orders or communication
from Billotte, was considering the likelihood of the B.E.F. having
to act on its own. He even envisaged his nine divisions withdrawing
to the coast. In the confusion, new and grim possibilities were opening up. On the nineteenth Lord Gort informed the War Cabinet in
London that he was studying the prospects of a retirement—should
this become essential—toward Dunkirk. The Cabinet disagreed
with this plan, preferring that the B.E.F. should try to push south
to the Somme. General Ironside was thereupon sent to Belgium to
instruct Lord Gort accordingly. But while he was away, the War
Cabinet was making fateful decisions. At a morning meeting on the
twentieth, the Cabinet members discussed the position of the B.E.F.
"Even on the assumption of a successful fighting retreat to the
Somme," recorded Churchill, "I thought it likely that considerable
numbers might be cut off or driven back on the sea."[2] Churchill
quoted from the minutes of the meeting: " 'The Prime Minister
thought that as a precautionary measure the Admiralty should as-

---

[1] W. Picht: *La Fin des Illusions: l'An 1940* (1940), p. 46.
[2] Churchill: *Second World War*, Vol II, p. 52.

semble a large number of small vessels in readiness to proceed to
ports and inlets on the French coast.' " The plans for Dunkirk
were in train.

Ironside returned to Downing Street late on the twenty-first
with Lord Gort's comments on the War Cabinet instructions. The
British Commander in Chief had objected to the southward march
on several counts, adminstrative and operational. Lord Gort's view
was supported by Ironside's own account of the disorder prevailing
in the north. The Cabinet now faced a grave quandary: Should the
B.E.F.—alone or with the French and Belgians—try to force its
way south to the Somme, or should it retreat westward to Dunkirk and attempt a hazardous sea evacuation? To Churchill it
seemed vital to confer on the matter with Reynaud and Weygand.
He left for Paris by air early on Wednesday, the twenty-second.

Weygand himself was only just back from his Ypres meeting
of the day before. To reach Paris he had had to make a roundabout
trip that he described to Baudouin as "a veritable Odyssey."[3] As
flying was impossible due to the bomb-wrecked northern airfields,
Admiral Abrial, Commander of the Naval Forces of the North, put
at his disposal the torpedo boat *Flore*. The general embarked at
Dunkirk in a violent air raid and reached Cherbourg at dawn on
Wednesday after a detour by way of Dover. When he called on
Reynaud at 9:30 to report, he looked fresh and alert. Recounting
the results of the conference, he told the Premier: "I have issued
my orders; the northern group of armies, supported by the English,
are to move south to meet Frère's army which is to reach the
Somme. I have no choice. I must try to close the gap, and thus
cut-off the German formations from the bulk of their advancing
forces."[4] Reynaud, as Baudouin relates, entirely approved these
instructions, and then advised Weygand of Churchill's imminent
arrival.

This time the rendezvous was Vincennes. Reynaud arrived
there with Churchill at noon, driving through a bright springtime
Paris "under a sky," wrote Reynaud, "whose very beauty seemed
implacable in those tragic days."[5] Weygand was awaiting them,

---

[3] Baudouin: *Private Diaries*, p. 37.
[4] Ibid., p. 38.
[5] Reynaud: *Fight*, p. 363.

along with Dill, Ismay, and Air Vice-Marshal Pierce. The new Supreme Commander struck Churchill as "brisk, buoyant and incisive," making "an excellent impression upon all."[6] In the map-hung operations room, Weygand explained his plans. He stressed his offensive intentions, the essential aim being to subject the panzer units in the Amiens-Abbeville-Arras area "to constant pressure"— as the official minutes stated—"to allow the German armoured divisions no opportunity to act on their own initiative but to keep them perpetually on the move, to inflict losses on them, and to threaten their rear."[7] Weygand's aggressive approach appealed to Churchill. His scheme for a combined Franco-British strike southward also confirmed the British War Cabinet's own conclusions as to the right action to be undertaken by the B.E.F. He and Dill formally "welcomed" the plan; and Churchill thereupon drew up a résumé of the decisions:

It was agreed—

1. That the Belgian Army should withdraw to the line of the Yser and stand there, the sluices being opened.

2. That the British Army and the French First Army should attack south-west towards Bapaume and Cambrai at the earliest moment, certainly to-morrow, with about eight divisions, and with the Belgian cavalry corps on the right of the British.

3. That as this battle is vital to both armies and the British communications depend upon freeing Amiens, the British Air Force should give the utmost possible help, both by day and by night, while it is going on.

4. That the new French Army Group which is advancing upon Amiens and forming a line along the Somme should strike northwards and join hands with the British divisions who are attacking southwards in the direction of Bapaume.[8]

On paper the plan looked sound and logical. It represented the only possible means of extricating the First Army Group from the disaster of encirclement or evacuation. "But men are made of flesh and blood," commented Captain Beaufre, of these hard-pressed northern troops.[9] The Franco-British armies had been almost constantly on the move since May 10. Hustled, dive-bombed,

---

[6] Churchill: *Second World War*, Vol. II, p. 57.
[7] Reynaud: *Fight*, p. 365.
[8] Churchill: *Second World War*, Vol. II, p. 58.
[9] Beaufre: *Le Drame*, p. 243.

impeded by hordes of Belgian refugees, now, in growing disorder, they were threatened with attack from the rear by the panzer formations heading up the Channel coast. In the situation facing them, concluded Beaufre as he surveyed their predicament from GHQ, Montry, a successful breakout "was too much to hope from human capabilities."[1]

Fatigue was bearing heavily on troops and staffs alike. Marc Bloch, a Sorbonne professor serving at 1st Army HQ, Attiches, noted signs of stress among his colleagues—"haggard eyes, ill-shaved beards, a nervousness that changed from extreme irritability to a mood of impossible euphoria."[2] General Prioux, arriving at Attiches on the night of the twenty-fifth to assume command in place of Blanchard, found a state of chaos. Sleeping officers, clerks, and orderlies lay indiscriminately about the floor on paillasses, among papers and equipment. No bedding facilities had been provided for Prioux. Finally his aide discovered an empty attic for him, furnished with a bare metal mattress. "Never had I been worse off since the start of the campaign," wrote the dismayed Prioux.[3] The strain had been telling hardest on General Blanchard himself —pleasant-mannered, reserved, a military theoretician rather than a fighting general. Bloch recalled seeing him in his office at Attiches, sitting silent and motionless for an hour while contemplating a map spread out before him, "as if to seek in it the decision that was eluding him."[4] Now, suddenly thrust into the role of Army Group Commander, Blanchard was rapidly becoming overwhelmed. As a British staff officer put it, he was "helpless in the face of the unorthodox black magic of the German high command."[5] When he visited British GHQ on the twenty-fourth, General Alan Brooke was struck by his lost, bewildered look. Blanchard was studying a map, and Brooke "gathered the impression that he might just as well have been staring at a blank wall. . . . The blows that had fallen on us in quick succession had left him 'punch drunk' and unable to register events."[6]

---

[1] Ibid.

[2] M. Bloch, *L'Étrange Défaite* (1946), p. 128.

[3] Prioux: *Souvenirs*, p. 144.

[4] Bloch: *Étrange Défaite*, p. 48.

[5] *The Diary of a Staff Officer at Advanced Headquarters North, B.A.F.F., 1940* (1941), p. 47.

[6] Bryant: *Turn of the Tide*, Vol. I, pp. 119–20.

In these crucial hours, as Blanchard took over from Billotte, no concerted counterattack from the north was in fact made. On the twenty-first—the day before Churchill's visit to Paris—the British, supported by light French forces, launched a limited assault on Arras that was briefly successful. But a forced withdrawal was made on the night of the twenty-third. And on the twenty-fourth Gort and Blanchard agreed to execute a combined attack on the twenty-sixth. But this never materialized: the routing of the Belgians, now near total defeat, compelled Lord Gort to pull back his troops in order to protect his left flank. Early on the twenty-fourth Weygand sent a peremptory call to First Army Group: "I confirm the orders issued to you. . . . Salvation lies in the continuation of your manoeuvre southwards. I rely on the fierce resolve of all."[7] But resolve was no longer enough—although the spirit of many of these dogged northern troops was still unbroken, despite the many setbacks. "So we are encircled! It's flabbergasting!" wrote Captain Barlone of the 1st Army's 2nd North African Division, as his unit dug in near Orchies, northwest of Valenciennes, on the twenty-third. "Shall we succeed in breaking through the circle . . . ? The whole of the North of France, Belgium, our lines of fortifications, our immense quantities of material, hundreds of thousands of men . . . are perhaps about to fall into the hands of the Boches. The Army is now aware of it, but it is in no wise discouraged."[8] What was paralyzing the initiative of the First Army Group, in its tightening circle, was the indecision, misunderstanding, and lack of communication at command level, and the conflicting French and British interests that now began to emerge.

If the First Army Group was unable to join up with the southern armies, as now seemed probable, it was doomed as a fighting force; and the primary aim of the B.E.F. must be to disengage and evacuate while there was yet time. Churchill had this in mind when he telephoned Reynaud on the afternoon of the twenty-third to say, as quoted by Reynaud, "that because of the position of the German armoured divisions, he was wondering whether it would not be better if the British Army fought in retreat towards the coast." Reynaud replied: "Weygand is satisfied.

---

[7] Beaufre: *Le Drame*, p. 244.
[8] D. Barlone: *A French Officer's Diary* . . . , trans. L. V. Cass (1942), p. 53.

We ought not to change anything. We must follow the path which we have traced out."[9] But the British War Cabinet was increasingly worried by the apparent absence of coordination between the Allied armies. That morning Weygand had declared that they were "working hand-in-hand,"[1] and Reynaud had so informed Churchill. Late that night Churchill expressed his misgivings in a cable to Reynaud: "General Gort wires that co-ordination of northern front is essential with armies of three different nations. He says he cannot undertake this co-ordination, as he is already fighting north and south and is threatened on his lines of communications. At the same time Sir Roger Keyes[2] tells me that up to 3 p.m. to-day Belgian Headquarters and King had received no directive. How does this agree with your statement that Blanchard and Gort are *main dans la main*? . . . Nevertheless, we are instructing him to persevere in carrying out your plan."[3]

Weygand, however, began to suspect that the B.E.F. was abandoning his plan. Reporting to Reynaud and Pétain next morning, Friday, the twenty-fourth, he told the Premier that according to a telegram from General Champon, France's liaison officer with King Leopold, the British had pulled out of Arras unnecessarily and were moving back to the Channel ports. This, he said, obliged him to modify his maneuver, so that the junction between the northern and southern forces would now be made between Amiens and the sea instead of farther east between Amiens and Péronne. An ominous note crept into Weygand's review. If the junction was not effected quickly, he declared, "it would be very difficult to avoid the capitulation of the armies in the north, for they were already suffering from a shortage of munitions and even of victuals."[4] Reynaud asked him what he thought would happen if the northern formations were forced to surrender. Weygand replied that all the remaining French forces would be in position on the Somme, the Ailette Canal, and the Aisne, but "in these circumstances it would be very difficult to resist the German drive." Later that day he sent Reynaud a formal note: "I have the honour to inform you that, as a result of the withdrawal dur-

---

[9] Reynaud: *Fight*, p. 369.
[1] Baudouin: *Private Diaries*, p. 42.
[2] Churchill's liaison officer with King Leopold.
[3] Churchill: *Second World War*, Vol. II, p. 61.
[4] Baudouin, *Private Diaries*, p. 44.

ing the night of May 23 to 24 of the British Army on the Haute-Deule canal, the importance of which I realised this afternoon, I have directed the Commander of Number One Army Group, if he considers the manoeuvre previously ordered can no longer be carried out, to form a bridgehead as extensive as possible in front of the three northern ports . . ."[5] Within four days of its launching, the Weygand Plan was dead.

Now Weygand was considering the gloomiest eventualities. That evening he called Baudouin to Vincennes, where he had been discussing with General Georges the future of the French southern armies in the event of the surrender of the northern forces. He told Baudouin that he calculated he could then call on fifty divisions, of which eighteen were static formations. These would have to hold a 180-mile front from the Somme to the Aisne, as far as the Maginot Line. "Fifty divisions along this front would only constitute a sand-dune," he said, "and would not be able to withstand the pressure of 150 divisions and 10 armoured divisions. . . . I think that if there is a surrender in the north, the French Army ought to resist desperately on the Somme and Aisne positions. Then, when the enemy has broken this resistance, what is left of the French Army should continue to fight where it stands until it is annihilated."[6] Weygand added that he and Georges had come to this conclusion after searching the map in vain for a possible defensive line that could be held by fifty divisions. He asked Baudouin to pass their thoughts on to Reynaud. The two men went on to talk about the state of France and her ability to continue fighting. Finally Weygand confessed "with tears in his eyes" that he was uncertain whether the national morale would support a fight to the end, such as he had foreshadowed.[7] Baudouin drove back to the Quai d'Orsay to report to the Prime Minister. Reynaud also was full of doubts about French staying power—fierily declaring that he would resign if public opinion accepted a German peace offer. "I have always advocated war to the end!" he exclaimed.[8]

At Führer Headquarters, Germany, Hitler too was contemplating "war to the end." His two previous directives on the

---

[5] Reynaud: *Fight,* p. 369.
[6] Baudouin: *Private Diaries,* p. 46.
[7] Ibid., p. 47.
[8] Ibid.

Western offensive, of February 18 and May 14, had been implemented with an almost machinelike accuracy: indeed his sole fear had been that his forces would overreach themselves in their headlong advance westward. Now, on May 24, he issued his clear and uncompromising order for total military victory—Directive No. 13: "The next object of our operations is to annihilate the French, English and Belgian forces which are surrounded in Artois and Flanders. . . . The Army will then prepare to destroy in the shortest possible time the remaining enemy forces in France . . ."9

Whatever Lord Gort found himself compelled to do through lack of direction or coordination, or sheer military necessity, in London, Churchill and the War Cabinet were under the impression that the Weygand Plan was proceeding and Gort was cooperating in it. Late on the twenty-fourth, Churchill telegraphed Reynaud: "We have every reason to believe that Gort is still persevering in southward move. All we know is that he has been forced by the pressure on his western flank, to keep communication with Dunkirk for indispensable supplies, to place parts of two divisions between himself and the increasing pressure of the German forces, which in apparently irresistible strength have successfully captured Abbeville, are menacing Calais and Dunkirk, and have taken Saint-Omer . . ."1 This cable did not reach Reynaud until 1 p.m. on the twenty-fifth. Meanwhile, during the night Blanchard had notified Weygand that a Franco-British attack was being launched on the twenty-fifth in the eventual direction of Bapaume; and a few hours later Weygand informed Reynaud's office that the British were still in contact with the French 1st Army and he had suspended the order to withdraw on the ports.

Following on earlier reports that Lord Gort was pulling out and that the Weygand Plan was canceled, this was typical of the contradictions and uncertainties surrounding the Flanders operations. Amid the welter of conflicting messages and orders passing between London, Paris, and the various headquarters, priceless

---

9 H. R. Trevor-Roper, ed.: *Hitler's War Directives, 1939–1945* (1964), p. 27.
1 Reynaud: *Fight,* p. 372.

time was being lost and grave misconceptions created. For days Churchill had been increasingly worried about the faulty state of Franco-British liaison. On the twenty-second he had decided to remedy this by appointing a personal liaison officer between himself and Reynaud. The man he chose was General Edward Spears, whose knowledge of France and close acquaintance with many French political and military leaders dated from World War I. Now, on the morning of the twenty-fifth, Spears presented his credentials to his old friend Reynaud at the Quai d'Orsay. Henceforth he would have unrestricted entrée to Reynaud and his colleagues and participate in top-level French councils.

Any illusions about the First Army Group's ability to counterattack were dispelled at a meeting of the War Cabinet, held at noon in Reynaud's War Ministry office. Present besides Reynaud were Weygand, Pétain, Darlan, Baudouin, and Spears. After preliminary discussions Weygand introduced a staff officer from the First Army Group, Major Fauvelle, who had a report to make. Fauvelle had left General Blanchard's headquarters at Lille twenty-four hours before, reaching Paris after a laborious sea-and-land journey that took him as far as London. He was badly unnerved. "I have in my time seen broken men," Spears noted, "but never before one deliquescent." In answer to a question of Weygand's, he declared: "I believe in a very early capitulation." Fauvelle went on to describe how the 1st Army troops were "stupefied" by bombing, had no more bread, had lost all their heavy guns and almost run out of ammunition. Listening to him, "I felt cold fingers turning my heart to stone," wrote Spears.[2] Weygand's reaction was to launch an angry diatribe on the defects of the prewar French Army—clearly aimed at Pétain, archadvocate of the defensive theory of war, which, Weygand claimed in rasping tones, was responsible for the current troubles. Across the table Pétain sat silent, his head bowed. Speaking again, Fauvelle disclosed with the aid of a map tracing he had brought with him that only three of the 1st Army divisions were in a condition to attack, and these were supported by a single artillery unit. The British, he reported, seemed to be chiefly interested in preparations to re-embark, while the fighting capacity of

---

[2] E. L. Spears: *Assignment to Catastrophe* (1954), Vol. I, p. 189.

the Belgians was highly dubious. He reiterated that he believed early surrender inevitable. Weygand was so impressed that he thereupon announced his intention to order Blanchard to fall back on the Channel ports. "Blanchard is attacking southwards at this moment," Reynaud broke in indignantly. "You cannot countermand that offensive."[3] Finally Weygand instructed Fauvelle to fly back at once to Blanchard. "General Blanchard is a real leader of men," he said. "I leave it to him to do all he can to save the troops under his command. . . . They can only pass away with honour when there are no more guns to be fired. Until then, they must fight on, whether it is to break through to the south, or to fall back towards the ports. That is for General Blanchard to decide."[4]

Weygand did not seem to realize the immense individual burden being imposed on Blanchard. This was brought home to Spears just after the meeting, when Fauvelle told him: "Blanchard is exhausted by his attempt to command both the army group and his own army."[5] The startled Spears thought the matter important enough to be mentioned to Reynaud and Weygand, and asked Reynaud's *chef de cabinet* to do this.[6] For the rest, he endeavored to inject a little spirit into the faltering Fauvelle, who now talked in terms of France being lucky to avoid total defeat in the field— "*capitulation en rase campagne.*"

At seven that evening President Lebrun, Reynaud, Pétain, three ministers, Weygand, Darlan, Vuillemin, General Buhrer, and Baudouin, assembled at the Élysée Palace for a meeting of the War Committee. An air of uninhibited pessimism marked the assembly. The tone was set by Weygand in his opening statement on the military situation. After a résumé of the operations to date, he said: "It is my duty to prepare for the worst, that is to say for the eventuality that we may no longer have at our disposal the troops which comprise the northern group of armies."[7] Continuing, he

---

[3] Ibid., p. 191.
[4] Baudouin: *Private Diaries,* p. 49.
[5] Spears: *Assignment,* Vol. I, p. 197.
[6] On the night of the twenty-fifth, General Prioux assumed command of the 1st Army.
[7] Baudouin: *Private Diaries,* p. 51.

gave a chilling picture of future prospects. By mid-June, he told his grave-faced audience of political and military chiefs, the French Army would dispose, in all, 60 divisions. "In front of us," he said, "we have 130 to 150 divisions, of which nine are armoured. We are thus called upon to fight against odds of three to one. Nor is this all, for our tank formations have been reduced by four-fifths." The only strategic solution, Weygand asserted, was to "find a shorter line." His final conclusion was that the army "must hold on to the present Somme-Aisne position, and defend it to the bitter end. It contains many weaknesses . . . where it can be pierced. If that happens the fragments must constitute breakwaters, and each section of the army must fight to the last to save the honour of the country."

The meeting listened silently to the bleak forecast. Reynaud spoke next, agreeing with Weygand's insistence that the army's honor must be saved by "a fight to the death." Then he touched on the implications of military defeat. "In such circumstances," he asked, "is it not indispensable to avoid the capture of the Government if the enemy enters Paris?"[8] President Lebrun posed a more ominous question. In the event of the army's total destruction, he asked, "what freedom of action would the French Government enjoy if any offer of peace were made to it? Would not this freedom of action be greater before the destruction of the French armies?" Lebrun admitted that France had signed commitments that prohibited her from concluding a separate peace—"but if Germany makes any relatively advantageous offer we ought nevertheless to examine it closely and objectively." The answer came from Weygand. He appreciated the President's problem, he said, and he was aware that a cessation of hostilities was an inter-Allied matter. He also accepted that it was not necessary to adopt immediately the "extreme solution" which he had proposed, that of the army fighting to the end to save its honor, "without discussing the consequences of such a course with England."

A separate peace: the momentous issue, hitherto unvoiced but probably in the mind of more than one member of that committee for some days, was now out in the open. Perhaps to everyone's relief it was President Lebrun who first spoke the words. The men-

---

[8] Ibid., p. 53.

tion of them had at least allowed Weygand to retreat slightly from his fight-to-the-death position. But here Reynaud intervened, to stress that, if France received a peace offer, Britain must be fully consulted. "We are, as you know, tied by a definite engagement," he reminded the committee.[9] Weygand's reply was that since Britain was threatened with the loss of her British Expeditionary Force, the nucleus of her future army, she might well understand the French predicament. All this time Pétain had made no comment. Now he broke his silence to ask "if there was to be complete reciprocity of obligations between France and England." Insofar as Britain had fielded only ten divisions compared with France's eighty, he said, the French contribution—in suffering as well as military effort— was much larger than that of the British.[1] The aged marshal was airing a resentment about unequal Franco-British sacrifice that had burned in his mind ever since the years of World War I. The discussion went on, moving in favor of a speedy consultation with Britain. Finally Reynaud announced that he would visit London the next day, "and would explain clearly to the English the inequality of a struggle of three to one." He would say that despite this the French government was prepared to continue the fight, "even if that were nothing more than one for honour." He was careful to emphasize that Britain might well tell France that she was bound by her signature to fight on even though the struggle was hopeless.[2] The last word came from Weygand. The British must be told, he said, that a fight to the end "would inevitably mean the total destruction of all the French armed forces." What he was concerned about was the maintenance of order in the country, for without the army "no one could say what troubles might ensue."[3]

The meeting ended at ten past nine. In the dusk of the Paris evening the members left the Élysée Palace for their ministries, offices, and headquarters. This was the last War Committee meeting to be held before the armistice. Later it would become notorious for what was said, or alleged to be said, during its course. Grave doubts were raised about the accuracy of the minutes drafted by Baudouin, the War Cabinet Secretary. Some members

---

9 Ibid.
1 Ibid., p. 54.
2 Ibid., p. 55.
3 Ibid., p. 56.

claimed to possess versions differing from that of Baudouin. Heated controversy was to rage as to whether or not Reynaud himself talked about the possible granting of an armistice.[4] But one certainty was that the meeting revealed the basic split now developing between the members who were inclined toward a separate peace with Germany and those who wanted to honor France's pledge to Britain and fight on to the end, if necessary from North Africa.

In the wake of the westward-racing tanks of Von Kleist's and Hoth's panzer groups and their accompanying motorized divisions stretched a lengthening corridor of no man's land. Until the German infantry formations could arrive to fill this gap, it remained highly vulnerable to Allied attack. And in the late May days while the First Army Group battled stubbornly in Flanders, the French High Command placed its dwindling hopes on the counterblow from the south, as ordered in the Weygand Plan. Adequate forces were available. Poised behind the river lines from the Channel to the Ailette stood the best part of three armies—the newly formed Third Army Group of General Besson. The three divisions of General Robert Altmayer's 10th Army Detachment flanked the Lower Somme from Abbeville to the sea; to their right the seven divisions (some of them still arriving) of Frère's 7th Army guarded the Somme and part of the Lower Somme; and to their right again, Touchon's 6th Army covered the south banks of the Aisne and Ailette. (In a gallant action against heavy odds, troops of De Lattre de Tassigny's 14th Division had defended Rethel until forced to withdraw on May 19.) According to the Weygand Plan, the northward blow was to be struck by the 7th Army which, at least by the twenty-third, was able to pass from a defensive to an offensive role owing to the paucity of enemy troops facing it north of the Somme. But despite clear orders from Weygand, the expected thrust from the 7th Army failed to develop.

On the twenty-fifth Weygand conferred at Les Bondons with

---

4 Weygand's version of the minutes (*Recalled to Service*, pp. 428–35) includes a remark by Reynaud—"it does not follow that our adversary will grant us an immediate armistice"— alleged to have been struck out of the draft by the Prime Minister himself, after the meeting.

Georges, Doumenc, Koeltz, and Roton on matters of general future strategy. By now he was realizing that the First Army Group's counterattack was "gravely compromised." "As for the army that was to debouch from the Somme to meet it," he wrote, "General Georges had firmly hoped at first to stage an attack 'of a certain value' about 23rd May. But the days that passed brought increasing difficulties for the commander of the 7th Army in his double effort to form the manoeuvring force necessary for that attack while completing his defence line on the Lower Somme."[5] By this failure of the southern force, the doom of the First Army Group was doubly sealed. Now, short of a miracle, a major Allied disaster was inevitable.

But one French formation on the Somme set a stirring example. In a fierce four-day battle at Abbeville, distinction was won by De Gaulle's 4th Armored Division. Ten days before, the 4th had been in action around Laon, and since the twenty-second had covered 110 miles in a westward move to Grandvilliers, south of Abbeville. "From its birth in the fields of Montcornet, it had never stopped fighting or marching," wrote De Gaulle.[6] Gathering additional equipment en route, it now comprised 140 fully operational tanks and six infantry battalions, supported by six artillery groups. The morale of the troops was high, exuding, as De Gaulle said, "an atmosphere of keenness." Now, on the night of the twenty-sixth–twenty-seventh, General Altmayer of the 10th Army Detachment ordered De Gaulle—promoted to general two days earlier—to attack the powerful enemy bridgehead south of Abbeville. De Gaulle marked out three successive objectives and attacked at 6 p.m. on the twenty-seventh. By nightfall the first objective had fallen. By next evening, after heavy and costly fighting in which a third of the tanks were knocked out, the next objective was reached. The troops were jubilant: an air "of victory hovered over the battlefield," commented De Gaulle.[7] When the assault was resumed on the twenty-ninth, against the formidable Mont Caubert, the Germans had received strong reinforcements: De Gaulle had likewise been reinforced by the 5th Light Cavalry Division. At 5 p.m.,

[5] Weygand: *Recalled*, p. 95–6.
[6] C. de Gaulle: *War Memoirs*, Vol. I: *The Call to Honour*, 1940–42 (1955), p. 50.
[7] Ibid., Vol. I, p. 52.

without the air support he had requested, his troops pressed forward
to the slopes of the hill but failed to gain the crest. Next day the
4th was relieved by General Fortune's 51st Scottish Division. The
net result of the operation was that the bridgehead was reduced by
three quarters and the enemy could no longer "debouch from it in
force."[8] The 4th took five hundred prisoners and a large haul of
arms and equipment.

Not all senior commanders were showing De Gaulle's drive
and leadership. In the last days, ranging among command posts and
headquarters, Weygand had been casting a hard and searching eye
on his generals. Like Joffre in August 1914, he had made a ruthless purge of the incompetents. On the twenty-fifth a War Ministry
communiqué appeared, headed "Penalties," which announced the
removal of fifteen French generals, including army and corps commanders, several divisional commanders, and other high officers.
All had been replaced by men of Weygand's choice. Reading the
communiqué, Pétain took strong exception to the dismissals. "I
cannot allow the army to be blamed for errors of policy," he complained to Baudouin next day. "The real culprit is Daladier, for it
was he who created the Popular Front." The old marshal switched
to another subject: the proposal to fight to the end, with which
he vehemently disagreed. "It is at once easy and stupid to talk of
fighting to the last man," he said. "It is also criminal in view of our
losses in the last war and of our low birth-rate. In any case what is
the use of saying it when it cannot be done? A part of the army
must be saved, for without an army grouped around some leaders
to maintain order a true peace is impossible, and the reconstruction
of France will have no point of departure."[9]

But that same day Weygand, with the final battle for France
in mind, was steeling the armies of the Somme-Aisne River Line to
nothing less than a fight to the finish. In a General Order of
Operations, published on May 26, he declared:

1. The battle on which depends the fate of the country will
be fought without thought of retreat on the position we occupy
at present. All commanders, from the army commander to the

8 Ibid., Vol. I, p. 54.
9 Baudouin: *Private Diaries,* p. 57.

head of a section, must be animated by the fierce resolve to
fight to the death where they stand. If the leaders give the example, their troops will hold fast, and they will be right, in case of
necessity, in forcing their obedience.

2. To be certain of halting the enemy, it is necessary to show
constant aggressiveness. If the enemy shows offensive intentions
in a sector, he must be replied to by strong and rapid counter-
preparations. If the enemy succeeds in forming in our front
one of those bridgeheads of which he makes use for thrusting
in his tanks and passing on to the armoured attack, however
minute the bridgehead may be the enemy must be pushed back
at once to his lines, by crushing him under artillery fire and
bombing and by counter-attacking. Infiltration must be replied
to by infiltration. If a unit finds that the next unit has had to
give way, it must on no account retreat; it must try to restore
the situation, and if it cannot do that it must form a hedgehog
and constitute a bastion of resistance. That is as true for a
division as for a regiment, a battalion, a company.

3. All behind the principal line, from the front to the greatest
depth possible, must be organised in a chequer-work of centres
of resistance, particularly on the principal routes of access, by
which the Germans have always progressed up to now. Keep
a close watch on demolitions.

4. All generals of divisions should see their colonels very
frequently, the colonels their battalion commanders, the battalion
commanders their companies, the captains and lieutenants their
sections and men—*Activity-Solidarity-Resolution*.[1]

This was a ringing "last-ditch" call, with the accent on un-
yielding resistance. Two days later Weygand followed it up with a
General Instruction that was more specifically offensive in tone:

> In view of the general situation and of the character of the
> fighting in progress in the north, the commanders of all the
> echelons have the imperative duty of doing everything possible
> to keep the enemy threatened and anxious along the whole
> front.
> There is only one way to do that, to be constantly on the of-
> fensive, with all concerned, whether directing or directed, giving
> proof every moment of a resolute will to aggression.
> It is not a question only of offensives arranged by the higher
> echelons, which always demand resources and time during
> which the enemy has freedom of movement, but also, and espe-
> cially at the present time, of operations quickly arranged by the
> lower echelons down to the section and even the fighting group.

---

[1] Weygand: *Recalled*, pp. 97–8.

For the preparation of these operations and for success in them, everyone must call upon all the resources of an imagination unceasingly active, and on cunning as well as force. The enemy must feel that he is in the presence of men determined to strike at him without cessation, men whose astuteness and activity he finds formidable, and not courageous adversaries who remain inactive.[2]

In an elegant room at Admiralty House, London, Reynaud was conferring with members of the British Cabinet. He had flown to England early on this morning of the twenty-sixth as a result of his undertaking, given at yesterday's War Committee meeting. But besides the question of France's ability to continue fighting, he had another serious and urgent issue to discuss: Italy's threat to enter the war alongside Germany.

Since the signing of the Pact of Steel in May 1939, Italy had stood firmly aligned with Germany. From across the Alps, Mussolini had watched the Allied reverses with mounting satisfaction and a growing confidence that the moment had come for Italy to move in and gather the spoils of an easy victory. Convinced of the Duce's ultimate intentions, Reynaud had brought up the matter with him soon after becoming Premier the previous March. Again in April, when Mussolini publicly congratulated Hitler on his recent successes, Reynaud sent him a personal letter couched in pacific terms. "A war between us," wrote Reynaud, "would be a sacrilege against our common heritage." Mussolini's reply was a calculated snub: "Italy is and means to stay the political and military ally of Germany in adherence to the Treaty of May, 1939 . . . ."[3] Now, as Italian intervention seemed imminent, Reynaud proposed to try and buy the Duce off. His plan was that France and Britain should make Italy certain concessions involving the status of Gibraltar, Malta, Suez, Djibouti, and Tunis. This scheme he was putting before the British Ministers. After an initial private talk, Churchill and Reynaud were joined by Chamberlain, Lord Halifax, Attlee, and Eden. "We were not able to show any favour to these ideas," noted Churchill—though Reynaud thought that Halifax was impressed by his arguments.[4] In Churchill's view, the Allies could

---

[2] Ibid., p. 99.
[3] Reynaud: *Fight,* p. 403.
[4] Churchill: *Second World War,* Vol. II, p. 109.

offer Mussolini nothing he would not be able to obtain by a Nazi victory. Reynaud stressed the added dangers that would face Britain if Italy's entry made certain the loss of the Battle of France. Moreover, "I thought it my duty," he records, "to warn them that I would have difficulties with my Government if the Battle of France were lost, for Pétain would speak in favour of an armistice. It can be guessed how painful this confidence was . . . but I considered it my duty to take any step in order to defend the soil of France."[5] The sole comfort Reynaud gained from the meeting was Churchill's promise that the Cabinet would consider the matter and inform him the next day. The burning question as to whether and on what conditions Britain might permit France to break off the fight, Reynaud did not bring up. His own note on the matter states: "I did not speak to the British statesmen about continuing the war in North Africa, because I did not wish to weaken the effect of my repeated demands made to secure the co-operation of their air-craft."[6]

Met by Boudouin on his return to Le Bourget that evening, Reynaud confessed that he had had a trying interview. "The only one who understands is Halifax, who is clearly worried about the future," he said. "Churchill is always hectoring, and Chamberlain undecided."[7]

While Reynaud parleyed in London, events on the northern front were moving to a swift climax. The last coordinated resistance of Blanchard's armies was crumbling. Late on the twenty-fourth the Belgian 4th Corps, stationed on the Lys, was thrown back on a 13-mile front between Menin and Courtrai by a powerful enemy attack, supported by tanks. Learning this early on the twenty-fifth, Lord Gort saw himself in an awkward position: his forces, on the right of the Belgians, risked being separated from them at Menin, and the Belgian Army would, he believed, be forced to retreat northward instead of westward. Above all, it seemed that the Franco-British counterattack to the south (planned for the twenty-sixth) would finally have to be abandoned. That morning

---

5 Reynaud: *Fight*, p. 405.
6 Ibid., p. 406*n*.
7 Baudouin: *Private Diaries*, p. 58.

Inside the Maginot Line

RADIO

ABOVE:
*President Lebrun with
Colonel Charles de Gaulle*
BELOW:
General Gamelin

ABOVE:
General Georges
BELOW:
General Weygand

Paul Reynaud (front center), France's new Prime Minister, with his Cabinet, March 1940, and Edouard Daladier, whom he succeeded, seen on his right

ABOVE:
General Huntziger
BELOW:
The Germans enter Paris

Aftermath of Dunkirk: French troops landing in Britain, June 1940

The French delegates arrive for the Armistice talks, June 21, 1940

Armistice negotiations in progress:
General Huntziger (extreme left), Field Marshal Keitel (extreme right)

France's new leader, Marshal Pétain, June 1940

Sir John Dill visited his headquarters and was so worried about the German breakthrough that he telegraphed London. By evening Gort was becoming alarmed at the widening gap between his forces and the Belgians, and decided to pull back to cover Ypres. He could not get in touch with Blanchard, who was in urgent conference at the Belgian GHQ at Bruges. Calling at Attiches next morning, he found that Blanchard had already resolved to cancel the southward counterattack and retire westward, owing to the dangerous situation of both 1st Army Group's flanks. After an hour's tense conference they agreed on a joint plan to withdraw the main bodies to the left bank of the Lys—subject to there being no further deterioration on the Belgian front. "I had not so far discussed with General Blanchard a further withdrawal to the sea," recorded Gort. "However, the possibility could not have been absent from his mind."[8]

Returning to his headquarters at midmorning, Gort found a telegram from Anthony Eden in London: ". . . Only course open to you may be to fight your way back to West where all beaches and ports east of Gravelines will be used for embarkation . . ."[9] Later that day, Sunday, the twenty-sixth, he received a further telegram from the War Office, which ended: "You are now authorised to operate towards coast forthwith in conjunction with French and Belgian Armies."[1]

But the Belgians were now in desperate straits. Twice that day Blanchard visited Belgian GHQ, striving to keep their flagging resistance alive. His overriding problem was the plugging of the breach around Courtrai. On his first visit King Leopold declared that he had no reserves left and his troops were incapable of staging another attack: he asked instead for a Franco-British counterblow in the threatened Menin-Courtrai sector. General Michiels, Leopold's Chief of Staff, thereupon sent Gort a call for immediate aid, explaining that the Belgians were no longer in a position to retire to the Yser as this would involve the destruction of their last available units. Revisiting Bruges that evening, Blanchard had to tell Leopold that Lord Gort was unable to counterattack at Courtrai and that the British were evacuating their positions on the

---

[8] Reynaud: *Fight*, p. 378.
[9] Ibid., p. 379.
[1] Ibid.

Belgian right for a line farther west, based on Ypres and Lille. This hard news came after the Belgian High Command had addressed to General Champon the following ominous note for forwarding to General Weygand, dated the twenty-sixth: "The Belgian High Command requests you to inform the Supreme Commander that the situation of the Belgian Army is grave. The High Command intends to continue the struggle to the extremity of its resources. At the present moment the enemy is attacking from Eecloo to Menin. The limits of Belgian resistance have very nearly been reached."[2]

On the right flank of the First Army Group's wavering line, the French 1st Army was making its way westward. On the twenty-fifth Weygand had telegraphed Blanchard: "The Prime Minister and I have received Major Fauvelle. We quite understand the situation. You will remain sole judge of the decisions to be taken to save what can be saved, and above all the honour of the flags of which you are the guardian."[3] But already on the twenty-sixth the honor of these flags seemed in mortal danger. That morning, it is recorded, "the situation was so tragic"[4] that as the 1st Army prepared to withdraw to the Lys, General Prioux ordered the burning of its standards.[5]

In the Mons-en-Pevelle sector, just north of Douai, the 2nd North African Division was pulling back at the rate of some 20 miles a night. In bloody engagements on the Dyle and at Fort Maulde, the 2nd North Africans had taken severe punishment: their regiments, 3,000 strong at the outset, had been reduced to about 1,300 men. But now, on the twenty-sixth, they were suddenly buoyed by the news that Frère's 7th Army was counterattacking from the south and would join up with the 1st near Bapaume, well south of Arras. The division was hurriedly swung round to face southward. The troops "attack with great courage," noted Captain Barlone, of the 2nd North Africans. "Heavy losses among the officers, who always lead." That evening the rumor

---

[2] J. G. P. M. Benoist-Méchin: *60 Jours qui Ebranlèrent l'Occident* (1956), Vol. I, p. 295.

[3] Weygand: *Recalled*, p. 81.

[4] H. Bidou: *La Bataille de France, 10 mai–25 juin 1940* (1941), p. 127.

[5] Another account, by Benoist-Méchin (*60 Jours qui Ebranlèrent l'Occident*, p. 293), states that General Blanchard gave the order.

swept the division that the counterblow had succeeded. "That shows the Weygand touch!" wrote Barlone. "We dance for joy."[6] But next morning spirits sank when it was learned that Frère's army had not advanced north after all. The 1st Army had merely been fighting a local action against advancing Germans on the north of the corridor. All that day, the twenty-seventh, the retreat was to continue. Under constant attack Barlone's troops battled their way back across the Lys. Nearby was a French armored unit, diminished to three tanks from an original half-brigade of 88, but still fighting. "At two to one," the commander told Barlone, "we should have had the Boches as easily as winking. But four to one, what can you do?"[7]

Even in the turmoil of retreat, French customs died hard. That day a reconnaissance officer, Captain de Vibraye, arrived around lunchtime at the command post at Houplin of General Mellier, commanding the 1st Army's 1st Moroccan Division. In an impromptu messroom littered with half-open cases, haversacks, bottles, loaves of bread, tins of conserves, the general and his staff of ten were taking *déjeuner*. The cutlery was poor and the meal plain, but De Vibraye noted with wry amusement the white tablecloth and fine antique glassware, the choice vintage wines standing alongside the *vin ordinaire*. "For Frenchmen the ritual of the midday meal never loses its importance," he remarked dryly.[8]

On the twenty-sixth, in a morning talk with Boudouin at Vincennes, Weygand had been voicing pessimistic views on the war situation. He had passed a restless night reflecting on the previous evening's War Committee meeting. In his opinion, the government should be announcing its clear intention to remain in Paris whatever happened, not only for the sake of the army's morale but to prevent possible revolutionary trouble in the capital. "It is a matter of the maintenance of order and the preservation of power," he said.[9] He broached the question of fighting to the last man, on which he had hitherto been so uncompromising. While he still rec-

[6] Barlone: *French Officer's Diary*, p. 54.
[7] Ibid., p. 55.
[8] T. de Vibraye: *Avec mon Groupe de Reconnaissance* (1943), p. 205.
[9] Baudouin: *Private Diaries*, p. 56.

ognized the need for preserving national honor, he now talked about avoiding a useless massacre. Weygand's thoughts turned to the battle in the north. He complained of "the defection of the English," which he claimed had forced him to abandon his offensive plans. "It is now necessary to do our best to save our army in the north," he added. He was a little more hopeful about the southern front, where he thought the troops were fighting well. But he admitted that they would have a "terrible task" to hold the Germans once the line broke under the massive enemy superiority. As the general was leaving his office, Baudouin—a confirmed admirer of Weygand—was struck by an oddly mystic vision. Weygand's "countenance, in all its delicacy and gravity, stood out against the harsh wall of the casemate, vaulted like a cell. The castle was merged into the monastery, and the soldier was merged in the monk. I bowed in silence," recorded Baudouin.[1]

Weygand could now do little more for the isolated northern armies than issue fighting calls to their commanders. On the twenty-fifth he had radioed Lord Gort: "In view of the gravity of the circumstances, General Weygand appeals personally to Lord Gort. The British Army should participate vigorously in the necessary general counter-attacks. The situation demands hard hitting."[2] Two days later, at the Premier's midday conference, he told Reynaud that he had just dispatched a strongly worded message to General Champon, for transmission to King Leopold. "There will probably be reactions to these rigorous telegrams on the part of the two Governments," he added. "Tell them that you can do nothing and that I am a swine. Not only do the English not attack, but they retreat, and the Belgians are giving way." "But I think your telegrams are very moderate," answered Reynaud.[3]

More constructively, on the twenty-sixth Weygand sent Doumenc's deputy, General Koeltz, north to the First Army Group as his personal agent. In view of the prevailing command difficulties, Blanchard had asked for an "authorised co-ordinator."[4] Koeltz's task was thus to "direct the command in my name," as Weygand put it; and in particular to ensure that a bridgehead as ex-

[1] Ibid., pp. 56–7.
[2] Weygand: *Recalled*, p. 82n.
[3] Baudouin: *Private Diaries*, p. 59.
[4] Weygand: *Recalled*, p. 82.

tensive as possible was maintained in the Dunkirk area. On the twenty-seventh Koeltz attended a conference at Cassel, 20 miles south of Dunkirk, attended by Admiral Abrial, Generals Blanchard, Prioux, Fagalde, and two British generals, one of whom represented Gort. At this meeting "it was agreed," in words quoted by Weygand, "that, Dunkirk being of precarious service-ability because of bombing, it is desirable to reinforce the occupation of Gravelines and to make an effort to install ourselves in Calais."[5] But events had already outpaced this decision: after the fall of Boulogne and Cape Gris-Nez on the twenty-fifth, Calais had been captured on the twenty-sixth. And even as the Allied commanders conferred at Cassel, a salvo of shells crashed on the small hilltop town. Dunkirk itself was now directly menaced.

---

[5] Ibid., p. 83.

Chapter 14

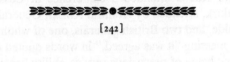

DOUBLE REVERSE: BELGIUM AND DUNKIRK

"We are going to call on all the forces of the Empire."

(Winston Churchill)

A T 6 P.M. ON MONDAY, May 27, while Weygand was in conference with Generals Georges, Doumenc, and Besson at Vincennes, he received a message from Lieutenant Colonel Morel, GHQ, Northeast, originating from General Champon at Belgian GHQ: the Belgian Army had abandoned the struggle and a ceasefire was expected to take effect as of midnight. "The news came like a thunderclap," Weygand recorded.[1] At once he cabled Morel:

1. I am immediately advising the Government of the fact.
2. Pending new instructions, I order Blanchard to sever his contacts with the Belgian troops.
3. In agreement with General Gort, Blanchard will take all the necessary urgent decisions to guard against this act of desertion.[2]

Then Weygand rang Baudouin at Reynaud's office to announce that he had very important news for the Prime Minister. All he would add in answer to Baudouin's queries was: "It is very serious."[3] At 6:45 he arrived at the War Ministry and handed Reynaud the message, which ran as follows:

---

[1] M. Weygand: *Recalled to Service*, trans. E. W. Dickes (1952), p. 84.
[2] P. Reynaud: *In the Thick of the Fight*, p. 432.
[3] P. Baudouin: *The Private Diaries . . .* , trans. Sir Charles Petrie (1948), p. 60.

General Champon has telegraphed to say: "The King of the Belgians has sent an envoy to the German High Command to inquire under what conditions it is possible to conclude hostilities between the Belgian and German Armies. The King proposes that the cease-fire should begin at midnight tonight. I have taken note of the communication made by the Chief of the Belgian General Staff, and I have added that the discussion of this condition cannot validly be accepted, nor can it take place except in the presence of accredited representative of the three Commands, Belgian, French and British, as the three Armies form an entity, and the Belgian Army cannot act alone."

General Champon is going to establish contact with General Blanchard, but he has asked that the latter be also informed. He would like also to receive instructions.[4]

After two and a half weeks of fierce and increasingly hopeless resistance, the Belgian Army had been brought to the verge of defeat. With most of the country overrun, it had no alternative but to ask for a cease-fire. The disappearance of an ally at this critical stage was a heavy blow—as much psychologically as militarily—to the French and British, themselves struggling with increasing desperation against the German onslaught. In the atmosphere of growing disaster that marked these late May days, the Belgian leader, King Leopold, was to become the target for Franco-British resentment and recrimination—the convenient scapegoat for a situation that was not the fault of the Belgian Army. The French in particular claimed—unjustifiably—that they were caught unawares and grossly betrayed by the Belgian decision to stop fighting, of which, they asserted, Leopold had given them no warning. In fact there were a number of warnings, implicit and explicit. But in the heat of the moment and under the crushing enemy pressure, truth and rational judgment were thrown overboard—added to which there were the complicating factors of misunderstanding and garbled communications, the messages that went astray and orders that were overtaken by fast-moving events. The result was that the French leaders, striving to absolve themselves from blame, blackened the case against Leopold with their own twisted accounts. Thus when Weygand recorded (above) that he had learned that the Belgian Army "had abandoned the struggle," the fact was that Leopold proposed to ascertain the terms of a cease-fire. Likewise,

---

[4] Reynaud: *Fight*, p. 430.

he says that the news came like "a thunderclap," whereas he already well knew that Belgium would be giving up the fight at any moment. Even more guilty was Reynaud, whose broadcast of the twenty-eighth, announcing the news to the French people, was unmercifully and inaccurately slanted against Leopold. Churchill, too, was to endorse Reynaud's attitude by declaring that Leopold had acted capriciously and without notice.

Emotions ran hot, and controversy was to rage loud and long, over this sorry episode. It was an example of what could happen among the parties to a shaky military alliance when catastrophe threatened all of them, and the first of them collapsed under the strain.

Reynaud was conferring with Pétain when Weygand arrived. Soon afterwards Hubert Pierlot, the Belgian Prime Minister, and General Denis, the Belgian Minister of Defense, joined them. They had hastened to the rue Saint-Dominique from a meeting of the Belgian Council of Ministers at the Belgian Embassy in Paris, at which they had heard the news. Then the British ambassador, Sir Ronald Campbell, and General Spears were shown in. There followed a bitter and unhappy discussion. Reynaud, says Baudouin, "did not mince his words."[5] He inveighed against Leopold's so-called desertion of the Allies, his alleged failure to warn them of his surrender, and his consequent jeopardizing of the whole Allied situation. General Denis, with "tears in his eyes," tried to defend the Belgian Army against Reynaud's charges.[6] Pierlot protested vigorously that he was totally opposed to Leopold's action, and informed Reynaud of the decision made by the Belgian ministers that afternoon, that the Belgian government intended to continue the fight with all the means still at its disposal. Pétain and Weygand remained stonily silent during the tense exchanges. The marshal, as Pierlot recorded, was "obviously hostile."[7] Before the meeting ended, it was resolved that the Allied High Commands should be directed as follows: "The French and British Governments agree to instruct their Commanders-in-Chief, General Blanchard and

---

[5] Baudouin, *Private Diaries,* p. 60.
[6] Ibid.
[7] Reynaud: *Fight,* p. 436.

Lord Gort, to defend the honour of their flags by dissociating themselves entirely from the Belgian armistice."[8]

At ten that night a hurriedly summoned Council of Ministers met at the Élysée. Weygand claimed that the surrender had finally killed all chances of his plan and made more probable the gloomy predictions he had made at the War Committee meeting two days before. For Reynaud there was the problem of how he should break the news to the French public. During the early hours of the twenty-eighth he called Pierlot and Spaak, the Belgian Foreign Minister, to his apartment to decide on the framing of a radio announcement. At 8 a.m. he broadcast the tidings to his countrymen in a speech riddled with distortions and unwarranted abuse of Leopold.

I have to announce a grave event to the French people [he said]. This took place during the night. France can no longer count on the assistance of the Belgian Army. Since four o'clock this morning the French and British Armies have been fighting alone in the north against the enemy . . .

It is this Belgian Army which has suddenly surrendered unconditionally at the height of battle at the orders of its King, without warning its French and British comrades in the fight, and has thus opened the road to Dunkirk for the German divisions.

This same King eighteen days ago, who until then had pretended to attach the same value to Germany's word as to that of the Allies, had addressed to us an appeal for help. Following a plan prepared since last December by the Allied General Staffs we answered this appeal.

Now, in the full course of battle, without any warning to General Blanchard, without, indeed, a thought or a word for the French and British soldiers who came, in answer to his anguished appeal, to the help of his country, King Leopold III of Belgium has laid down arms. It is an action unprecedented in history.

The Belgian Government has told me that the King's decision was taken against the unanimous desire of the responsible Ministers. It has added that it is resolved to place at the service of the common cause all the resources of its country that it can still control and that, above all, it wishes to raise a new Army, and to collaborate in the task of arming France.[9]

---

[8] Weygand: *Recalled*, pp. 84–5.
[9] Reynaud: *Fight*, pp. 438–9.

Reverting to a less somber note, Reynaud spoke of the French fighting men and the certainty of eventual victory:

It is our soldiers we are thinking about. They at least can say that their honour is intact. Over the whole front they are making a magnificent effort. Every day throughout the 18 days of battle they have provided a thousand examples of heroism. . . . Our commanders and troops are forming a united body in which the country has entire confidence and which tomorrow will earn the admiration of the world.

We knew that dark days would come. They have come now. France has been invaded a hundred times and never brought down; let our brave people of the north remember this. It is through these trials that France's new army will be forged, the army that will make her greater than ever.

Our faith in victory is unbroken. The strength of every soldier and every citizen is increased tenfold. Ill-fortune has always served to make France greater. She has never been more single-minded than she is today.

On the new line which our great commander, Weygand, has just established on the Somme and the Aisne with the full accord of Marshal Pétain, we shall hold, and because we have held, we shall conquer![1]

To Frenchmen crowding around their radios that morning, the news of Leopold's capitulation came as a staggering shock. Recalling the stout resistance of his father, King Albert, in World War I, they saw his defection as hardly less than treason. Reynaud's withering and unjustified condemnation of Leopold did nothing to discourage this view. He was voicing the rage and chagrin of himself and all good Frenchmen at being deserted by an ally in mid-battle— allegedly without warning. But the charge that Leopold had failed to give warning was demonstrably untrue.

At noon on the twenty-seventh, at Belgian GHQ, Bruges, King Leopold handed Admiral Sir Roger Keyes, personal liaison officer between Winston Churchill and himself, a top-priority message for Lord Gort. In it the king said that he wished Gort "to know that his army is greatly disheartened. It has been incessantly engaged for four days and subjected to intense air bombardment, which the RAF have been unable to prevent. The knowledge that the Allied armies in this sector have been encircled, and that the

---

[1] J. G. P. M. Benoist-Méchin: *60 Jours qui Ebranlèrent l'Occident* (1956), p. 338.

Germans have great superiority in the air, has led his troops to believe that the position is almost hopeless. He fears a moment is rapidly approaching when he can no longer rely upon his troops to fight or be of any further use to the B.E.F. *He wishes you to realize that he will be obliged to surrender before a débâcle.*[2] The message was sent at 12:30 p.m.[3] Its air of finality was such that no doubt could have remained that a Belgian cease-fire was imminent. It was uncertain whether or not Gort—constantly on the move—received this message, but he had certainly had other previous warnings and was aware of Belgium's grave predicament. A message from the British War Office, firmly notifying the forthcoming surrender and dispatched about 6 p.m., failed to reach him before the surrender had taken place. Lord Gort first learned of this at 11 p.m., when he was visiting Dunkirk. He there met Weygand's envoy, General Koeltz, who asked if he had heard that a Belgian cease-fire was to take effect as from midnight. Gort expressed his astonishment, although, as he admits, he realized that Belgian resistance was virtually at an end.

Leopold himself was as much a victim of this top-level communications breakdown as Gort. Up to the twenty-sixth, he was ignorant that the Weygand Plan had been canceled—Weygand himself was to claim, wrongly, that the cancellation was caused by the Belgian surrender—or that B.E.F. had been ordered to withdraw to the coast and evacuate. That afternoon Admiral Keyes, telephoning his daily situation report to Churchill, was amazed to hear that the evacuation was already in progress: it had begun

---

[2] The Private Papers of Lord Keyes.

[3] When Leopold wrote this message he was hoping to hold out for another twenty-four hours. He was now putting off surrender almost from day to day. But during the course of the twenty-seventh, intensifying enemy attacks breached his line in several more places and it was obvious that his forces were on the point of total collapse. "Just before 5 o'clock," writes Admiral Keyes's biographer, Cecil Aspinall-Oglander, "being unable to be of any further assistance to the BEF, and having already flooded the Yser, mined its bridges and sent all the French troops still under his command to its western bank, King Leopold asked for an armistice in order to avert, not only a débâcle in his army, but also the further slaughter of his civilian population, who were crowding every town, village and road in the small corner of Belgium still left to them, and were being continually and mercilessly bombed."

that day, the twenty-sixth, without warning to anybody. "Mr. Churchill," writes Keyes's biographer, "was equally astounded that neither Keyes nor Belgian GHQ had been informed by Gort of this decision, which so vitally concerned the Belgian Army . . ."[4]

But beneath the question of actual surrender and adequate warning to the Allies lay a deeper issue. As the Belgian forces began to break up and surrender became inevitable, a tense drama was developing between Leopold and his ministers. Thirty-eight-year-old Leopold had decided to remain in Belgium and face the Germans as a prisoner rather than leave and set up a government that might carry on the fight from overseas. Quitting Belgium would mean deserting his people, he maintained; his duty was to stay and do what he could to mitigate the conditions of the Belgians under enemy occupation. In an anxious conference with Pierlot, Spaak, General Denis, and another minister at the château of Wynendael, near Bruges, in the early hours of the twenty-fifth, he had steadfastly restated his determination to remain, against all advice and entreaties. He told the ministers that by so doing he considered he was fulfilling his duties as head of state and Commander in Chief of the Belgian Army. To leave his army, he declared, would be desertion, and he must, whatever happened, share the fate of his troops. In vain the ministers pointed out that in failing to follow the example of the king of Norway and the queen of the Netherlands (who had both left their countries for Britain) he would be abandoning the Allied cause; and that by leaving Belgium he could, on the other hand, carry on the fight from abroad. Leopold was adamant. If he did not stay in Belgium, he said, he was convinced he would never return. He judged that the Allied cause was lost, and that within a few days France would collapse. He made it clear to Pierlot and his colleagues that they themselves were at liberty to leave the country if they felt they could no longer serve under him: in these circumstances—having no wish to be a dictator—he would form a new government of ministers who were willing to stay. Asked how long capitulation could still be put off, the king replied: "Twenty-four hours at the most."[5] This was the last interview the king had with his ministers.

---

[4] C. Aspinall-Oglander: *Roger Keyes* (1951), p. 367.
[5] Reynaud: *Fight*, p. 426.

Immediately afterward Leopold sent a message, signifying his intention, to King George in London. In it he said: ". . . In spite of the varied advice which I have been given, I feel that my duty impels me to follow the fate of my Army and to remain with my people: to act otherwise would mean desertion. I am convinced that I can best aid my people by staying with them, rather than in trying to carry on abroad. . . . I fully realize that my position will be very difficult, but my essential care will be to prevent my countrymen from being forced to join in any action against the countries which have helped Belgium in her struggle . . ."[6] From King George—or rather from Lord Halifax, who composed the reply—Leopold received little support or comfort. A British note of the twenty-sixth expressed "serious concern at seeing Leopold resolved to place himself under the thumb of the enemy," and warned him that his continued presence in Belgium would be ineffective in easing the hardships of German occupation.[7] As another instance of the breakdown of communications, Leopold did not receive this message until early on the twenty-seventh, when the Belgian Army was on the verge of collapse.

Reynaud, too, had on the twenty-sixth tried to persuade Leopold to leave Belgium—and thereby showed that he was aware of Belgium's impending collapse at least twenty-four hours before it took place. When about to fly back to Paris from his London conference on the evening of the twenty-sixth, he had found Paul-Henri Spaak waiting for him at the airfield. The agitated Belgian Foreign Minister told him of Leopold's inflexible attitude at the Wynendael meeting, and of the king's intention to capitulate and even form a new government in order to treat with the Germans. On reaching Paris Reynaud at once telegraphed the French ambassador asking him to urge Leopold to flee to Britain. Weygand's aide, Captain Gasser, had known of the forthcoming surrender as much as a week earlier. At the Ypres meeting on the twenty-first he was told by Leopold's brother, the Count of Flanders, that within eight days the fight would be over. In London, Churchill likewise expected the fall of Belgium. On the twenty-seventh, before the capitulation, he cabled Admiral Sir Roger

6 Ibid., pp. 426–7.
7 Ibid., p. 427.

Keyes: " . . . Trust you will make sure Leopold leaves with you by aeroplane before too late . . ."[8] But that cable never reached Keyes. Again, late that afternoon, after he had heard from Keyes that Leopold was asking for an armistice, Churchill directed Keyes to appeal urgently to him to leave Belgium. "I gave King Leopold the Prime Minister's message," reported Keyes later, "but he said that he had made up his mind that he must stay with his Army and people."[9]

The immediate reaction of the Belgian government in Paris was to repudiate Leopold publicly. After Reynaud's radio address, Pierlot led a delegation of ministers and members of Parliament to the Place de la Concorde to lay a wreath at the statue of King Albert I. Then he pronounced a speech from a text virtually imposed by Reynaud at their recent meeting: ". . . Belgium will be struck with stupefaction, but the fault of one cannot be imputed to the whole nation. Our army has not deserved the fate that has been meted out to it . . ."[1] That day, at the Belgian Embassy, the (now exiled) government released Belgian officers and officials from their obligation of obedience to the king, who was now deemed to be under German domination. Many of them, however, publicly proclaimed their loyalty.

Amid the chorus of condemnation one voice in particular spoke up for Leopold—that of Admiral Sir Roger Keyes. This bold and experienced British sailor—famous for his Zeebrugge exploit of World War I—had been in closest contact with King Leopold since his appointment as liaison officer on May 10. Living always under the same roof as Leopold, he had shared the king's intimate confidences on political and military matters and followed the progress of the battle from the Belgian viewpoint, as well as being in regular personal touch with the Allied commanders, and in telephone communication with Churchill. Keyes knew that Leopold had not betrayed the Allies and especially the British—whose eastern flank the Belgian Army was said to have jeopardized by its surrender: the British, Keyes maintained, had taken their own steps to guard the flank from the twenty-fifth on, after realizing

---

[8] W. S. Churchill: *The Second World War*, Vol. II: *Their Finest Hour* (1949), p. 80.
[9] Ibid., Vol. II, p. 81.
[1] Benoist-Méchin: *60 Jours*, p. 338.

that the Belgians were about to collapse. They had also, in his words, "abandoned the Belgians to their fate."[2] Now, reaching England early on the twenty-eighth after a perilous escape from Belgium, Keyes hurried from Harwich to London to report to Churchill and the king, and then to the lobbies of the House of Commons—he was a Member of Parliament—to defend King Leopold from what were, to his certain knowledge, the groundless charges in Reynaud's broadcast announcement. He was gratified that afternoon to hear Winston Churchill—informed of the true position by himself and Colonel Davy, head of the British Military Mission to Belgian GHQ—refer to the Belgian king's action in far more moderate terms than Reynaud, and counsel members to defer judgment until the facts were known. But a week later, in another Commons speech, Churchill himself—seemingly in the interests of Anglo-French solidarity rather than on the merits of the case[3]—was to condemn Leopold for surrendering "without prior consultation, with the least possible notice, without the advice of his Ministers and upon his own personal act," thereby vitally endangering the British positions.[4]

Weygand at least was to modify his initially severe judgment on the king. On mature consideration, together with study of the available documents, he came to this conclusion: "On May 27th the Belgian Army was in a perilous situation. The whole of its forces were still too far from the Yser for it to be able to take up position there in a reasonable time. Its right wing, threatened with envelopment, could no longer be extricated by the French any more than by the British, whose withdrawal on Dunkirk had already begun. The Belgian Command then evidently regarded itself as abandoned by its Allies."[5]

---

[2] Private Papers of Lord Keyes.

[3] A telegram to London from Sir Ronald Campbell on May 29 was significant. It reported that Frossard, the Minister of Information, had appealed to the British Press Counsellor in Paris to try to prevent prominence being given, in the British press and on the radio, to the calls by Keyes to suspend judgment on Leopold. Such an attitude by Keyes, Frossard feared, was conducive to defeatism at the moment when French morale had been raised through anger at Leopold's action.

[4] House of Commons: *Parliamentary Debates*, 5th Series (June 4, 1940), Vol. 361, Col. 789.

[5] Weygand: *Recalled*, pp. 85–6.

Psychologically disastrous though it was, the surrender hardly changed the military situation on a front where the Allies were already facing certain defeat and the British evacuation had already started—on the twenty-sixth—without the knowledge of Belgians or French. What it did was to hasten by a few hours the final crumbling of the Allied partnership in Belgium. Now, as the Belgians laid down their arms and Von Reichenau's troops pressed their encirclement of the beleaguered Franco-British forces around Dunkirk, the last show of unity in the field was breaking down. On the evening of the twenty-eighth, Blanchard, on a visit to the 1st Army commander, Prioux, at his command post at Steenwerck, admitted that his army group no longer existed because the Belgians were out of the fight and the British were returning to their island. And early on the twenty-ninth he radioed Weygand that some French divisions were (as Weygand reported over the telephone to Baudouin) "uncovered in consequence of the precipitate retreat of the English."[6] If blame were to be apportioned for the Belgian *débâcle,* it lay back in the interwar years; in the Pétainist decree of the thirties that the Franco-British defense line should be based not behind the French frontier but across the center of Belgium.

Favored by calm seas, the B.E.F. and a large part of the French 1st Army made their providential escape from the shores of Flanders. Day after day, from burning, smoke-covered Dunkirk Harbor and points on the nine miles of sand dunes that ran east to La Panne, the long lines of British and French troops boarded a motley fleet of large and small craft—exhausted, patient, harassed by constant bombing. Operation Dynamo—the great Dunkirk evacuation—had begun on Sunday, May 26. At 10:30 that evening the first transport steamed into Dover Harbor with 1,312 British troops aboard. On the twenty-eighth Lord Gort gave the B.E.F. the general order to withdraw to the Dunkirk bridgehead. "It will be impossible to carry out the embarkation," Admiral Darlan pessimistically predicted to Reynaud.[7] Initially even the British planners thought the operation could last no more than two days,

---

[6] Baudouin: *Private Diaries,* p. 60.
[7] Reynaud: *Fight,* p. 449.

saving a maximum of some 45,000 men. But it was to continue for more than a week, until over 338,000—including 115,000 French —had been picked up.[8] Technically and in terms of courage and endurance it was a brilliant and almost miraculous feat; but as Winston Churchill was to remind the House of Commons on June 4: "Wars are not won by evacuations." In the last days of May, as the loaded transports bore the bulk of two Allied armies out of continental Europe with almost nothing but their small arms, there was no room in Paris or London for complacency or self-congratulation. It was under the impact of a major catastrophe— with still graver prospects looming ahead—that the Supreme War Council met at Reynaud's office in the War Ministry on the afternoon of the thirty-first.

Although the Allied leaders had met twice before in Paris, this was the first Supreme War Council to be held since the start of the offensive on the tenth. As imminent defeat threatened France the council would meet twice more, in the provinces, under dire conditions of strain and growing disunity. But now, as Reynaud recorded, "the entire discussion took place in an atmosphere of friendliness and mutual trust."[9] (He was charitably overlooking Weygand's occasional querulous comments to Churchill, and Pétain's silent, veiled hostility.) Flying from London in the morning, Churchill was this time accompanied by Clement Attlee, Deputy Prime Minister. He also had with him Generals Dill, Ismay, and Spears, and British Ambassador Sir Ronald Campbell. The French were represented by Reynaud, Pétain (making his first appearance at a Franco-British meeting), Weygand, Darlan, Captain de Margerie, of Reynaud's staff, and Paul Baudouin. While other matters—the evacuation of Narvik and the impending entry of Italy into the war—were on the agenda, the most urgent topic was Dunkirk. This engendered some emotion, especially on Churchill's part. "Mr. Churchill twice had tears in his eyes when he was describing the martyrdom of the armies in the north, the terrible sufferings of the men," noted Baudouin.[1] But it was always Churchill, by turns grave, forceful, and persuasive, who dominated the

---

[8] In this great sea lift 693 British and 168 other vessels were engaged, with losses of 243 sunk (of which 226 were British).

[9] Ibid., p. 452.

[1] Baudouin: *Private Diaries*, p. 69.

meeting. The French "had accepted his leadership," remarked Spears.[2]

Early in the discussion of Dunkirk, a delicate point arose. Churchill disclosed that of the total number of troops already evacuated—165,000—only 15,000 were French. There were sound reasons for this (the relative distances from Dunkirk of the French and British), but the disparity brought a sharp query from Reynaud. "If not immediately corrected, it might entail grave consequences in the political field," he said.[3] Churchill had been well aware of the discrepancy: two days before, he had directed the Chief of the Imperial General Staff to increase the French quota: now he reassured Reynaud that orders had been issued that day to give French troops priority where possible. He went further and said that as he did not wish to see French troops bear new sacrifices, he would instruct that the final rear guard at Dunkirk should be made up of three British divisions. A telegram to this effect was dispatched to Admiral Abrial at Dunkirk after the meeting. Weygand pointed out that unfortunately there was no hope of evacuating all the French troops, as they were farthest from the coast. Of the twelve divisions still in Flanders, only four were in a position to be embarked, and at least five had been unable to cross the Lys. From Dunkirk the council turned to the crucial coming struggle on the Somme-Aisne front. On this issue the basically clashing interests of the French and British inevitably emerged. While Reynaud appealed strongly for all possible British manpower to be sent to France, Churchill insisted on the need to keep troops at home to combat probable invasion. The same, he pointed out, applied to British aircraft. Reynaud remained obdurate. "Remember," he said, "that we are going to throw all our land and air forces into the battle of the Somme and Aisne." "We are going to call on all the forces of the Empire," replied Churchill. To this Reynaud answered: "I am convinced that England appreciates the decisive and vital character of the battle which is about to begin in a few days. We shall stake all we have without sparing anything, and if we are beaten the French Army will have played its part. We have nothing in reserve, neither arms, nor clothing nor supplies." Churchill's final

---

[2] E. L. Spears: *Assignment to Catastrophe* (1954), Vol. I, p. 301.

[3] Reynaud: *Fight,* p. 450.

answer was frank and hardly encouraging. As Baudouin recorded it, "he would do all he could to help France, but the French Government must not harbor any illusions concerning the assistance it could expect from England."[4]

Churchill was not impressed with Pétain at this first encounter. Watching Pétain talk to a group of men after the meeting ended, he summed him up as apathetic and defeatist, even ready to accept a separate peace. Churchill listened with satisfaction as General Spears warned the group—with Pétain particularly in mind—that if France's "foreign policy" changed as a result of further military setbacks, she could expect blockade and bombardment of her German-held ports.

During the conference Churchill had mentioned that Lord Gort was under orders to return to England—his role as Commander in Chief of the B.E.F. being about to terminate—and asked if Blanchard was being likewise withdrawn. Weygand was noncommittal, "since the situation of the French Army," as he later put it, "was entirely different."[5] By this he meant that there were considerable French forces still outside the Dunkirk perimeter. At that moment the majority of five 1st Army divisions (the 1st Moroccan, 2nd North African, and the 15th, 4th, and 25th), encircled to the south of the Lys, were making their last stand. Two days before, the 1st Army commander, General Prioux, had been captured with his staff at Steenwerck; and for the last seventy-two hours these divisions had been battling to break through toward Dunkirk and now they were exhausted and near the end of their ammunition. After refusing two calls to surrender, General Molinie of the 25th Division, the senior commander, was to capitulate at eight o'clock that evening. Over the vital initial phase of the evacuation, Molinie's force had stopped six German divisions from advancing on Dunkirk. Next morning the enemy would pay tribute to the high fighting qualities of these troops: two French battalions were to parade, with their arms, before the German General Wegner and a German detachment in the Grande Place at Lille.

Some units of these divisions had a luckier fate. They had already crossed the Lys, under orders, and after a nightmare trek

4 Baudouin: *Private Diaries*, p. 72.
5 Weygand: *Recalled*, p. 88.

north they reached the Dunkirk bridgehead to make their escape from the bomb-scarred beaches. One such contingent was that of Captain Barlone, 2nd North African Division.

On the 28th Barlone was at Erquinghem on the north bank of the Lys, without instructions and out of contact with divisional headquarters. That evening, still without orders, he decided to make for Dunkirk. Through the night he and his men fought their way, with their horse-drawn vehicles, along roads almost impassable because of a vast one-way traffic of transport, guns, and tired, plodding French and British troops. At one point it took four hours to cover half a mile. Constant air strafing and a fleeting tank attack increased the chaos. By dawn on the twenty-ninth, Barlone's unit was a dozen miles from Dunkirk. In the brightening light the great columns of men and transport stretched across the flat plain in "indescribable disorder."[6] German artillery opened up, causing heavy damage and worse congestion on the roads. Troops struggled to heave wrecked vehicles and guns into the ditches. Somehow keeping together, Barlone and his men reached Bergues, entry point to the inner bridgehead around Dunkirk. Here British police were directing British to the left of the northward-running canal that joined Bergues to Dunkirk, and French to the right. Under intensifying artillery fire Barlone's party pressed on—repeatedly plunged into the roadside ditches that were now filling with water as the defensive flooding of the plain began. After six more miles they finally struck the coast at Bray-Dunes, about six miles east of Dunkirk.

Bray, small peacetime resort complete with its casino, was a vast park of trucks, lorries, and equipment jettisoned by troops on their way to the beaches. Threading their way through this debris of an army, Barlone's men met an officer of the 2nd North Africans who reported that the remnants of the division were re-forming near La Panne, to the east. They moved off along the railway tracks. Over the dike-crossed plain to their right, the floodwater was slowly rising. They stared aghast at what Barlone called "the heart-rending sight of tens of thousands of abandoned vehicles and wandering horses." "An impression of awful and irretrievable disaster," he

---

[6] Barlone: *A French Officer's Diary 23 August 1939– 1 October, 1940*, trans. L. V. Cass (1942), p. 57.

added.[7] Upon his arrival at La Panne, Barlone found that the divisional commander, the admired and respected General Dame, had been wounded and captured while supervising the retirement of his troops. Most of his staff had likewise been taken, leaving Colonel Sevestre of the 13th Algerian Rifles to lead the division. Barlone's men dug in among the dunes to sleep. Next morning, the thirtieth, Sevestre ordered a count to be made of officers and men to be embarked. The total was 1,250—all that remained of the 18,000-strong 2nd North African Division.

At noon Sevestre instructed Barlone and a fellow officer to embark about half the division—550 men—at Dunkirk, nine miles to the west. They set out, following the railroad tracks. At Malo-les-Bains, just short of Dunkirk, they ran into growing confusion: there were no military police or signposts to point the way through the battered town to the embarkation area. Taking shelter against the shelling in the lee of a large pumphouse, they waited until 9 p.m. before they received orders to embark. To reach the quayside allocated to the French they had to cover half a mile and cross two footbridges under continued heavy shellfire. Barlone sent the men forward in parties of ten, in single file. As he vividly described it, Dunkirk was an inferno of smoke from the burning oil tanks, fanned downward by the westerly wind. Flames leaped from blazing buildings. The ground was churned by shell and bomb craters and littered with fallen masonry and displaced paving stones. Over large tracts buildings had been flattened, leaving solitary crags of wall standing; and in the background giant cranes jutted skyward, while from overhead bombers pounded the stricken port, unopposed by Allied fighters. Through this havoc Barlone's troops gained the quayside, with four dead and a number of wounded—to find that the boats allotted to them had already sailed. Angry and dejected, they moved out to the dunes, beyond the worst of the bombing and shelling. Snatching what rest they could, they were roused in the early hours with orders to return to the quayside. This time there was no mistake. Now at last, at 3 a.m. on the thirty-first, the ships were waiting for them. In the faint light of dawn they boarded two small cargo boats, the *Keremah* and *Hebe*. An hour later the weary, much-tried men of the 2nd North African

---

[7] Ibid., p. 58.

Division steamed out through heavy shelling. At eight o'clock they sailed into the haven of Dover Harbor.

That day 68,000 Allied troops reached England from Dunkirk, the largest number to be landed on any day of Operation Dynamo. But enemy pressure was increasing dangerously on the steadily contracting bridgehead, and despite the valiant efforts of the R.A.F.—five fighter squadrons were operating almost continuously over and inland of the bridgehead—Allied losses were mounting. On June 1 Churchill warned Weygand that the evacuation might have to end that night, and that General Alexander (Lord Gort's successor in command of the British forces) had been ordered to confer with Admiral Abrial on the question of stopping it forthwith or continuing it until next day at the latest. But by dawn on the second there were still some 4,000 British within the bridgehead and a much larger body of French—including the men of General Fagalde's XVI Corps and General de la Laurencie's III Corps —defending the perimeter. The evacuation, it was decided, must go on—whatever the cost—until every possible man had been taken off. So, through the second and third, and into the early hours of the fourth, it continued. The British rear guard was evacuated by midnight on the second, but still many French remained. Ships that returned empty to Dover before dawn on the third—embarkation could now only take place during the dark hours—sailed back to Dunkirk that night to bring out these stubborn defenders. At 3:30 a.m. on June 4 the last ships of Operation Dynamo left the shores of Dunkirk. The French troops landing at Dover on the fourth numbered 26,175. But over 30,000 stayed on, to be taken prisoner —the men of the Fortified Sector of Flanders and the 68th, 12th, and 32nd Divisions—"the last squares of resistance," as Weygand recorded, "who had devoted themselves to the salvation of their comrades."[8] Among the latest to leave the bomb-wrecked port were Admiral Abrial and his deputy, Admiral Platon, who for nine days had directed the great sea lift (along with Admiral Ramsay at Dover) from their front-line command post at Bastion 32.

In these desperate hours there had been tensions and differences between the Allies—aggravated by the collapse of communications and the bewildering speed of events—on matters of com-

---

[8] Weygand: *Recalled,* p. 89.

mand, priorities, shipping commitments, defense responsibilities. What was remarkable in the circumstances was the cooperation that enabled 338,000 men of two national armies to be shipped and safely transported despite prodigious handicaps.

For the moment at least, the bulk of the British Army was driven off the Continent—knocked out of the main theater of the struggle against Hitler. To a large extent it was the victim of the strategic misjudgments and the underestimates of German strength of which British as well as French leaders had been guilty in the interwar years. Its fighting qualities remained unquestioned; but since the B.E.F. had marched north into Belgium less than four weeks before, it had had no real chance to show those qualities. Nevertheless, the British troops had played a full and valuable part in the campaign, manning the difficult line between the Belgians and the French Ist Army. Caught in the great retreat, they had battled their way back from the Dyle to Dunkirk with stubborn fortitude. Now, as they reached England devoid of almost all their arms and equipment, but with their morale still high, all that these quarter of a million survivors of the B.E.F. could do was to set about retraining and re-equipping—the nucleus of the expending armies that would fight Hitler wherever possible and whose ultimate aim was to go back to continental Europe.

Meanwhile a considerable British force—some 140,000 troops of various arms that had not been involved in the disaster to the northern armies—remained in France. And in the immediate aftermath of Dunkirk, Churchill was proposing to strengthen this force with more divisions in order to give the French continuing British support. Appointed to command this residual B.E.F. was General Alan Brooke. Brooke was to return to France on June 12, but his command was to be short-lived. On the fourteenth, with the French situation becoming increasingly desperate and the British, in their positions in Brittany, no longer able to provide effective help, he would receive the order to evacuate. Within the next days nearly 150,000 British and some 47,000 Allied troops were embarked for England.[9] Brooke himself sailed from Saint-Nazaire on the

---

[9] These figures are quoted in A. Bryant: *The Turn of the Tide* . . . (1957), p. 185. Churchill: *Second World War*, Vol. II, p. 171, gives the total as 136,000 British and 20,000 Polish troops evacuated.

nineteenth, among the last to leave France. But not all the British escaped: the 51st or Highland Division, fighting courageously alongside the French 10th Army in Normandy, was on the eleventh surrounded and captured at Saint-Valéry-en-Caux.

Amid the massive defeat of Dunkirk, the Allies registered one triumph. The *Luftwaffe*, making a maximum effort to smash Operation Dynamo at the Dunkirk docks, on the beaches, and in the sea approaches, was decisively worsted by the R.A.F., numerically inferior but now showing its clear mastery in quality. Strained to the limit, time and again the British Spitfires and Defiants broke up the enemy formations before they could bomb their targets. Often the Allied troops cursed the absence of their own planes over the Dunkirk bridgehead. But the fighters were engaged in bitter battles farther inland, and their victories went unnoticed by the men crowding on the dunes and jetties and exposed to the bombers that got through. Inflicting four times the losses that they themselves suffered, the planes of the R.A.F. assured the success of the Dunkirk "deliverance."

But how far had Hitler himself assisted in the deliverance? It was the Führer who expressly assigned the *Luftwaffe* the role of finishing off the Allies at Dunkirk, while halting the German armored divisions. At a conference at Charleville on the twenty-fourth, attended by Wilhelm Keitel, head of OKW; Alfred Jodl, OKW's Chief of Operations, Walther von Brauchitsch, Commander in Chief of the German Army, and General von Rundstedt, he had rejected a proposal by Brauchitsch for a full-scale armored assault in the region Vimy–Saint-Omer–Gravelines, aimed at the rolling up and destruction of the First Army Group. Pointing out that the First Army Group's fate was sealed in any case, Hitler stressed that the paramount task was to prepare without delay for the next phase of the battle—on the Somme front and as far as the western end of the Maginot Line. For this purpose—to the consternation of some of the generals present—he ordered the armored divisions to regroup in the Saint-Quentin area and prescribed that the completion of the Flanders battle be left to the infantry and the *Luftwaffe*. His decision seemed so bizarre to the commanders who, after a long chase, were poised to destroy the Franco-British armies that it raised queries as to whether he had ulterior motives for it. Hitler admitted soon afterward to Von Kleist that he might be losing a unique opportunity in not occupying Dunkirk before the

British escaped, but added that he did not want his tanks to become bogged down in the Flanders mud. To other questioners he explained that he wished to ascertain the amount of wear and tear sustained by his armor before committing it to further action; or simply that he was anxious to preserve the panzer forces for the next campaign. Von Rundstedt was to suggest that the Führer was deliberately letting the B.E.F. get away, with a view to easing the path for future peace talks with the British. Von Kleist, on the other hand, maintained that Hitler had allotted the honor of making the final attack to the *Luftwaffe* on the persuasion of Göring.

Two days later, on the twenty-sixth—as Weygand issued his fight-to-the-death call to the Allied troops and General Gort was instructed from London to prepare to evacuate the B.E.F.—Hitler formally ordered the *Luftwaffe* to liquidate the Dunkirk pocket. His order was promptly relayed to Kesselring's and Sperrle's Second and Third Air Fleets. East of Dunkirk, the XXXIX Armored Corps had already been halted for forty-eight hours at La Bassée; and now General Guderian, preparing to launch the XIX Armored Corps against Dunkirk from the south, received a "stop" order confirming that of the twenty-fourth. With this was repeated a general directive to the German Army not to proceed beyond the Aa Canal (which linked the Lys River with Gravelines on the coast). No explanation was given to Guderian, save that the reduction of Dunkirk was entrusted to the air force. The XIX Panzer Corps commander was astounded. To him it seemed unintelligible that Germany's armored forces should be withheld from attacking at the crucial moment of the battle. However, Hitler's intentions were made clear that evening when the XIX Armored Corps was relieved by the XIV Corps, an infantry formation of Von Kluge's 4th Army. On the twenty-ninth the Führer clinched the matter: after a conference with his army chiefs at Cambrai Airport on future plans, he notified Guderian that he was giving him the command of an armored group that would bear his name and whose assembly point would be at Signy-le-Petit, southwest of Charleville and 150 miles from the coast.

For General Heinz Guderian and the men of the XIX Armored Corps it had been a tough, exhilarating, brilliantly successful campaign, even though they were denied the final kill. In tribute to his troops Guderian issued this order on the twenty-sixth:

Soldiers of the XIX Armoured Corps!

Sixteen days of battle in Belgium and France are behind us. Six hundred kilometres separate us from the frontiers of the Reich. We have gained the shores of the Channel and the ocean. . . . You have crowned your achievement by the capture of the fortified ports of Boulogne and Calais.

I had asked you not to sleep for 48 hours. You have held out for 17 days. I made you ensure the safety of your flanks and rear. You have done this without fail.

With an exemplary confidence and invincible faith in the accomplishment of your task, you have obeyed all my orders with whole-hearted devotion.

We bow respectfully before our dead comrades in the certainty that their sacrifice will not have been in vain.

Let us now arm ourselves for fresh exploits.

For Germany and our Fuehrer Adolf Hitler![1]

While the great sea lift went ahead, in Paris the War Cabinet was grappling with manifold problems. Almost simultaneously it was confronted with the Belgian surrender, the loss of an army and vast quantities of material in Flanders, the withdrawal of British aid, the virtual certainty of Italy's intervention. But above all other preoccupations, one in particular stood out. Within days the Germans would launch their offensive on the Somme-Aisne Line. Since the War Committee meeting of the twenty-fifth, Weygand had been weighing the problem with growing uneasiness. He was highly pessimistic about France's ability to continue fighting without British support. Consulting Pétain on the matter at his office on the Boulevard des Invalides on the morning of the twenty-eighth, he found the marshal in like mind. Late that day he embodied his views in a memorandum "showing the gravity of the situation, the extent of the risks run, and the necessity of informing our British Allies and asking them for the most extensive aid possible."[2] Next morning he submitted the paper personally to Reynaud at the rue Saint-Dominique, reading it aloud to him in the presence of Pétain and Darlan. It made a realistic document.

The resolution to defend ourselves to the death on the existing positions [it began] and the prohibition of looking back

---

[1] H. Guderian: *Panzer Leader,* trans. Constantine Fitz-Gibbon (1952), pp. 119–20.

[2] Weygand: *Recalled,* p. 105.

issued to all the subordinate commanders, do not relieve the Commander-in-Chief of the duty, in view of the gravity of the circumstances, of examining every possibility.

The French Army is bringing into play for the defence of its present positions all the forces left at its disposal by its successive reverses on the Meuse and in the north. Should this defence be finally dislocated, the French Government would have to take decisions of capital importance . . .

Owing to the enormous disproportion in forces and resources between the attack and the defence—this latter partly improvised in the course of the battle—it is possible that, in spite of the heroic efforts of all, the positions at present defended may come to be seriously broken into. In that event, the power of penetration and exploitation which the enemy draws from his armoured units and his air force might enable him rapidly to reach the vital centres of the country. In particular, the French Army might be powerless to stop an enemy raid on the Paris region, where an important part of our war industries is concentrated. In this case France would be unable to continue a struggle assuring a co-ordinated defence of her territory.

Weygand went to show that in World War I it was possible to plug breaks in the line "because the armies did not possess an organ of exploitation comparable to the tank-aircraft combination." Similarly, in the war of 1870, it was possible to raise new forces to re-place the armies destroyed in the field and so prolong French resistance. But today, he added, France would be given no time to organize new armies and train them in the use of modern weapons, nor did she possess the necessary arms, uniforms, and equipment. Weygand pointed out that since he had described the military situation at the War Committee meeting of the twenty-fifth, the French Army had strengthened its positions on the Somme and the Aisne; but the Belgian "defection" had freed the German armored divisions for action against the French defense lines.

> The urgency is great, and for that reason the Commander-in-Chief considers it necessary that the British Government shall be asked to give all the aid in its power to our lines of defence.
>
> That is to say: two or three divisions formed in England; units of tanks and of anti-tank and anti-aircraft artillery; the aid of air forces based on England. It seems, on the other hand, quite equally necessary that the British Government should know that a time may come when France would find herself, in spite of her will to do so, completely unable to continue a militarily effectual struggle to protect her soil.

That time would be marked by the definitive rupture of the positions on which the French Armies have received orders to fight without thought of retreat.[3]

Weygand finished reading. Then, to drive home his point, he said to Reynaud: "I hope to stand on the Somme-Aisne line, but it is my duty to tell you that I am not sure of being able to do so."[4] Pétain broke in to congratulate Weygand on his memorandum and express his agreement. After some discussion Reynaud put a startling proposal. If the Somme-Aisne front were pierced, he said, the only intact French force would be the navy. "It is in consequence necessary," he added, "for the Government to organise resistance in a part of France resting on the sea, and round which the remaining troops can be disposed in the form of a crescent."[5] The Premier led the others to a large map of France standing on a circular table at the end of the room. Appropriately, noticed Baudouin, a portrait of Sébastien de Vauban, the great fortifications expert, gazed down on them from the wall above. Indicating Brittany and the Cotentin Peninsula, Reynaud declared that these were the only regions in France where resistance could be maintained on the basis of supply by sea. He asked Weygand to study the possibility of setting up a defense line covering Brittany and Cotentin, or even Brittany alone. "It is essential," he said, "that France should fight to the end, for a heroic defence will give her the right to survive and rise again."[6] Weygand's reaction was mixed. He told Reynaud that he entirely supported the basic conception, but doubted whether the army had the material and equipment necessary for turning Brittany into a fortress. Pétain and Darlan both approved in principle. The meeting ended, and Weygand hurried off to discuss the scheme with Georges at Les Bondons. As he left his office, Reynaud confessed to Baudouin how gratified he was to see Pétain and Weygand resolved to continue the fight. Only last evening Pétain had been talking of treating with the enemy in the event of the Somme-Aisne front being broken. "If the French Army is completely defeated," Reynaud told Baudouin, "I am not opposed to a request on our part for a suspension of hostilities, but

---

[3] Ibid., pp. 106–7.
[4] Baudouin: *Private Diaries*, p. 63.
[5] Ibid., p. 64.
[6] Ibid.

I am convinced that the enemy would impose dishonourable conditions upon us, and it would then be necessary to fight in the Breton redoubt."[7]

Anxious to put his Breton redoubt proposal on formal record, that day Reynaud sent Weygand the following note:

> . . . Because, in the eventuality previously mentioned, the whole of the national territory could no longer be defended does not necessarily mean that we would be able to suspend hostilities in circumstances which would be compatible with the honour and vital interests of France.
>
> Therefore, since, in view of this eventuality, the enemy would be in a position to make rapid thrusts over the whole area of the territory, I am asking you to have the goodness to study preparations for putting into a state of defence a national redoubt around a naval port which would give us the use of the sea, and especially lines of communication with our allies. This national redoubt ought to be equipped and provisioned—especially in ammunition—like a true fortress. It would comprise the Breton peninsula. Thus, the Government would remain seated in metropolitan France, and continue the war by using our naval forces and our Air Force, which would be employed in North Africa . . .[8]

Reynaud enlarged on the idea at the War Cabinet meeting on the morning of the thirty-first. He now explained that he visualized the government's retirement to Brittany only after a final defeat that left France faced with dishonorable surrender. The government, it was agreed, would in these circumstances reside at Quimper, capital of Finistère Department; and Baudouin was directed to arrange at once with the governor of the Bank of France that all gold still in France should be moved to Brest and a note reserve created there. But Weygand, after considering the military aspects of the plan for forty-eight hours, had become distinctly cool toward it. Confirming what he had hinted at on the twenty-ninth, he told the meeting that if the Somme-Aisne Line were broken he did not see what troops or material would be disposable for the defense of a Breton redoubt. "That is all there is to it," he concluded flatly.[9] As he argued later, "the organisation of a *veritable fortress* depended

---

[7] Ibid., pp. 64–5.
[8] Reynaud: *Fight*, p. 444.
[9] Baudouin: *Private Diaries*, p. 68.

on the availability of effectives and of engines of war of every sort, particularly anti-tank and anti-aircraft. We were short of all these on the line of defence which we were organising in the utmost haste, and there could be no question of depriving it of any element."[1]

Outside the War Cabinet Reynaud put the scheme to Georges Mandel, who opposed it on other grounds. Mandel thought it would be impossible for the government to function properly from Finistère, and also that, in moving to Brittany, it would appear to be leaving the country to its fate. Nonetheless, Reynaud still stubbornly maintained that it was of crucial importance for the government not to quit France until it had "resisted to the last."[2] His concept seemed destined to come to naught. Setting aside Mandel's objection, it would need not only substantial manpower and material resources, but also time, to turn this great rock-girt peninsula of northwest France—some 70 miles wide at its neck or narrowest point—into a national fortress. The project would be mooted again in the dark days of mid-June; but by then defeat was too near, in any case, for it to be implemented.

Meanwhile Weygand and his staff were busy on more conventional defense problems. Up to June 3, two army groups, Prételat's Second and Besson's Third, were guarding northern France from east to west (their junction point being Attigny on the Aisne). But on that date, in consultation with Generals Georges and Koeltz at Montry, Weygand decided to strengthen the western half of the long defense line. He ordered the formation of a Fourth Army Group under General Huntziger (General Requin's 4th Army and General Freydenberg's 2nd Army), to be interposed between the Second and Third Army Groups. Thus, as the High Command saw it, each of the two most likely axes of enemy advance would be specifically barred by a French army group. Besson's Third (from the coast to the Aisne north of Rheims) would protect the lower Seine, and Huntziger's Fourth, lying immediately to the east, would defend the plains of Champagne. In addition, Georges created two reserve groups in Besson's zone and one in Huntziger's zone. Weygand was keeping in constant touch with his

---

[1] Weygand: *Recalled*, p. 109.
[2] Reynaud: *Fight*, p. 445.

army commanders in the threatened sectors. He expressed strong confidence in them all. Requin, commanding the 4th Army in Champagne, possessed "qualities of intelligence and judgment"; Touchon, of the 6th Army, was "a sound commander who was generally agreed to be one of the most experienced soldiers in our army"; General Frère, of the 7th, was "a man of exceptional professional and moral quality who knew the way to men's hearts"; and General Robert Altmayer, of the 10th, had "the qualities of special energy which I had appreciated in him for many years."[3]

But the caliber of the generals was not always matched in the lower echelons. From a British observer came a disquieting account of the state of the 6th Army. Reconnoitering with a colleague in the Soissons-Rethel-Rheims area on May 29, the British GHQ military adviser to Air Marshal Barratt, Colonel Woodall, found no signs of digging in, no tank traps, no trench system, and only the flimsiest road barriers. Few troops were about and tanks and guns seemed nonexistent. Woodall was the more surprised as his headquarters had heard from General Georges that the Aisne Line was "strongly held."[4] He asked a battalion commander near the Aisne why there was no trench system, and the officer replied that his troops were Algerians. "Algerians never dig," he added. Behind this and adjoining sectors there was no second defense line. What antitank obstacles there were were practically useless. Next day, at General Touchon's 6th Army headquarters, Woodall was told that it was true—Algerians never dug. He was assured that the Germans could break through with ease anywhere along the broad 6th Army front (each division held some 17 miles). The 6th Army was "*épuisé*," officers declared with a shrug. In any case, in the hard fighting it had had over the last ten days, it had lost half its equipment.[5]

Yet General Georges himself was apparently hearing nothing but good of the army's morale. At Les Bondons on June 2 he told Colonel Woodall that "a new spirit had become evident among the French troops," who "realised at last that they were faced with inglorious defeat and the loss of their country."[6] The spirit of Verdun

---

[3] Weygand: *Recalled*, p. 120.
[4] *The Diary of a Staff Officer at Advanced Headquarters North* . . . (1941), p. 51.
[5] Ibid., p. 52.
[6] Ibid., p. 57.

was aroused, he added. But the conditions, conceded Georges, "were less favorable than in 1918."

The French could hardly blame everything on unfavorable conditions. They were not even taking full advantage of the precious lull in the fighting to press on with vital defense construction. By the start of June, utilization of civilian resources had hardly begun. Manpower shortage was holding up essential military works. On June 2, General Besson declared to Weygand that he could make better tank traps if he had more men. At the War Cabinet meeting on the third, Reynaud told Weygand and General Colson, Chief of Staff at the War Ministry, that he was ready to order the requisitioning of civil stocks and materials. Colson, as Baudouin recorded, said "he would have to examine with the Minister of Munitions what was possible in the way of tools, and particularly those for digging."[7] Reynaud reiterated the need for starting defense works, for which, he said, large civilian forces could be used. "Time presses," he repeated. Next day General Spears asked him how the defenses between the Somme and Paris were progressing. "He made a quick movement of exasperation," Spears writes, "and I gathered he could not get the General Staff and General Colson even to ask him for the civil workers he could have provided."[8] Some days before, a British journalist in Paris was mildly astonished to observe a gang of workmen busy renovating the base of one of the statues on the Pont du Louvre over the Seine.

In the last three weeks France had suffered multiple blows. Now, as May moved into June, the authorities seemed powerless to muster the national forces into a united war effort. Recently French Senator Jean Bardoux had made his own somber diagnosis of the situation when he noted in his journal: "The shadow of 1870 is spreading over the country."[9]

---

[7] Baudouin: *Private Diaries*, p. 76.

[8] Spears: *Assignment*, Vol. II, pp. 36–7.

[9] J. Bardoux: *Journal d'un Témoin de la Troisième . . . 1940* (1940), p. 332.

Chapter 15

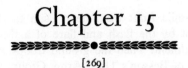

THE BATTLE OF FRANCE

"The fate of our Country . . . depends on your tenacity."

(General Weygand to his troops)

T HE LONG, battle-stained German columns had turned south from the plains of Belgium and Flanders. For 200-odd miles along the north banks of the Somme, the Ailette, the Aisne, and eastward to Longuyon, the *Wehrmacht* stood massed for the next phase of the offensive. Across the narrow river line, Von Bock's and Von Rundstedt's Army Groups A and B, ranged from east to west, faced the active remnants of the French Army—some 140 divisions against 49.[1] In the vanguard of the German infantry was the whole armored strength of the German Army—ten panzer divisions, formed now into five corps of two divisions each. Hoth's, the most westerly, was to attack between Amiens and the sea; Von Kleist, with two corps, was to strike from the Somme bridgeheads at Amiens and Péronne; and Guderian, also with two corps, was to drive south from the Aisne. And ready on the airfields was arrayed the almost-intact might of the *Luftwaffe*.

In the early hours of Wednesday, June 5, Hitler hurled his forces into the Battle of France.

---

[1] German losses to date were, according to Hitler's headquarters, 61,418 officers and men killed, wounded, and missing. French losses, according to the French General Staff, were some 370,000 men of the 7th, 1st, and 9th Armies. Material losses amounted to a quarter of France's field artillery, a third of her tanks, the majority of her transport.

On a 120-mile front from near Laon to the Channel, the dawn sky was lit by the flash and flare of a thunderous air and artillery bombardment. Then the ground troops moved in against the three armies of Besson's Third Army Group. German infantry attacked in the Ailette sector and the tanks of one of Von Kleist's two panzer corps broke out from the Péronne and Amiens bridgeheads. At GHQ, Montry, Captain Beaufre was roused by an early telephone report and passed the news to Weygand and Doumenc. Soon after 8 a.m. Weygand was at Les Bondons, watching the developments with General Georges. Since Weygand's assumption of command, Georges had seemingly become a changed man. Weygand found him now "in the best of spirits." He urged him "to neglect nothing, appeals, encouragement, rewards, that could maintain in men's hearts resolution, emulation, and tenacity."[2] And the Supreme Commander himself marked this grave moment with a ringing order to the French Army:

> The Battle of France has begun.
> The order is to defend our positions without thought of retreat.
> Officers, non-commissioned officers, and soldiers of the French Army, may the thought of our Country, wounded by the invader, inspire in you the unshakable resolve to stand fast.
> The examples of our glorious past show that determination and courage have always carried the day.
> Hold fast to the soil of France, look only ahead of you; in the rear the Command has made its arrangements for your support.
> The fate of our Country, the safeguarding of her liberties, the future of our sons depend on your tenacity.[3]

That evening, in Paris, a crowd of journalists and war correspondents assembled for the usual briefing from the War Ministry's official spokesman, Colonel Thomas. One change marked the familiar procedure. They had been called to the Quai d'Orsay instead of the War Ministry, their normal rendezvous place. There, gathered in the large ornate Clock Room, they listened tensely as the tall, bespectacled colonel began his statement. "Today,"

---

[2] M. Weygand: *Recalled to Service*, trans. E. W. Dickes (1952), p. 122.
[3] Ibid., p. 121.

he announced, unwontedly serious, "has begun the greatest battle of the war . . ."[4]

At this anxious moment, Reynaud's thoughts turned to the leader across the seas—head of a friendly nation whose vast untapped resources might yet, he hoped, save France. From his apartment in the Place du Palais-Bourbon he put through a direct telephone call to President Roosevelt in Washington. "In the midst of our struggle to the death," he said, "an irresistible impulse urges me to speak to you directly as man to man." As movingly as he could, Reynaud went on to describe France's predicament and danger. "But, Mr. President," he added, "to continue this struggle during the decisive weeks which are coming, to intensify it until victory, we have immediate need of all the available planes of your army and navy, which it is materially possible for you to send us. Can you stretch a hand across the ocean to help us save civilization? . . . The problem of destroyers is equally urgent. Anything done about all this would strengthen us very much. It could be decisive. It could reverse the course of history."[5]

For the men of the Somme and Aisne armies, Weygand's phrase "without thought of retreat" was no heroic platitude. The whole defense plan for this great battle was built on the basis of units fighting where they stood. In the hurried days of late May, as Besson's and Prételat's divisions prepared their defenses behind the rivers, the High Command had introduced a new tactic. No longer was there to be a thin defense line which, if broken, would be reformed farther back. Now the line was designed as a band of strong points, extending in depth as well as length—a *quadrillage*, or checkerboard of fortified positions such as villages or small woods, chosen mainly with the aim of denying the roads to German tanks. From these mutually supporting *points d'appui* counterattacks were to be made; and from them there would be no withdrawal, even if bypassed by the enemy. Gamelin had foreshadowed the tactic— nothing less than aggressive defense in depth—when he had specified "kernels of resistance" in his order of May 16 after the Meuse breakthrough. Weygand, two days before his order of the twenty-

---

4 G. Waterfield: *What Happened to France* (1940), p. 95.

5 P. Reynaud: *In the Thick of the Fight*, trans. J. D. Lambert (1955), pp. 461–2.

sixth, in which he prescribed "a chequer-work of centres of resistance," had laid down the new procedure in precise terms in a secret "Note on the Action to be taken against Armoured Units supported by Aircraft" for distribution to all commands.

. . . For the notion of the line [he ordained], there must be substituted the mastery of all communications.

Experience has just shown that every defence post barricaded on all sides, bristling with firearms levelled in every direction, and under a commander determined not to surrender, is impenetrable for tanks.

Every commander of a large unit must therefore take possession of all the communications in his zone by establishing a complete chequer-work of defence areas supplied with anti-tank arms or 75mm guns, without hesitating to give that zone even an exaggerated depth.

Every commander of a small unit must establish, on the site which he has been ordered to defend, a closed defence post, taking advantage of any local feature, a locality or cover, and solidly barricading every means of access.

He must realise that the strength of this key-point will be what his resolution, his activity, and his troops' work make of it. The barricades must be solid and all weapons protected and dug in . . .

The artillery must always be contained within the defence posts. Apart from its tasks of protecting the approaches to the neighbouring strong points and harassing the enemy movements, it contributes to the anti-tank defences of the strong-point in which it is installed . . .

Each of the commanders responsible for the defence of a stronghold will resist in it without thought of retreat. He is the defender there of the honour of his flag . . .

The effects obtained by the attacks of armoured units have been greatly increased by the moral effect produced by the aircraft accompanying them.

Established in strong-points guarded on all sides, as just described, the troops will have confidence and the means of sustaining every attack, even from aircraft. All movable weapons must fire against the attacks of aircraft flying low. It is sufficient for this that commanders make sure of their installation in dugouts, under shelter, or behind splinter-proof shields. Defence against aircraft is an integral part of the organisation of a strongpoint, and the ordering of fire is an obligation of the commanders . . .

This system of defence must be completed by the offensive action of our tanks and armoured cars—local clearing actions carried out by elements of inconsiderable size; or counter-attacks carried out by mechanised large units under the orders of their commander . . .

Everyone will feel that he is under command; surprises will be avoided, fear will disappear, and duty will be carried out without flinching.[6]

With this note Weygand had canceled at one stroke French defense doctrines that had stood for decades. But his exacting formula depended for its success on the possession of armor, aircraft, and reserves to counterattack the enemy forces that bypassed the French strong points. (In fact, none of these would be forthcoming.) As the day of the assault approached, he remained insistent that his troops must at all costs stand fast in their entrenched bastions. He would brook no thought of retirement for any reason. At a meeting with Prételat, commanding Second Army Group, and Huntziger, at Châlons on June 2, he rejected Prételat's suggestion for a preliminary strategic withdrawal. Visiting General Robert Altmayer at his 10th Army headquarters on the fourth, he reiterated fiercely: "The Somme, the Somme! Hold there till the 15th June, when I will have my reserves."[7]

Early on the afternoon of the fifth, Weygand was reviewing the first results of the fighting with Besson at his Ferrières command post. Both were confident that the holding tactics were proving successful. Although the enemy infantry had crossed the Ailette in the 6th Army sector, it had not gained a foothold on the dominating high ground. On the left, the initial tank breakout from the Amiens bridgehead had been followed by further assaults on the 10th Army front, extending as far as the coast, but these appeared to be checked. Only in the center was the situation less happy: here a massed armored onslaught from the Péronne bridgehead had penetrated as far as Roye, some 20 miles south. Assessing the day's operations, Weygand later commented: "The defence posts held, in spite of encirclement and in spite of bombing." But "only one anxious question faced us," he added. "Would the intervention of our local and general reserves enable these posts to be supported strongly enough and liberated by destroying the armoured units that

---

[6] Weygand: *Recalled*, pp. 410–2.
[7] A. Laffargue: *Justice pour Ceux de 1940* (1952), p. 172.

had penetrated our positions? That was the whole problem of the battle."[8]

By evening General Besson likewise was worried about the armored penetrations. He even began to consider partial withdrawal. So uncertain did the position appear to him that during the night of the sixth–seventh he issued instructions to Third Army Group that Captain Beaufre, at GHQ, Montry, quoted as "in formal contradiction" to those of Weygand.[9] Learning of this early on the seventh, Weygand promptly directed Beaufre to call Generals Georges and Besson, along with Doumenc, to a conference at Montry. The meeting assembled at 8 a.m. While the generals were in session, Beaufre wondered whether Besson was going to be relieved of his command as a result of contravening Weygand's express orders. As soon as they emerged from the Supreme Commander's room he buttonholed his chief, Doumenc, to ask what had happened. To Beaufre's astonishment Doumenc replied: "Besson defended his case very well." "What?" asked Beaufre, "a strategic retreat (*manoeuvre en retraite*)?"[1] Doumenc nodded. Beaufre was astounded. As he saw it, Weygand was admitting the failure of his plan before it had been properly tried out. If the plan were abandoned, the troops would be unable to withdraw their material from the *points d'appui* and would finally lose all faith in the role that had been assigned to them. "We are opening the way to a rout that can only accelerate," he noted in consternation.[2]

Weygand's "hold fast" order was apparently also troubling General Frère. At noon a Supreme Command liaison officer, returning from the 7th Army command post near Forges-les-Eaux, informed Weygand that Frère too had issued a conflicting instruction. Weygand hurriedly radioed General Georges to countermand this. But the position remained so confused that he called Georges and Besson to another conference that evening. It then transpired that Frère's order was only provisional and involved no withdrawal without confirmation. Nevertheless, as Weygand realized, "the situation on the fighting front as a whole had grown worse."[3]

---

[8] Weygand: *Recalled*, p. 122.
[9] A. Beaufre: *Le Drame de 1940* (1965), p. 256.
[1] Ibid.
[2] Ibid., pp. 256–7.
[3] Weygand: *Recalled*, p. 125.

In the 6th Army zone the enemy infantry was converging on Soissons and edging forward on the plateaus south of the Ailette; and Touchon had withdrawn part of his artillery. On the central 7th Army front the German armor was held outside the Péronne bridgehead, although more tanks were being brought up. Here the threat of a further advance was frustrated by a determined bomber attack —Besson had called up his entire resources of fifty aircraft. On the 10th Army front the two divisions of Hoth's panzer corps had driven as far as Hornoy, 20 miles southeast of Amiens. Now the truth stood out clear and unmistakable on the Montry operations maps: with the Ailette forced and the Somme crossed along almost its entire length, Besson's two wings were giving way.

At 6 p.m. Weygand had to accept "that the defence of the Third Army Group must be progressively withdrawn to a line traced by the Bresle, the Hornoy ridge, Poix, Conty, Ailly-sur-Noye, Moreuil, the Avre, and the Aisne, to which important forces had already been thrown back."[4] As the waves of panzers and the motorized divisions headed deep beyond the sacred river line from which there was to have been no retirement, all Weygand could do for his hard-pressed armies—many of whose units, by-passed and encircled, were fighting on doggedly in their "hedgehogs" without hope of relief—was to issue a special order praising their courageous spirit. "After the manoeuvre in progress," he added, "which will place our forces once more solidly facing the enemy, they will at once prepare the same deep chequer-work system, the same artillery organisations, and the same obstinate struggle against the tanks, in order to be ready for fresh successes."[5] The words could not hide the fact that the French Army was in retreat. Already by the end of Thursday, June 6—the second day of the Battle of France—Weygand's plan was in ruins.

Now, from the Channel to the junction of the Ailette and Aisne, there was no stopping the German advance. In growing disarray the French struggled back from river line to river line—the Bresle, the Avre, the Oise, the Seine, the Ourcq. On the seventh one of Hoth's panzer divisions—the 7th, commanded by Rommel

---

4 Ibid., p. 126.
5 Ibid., p. 128.

—raced on 28 miles to reach Forges-les-Eaux, 25 miles from Rouen
on the Seine, and cut off on the Bresle the left part of Altmayer's
10th Army, consisting of the IX Corps and the British 51st Division. Late that evening Colonel Bourget, Weygand's Chief of Staff,
telephoned Baudouin in Paris to report the news. To lessen the
shock he began by speaking of "a mishap of a tactical nature."
Baudouin's "heart stood still" as he asked what Bourget meant. The
colonel explained and asked where he could find Reynaud. Baudouin told him to go at once to Reynaud's private apartment and
inform him. Then, as Baudouin records, he "took up the receiver
with a trembling hand" and warned Reynaud that Bourget was on
the way, giving the gist of Bourget's report. Reynaud seemed
stunned by the tidings. "Is it possible that our hopes are crumbling?" he asked. "No, it is not possible," replied Baudouin in a for-

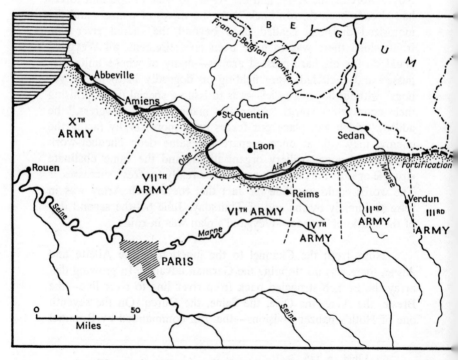

3.   The Battle of France: the French positions on June 5, 1940.

lorn attempt to reassure him. "But I know, I am convinced," wrote Baudouin, "that the battle is lost."[6]

Next day, as Rommel pressed on southwestward toward El-beuf, the 10th Army was split in two and the Seine exposed from Vernon to its mouth. In the center, Frère's 7th Army was falling back to Saint-Just-en-Chausée, 50 miles north of Paris. Weygand then ordered it to cover the eastern approaches to Paris as far as the Ourcq. By that evening, June 8, the battle of the Somme was lost. For the men of Altmayer's and Frère's armies and for General Hering's newly named "Army of Paris" there was one immediate task: to hold the lower Seine and the defenses around the capital.

War came that day to Vernon, a small pleasant town on the Seine with its ancient church and tree-shaded avenues, 50 miles from Paris, as it did to other towns of Normandy—suddenly and brutally. As shopkeepers opened their shutters in the early sun, one grim sign had already banished the semblance of peace. Through the streets passed endless columns of refugees. They carried babies, trundled burdened wheelbarrows and pushcarts, humped on bent shoulders all their worldly goods. Jostled by cyclists, horse-drawn carts packed with women and children, loaded cars bearing the registration plates of the Nord, Pas-de-Calais and Somme departments, troop-crammed army vehicles festooned with the faded greenery of camouflage, slowly the great procession moved on under the vault of plane trees. Most of these fugitives had been on the road for some days, often bombed and machine-gunned as they marched. Their faces bore the marks of fatigue and strain and on their clothes were the dust and grass that bespoke nights spent in ditches. Now, as they shuffled over the bridge that crossed the Seine to the quiet town of Vernon, all their troubles seemed past. But hardly had the refugees got clear of Vernon when German bombers roared over the town and turned it into an inferno of fire and destruction.

The German Stukas were ranging unopposed everywhere behind the disorganized 10th Army. Traveling with Captain Gasser from bomb-wrecked Pontoise toward Rouen to meet General

---

6 P. Baudouin: *The Private Diaries (March 1940 to January 1941)*, trans. Sir Charles Petrie (1942), p. 86.

Altmayer late on the afternoon of the seventh, Weygand viewed for himself the chaos caused to the 10th's communications by methodical bombing. "The aircraft had a free field," he noted angrily. "One after another, we saw the principal railway stations and cross-roads sending up smoke from fires caused by bombs."[7] While he talked with Altmayer at his command post at Lyons-la-Forêt, bombers came over and demolished Altmayer's telephone lines to all his corps. At this crucial moment when the 10th Army faced the threat of being cut in two, his only remaining means of contact was by unreliable radio or dispatch rider. Happily, Weygand and Altmayer were able to learn the Germans' immediate line of advance from orders carried by a recently captured prisoner. But, as Weygand said, the incident gave him the opportunity "to verify both the method by which the German Air Force succeeded in destroying the Command by depriving it of means of action, and also the almost complete absence of risks it enjoyed owing to our shortage of aircraft."[8]

Swift and overpowering as was the German onslaught on the river front, this time it was no Meuse breakthrough. The French troops had never fought more stalwartly since the start of the offensive four weeks before. Many formations were surrounded as they stood resisting on their appointed ground. Typical of these was General Mordant's 16th Division (7th Army). South of Amiens, at Dury, Saint-Fuscien, and Boves, three Côte-d'Or regiments of the 16th were swamped by the massed tanks of two of Von Kleist's divisions. Encircled artillery battalions fired over open sights. The 19th Reconnaissance Group and its reserve companies were overrun by the enemy's 29th Motorized Division while carrying out gallant but futile counterattacks. The odds against Mordant's troops were increased when a third panzer division crashed forward through the French defenses. By June 7, the 16th Division was reduced to three artillery battalions and four infantry battalions out of twelve. But cut off in their islands of resistance they fought on, while General Voirin's 24th Division took over the sector. Through the eighth and ninth the battle continued against tanks attacking in groups of fifty to a hundred. At Le Bosquel the

---

[7] Weygand: *Recalled*, p. 130.
[8] Ibid., p. 131.

50th Infantry Regiment was engaged in savage hand-to-hand combat: its colonel, and the colonel of the 63rd, bypassed by the panzers, held out doggedly in their command posts. By now, amid the confusion of conflicting orders, some formations were retiring and some were still standing fast—like the battalion of the 2nd Colonial Division, which battled on, totally surrounded, while the division on its right withdrew in good order.

As the front began to crumble, a sense of helplessness was invading some higher commands. Visiting the 7th Army command post at Forges-les-Eaux with General Doumenc on the seventh, Captain Beaufre saw staff officers in the streets firing up at enemy planes with a kind of "resigned fury."[9] Next day, at General Georges's headquarters in Les Bondons, he was struck by the pernicious atmosphere. Officers manning the telephones no longer seemed shocked or surprised at the bad news arriving almost continuously. They took the messages with cynical indifference while other officers slouched silently in their chairs. That morning, as Beaufre brought the operations map up to date, the aide major general, Operations, whom he knew as a stiff and severe instructor in his cadet days at Saint-Cyr, watched him, openly in tears. Beaufre steeled himself to appear calm and businesslike.

At dawn on Sunday, June 9, fell the second blow: the Germans launched their attack on the Aisne. Now, away on the right, the French 4th Army (Huntziger's Fourth Army Group) was in the battle. Once more, Weygand issued a stirring order. "Feeling that the drama was approaching," he wrote, "I sent out a supreme appeal to the troops":

> The German offensive is now launched along the whole front from the sea to Montmedy. Tomorrow it will extend to Switzerland.
> The order remains, for each one, to fight without thought of giving ground, looking straight ahead, where the Command has placed him.
> The Commander-in-Chief is fully aware of the efforts and the valour with which the armies engaged and the air force are unremittingly setting a magnificent example. He thanks them for it. France asks of them yet more.

---

[9] A. Beaufre: *Le Drame de 1940* (1965), p. 257.

Officer, NCO's, and soldiers, the salvation of our Country requires of you not only your courage but all your stubbornness, all the initiative, all the fighting spirit of which I know you are capable.

The enemy has suffered considerable losses. His effort will soon reach its limit.

We have come to the last quarter of an hour. Stand firm.[1]

When the Germans struck on June 5, Reynaud was busy reshuffling his Cabinet. He was vitally concerned at the widening breach between those who, with him, were sworn to fighting on (even from North Africa), and those who wanted an early armistice. Among these last he well knew Pétain to be the leader, closely backed by Weygand. Beneath Pétain's apathy and Weygand's belligerence he sensed a fatal pessimism, an attitude that admitted defeat in advance, a desire to save the army from total destruction at all costs—and, more sinister, perhaps a conviction that there could be worse things than a German victory. He suspected that since the failure of the Weygand Plan they were planning to form a "coalition" to demand an armistice in the event of the forthcoming Somme battle being lost.[2] While he realized that their public image as famous war leaders was of value to national morale and that therefore he could not afford to reveal an open disagreement with them—let alone dismiss them—he had decided to strengthen the anti-armistice group in the Cabinet by getting rid of other suspected defeatists and bringing in more of his own supporters. Chief among the dismissed were Daladier, recently War and National Defense Minister, and since then precariously in office as Foreign Minister; and De Monzie, Minister of Public Works, known to be pro-Italian. Included in the new appointments—along with Baudouin as Under-Secretary of State for Foreign Affairs, Prouvost as Minister of Information, and others—was, as Under-Secretary for War, that ambitious, far-seeing professional soldier who was fast making a name for himself as a man of both action and ideas, Charles de Gaulle. Reynaud had been impressed with De Gaulle ever since he had brought him his proposal for an armored corps in 1934, and subsequently had often discussed technical and other matters with him. Now De Gaulle's notable service with the 4th Armored Division confirmed him in Reynaud's

---

[1] Weygand: *Recalled*, p. 136.
[2] Reynaud: *Fight*, p. 382.

eyes as a fighter who could be a valuable Cabinet ally against the armistice seekers.

De Gaulle first heard of his appointment indirectly. On the fifth he visited General Frère at his command post to ask for orders for his 4th Armored Division. Busy dealing with the disquieting messages already coming in from the front, Frère said to him: "We're sick. Rumour has it that you're to be Minister. It's certainly late in the day for a cure. Ah! at least let's save our honour."[3] Next morning De Gaulle learned the news officially from General Delestraint, Inspector of Tanks, who had heard it in a radio announcement. He said a hasty good-bye to his division and left to report to Reynaud in Paris. At the rue Saint-Dominique he found the Premier "assured, lively, incisive." Reynaud spoke about Pétain. He explained why he had included the marshal in his Cabinet, even though neither he nor De Gaulle doubted that the armistice-seekers would aim to use him as a figurehead.[4] "It's better to have him inside than out," he said. De Gaulle was dubious. "I'm afraid you may be forced to change your opinion," he replied. " . . . Defeatism may easily submerge everything." Reynaud told him that he wanted him to go as soon as possible to London "to convince the English that we will hold out, whatever happens, even overseas if necessary."[5]

When Reynaud told Pétain of De Gaulle's appointment, the marshal showed marked displeasure. It was "even more distasteful" to Weygand. "What is your complaint against him?" Reynaud asked. "He's only a stripling," answered Weygand. (De Gaulle was then fifty.[6]) On the eighth, while awaiting arrangements to be completed for his London visit, De Gaulle paid Weygand a courtesy call at Montry. The Supreme Commander appeared "calm and master of himself." He lost no time in revealing his thoughts on the war to De Gaulle. "You see," he said, "I was not mistaken when I told you, a few days ago, that the Germans would attack on the Somme on 6th June. They are in fact attacking. At this moment they are crossing the river. I can't stop them." "All right!" rejoined De

---

[3] C. de Gaulle: *War Memoirs*, Vol. I: *The Call to Honour*, trans. J. Griffin (1955), p. 58.

[4] In his own account, Reynaud does not show that he suspected this at the time he invited Pétain to join his Cabinet.

[5] De Gaulle: *Memoirs*, Vol. I, pp. 59–60.

[6] Reynaud: *Fight*, p. 460.

Gaulle. "They're crossing the Somme. And then?" "Then? The Seine and the Marne." "Yes," persisted De Gaulle. "And then?" "Then? But that's the end!" "How do you mean? The end? And the world? And the Empire?" Weygand gave a hollow laugh. "The Empire? But that's childish! As for the world, when I've been beaten here, England won't wait a week before negotiating with the Reich."[7] De Gaulle gave up trying to argue. In a last word to Weygand he told him flatly that the government had no intention of giving up the fight, however badly it went. Talking to various staff-officer friends before leaving Montry, De Gaulle became more convinced than before that the senior echelons of the Command believed that the battle was lost and would soon be openly calling for a cease-fire on some terms or other. Back in Paris, he reported his impressions to Reynaud, and urged that Weygand—now frankly defeatist—be replaced. Reynaud demurred, and asked whom De Gaulle would suggest as a successor. De Gaulle proposed Huntziger, then commanding the Fourth Army Group: "although he is not ideal, he is capable, in my opinion, of rising to the level of a world strategy."[8]

Weygand himself had mixed views about De Gaulle. He had met him occasionally when De Gaulle was attached to the Ministry of National Defense, but he was more familiar with his writings and strongly disagreed with his case—backed, as he knew, by Reynaud—for a small professional and mechanized army. (This he dismissed as "a very seductive idea" which ignored the fact that modern war demanded large numbers of both men and mechanized equipment—the men being obtainable only through conscription.[9]) Recently, on the eve of the Abbeville operation, he had taken exception to a letter De Gaulle had addressed to him criticizing the way the High Command was using its armored forces. Before reprimanding him for this irregular conduct, Weygand had decided to wait and see how he handled the Abbeville action. He had to admit that this was conducted "brilliantly," and forthwith mentioned De Gaulle in dispatches and appointed him acting

---

[7] De Gaulle: *Memoirs*, Vol. I, pp. 60–1.

[8] Ibid., Vol. I, p. 62. In a recent conversation with Baudouin, Weygand had mentioned Georges as the best man to replace him, with Huntziger as second choice.

[9] Weygand: *Recalled*, p. 134.

Brigadier-General.[1] But Weygand's recognition of De Gaulle as an outstanding commander was tempered by a mistrust of him as being too intimate with Reynaud.

Meanwhile Reynaud faced another problem. The grim logic of Dunkirk was that it had isolated France as well as Britain. Just at the moment when France most needed British aid, that aid was virtually cut off. To prepare for Hitler's expected assault, Britain required all her resources herself—and in any case these were gravely depleted. The dilemma (especially in the matter of how much air assistance Britain could give France) had been apparent even before Dunkirk. Now it was intensified. In the first days of June appeals flowed thick and fast from Paris to London. On the second Reynaud telegraphed Churchill: "The battle which is about to take place on our front possesses such a supreme significance to our common cause that I wish to draw your attention again to the necessity for the twofold assistance of the British Army and Air Force."[2] He went on to ask for three divisions, at least as many bombers as had taken part in the "battle of northern France," and a larger force of fighters—to be based on French airfields. From then on, the calls were repeated almost daily. In London, Churchill and his War Cabinet studied them carefully, well aware that they could not meet the requests in full but ready to stretch British resources to the limit. Back went Churchill's replies, frank, rational, never raising false hopes. On the fifth he told Reynaud that the movement of the 52nd Division had been accelerated and would begin next day. On the seventh he radioed that in the last twenty-four hours British air aid had been further increased, specifying the heavily stepped-up sorties of heavy and medium bombers and fighters. He added that Britain was at once augmenting her fighter force in France to five full-strength squadrons. But still Reynaud was not satisfied. He telegraphed Churchill on the eighth: ". . . I thank you for your efforts, but the situation requires more powerful ones still, including especially the basing of fighter squadrons in France. . . . My duty is to ask you to throw all your forces into the battle, as we are doing."[3] To General Spears, attending the

[1] Ibid., p. 135.
[2] Reynaud: *Fight,* p. 462.
[3] Ibid., p. 474.

meetings of the French War Cabinet, fell the often thankless task of explaining the British position and meeting the charges that Britain was not doing enough. In these tense sessions his most persistent adversary was Weygand.

It was largely on Weygand's insistence that Reynaud kept pressing Churchill for more aid. Like Pétain, Weygand nursed a bitterness against the British, seemingly dating from the 1914–18 war. He blamed them for the failure of the junction maneuver of late May; and now, as the French took the shock of the fresh German offensive, he assailed them for their lack of support. At the start of the morning War Cabinet meeting on the fifth, he walked in and handed Reynaud this note: "The Commander-in-Chief must point out that our appeals to the British Government have been of no avail. We are meeting the German attack without the advantage of any new British assistance. Neither fighter aircraft nor fresh divisions."[4] Trouble flared at the meeting of the sixth when Weygand, as Spears recorded, "wanted a row."[5] After remarks reflecting on the British government and the B.E.F. at Dunkirk, he abused the R.A.F. for its current inactivity. Spears retaliated sharply, and the temperature mounted until, in Spears's words, Weygand was "grey with rage."[6] As Baudouin noted, at one point he burst out that "he was not prepared to tolerate the British attitude which was to blame the French High Command for the entire absence of goodwill to be found among those who were controlling British policy."[7] Finally a pause came and Reynaud diplomatically changed the subject. Next day, commenting on the operations on the extreme left, Weygand tilted at the harassed British 51st Division, which he accused of "fighting indifferently." General Fortune, the 51st commander, did "not understand the seriousness of the struggle," he complained.[8]

Pétain brooded in silent agreement. Remote, enigmatic, gazing morosely at the carpet, the eighty-four-year-old marshal sat through these ministerial meetings like an ancient ghost, a wreck of the famous soldier who had saved the French Army in 1917.

4 Ibid., p. 464.
5 E. L. Spears: *Assignment to Catastrophe* (1954), Vol. II, p. 75.
6 Ibid., Vol. II, p. 78.
7 Baudouin: *Private Diaries*, pp. 82–3.
8 Ibid., p. 85.

Now he wore a sober civilian suit, pince-nez glinted over the faded blue eyes, and the once-flowing mustache was clipped and white. Increasing deafness prevented him from following much of the proceedings. Often when he did speak he seemed to be living in the past. At a meeting in late May he was heard to say: "We don't seem to be making much use of carrier pigeons. There should be a dove cote in the rear, which is permanently linked up with Supreme Headquarters."[9] He repeated the bizarre idea a week later. But beneath the cold, blank-faced exterior burned fierce animosities—none stronger than his old grudge against Britain for bearing, now as in World War I, less than her fair share of military effort and sacrifice, and so being responsible for France's present plight. "England has got us into this position," he protested at the War Cabinet meeting on the ninth. "It is our duty not to put up with it, but to get out of it."[1] General Spears, meeting the marshal—an old and admired friend—a fortnight earlier for the first time after many years, had been sadly disconcerted. "If appearances meant anything," he noted, "Pétain barely grasped the situation."[2] Since then, in and out of the conference room, Spears had formed the impression that Pétain considered the war lost, further resistance useless, and a speedy peace with Germany essential.

Spears was particularly incensed at Weygand's attacks on Britain, a regular feature of the morning conferences. He decided to try and persuade Pétain to restrain him—on the grounds of military honor if nothing else. On June 6 he called on the marshal at his office next to 4*bis,* boulevard des Invalides. Upstairs in his long, low-ceilinged study, Pétain received him amicably. Seating Spears beside him at his desk, he showed him a map of northern France. "This is like old times," he said, "but we have never looked at anything like this." Pétain then proceeded to demonstrate Germany's crushing superiority, stressing the almost total absence of help being provided by Britain. He went on to lament the French Army's predicament, its lack of reserves and loss of equipment. With rising anger he inveighed against the schoolmasters and especially the politicians as answerable for France's decline. "The country has been rotted by politics," he exclaimed. Then he turned on De

[9] Reynaud: *Fight,* p. 458.
[1] Baudouin: *Private Diaries,* p. 89.
[2] Spears: *Assignment,* Vol. I, p. 201.

Gaulle, airing a long-standing grievance about a book published by De Gaulle—once a member of his staff—without acknowledgement of the substantial help given by himself. Spears tried to switch the conversation to the subject of French resistance, to fire the old marshal with a spark of fighting spirit and show that measures could still be taken to destroy the panzers first and then deal with the German infantry and artillery: the United States, he said, would provide the planes, if given time. But Pétain's tired defeatism was impervious to plea or argument. His thoughts wandered aimlessly. At a chance remark of Spears, he hunted for a speech he had made on Joan of Arc at Rouen in 1937 and insisted on reading it out at length.[3] Spears listened in pity and dismay to this "old man's tremulous evocation of a heroic past." Barely escaping the offer of another speech-reading, he rose to go. As he did so, he made a last effort to bring up the matter of Weygand's anti-British attitude. But Pétain, busy showing him to the door, seemed not to hear. Spears gave up the attempt.[4] In the hall he tried once more to rally Pétain to the notion of holding out, along with Britain. Again the marshal showed no reaction. Instead he ushered Spears to a small room where he took from a pedestal a small, finely wrought statuette and handed it to him. It portrayed Pétain on horseback, leaning forward toward two World War I *poilus,* who were looking trustingly up at him. Spears was fascinated. He expressed his admiration of this striking piece of symbolism. "That is the epitome of the 1917 mutinies," he said. "It is the whole story of the way you handled them." "I wish that group to commemorate me to the French people one day," replied Pétain. Returning thoughtfully to the British Embassy, Spears read another message into what Pétain had been trying to convey to him: he was the "grandfather" of his country, and "a grandfather does not abandon his children whatever the motive may be." Next day Spears informed Churchill that he was convinced Pétain would never quit France.[5]

Each day, around Reynaud's conference table in the War Ministry, one issue became more pressing: What would happen if

---

[3] Ibid., Vol. II, p. 84.
[4] Ibid., Vol. II, p. 88.
[5] Ibid., Vol. II, p. 90.

the Battle of France were lost? On June 6, when Weygand reported the position as still "satisfactory," he broached the burning question and then bluntly asked Reynaud: "Are you going on with the war? And with what—if the Paris area, which contains 70 per cent of the war industry, is captured?" Reynaud replied that Britain and the United States would provide arms, but that France must hold out in some part of France, by which he meant the Breton redoubt. Weygand countered by reiterating that he could guarantee no defense in Brittany. "All right," Reynaud retorted, "if we are refused a peace that is commensurate with the honour and vital interests of France, we shall continue the war in North Africa." Later Weygand returned to the Breton redoubt theme, which he dismissed as belonging to the "domain of fantasy." From Pétain came the bleak verdict that if the present battle were lost the only recourse would be to negotiate with the Germans. "If we can obtain conditions that are possible," interjected Reynaud.[6] Next day's German breakthrough toward the Seine heightened the urgency of the problem. "We are at the end of our reserves," Weygand told Reynaud at the morning War Cabinet meeting of the eighth. ". . . I have no more formations at my disposal."[7] That evening Chautemps, President of the Council, declared to Baudouin over dinner at the Hotel Matignon: "We must put an end to it. It is useless, and we ought to stop before the whole country is destroyed. Marshal Pétain sees the position the clearest."[8]

In his quiet office under the shadow of the Invalides, Pétain mused glumly on the fate of France. He had drafted some conclusions and proposals into a memorandum. This he submitted at the morning Cabinet on the ninth, reading it out himself. After covering other points he touched on the predicament of the French armies. "No outside assistance," to quote Baudouin's version of the memorandum, "could be expected immediately. Such being the case, the Marshal asked that the Commander-in-Chief should be consulted as to the line to be taken after the fall of Paris, which in

---

[6] Baudouin: *Private Diaries*, p. 84.
[7] Ibid., p. 87. Weygand and Georges had already drawn upon a number of divisions from the armies in the Maginot Line, the Alps, and North Africa, and some of these were still in transit.
[8] Ibid., p. 88.

the writer's opinion was inevitable. The memorandum closed on the necessity of seeking an armistice with a view to the cessation of hostilities; that was, of course, if the conditions of such an armistice, though hard, should prove acceptable . . ."[9] The matter of an armistice was promptly taken up by Reynaud. His views on this now seemed to have hardened. It was useless to ask for an armistice, he argued, for no honorable terms could be expected from Hitler: he was aiming at the destruction of France. Moreover, it would be highly unwise to sever France's ties with Britain. Reynaud asked Baudouin's opinion. Baudouin replied that an armistice appeared unavoidable: the decisive battle was lost.

As the dismal discussion continued, Weygand strode in—with reports of that morning's Aisne assault and of the battle situation worsening still further. He believed, he said, that his armies "were coming to the end of their strength."[1] He drew a stark picture of exhausted troops subjected to overwhelming bombing and tank attacks during the day, and then having to march through the night. He told how his generals had seen officers, moving forward almost light-headed with fatigue and hardly able to understand their orders, urging on their men to their defense positions. The troops themselves fell asleep at their posts and had to be roused to fire. Looking at Reynaud, Weygand felt that the Premier was not grasping the significance of what he was saying—which was, in effect, that the French Army was already beaten. "A wall was rising between the two of us," he recorded.[2] But Reynaud's thoughts were turning stubbornly once more to the Breton redoubt. If by any mischance the armies collapsed, he asked Weygand, would it be possible to move part of them toward Brittany? British divisions landing there could be retained for the defense of the fortress. Again his hopes were dashed. The condition of the troops, Weygand replied, would never permit of their being transported to Brittany. Reynaud, too, may well have sensed the "wall" that stood between himself and Weygand.

From west and north, the German tide was surging toward Paris. In five days it had swept down through the Somme, Oise, and

---

[9] Ibid.
[1] Weygand: *Recalled*, p. 137.
[2] Ibid., p. 138.

Aisne departments to reach, at some points, within 50 miles of the capital. With striking speed it was engulfing the quiet towns, peaceful villages, and green hills and valleys that bordered the ancient province of the Ile-de-France. At ten that morning, as the last bridges at Rouen were destroyed, isolated enemy spearheads were poised to cross the Seine. Fighting raged in the forest of Compiègne, where the famous "Iron Division" of Nancy (the 11th Division) stood firm while the 7th Army fell back to the Oise; and shortly to the southeast the 6th Army struggled to hold Villers-Cotterêts. Farther eastward the new threat was developing on the Aisne. The initial assault by German infantry, between Neufchâtel and Attigny, had fallen on De Lattre de Tassigny's 14th Division and Klopfenstein's 2nd Division. Resisting stoutly, at first these gave little or no ground. But before the day was out the Germans would hack their way through the 2nd Division's left flank to gain a bridgehead at Château-Porcien. Late that night, at GHQ, Montry, Weygand surveyed the overall situation with misgivings. In his May 29 memorandum to Reynaud he had foreshadowed a time when the French Army would be unable to continue the fight. "That time," he had said, "would be marked by the definitive rupture of the positions on which the French armies have received orders to fight without thought of retreat."[3] The moment had come, Weygand now considered, to warn Reynaud once again, in crystal-clear terms. "Faithful to the line of conduct I had assigned to myself of hiding nothing from the Government," he decided to draft another memorandum.[4] Before retiring, he penned this document:

> . . . Our armies are fighting heroically. They are inflicting considerable losses on the enemy. But the reduced number of our divisions makes reliefs impossible. Fatigue, lack of sleep, and losses are diminishing their power of resistance.
>
> On the morning of this sixth day of fighting (Weygand was taking his report to the 10th), I have to report that the enemy attacks are compelling us to make deeper and deeper withdrawals. Each day the enemy is extending his offensive eastwards. Thanks to the number of fresh units he has available, he is able yet further to extend his operations; the front stretches already from the Channel to the Argonne.
>
> At one point in this front, German armoured units have suc-

---

3 Ibid., p. 107.
4 Ibid., p. 138.

ceeded, by the rapid exploitation of a partial success, in cutting into two the forces of our armies on the left and seriously threatening the Lower Seine.

Our armies are re-establishing themselves on the Lower Seine front, the position guarding Paris, and the Marne, the last line on which we can hope for effectual resistance.

I ended my note of 29th May by pointing out that a moment might come when France, in spite of her will, might find herself unable to continue a militarily effectual struggle for the protection of her soil. I added that that moment would be marked by the definite rupture of the defence positions on which the French armies had received the order to fight without thought of retreat.

I am far from having lost all hope of halting the enemy, as my order of yesterday bears witness. Our armies are fighting and their manoeuvres are still co-ordinated.

But the events of the last two days of fighting make it my duty to warn the Prime Minister that the definite rupture of our lines of defence may occur at any moment.

Either through the adversary's success in seizing the crossings over the Lower Seine and entering the Paris region from the south.

Or through his success in Champagne in another deep incursion of armoured forces.

Or, finally, through our divisions, overcome by fatigue and diminished by losses, becoming powerless, under the pressure of an enemy three times as strong as they, to establish themselves solidly on the line of the Lower Seine, the Paris position, and the Marne.

If this should happen, our armies would continue to fight until their forces and their resources are exhausted. But their scattering would only be a matter of time.[5]

Even as Weygand wrote, events were shaping disastrously on the Aisne front. The bridgehead at Château-Porcien, forced by the German infantry, was the cue for Guderian's waiting armor. During the night of the ninth–tenth he was to send his 1st Panzers across the bridgehead, and early on the tenth tanks and infantry would drive forward as far as the Retourne River (south of and roughly parallel to the Aisne), to be checked late in the afternoon by a counterattack from the reserve light-armored group led by General Buisson. Meanwhile Guderian's 2nd Panzers would likewise cross at Château-Porcien and head across the plains of Champagne in

---

[5] Ibid., pp. 138–9.

a race for Reims. As evening fell the historic cathedral city, bruised and battered in World War I but never taken, was in danger of capture. To the east, Requin's 4th Army, now outflanked, would pull back toward the Marne. Like the Somme battle two days before, by the night of June 10 the Battle of the Aisne was lost.

As the German onrush continued, Reynaud could no longer put off the grave and weighty decision: in an atmosphere reminiscent of the hectic hours of mid-May he notified the Council of Ministers on the afternoon of June 8 that the President and ministers would leave Paris for prearranged places in Touraine. Twenty-eight hours later, at 9 p.m. on the ninth, Reynaud and his colleagues gathered solemnly in a salon at the Élysée Palace for another ministerial council. Its purpose was to endorse the evacuation decision. With President Lebrun in the chair, they listened to a frank report from General Weygand. "Strong impression of gloom," noted the President.[6] "The Ministers would have sincerely wished to remain in Paris," commented Yves Bouthillier, Finance Minister. "Their duty was to leave in order to ensure the Government's freedom of decision, that is to say, its very existence. The Ministers were aware of the inevitable necessity that was forced on them. Up to now they had known that the appalling thing—the Wehrmacht marching on Paris—was threatening. . . . Now they were sure of it."[7] Through the tense proceedings one member stayed silent: Marshal Pétain sat seemingly asleep, oblivious to what was going on. Lebrun noticed this and turned to him. "Don't you wish to give your opinion, *Monsieur le Marechal?*" he asked. "These gentlemen are anxious to hear it." Pétain stirred in his chair. "I've nothing to say," he replied.[8] Afterwards the worried Lebrun spent a sleepless night—his last in the Élysée Palace—wondering if the situation were as critical as it appeared. He recalled that France had faced a similar crisis in 1914. In an effort to glean assurance, he rose and consulted the *Mémoires* of the great war leaders, Joffre and Foch. Joffre was hardly comforting. "From everywhere," Lebrun read, in relation to the threat to Paris in August

---

[6] A. Lebrun: *Témoignage* (1945), p. 73.

[7] Y. Bouthillier: *Le Drame de Vichy* (1950), Vol. I, p. 47.

[8] Lebrun: *Témoignage*, p. 73.

1914, "the echo reached me of weaknesses that made me fear for
the breakdown of the troops' morale. The discouragement began to
appear . . . even at GHQ. I was afraid that the retreat might turn into
a rout. . . . The Government had to be made aware that in four or
five days the German cavalry would arrive outside Paris . . ." Foch
was equally disheartening. "The enemy's march towards Paris . . .
proceeded at a dizzying pace," read the President. ". . . Our troops
were pulling back under violent pursuits. . . . Companies were
wandering about at random, incapable of any action for want of
orders . . ." Lebrun reflected that nonetheless this much-tried army
had managed to make its magnificent stand on the Marne. The
wakeful President asked himself if the army of 1940 were capable
of such a superhuman recovery.[9]

---

[9] Ibid., pp. 73–4.

Chapter 16

START OF THE GREAT ROUT

"I shall urge the Government to request an armistice."
(Marshal Pétain)

ASSEMBLED IN THE CLOCK ROOM at the Quai d'Orsai, the newspapermen impatiently awaited their usual morning briefing from Colonel Thomas. The colonel was late. Minutes passed and still—contrary to his unvarying practice of the last nine months—he failed to appear. Colonel Thomas never did arrive on that morning of Monday, June 10. Along with a host of other officials, the War Ministry press spokesman had left Paris. The government's hurried exodus from the capital had begun.

Heading southwest for Tours, all day and into the night the government convoys rolled out of Paris via the Porte de Châtillon. By car, bus, and truck, it was a migration of almost the entire French administrative machine, along with ministers, senators, and deputies. History was being repeated, for on September 2, 1914, another French government had left the threatened capital for Bordeaux. Now, for many involved in the evacuation, this was a mournful moment. Bouthillier, leaving his offices in the Louvre at three o'clock with senior Ministry of Finance officials, was to remember June 10 as "a day of unspeakable grief." On the way through Paris he contemplated sadly the vistas of historic buildings, the impressive mass of the Arc de Triomphe. "What is noble, ancient and beautiful is the natural prey of barbarians," he reflected.[1] Baudouin, too, felt a wave of sorrow as he cleared the safe and the

---

[1] Y. Bouthillier: *Le Drame de Vichy* (1950), Vol. I, pp. 20–1.

drawers of his desk and left the Quai d'Orsai early that evening. Traversing the sunlit boulevards, he tried "to keep this memory of an unsoiled Paris that he would never see again."[2]

Despite the alarms of May 15, which might have provided a lesson, the evacuation caught everyone unawares. A plan was said to have been drawn up by the Ministry of War and National Defense, but the previous morning Baudouin had been horrified to find that preparations were almost nonexistent. Only at that late stage were the Ministries of War and National Defense, the Interior, and the Police Prefecture collaborating in a hasty last-minute scheme. The sudden evacuation order threw most departments into chaos as they struggled to improvise the removal and the packaging and transport of files and archives. In the offices of the Ministry of Finance there was every sign of headlong departure. Already on Monday morning the bureaus were deserted, the corridors empty, some doors locked and others still open—allowing casual visitors to enter and read papers that had been left lying on the desks. In the courtyard clerks and workmen were hurriedly nailing up boxes. At the rue Saint-Dominique, De Gaulle spent the day supervising the move, in a confusion of packing cases, incessantly ringing telephones, and belated callers tramping through half-cleared offices. The difficulties of the evacuation were enhanced by the need to keep it secret from the public as long as possible. Another complication arose from the fact that the evacuation was originally arranged by rail: when it was changed to a road operation there was an unprecedented call for trucks. The Air Ministry alone needed six hundred. This widespread demand was to denude the Paris region of most of its military transport.

Weygand had been strongly opposed to the whole government withdrawing at one time. He advocated the more important ministers staying in Paris until "the last moment." ("Weygand," Reynaud wrote later, with feeling, "had always been in favour of allowing public authorities to fall into the hands of the enemy."[3]) This view coincided, in fact, with the ministerial council's initial decision on the eighth, when it was agreed that Reynaud and the Ministers of the Interior, Air, and Marine should remain "as long as the situa-

---

[2] P. Baudouin: *The Private Diaries (March 1940 to January 1941)*, trans. Sir Charles Petrie (1942), p. 95.

[3] P. Reynaud: *In the Thick of the Fight*, trans. J. D. Lambert (1955), p. 480.

tion allowed." On the ninth, Weygand wrote to Reynaud reiterating this proposal; but that evening the Council of Ministers—perhaps even as a result of Weygand's own gloomy survey of the position— changed its views and resolved on the evacuation forthwith of all ministers, with no exceptions. One convinced supporter of wholesale government withdrawal was Mandel, Minister of the Interior. Now Mandel went further: on the tenth he urged the Paris councilors to follow the government's example. Meeting in the Hôtel de Ville at six that evening, they agreed to leave Paris; but seven councilors, they proposed, should remain in the capital "representing the people of Paris, whatever the circumstances."[4]

Reynaud himself would be one of the last ministers to leave. Dynamic and determined, yet beginning to show signs of strain, for him this was a day not only of complex administrative decisions but of mounting crises and fresh problems. During the night he had summoned De Gaulle—just back from his visit to Churchill in London—to his flat in the Place du Palais-Bourbon to discuss the worsening position on the Seine front and the armored threat impending in Champagne, both of which intensified the danger to Paris. Another blow now menaced France: André François-Poncet, the French Ambassador in Rome, had warned Reynaud that Italy was expected to declare war at any moment. De Gaulle could only counsel maximum resistance, to be continued if possible in North Africa. The new Under-Secretary was with Reynaud again next morning when Weygand called. While drafting his memorandum the previous night, the Supreme Commander had not decided when to submit it to Reynaud. He was waiting to see whether the events of the next few hours endorsed his conclusions. An alarming early report brought back from the Seine sector by Colonel Bourget decided him. He scrawled his signature across the bottom of the document, dated it June 10, and hurried from Montry to the rue Saint-Dominique. Marching into the room, he declared brusquely: "I have something important to say." He sat down and expounded his view of the situation. "His conclusion," recorded De Gaulle, "was obvious. We must, without delay, ask for an armistice."[5] Wey-

---

4 Ibid., p. 481.
5 C. de Gaulle: *War Memoirs*, Vol. I: *The Call to Honour*, trans. J. Griffin (1955), p. 67.

gand explained that things had reached the point where everyone's responsibilities must be clearly established. That was why, he said, he had put his opinion on paper. He then handed Reynaud the memorandum.

An angry scene followed. Reynaud heatedly challenged Weygand's conclusions. Weygand replied with equal force—insisting that the battle was lost and France must capitulate. "But there are other prospects," interposed De Gaulle. "Have you something to suggest?" queried Weygand derisively. "The Government has not suggestions to make, but orders to give," De Gaulle retorted. "I am sure it will give them." Finally the wrathful Prime Minister virtually showed Weygand the door. "We separated," noted De Gaulle, "in a most heavy atmosphere."[6]

The fact was that the rift between the Prime Minister and the Commander in Chief had become irreconcilable. They "had ceased to speak the same language," admitted Weygand.[7] The dissension overshadowed that morning's War Cabinet meeting—the last to be held in Paris or elsewhere. Nothing could now shake Weygand's certainty—reinforced by the latest battle reports—that the French Army was finished and an immediate cease-fire was necessary. When Reynaud asked him how soon the Germans might occupy Paris, he answered gloomily: "In twenty-four hours, if they know how weak we really are," though he admitted it might be longer. At the meeting they discussed Weygand's memorandum. In reply to a comment on it by Reynaud, Baudouin—in recent days an increasingly convinced pro-armistice man—came out in strong support of Weygand. Baudouin suggested that if Pétain had been present he would have insisted on the immediate examination of armistice terms. "The situation gets worse every day," he added.[8] Here De Gaulle—present at a War Committee for the first (and only) time—spoke up for Reynaud. "If the situation gets worse," he countered sharply, "it is because we allow it to do so." From Weygand came the swift retort: "What do you suggest?" "It is not my business to say what should be done," replied De Gaulle. In a confidential talk with Baudouin afterwards, Weygand told him that

---

[6] Ibid., Vol. I, p. 68.

[7] M. Weygand: *Recalled to Service*, trans. E. W. Dickes (1952), p. 140.

[8] Baudouin: *Private Diaries*, p. 93.

he agreed with his views about asking for an armistice, "for the fighting had become meaningless." He added that he had not voiced his opinion fully at the meeting as he was waiting for Pétain to be present and back him.[9]

In a Paris of departed deputies and empty ministries, one piece of government business remained to be done. Hurriedly meeting that evening for the last time, the Council of Ministers settled final evacuation arrangements. Then those who had stayed took the road to Tours. The whole proceeding had been carried out in such confusion that nobody had officially informed General Hering of the decision to evacuate. The Military Governor happened to learn of this in conversation with Mandel. "You ought to be happy," Mandel told the indignant Hering. "It was you who wanted it."[1]

In the midst of that day of upheaval, Italy struck her expected blow. At 4 p.m. François-Poncet telephoned Reynaud from Rome: Galeazzo Ciano, the Italian Foreign Minister, had just informed him in the name of the king that Italy would be at war with France and Britain as of midnight. Baudouin, notified soon afterward, hurried to the rue Saint-Dominique to confer with him. Reynaud was already composing a broadcast speech announcing the declaration. He read it to Baudouin, who asked him to delete "some lively passages" that seemed unnecessary.[2] Late in the afternoon the voice of the French Premier came over the radio, presenting listening Frenchmen with one more ordeal to be faced in this time of trial. "At this very moment," they heard Reynaud say, "when France, wounded but undaunted and upright, is struggling against the hegemony of Germany, when she is thus fighting for the independance of all other peoples as well as her own, Mussolini has decided to stab us in the back. . . . The world, which is watching us, will pass judgment. You are aware of the efforts of reconcilation and the enduring patience we showed towards the Italian Government. . . . It has been in vain. Mussolini has decided that blood must flow. . . . France enters this war with a clear conscience, and for her this is not meaningless. . . . During her long and glorious history,

---

[9] Ibid., p. 94.
[1] A. Kammerer: *La Vérité sur l'Armistice* (1944), p. 71.
[2] Baudouin: *Private Diaries*, p. 95.

France has passed through greater trials. It has been then that she has astonished the world. France is indestructible."[3]

Weygand learned the news late in the afternoon at Vincennes. He contemptuously summed up Italy's action as a cowardly move to "satisfy its greed for booty with the minimum risk."[4] Now he was presented with another pressing defense problem: to protect the Franco-Italian frontier he had no more than six divisions—the residue of General Olry's Army of the Alps that had been heavily reduced to strengthen the Somme-Aisne front.

At GHQ, Montry, the tidings came as a crowning blow to the despondent staff. Dining in the mess hall, officers listened disgustedly to an Italian radio broadcast blaring out a stream of speeches, interspersed with cheers and the jubilant chanting of *"Giovinezza."* As Captain Beaufre records, there had already been tentative talk around the corridors of Montry about the need for a cease-fire in order to save France from total ruin. Now this latest news hardened the view in favor of an armistice—in the literal sense of that word as a suspension of fighting. Loyal and spirited staff officers were ruling out all thought of peacemaking with the enemy.

At 6 p.m., in Paris, Pétain telephoned his old friend General Serrigny to come and see him at his office. Seventy-year-old Bernard Serrigny had known Pétain for forty years and served with him throughout World War I. As Pétain's Chief of Staff he had been one of his closest advisers during the army crisis in 1917. His relationship to Pétain was like that of Weygand to Foch, and he used to say of the great man, "I served him as a mirror to clarify his thoughts."[5] Now, in answer to the call, Serrigny hurried to the boulevard des Invalides. Upon his arrival he was told by Captain Bonhomme, Pétain's orderly officer, that General Bineau, the marshal's Chief of Staff, and a colleague wished to talk to him before he saw Pétain. The venerable Bineau—almost as old as Pétain— was highly anxious about the military situation. The Germans, he said, were preparing to cross the Seine between Vernon and Mantes by means of pontoon bridges, and there were practically no troops

---

[3] Reynaud: *Fight*, pp. 477–8.
[4] Weygand: *Recalled*, p. 142.
[5] B. Serrigny: *Trente Ans Avec Pétain* (1959), p. 1.

to oppose them. As for French aircraft, this was conspicuous by its absence. Bineau added that the authorities were considering the evacuation of Paris and that Communist troubles were feared. Primed with this alarming picture, Serrigny went in to Pétain. The marshal seemed calm but betrayed his emotion by the tell-tale blinking of an eye. He led Serrigny to a map and described the position in stark terms.

"Where are the reserves?" asked the startled Serrigny.

"There are none," replied Pétain blankly.

"How long can the front go on holding?"

"About three days, Weygand says, on condition it is not totally engaged."

"What do you plan to do in the circumstances?" queried Serrigny.

"Urge the Government to ask for an armistice. There is a Council of Ministers tomorrow evening. I will propose it then."[6]

"That's too late," retorted Serrigny. "You must act immediately while France still possesses the semblance of an army and Italy has not entered the lists, and use a neutral as an intermediary in the negotiations. Roosevelt seems to me the person, for he could exert pressure on Hitler."

Pétain considered briefly. "You are right," he said. "I'll go and see Reynaud so that the decision can be taken this evening."[7]

They left Pétain's office together, and Serrigny dropped off the marshal at Reynaud's door in the rue Saint-Dominique.

That same evening, in an office in the drab, tall-windowed Ministry of the Interior, on the Place Beauveau, two other men were talking. Roger Langeron, Paris Prefect of Police, was in conversation with Minister Georges Mandel. They, too, were old friends. "I've managed to get my colleagues to leave," said Mandel. "I'll be leaving soon—the last to go."[8] Looking at Langeron, he added: "You are going to fulfill the mission that the Government's

---

[6] There was in fact a Council of Ministers on that evening of the 10th. It is doubtful whether Pétain could have known that there would be a Council on the 11th, when the government was dispersed around Tours.

[7] Serrigny: *Trente Ans*, pp. 173–4.

[8] R. Langeron: *Paris, Juin 1940* (1946), p. 7.

given you, and of which I officially informed the Paris Municipal Council some days ago. Together with the Prefect of the Seine you will represent the French Government in face of the enemy."[9]

Langeron nodded. His mind went back to a talk he had had with Mandel some months before. Now he recalled this to the Minister. Mandel, he said, had predicted that Weygand would eventually replace Gamelin, and had then asked him (Langeron): "But don't you think that in the event of trouble he would be ready to act like Hindenburg?" Langeron went on to quote his own answer: "The position's already been filled. It's Pétain who will be Hindenburg."[1]

As the great government cortege streamed out of Paris, from behind the battle front another exodus had started: French GHQ was pulling back. In a grim "admission of defeat," heading along the southbound roads was the whole complex, cumbersome command apparatus of the French Army—the tripartite headquarters of La Ferté, Montry, and Vincennes. The move had been inevitable since June 8, when the German advance had begun to threaten La Ferté—already under bombing—and Besson's command post at Ferrières. Weygand was stubbornly determined to postpone it as long as possible. He spoke about evacuation arrangements to Doumenc, who assured him that plans had been made for an emergency rear headquarters. The location chosen was Briare, about 100 miles south of Paris in the Loire Department, and about the same distance east of Tours. Two days were needed for the transference if it were not to interfere with operations. Weygand agreed to various preliminary removals (administrative and other elements), but stressed that the Chiefs of Staff and their staffs must remain until forced to withdraw. By next day Georges had been driven out of his Les Bondons command post and was sharing quarters with Besson at Ferrières; and the Germans were pressing forward to menace GHQ, Montry, itself. But the tenacious Commander in Chief refrained from ordering Doumenc to retire.[2]

Now, on the tenth, with his forces battling on the last ordained

---

[9] Ibid., p. 11.
[1] Ibid., pp. 11–12.
[2] Weygand: *Recalled,* p. 135.

line of defense—the Lower Seine, the advanced position before Paris, and the Marne—Weygand saw the fate of Paris and the French Army hanging in the balance. Reports he received during an afternoon visit to Ferrières brought home to him the desperate predicament of the French defenders. Liaison officers just back from the front told gloomy tales of German air supremacy, heavy losses of guns abandoned in the course of retreat, troops cut off by prematurely destroyed bridges. Yet while a glimmer of hope remained that the line would hold, Weygand still delayed giving Montry the withdrawal order. But the bad news continued to come in. By early evening Villers-Cotterêts had fallen, enemy units had reached the Ourcq and the Marne, at several points the Seine was actually crossed. And on the Aisne front, tanks had pressed forward to the Retourne. Weygand re-examined the situation. "I decided, with death in my soul," he recorded, "to leave for Briare."[3]

Dining with his staff at Vincennes, Weygand presided for the last time "at that table, where," he said, "no doubt, in the time of illusions, there had been plenty of gay talk."[4] Afterwards the GHQ party, subdued and sorrowful, drove through the silence of the empty Bois de Vincennes to the Neuilly-Plaisance station to board the special train that waited to take them to Briare. "We carried off our mourning," commented Captain Beaufre, "in sumptuous salooncoaches."[5]

Military and civil affairs were marching in fateful unison. As the Supreme Commander's train steamed through the night from threatened Paris, along the refugee-packed roads toward Orléans headed an official car carrying General De Gaulle and the French Prime Minister.

---

[3] Ibid., p. 142.
[4] Ibid.
[5] A. Beaufre: *Le Drame de 1940* (1965), p. 260.

Chapter 17

THE OPEN CITY

"Paris will be taken perhaps, destroyed quarter by quarter. . . . We must never give it up."

(A French captain)

I N ITS NEARLY 2,000 years of existence, Paris—the ancient stronghold of the Gallic tribe of the Parisii, the Lutetia of the Romans —had had a stormy history. It had started by being razed to the ground in Caesar's time, and since then it had known invasion, siege, bloody civil strife. Sacked by the barbarians, beleaguered by the Normans, captured by the English, it had moved through its early centuries to become the fine and growing capital of Louis XIV. After the terrors of the Revolution, in 1814 and again in 1871 it saw victorious enemy troops parade down the Champs-Élysées; and in the tense first days of September 1914, it nearly fell to Von Kluck's advancing army. Now, in June 1940, this city of close to three million people, Europe's most elegant and civilized capital, faced another ordeal. As the French defenses wavered and the Germans edged nearer to the gates of Paris, hanging over the city were the dire alternatives of a resistance that would bring irreparable destruction, or the shame of a bloodless surrender and occupation.

Weygand regarded Paris as an "open city" insofar as it had no defense within its own boundaries, but was to be defended on the "advanced position" some 18 miles in front of the capital. On the tenth he thus informed Reynaud, notifying his intention not to attempt a defense based on the capital's rings of old fortifications or forts. His view was that if the advanced position were breached, Paris itself could no longer be defended. But despite this, right up to

—and beyond—the day of the government's evacuation, no formal declaration about the city's status was made. Without clear information, Parisians were wondering apprehensively what the fate of Paris would be if the Germans reached the capital. On the seventh General Vuillemin, anticipating air attacks on Paris—the city had had a foretaste of bombing in a heavy daylight raid on the third— had asked Weygand to suggest to the government the wholesale evacuation of the town. In passing on the air chief's proposal, Weygand could do no more than advise the evacuation of young people under sixteen. On the ninth, a broadcast by General Hering claimed that Paris would be defended street by street. Likewise, a statement by a French government spokesman in the London *Daily Telegraph* on the tenth announced that the French would "defend every stone, every clod of earth, every lamp-post, every building" of the city. Reynaud himself, in an impassioned plea to President Roosevelt for aid on the tenth, used the conveniently noncommittal phrase: "We shall fight in front of Paris; we shall fight behind Paris."[1]

Langeron, the robust and determined Police Prefect, was becoming exasperated at the ambiguities and indecisions. More than once, at the Military Governor's daily conference, he protested vigorously. On June 4, he recalled, General Hering had written to Weygand asking for guidance. "I am resolved to defend the capital to the last," Hering had said. Then he had inquired whether certain "military elements" (firemen, guardians of the peace, army units retained for feeding purposes) should stay in Paris or follow the withdrawal of the defense troops. After three days Weygand had answered that they were "to remain in place in all circumstances."[2] But, Langeron complained, the uncertainties had continued, producing needless anxiety among Parisians. He noted that an appeal for unemployed men on June 9 caused the public to believe Paris would in fact be defended. But in his own mind he was sure it would not. A few days before, with Henri Giraud, Director-General of the Travaux de la Seine, he had visited Weygand at Vincennes. In his small, map-hung office—Gamelin's old room—that looked out over a wide moat, the Commander in

---

[1] P. Reynaud: *In the Thick of the Fight,* trans. J. D. Lambert (1955), p. 478.
[2] R. Langeron: *Paris, Juin 1940* (1946), p. 17.

Chief had explained to them that the only possible defense of Paris lay in a line well in front of the capital. "I came away from that interview," recorded Langeron, "with my heart wrung, convinced that Paris would be abandoned."[3]

General Hering was equally frustrated—chiefly through doubts about whether he was supposed to defend Paris or not, and if so, exactly how he was to do it. Although he had been labeled by Reynaud as "lazy and too old,"[4] Hering had shown drive and initiative in attempting to strengthen the Paris defenses. At the end of May he told Senator Bardoux that he had built up a stock of ammunition and had a number of guns, and had also organized strategic points for eventual flooding and destruction, guarded by groups of *gardes mobiles* and military cyclist squads. But, he lamented, he had "no more than 60,000 men."[5] (These would soon be drafted into the Army of Paris—the force that formed part of the defense line north of the city.) On June 3 he had unavailingly asked Weygand, in the event of general withdrawal, to uncover Paris and allocate him three divisions for the defense of the capital. Now, in addition to being responsible for defending and maintaining order in a Paris without troops, he found himself appointed commander of the Army of Paris.

In some concern, on the morning of the eleventh Hering sent his deputy, General Lannurien, to Weygand at his new GHQ at the Château du Muguet, near Briare, to inform him that he could not fulfill both these functions simultaneously. Received by Weygand in the grounds of the château, Lannurien delivered his message. Then the Commander in Chief announced his formal decision on the status of Paris: the capital was to be officially declared an open city. Walking nearby were Reynaud and Pétain, who had been in conference with Weygand that morning. Weygand and Lannurien approached them, and Weygand notified them of his resolve—which was in pursuance of the note he had sent Reynaud the previous day. "They neither objected nor expressed approval," he recorded.[6] He

---

[3] Ibid., p. 19.

[4] P. Baudouin: *The Private Diaries (March 1940 to January 1941)*, p. 89.

[5] J. Bardoux: *Journal d'un Témoin de la Troisième . . . 1940* (1957), p. 334.

[6] M. Weygand: *Recalled to Service*, trans. E. W. Dickes (1952), p. 147.

had finally arrived at the decision after an assessment of the latest battle situation in front of Paris. Although the central sector was holding, it was threatened with imminent encirclement from both flanks—on the Seine and Marne. "To defend Paris in such conditions," Weygand wrote later, "would have condemned the city to irreparable loss of human lives and of national treasures, for that resistance would have resulted in partial destruction."[7] Late that night Lannurien arrived back at the Invalides to communicate the order to Hering. He also brought Weygand's answer to Hering's specific question. "General Hering," he directed, "will assume command of the 'Army of Paris' and will remain with it, whilst General Dentz, commander of the Paris region, will stay on the spot until and after the Germans enter the town, if this proves to be the case. Thus the continuity of the capital's life will be ensured without any break."[8]

Rightly, Hering needed Weygand's personal confirmation of the momentous "open city" order. Next morning he telephoned GHQ, Briare, to request this. Weygand's reply came through as Hering was holding his morning conference in his office at the Invalides—aptly interrupting Langeron in a question on the defense of Paris. Speaking directly to Hering from his desk at the Château du Muguet, Weygand dictated this message:

1. Paris an open city.
2. Neither the line of the old forts nor the fortified girdles nor the city will be defended.
3. No destruction of bridges, and no other destruction in the city. The combatant troops must not pass through the city; they will by-pass it through the outer boulevards. Organise the maintainance of order accordingly.[9]

In his instruction of the eleventh, Weygand had named General Dentz. A burly Alsatian, commanding XII Corps of the Army of Alsace, Dentz had been urgently called to Paris on June 2 with orders to report to the Military Governor. Next day, as Hering was warned to organize a defense line running from Pontoise to Trilport between the Oise and the Marne, Dentz was put in charge of the Paris Region in place of General Lanoix. Now, eight days later,

---

7 Ibid.
8 Reynaud: *Fight,* p. 482.
9 Weygand: *Recalled,* p. 148.

he took over from Hering as Military Governor. While Hering would lead the Army of Paris in its withdrawal south of the capital, Dentz, with his small staff, had the repugnant task of staying behind and handing Paris over to the Germans. To aid him in his role of maintaining law and order he would have the Prefect of the Seine, Achille Valley, and Langeron, the Police Prefect. Weygand had chosen Dentz for "the qualities of authority, self-sacrifice and coolness which I appreciated in him," he said later.[1] The soldierly Dentz found the mission little to his taste. He even appealed to Weygand to relieve him. The general's answer was terse: "My decision is formal. You are staying in Paris."[2]

Paris would be spared the threat of destruction. Instead, its streets would echo once more to the tread of German troops, and it would suffer an occupation whose length and severity none could foresee. Militarily, Weygand's decision was undoubtedly sound. Any desperate guerrilla resistance that the French would offer in the capital's great built-up area—while, at the most, badly harassing the enemy and delaying the final outcome of the battle—could not change the fact that by mid-June the French Army was a beaten force. The Germans now had to their credit an almost uninterrupted run of success including two major victories—the Meuse and Flanders—and their manpower and material resources were still almost intact; whereas the French had experienced nothing but defeat, coupled with immense losses in men and equipment. Against this background military recovery would have been impossible. In the crisis days of 1914 resistance had been stiffened by President Poincaré's dour watchword, "*Tenir et durer* (Hold on and endure),", and the fighting generalship of Gallieni and Joffre. But now there was no miracle of the Marne in sight, no Russian front to draw off 70,000 German troops. By contrast there was the fearsome evidence of what had recently happened to another resisting capital—Warsaw. But there were spirited Frenchmen who at this juncture would have continued the struggle against all odds. On the day the Battle of France opened, Senator Bardoux received this letter from a serving captain, Roger Denormandie: "I implore you, tell the civilians, the Parisians, your women and Members of Parliament, to

---

[1] A. Laffargue: *Le Général Dentz* (1954), p. 10.
[2] Ibid., p. 11.

let us fight to the end. Paris will be taken perhaps, destroyed quarter by quarter: we must never give it up, never. . . . Let us fall one after the other, but do not have us capitulate. Never. We cannot do this, for the sake of our country, our traditions, our honour . . ."[3]

Paris in springtime had never looked lovelier. The unvarying sunshine of those weeks enhanced the majestic monuments and the long vistas of the avenues, picked out in a gay enchanting light the colors on the boulevards and the new green of the chestnut trees. But few Parisians were appreciating these beauties. Since the false alert of mid-May they had been in a constant state of apprehension. Steadily the population was leaving the city, spurred on by the calamitous war news and the growing streams of refugees from the north. At the start of June's second week the fear that had lain over the capital intensified sharply. Now, as the battle drew near, Parisians were moving out of the city in a great trek southward. Shops, restaurants, and places of entertainment were closing: on the eighth one of the few theaters still open performed, to a tiny audience, a comedy ironically called *"Pas d'Amis, Pas d'Ennuis* (No Friends, No Worries)." That day one observer thought Paris was beginning to seem like a city in a state of siege. "A day worse than the 16th May," Bardoux noted on Sunday, the ninth. "Empty streets. Taxis being stormed. A rush for the stations. The battle is at our gates."[4] At night distant gunfire could be heard. After dark almost the only people on the deserted main thoroughfares were the armed guards outside the government buildings and underground stations. On the evening of the tenth, Langeron dined with his wife and two friends in the restaurant of the stately Ritz Hotel, which was empty except for one other party. But despite the bleak communiqués and the story told by the war maps, up to now Parisians had felt that all was not lost as long as the government remained in Paris. The news of its departure flashed around the city early on the eleventh, causing consternation and something akin to panic. Abandoned by its government, the capital now began to be abandoned by its citizens, in an exodus that in a few days reduced the population of three million by over a million. In the crowded 14th

---

[3] Bardoux: *Journal,* p. 349n.
[4] Ibid., p. 355.

Arrondissement, south of the river, a mere 49,000 Parisians remained out of a total of 178,000.

Through the main streets and across the bridges, heading southward, crawled an endless procession of cars loaded to the roof, horse-drawn vehicles, pushcarts, cyclists, and pedestrians, mingled with fugitives from farther afield passing along the boulevards Saint-Germain and Henri-IV, with their herds of cattle, flocks of sheep, horses, cages of fowls. These migrating countrymen, noted Langeron, gave the squares of Paris the appearance of vast fairgrounds. The southern rail termini, like the Gares Montparnasse and d'Austerlitz were besieged by thousands of Parisians frantically seeking trains. Those unable to find places surged back exhausted to the nearest *métro* station to camp for the night and try again next day; but by Tuesday every terminus was closed except the Gare de Lyon. Families surrounded by their portable possessions waited on street corners, vainly trying to hail taxis. Departing dog owners, unable to take their pets, carried them to nearby drugstores for lethal injections. Other dogs, abandoned, roamed the streets hungrily. And everywhere along the route of the refugees lay the debris of their passage: broken furniture, paper, straw, open cases, umbrellas, lost clothing, burst tires. It was a pathetic picture of a metropolis in flight.

Paris was now a city virtually without news and information. The Paris dailies stopped publication on the tenth, most newspaper offices and correspondents having followed the government to Tours; and Parisians were left with the far from reliable radio. And with most foodshops and restaurants shut—the famous Maxim's closed its doors after lunch on the eleventh—those who stayed had a hard search for provisions and had to be satisfied with what they could get. One shopper was glad to accept chocolate and spiced bread. But amid the chaos and confusion of a city on the move, there were small oases of peace and normality. On a corner of the rue Saint-Antoine stood, as usual, the fruit sellers and flower sellers—these last awaiting customers who now had other preoccupations.

There was a darker side to the evacuation. Bringing an echo of the *débâcle* at the front, small groups of tired, disheveled soldiers were passing through the streets on the way south. And military units stationed in Paris started seizing private cars from garages, sometimes at revolver point. On receipt of the government evacuation order, anxious officials had commandeered trucks needed for army use—the Musée de l'Armée, in the Invalides, requisitioned two trucks to rescue its historic exhibits—and left piles of valuable military stores, like gun parts and aircraft components, lying abandoned for lack of transport. To intensify the city's dark mood, on the eleventh, a vast smoke cloud descended on Paris, enveloping the streets in gloom and forcing motorists to use their headlights. The city was wrapped in a strange silence, and at one time it was impossible to see across the Place de la Concorde. No one seemed to know the cause of the great pall. It was later learned that General Dentz had ordered the firing of gasoline dumps on the outskirts of Paris.

The uncertainties of the Parisians were increased by the delay in pronouncing on the status of Paris as an open town or otherwise. For all they knew, the city was coming under full German assault in a matter of days, perhaps hours. On the tenth, right in the heart of the capital, appeared clear signs that Paris would be vigorously defended. Along the Champs-Élysées, the avenue des Grandes Armées and the avenue Foch were parked some 500 buses (later replaced by dust carts), drawn up in diagonal lines at 50-yard intervals—allegedly to prevent troop-carrying planes from landing. Doubts were set at rest on the morning of the twelfth, when placards were posted all over the town proclaiming that Paris was an open city. "To the people of Paris," ran the notice. "General Hering, called to assume command of an army, has placed the military government in the hands of General Dentz. Paris is declared an open city, and every measure has been taken to ensure, in all circumstances, the safety and provisioning of its inhabitants. General Hering."[5]

The only apparent effect of the announcement was to speed up evacuation. Amid the relief that Paris was to be spared devastation was another feeling: for tens of thousands of Parisians the thought of living under German rule was worse than that of enduring an all-out attack in their own streets and houses.

From his headquarters at the Police Prefecture in the boulevard du Palais south of the river, Langeron watched the life of

---

[5] Reynaud: *Fight,* p. 482.

Paris ebbing. The only "government" left in the city consisted of a few Paris councilors and the Prefect of the Seine. On Langeron and his 25,000-strong police force devolved the responsibility for controlling this fantastic exodus—and later, with his colleague the Seine Prefect, the more difficult task of ensuring law and order and the protection of Parisians when the Germans marched in. Langeron made every effort to encourage his men and stiffen their morale. On the tenth he had visited the Garde Républicaine and Garde Mobile and told their commanders that whatever happened the *gardes* would not leave the capital and would cooperate, as ever, with the Paris police. Two evenings after, he addressed a great police rally of all ranks, detailing orders and adding an exhortation on the spirit the police should show in the face of the enemy. The men listened in silence—"I feel they understood me," said Langeron. The meeting broke up to cries of *"Vive la France!"*

To fortify Parisians for their coming ordeals, on the thirteenth Langeron issued his own proclamation. "To the people of Paris," it ran. "In the grave condition being experienced by Paris, the Prefecture of Police continues its mission. This is to assure security and order for the capital. We shall fulfil this duty to the end. Parisians, I rely on you, as always, to make the task easy for me. Rely on me. I declare to you, once more, my deep affection and devotion. Langeron, Prefect of Police, Paris."[6]

In their growing isolation Langeron and the people of Paris had one good friend who was steadfastly standing by them: William C. Bullitt, United States ambassador to France. That day, among the flood of telephone calls to the Prefecture, Langeron received one from Bullitt. The ambassador was expressing—with what Langeron termed his "usual generosity of heart"—his admiration for the bearing and conduct of the police.[7] Behind the scenes, Bullitt had been closely involved in recent happenings. As early as June 1 he had been asked by Reynaud and President Lebrun if, in the event of Paris being declared an open city, he would hand over the capital to the Germans. Bullitt had informed Washington, recommending the acceptance of this request; but the United States government had taken the view that Bullitt

---

[6] Langeron: *Paris*, pp. 29–30.
[7] Ibid., p. 31.

would be better employed in doing everything possible to strengthen and prolong French resistance. This meant, in effect, that he should accompany the government if and when it left Paris. Bullitt, however, not having been specifically forbidden to stay in the capital, decided on his own initiative to remain, holding himself ready, if called upon, to act as intermediary in the hand-over of the city and render any help he could in easing the situation of Parisians under German occupation. As ambassador of a benevolently neutral state, he might not be in a position to do more than offer moral support, but this he was prepared and anxious to do, to the full extent of his powers.

In the three days since the government had left, the German advance on Paris had continued remorselessly. Now, on the afternoon of the thirteenth, leading units were reported on the outskirts of the city, at Pierrefitte, Drancy, Bobigny, Noisy-le-Sec, and many other points. In Paris itself the great trek of cars, carts, and silent, shuffling pedestrians continued. With the Germans close behind, it was moving at a quicker pace. Shops that had stayed open until now put up their shutters, some shopkeepers nailing down the slats with grim finality. Streets not on the evacuation route were almost deserted, and except for vehicles heading out of Paris all motor transport had vanished. Gasoline being scarce, even the police were reduced to horse-drawn carriages. The absence of cars, as one eyewitness noted, gave Paris an oddly old-fashioned look: one might have been back in 1900. At high noon an English observer—one of the few Britons still in Paris—watched, fascinated, as a solitary cow ambled across the Place de la Concorde, followed by a group of black-clad peasants. Over the river the Latin Quarter was eerily quiet. Alone of all its normally crowded cafés the famous Deux Magots still welcomed customers, but only a handful of stragglers occupied its marble-topped tables. At 7 p.m. the Deux Magots, too, shut its doors. The last loyal patrons drifted away. Unusually, rain had fallen, condensing the persistent smoke pall into a sooty precipitation. Heavy gunfire mingled with the rumble of thunder. Sunk in a numb apathy, all Paris seemed to be closing down.

But at distant Tours there were strange and sinister suspicions about what was happening there. Late that afternoon at a Council of Ministers meeting, General Weygand was informed of a story that had been telephoned from Paris to his aide, Captain Gasser. Gasser had heard from a duty officer at the Ministry of Marine that a Communist government had seized power in the capital and the police and *gardes* had been disarmed. To Weygand, communism was like a red rag to a bull: fear of a Communist rising as France faced defeat was one of his chief reasons for not wanting the French Army totally destroyed. Now he hastily left the conference room to telephone General Dentz in Paris. As Minister of the Interior, Mandel also hurried out, to call Langeron. At the Police Prefecture Langeron picked up the telephone receiver and heard Mandel's voice.

"Nothing new?"

"No," replied the Police Prefect.

"No incidents?"

"None."

"It's just that . . ." Mandel hesitated. He sounded almost apologetic.

"What do you mean?" Langeron was mystified.

"Oh, well, here it is. It's been reported to us that there have been some incidents in Paris."

". . . As regards incidents, there are none." Langeron replied emphatically. "I am perfectly informed, and in full control of the situation."

"Oh, well, this is why I've put this question to you. Someone of importance has told us, a few minutes ago, that the Communists were in control of Paris and that Thorez[8] was at the Élysée Palace."

Langeron was astounded. "You can tell him this," he retorted forcibly. "Paris is in anguish, but it is calm. There have been no incidents, and there won't be any. The Communists aren't moving, no one's moving. Thorez is not in Paris, and there's no one at the Élysée but the Gardes Républicaines whom I've placed there!"[9] Mandel seemed satisfied, and he hung up. Weygand received an equally reassuring reply from Dentz, and both returned to the conference room to deny the grotesque rumor.

---

[8] Maurice Thorez was leader of the French Communist party.

[9] Langeron: *Paris,* pp. 35–7.

In Paris, at 9 p.m., the Police Prefecture intercepted a radio message from the German High Command calling on the Military Governor to ensure order during the passage of the German troops, and to send envoys to Sarcelles, 10 miles north of Paris on the road to Beauvais, to receive capitulation terms. Langeron passed on the message to General Dentz at the Invalides. Dentz ignored it, refusing to have any parley with the enemy. Soon afterwards Weygand telephoned him again from Briare. "Are the Germans there?" he asked. "No, General, not yet," Dentz answered, "but they will be tomorrow." "No incidents occurring in Paris?" queried Weygand. "Is the city calm?" "Very calm, but sad. I've had the Police Prefecture and the Hôtel de Ville guarded. And I've ordered bills to be posted advising Parisians to adopt a dignified attitude."[1] Dentz had also taken another precaution: late that afternoon he had ordered the firing of gasoline dumps sited in the path of the advancing Germans on the city outskirts.

Just before midnight the German High Command radioed again, peremptorily ordering the envoys to be sent to Sarcelles at five next morning, under threat of military action against Paris. Dentz now had no alternative but to accede, and made arrangements for two of his staff officers to be at the rendezvous as ordered. As Paris waited tensely, the last French troops from the abandoned northern line moved through the blacked-out city. Traversing the outer boulevards between the Porte de la Chapelle and the Porte d'Italie were the tired remnants of General Mordant's 16th Division—the 7th Army men who had fought hard and bitterly over the last eight days, edging back from south of Amiens to make their final stand on the Oise and Nonette. Paris was now open to the Germans. In the early hours of the fourteenth, Roger Langeron, on all-night duty in his office, noted in his journal: "Tomorrow we shall be cut off from the rest of the world."[2]

---

[1] Laffargue: *Général Dentz*, p. 13.
[2] Langeron: *Paris*, p. 40.

Chapter 18

SWASTIKAS OVER PARIS

"The frightful thing has happened."
(Roger Langeron, Paris Prefect of Police)

I
T BEGAN AT 3:40 A.M. with a solitary German motorcyclist cross-
ing the gray emptiness of the Place Voltaire[1] in the 11th
Arrondissement. From then on, as Friday, June 14, dawned over
Paris, the invasion of the capital steadily intensified.

Between five and eight o'clock reports flowed in to the
Police Prefecture of German detachments on the move all over
Paris: three carloads of troops arriving at Saint-Denis barracks;
two truckloads and half a dozen motorcyclists passing through the
northeasterly Porte de la Villette; German troops moving down
the rue de Flandre toward the gares du Nord and de l'Est; half
a dozen tanks making for Aubervilliers; dispatch riders proceeding
along the Quai des Grands-Augustins; patrols on the boulevard
Saint-Michel; a party of officers arriving at the Hôtel Crillon; a
score of motorcyclists heading down the Champs-Élysées; loudspeaker cars in the rue La Fayette, ordering people to stay at home
during the passage of German troops. By eight o'clock an apparently endless column of motorized troops was starting to move
southward across Paris in the direction of Montrouge, a solid
stream of armored cars and tanks, preceded by leather-coated
motorcyclists. Just five weeks after the launching of Hitler's assault in the west, Paris was under German occupation.

With over a million Parisians evacuated and the rest remaining tensely behind closed doors and shuttered windows, at first

---

[1] Now called the Place Léon Blum.

the German troops seemed to be moving into a deserted city. But gradually around breakfast time, people ventured out into the streets to watch the massive parade in awed and sullen silence. The march in was taking several routes and was not all composed of mechanized troops. Along the boulevard de Clichy and boulevard de Magenta, in the Montmartre area, rumbled an unbroken procession of horse-drawn artillery. Young and well-disciplined, the troops sat on their gun carriages staring straight ahead. The quiet crowd gathering on the pavements noted their fine equipment, powdered with the dust of the French roads.

Simultaneously, a huge supply column was on the move two miles to the southeast. It struck the river at the Palais de Chaillot and Trocadéro Gardens and then turned eastwards toward Vincennes. Both convoys were so long that they were still rolling by hours later. In the boulevard de Clichy there was a touch of irony as the German gunners passed a giant War Bond poster that declared: "We shall win because we are the stronger." A neighboring movie theater still advertised a war film with a placard showing a terrified Führer. Some watchers were surprised at the absence of mechanization among the columns. Near the Palais de Chaillot an early witness noted that, apart from the pneumatic tires on some vehicles, "we might have been watching an army of Napoleon's time."[2]

Many Parisians were first aware of the German entry when they saw the Nazi flags flying above the Paris rooftops. Shortly after dawn German soldiers, escorted by a gendarme, had scaled the 985 feet of the Eiffel Tower to hoist a swastika flag, an outsize banner that soon began to tear in the brisk breeze and had to be replaced after half an hour by a smaller one. This was followed by a rash of German flags that by ten o'clock were flying over all the capital's chief public buildings, including the Chamber of Deputies and the Senate, various ministries, and the Hôtel de Ville; along with the great hotels in the Champs-Élysées, the rue de Rivoli, and the Opéra quarter. At the Ministry of Foreign Affairs on the Quai d'Orsay, the Nazi banner was supplemented by a sentry posted at the entrance, with a notice stating that the Ministry was under

---

[2] N. Jucker: *Curfew in Paris: a Record of the German Occupation* (1960), p. 52.

the "protection" of the German Army. In their haste to raise the *croix gammée* over Paris, the German military police in charge of the flag-hoisting had given Frenchmen three minutes to lower their tricolors. And now, everywhere in their place the red, white, and black banners of Nazi Germany loomed balefully over the avenues and boulevards. Many of the German standards were so large that they hung halfway down the fronts of the buildings. It was impossible for Parisians to avoid seeing them at every turn. The Germans seemed to have deliberately used flags of great dimensions to rub in the shame of defeat.

One of the Germans' first acts was to visit the Invalides and demand their flags of the last war. At eight o'clock, from the windows of his office overlooking the river, General Dentz saw a field-gray German detachment cross the Pont Alexandre III and the Esplanade fronting the Invalides and halt at the entrance, mount guard on the doors and cut the telephone wires. German officers then marched into his office and unceremoniously ordered him to hand over the flags. Replying that he had no idea where they were, Dentz calmly suggested that, as they had occupied the Invalides, the Germans should look for them themselves. Unable to find them, they proceeded to remove the protective sandbags from the most sacred relic resting in the Invalides, the tomb of Napoleon.

Dentz had just been talking to Major Devouges, one of the two French envoys who had met the Germans at Sarcelles at five that morning. With his colleague, Lieutenant Holtzer, Devouges had reported at the town's *mairie* and then been escorted by a German officer to nearby Ecouen to hear the surrender conditions from the chief German envoy, Major Brink. Brink outlined the terms. They demanded cessation of military resistance by 9 a.m. along a given line, a guarantee of order by the French, the maintenance of normal public services, and a total curfew for forty-eight hours. Devouges protested at this last, asking how the public services could continue during a two-day curfew. Brink refused to compromise: he merely ordered Devouges to obtain a quick answer from his superiors. Devouges telephoned General Dentz, and after further negotiation with Brink succeeded in getting the impossible curfew condition removed. There was also the question of what constituted Paris. Devouges pointed out that he was authorized to cede only the city of Paris and not its environs. Brink refused to discuss this, threatening an immediate bombardment of the capital if the conditions were not accepted as they stood. Left with no choice, Devouges reluctantly signed the surrender instrument; and shortly afterwards, from his office in the Invalides General Dentz dispatched the following message to French GHQ at Briare:

> I am presented by the German High Command with the following note:—"In order to avoid Paris becoming a war zone, it is insisted that no resistance is offered, either by the troops or by the population, within Paris and as far as a line Saint-Germain–Versailles–Juvisy–Saint-Maur–Meaux." I transmit to you this condition, for which I am not answerable beyond the area of Paris itself. The other conditions—the maintenance of municipal police and avoidance of destruction of all bridges and installations necessary for public business—will be fulfilled under my supervision.[3]

But the impatient General von Studnitz, commanding the Occupation Army, had virtually ignored the surrender formalities. His troops had started moving in long before discussions had begun. By the time the surrender was signed they were well on the way to controlling Paris. In a swift, well-planned *coup* they were seizing all key buildings, policing the main crossings with tanks and machine guns, patroling the streets with armored cars and loudspeaker vans. All potential resistance had thus been forestalled by about eight o'clock. Not that much resistance was apparent: by nine, only two incidents had been reported at the Paris Prefecture from the outskirts—thirty guardians of the peace arrested and disarmed at Bondy, and one French soldier and a woman killed in a skirmish at Antony.

Just before eight a convoy of four cars sped through Paris to the Police Prefecture on the left bank a mile east of the Invalides. Two youngish officers, one a colonel, were shown into Langeron's office. Saluting politely, they requested him in French to report to Von Studnitz at his headquarters in the Hôtel Crillon at eleven o'clock. Langeron had been expecting the call. Throughout the past night he had been at the Prefecture receiving constant reports of German movements into the city, anxiously alert for signs of

---

[3] R. Langeron: *Paris, Juin 1940* (1946), p. 39.

trouble. Now, as the full tide of occupation flowed over Paris, he faced an unpredictable situation. His 25,000-man police force was loyal and dependable; but there was no gauging the attitude of the Germans—or of two million "occupied" Parisians. Langeron's main concern was whether he could establish, from the start, a workable liaison with Von Studnitz.

So far the Germans were not attempting to interfere with the city's communications. The telephone system was functioning as usual. Langeron was surprised that his officers were freely allowed to transmit their reports to the Prefecture from all over the town. With its busy offices, shrilling bells and blue-uniformed *agents* trooping in and out, the Police Prefecture was probably the most normal-looking establishment in Paris that morning. But from the capital itself all sign of normality had vanished. Under the bright June sun, central Paris presented a forlorn sight. Everywhere life seemed suspended: shops, offices, banks, institutions like the Bourse, were closed and barred; hotels were shuttered, cafés empty; parks, boulevards, and the great city squares deserted; and traffic almost nonexistent. The capital seemed suddenly and mysteriously abandoned by its inhabitants. It had resigned itself to a bloodless conquest.

If a single item could symbolize this conquest, it was the swastika planted over the Arc de Triomphe. Dominating the Place de l'Étoile and looking down Haussmann's twelve radiating avenues, the Arc de Triomphe, erected over one hundred years before, stood at the very hub of the grand imperial Paris created by Napoleon III. It also occupied a central place in the hearts of Frenchmen; for it guarded the Tomb of the Unknown Soldier and the Eternal Flame, enshrining the martial valor and patriotic pride of France. For many Parisians the sight of the Nazi flag flying above the great Arch was the most harrowing experience of the day, just as for the Germans it was the most triumphant. It spelled the German humbling of everything dearest to France—her capital, her military honor, even her national spirit. The Arc de Triomphe was thus the natural focus of German jubilation and the starting point of the ceremonial march staged to mark the German entry into Paris.

German troops had moved early into the Place de l'Étoile.

Soldiers manning light cannon and machine guns were posted round the Arc de Triomphe, facing four ways down the Champs-Élysées and the avenues Foch, Victor-Hugo, and Marceau, and a military band took position between the avenues MacMahon and Carnot. At 9:45, as the German flag broke over the Arc de Triomphe to the blare of gay music, two mechanized and infantry columns debouched from the avenues de Wagram and Friedland. Solemnly they saluted the generals standing at the base of the Arch—and, in a gesture of homage, the Eternal Flame and the wreath-decked Unknown Soldier's tomb. Then, with their motorcycles, tanks, and armored vehicles they wheeled into the Champs-Élysées, heading for the Place de la Concorde.

Chosen for this honor were the regulars of General von Koch-Erpach's 8th Division (VIII Corps) who as part of General von Kluge's 4th Army had seen hard fighting in Belgium and in France —around Maubeuge, Valenciennes, and Douai—and had recently been engaged with General von Küchler's 18th Army on the Somme and Oise, as the Germans had pressed toward Paris. These troops with their tired, impassive faces and first-class matériel represented the flower of Hitler's armies. They were typical of the formidable war machine that was now irresistibly overrunning France. Their presence here in Paris was like the realization of a nightmare that had long haunted French minds. For this was the second time in seventy years that German soldiers had marched on the Champs-Élysées. The oldest among the few Parisians who watched, grim and subdued, might even remember that earlier occasion in 1871. But this time the defeat and disaster were more total.

German news cameramen and radio announcers were installed in the Place de la Concorde to record the occasion for fifty-nine million Germans at home. The vast Place made a fine setting for the pomp and circumstance of the German parade. Over the Ministry of Marine, on its northern side, the Nazi flag floated proudly: and even the neutral United States Embassy, next to it across the rue Royale, now bore affixed to its entrance the sign *"Amerikanische Botschaft."* But inside the Embassy Ambassador Bullitt felt no enthusiasm for the German triumph. He was following the day's events in deep concern for the fate of Paris. As the threat to the capital had grown, he had been in close touch with Langeron, offering encouragement and whatever neutral aid was possible. The previous evening, when Von Studnitz's troops were approaching the northerly Porte Saint-Denis, Bullitt had sent an aide to request him to defer his march in until morning. And early on this Friday he managed to extract further concessions for the Parisians during a conference with Von Studnitz at the Embassy.

With his monocle, small mustache, and slightly *démodé* air of a cavalryman, General von Studnitz resembled an officer of the Kaiser's army. This at least was Langeron's impression as he was shown, with his fellow Prefect, Valley, into Von Studnitz's large first-floor salon in the Crillon at eleven o'clock. Wondering if all Nazi officers looked like this, Langeron decided that Von Studnitz was an exception. The general quickly came to the point. "Do you guarantee the maintenance of order?" he asked Langeron. "I guarantee it if I am left to carry out my duties undisturbed," Langeron answered. "If order is maintained and I can count on the safety of my troops," said Von Studnitz, "you won't hear from me." He dismissed Langeron after announcing that the population could move about freely, that there would be a 9 p.m. curfew, and that a daily conference would be held at German headquarters, to which the prefects were to send a representative.[4]

By noon Von Studnitz's forces had cast their net over the whole city. To their ubiquitous guns, tanks, banners, loudspeakers, and patrolling and parading troops were now added low-flying planes, which skimmed the Paris roofs with a deafening din. The official attitude of the Germans was a mixture of sternness and conciliation. A cruising loudspeaker van in the Place Saint-Sulpice warned that any hostile act against the occupying troops would be punished by death. Another in the Belleville quarter ordered arms to be handed in and announced that police and public services were continuing to function. (Gas and electricity supplies had been uninterrupted, and the *métro* services quickly resumed after a short break.) Elsewhere officers were mingling with small knots of Parisians, proclaiming that the French were free, that the Germans wished them no harm, that the British were to blame for the war. One officer stopped his car and escort in the Place du Châtelet to declare to the bystanders that the French were badly governed

---

4 Ibid., p. 46.

and that he could not understand why France had declared war on Germany.

All this was part of the studied propaganda drive that accompanied the German entry. Leaflets scattered in the Gare de Lyon area in the early afternoon stressed that, with the intervention of Italy, the choice for France was immediate peace or complete ruin. It ended: "Frenchmen, think of your poor children and unhappy wives. Act without delay to avoid the collapse of France. Call on your Government to end a hopeless struggle!"[5] Some efforts were more direct and personal. At lunchtime an open car carrying two German officers drew up outside the Hôtel de Ville. As they got out a small crowd collected. Then one of them delivered a speech in fluent French, on the same lines. He turned to a woman in the audience. "Madame, no doubt you want your husband back?" "Yes," replied the woman. "Well," said the officer, "my wife wants her husband back too. Once you've signed peace with us, we'll settle England's business in a fortnight."[6]

More Parisians were now emerging into the streets. Their first shocked stupefaction was wearing off, but they could still hardly credit what had happened to Paris. They watched the passing columns or listened to the loudspeaker announcements in dull-faced, muted groups. At this stage few attempted to fraternize, but there were some isolated and even flagrant cases. In the boulevard de Clichy where the artillery columns were still passing, a German officer's horse stumbled and he was pitched to the ground. On-lookers immediately ran out to pick him up and help him remount. Nearby, some women returning from market with full shopping bags thankfully accepted food from German army cooks who were preparing a meal for halted troops at a curb-side field kitchen.

Throughout the day the great convoys rolled interminably into Paris. (Most were passing straight through, to continue operations in the south.) For Parisians the sheer weight and mass of the armored invasion effectively shattered one illusion: that the Germans were starving and short of vital materials. Many were surprised at the tough, sturdy physique of the troops, and even more

---

[5] Ibid., p. 51.
[6] Ibid., p. 52.

so at the excellent equipment—from the formidable tanks and guns down to the leather jackets of the motorcyclists and the officers' prism binoculars. The onlookers came to the realization that this was not the ersatz army depicted by French propaganda—a discovery that provoked angry comments. Here and there the impressiveness of the German turnout produced murmurs of grudging admiration. In the rue La Fayette one woman waxed so enthusiastic that she had to be restrained from applauding. "Look, mother, get hold of yourself," a man warned her. "Some of our boys are dead." Elsewhere a cynic declared: "For men supposed to have nothing but rags to wear, they certainly get results."[7]

The general bearing of these troops caused agreeable surprise. They displayed little of the conqueror's arrogance as they moved through the Paris streets. Citizens who had expected a grim show of ruthlessness were relieved to find that the *Wehrmacht* was correct and well disciplined. (The dreaded Gestapo had not yet arrived.) It was certainly not seeking trouble. In the only two incidents reported to the police headquarters during the morning, three French soldiers were killed after firing on German troops at the Croix de Berny and on the Quai de Gallieni at Suresnes. Apart from one innocent victim of German bullets, no civilians were involved. Later that day, whenever off-duty Germans got into conversation with Frenchmen in the bars and bistros, they tried to placate them by explaining that the real enemies were the English. "The war will be over in a fortnight," declared a German private in the rue de Flandre. "We don't want to fight the French workers. They're our friends."[8]

At the best, loyal but dispirited Frenchmen ignored these overtures. Others, glad to discover that the Germans were not the ogres they had been portrayed, nervously responded. To Leo Leixner, a war correspondent accompanying the German entry, the majority of the Parisians he met seemed passive and acquiescent.

Leixner viewed conquered Paris from the vantage point of an advancing German armored column. He reported—admittedly for home consumption—that the few civilians they encountered in the

---

[7] H. Amouroux: *La Vie des Français sous l'Occupation* (1961), p. 22.

[8] Langeron: *Paris*, p. 52.

suburbs appeared resigned to events, and gratefully accepted the Germans' reassuring answers to their nervous questions. One woman confessed how happy she was that the first German soldier she met could be so kind. When the convoy stopped and an officer went into a shop to buy bananas, the frightened mothers hid their children behind them, but were soon won over after the officer bought chocolate and handed it round to the children. The small crowd of onlookers gave a sigh of relief. "My poor France," wept one woman. "This misfortune is not our fault." Leixner concluded that the general mood of Paris was one of relief. Overriding everything, he judged, was the comforting notion that the war was finished.[9]

The reality of defeat was brought starkly home to Parisians by two poignant sights among the German columns. One was the collection of French helmets and service caps fixed to the bonnets of the vehicles. The other was the pitiful procession of French prisoners accompanying the Germans. Exhausted, dirty, and ragged, they limped beside their captors. Some could hardly keep up with them and had to break into a trot. As they passed, people waved at them: some ran out and clasped their hands. The captives smiled back wanly. There was a dramatic moment in the Place de Clichy when a woman recognized one of the prisoners as her son. The man rushed to the curb and embraced her. Seeing this, a German officer came up and announced that, as a token of the Führer's consideration for unhappy France, he would release the prisoner, who was now free to go home. The incident brought the Germans high credit as news of it spread along the boulevard.

Around lunchtime, small gatherings in the bars began to exchange impressions of the Germans. In one bistro near the Sacré-Coeur the general consensus was that they might have been worse: they were correct, soldierly and magnificently equipped. Less favorable were some of the views on Prime Minister Reynaud, who was accused of deceiving France about the military strength and readiness of Germany during the eight months of the "*drôle de guerre.*" England was also criticized for her lack of preparedness which had contributed to the French reverse. Parisians were finding their

---

[9] Amouroux: *La Vie des Français*, p. 21.

scapegoats, and gleaning their crumbs of comfort from the fact that no terrible fate had overtaken the capital during the morning. But beneath the surface calm of Paris lay the fears and forebodings of a conquered city that faced an unguessable future. Early that afternoon Langeron toured the Latin Quarter and other districts to find a tense and silent town which had, as he put it, withdrawn into itself and seemed to be waiting. The only part of Paris to display any life was its heart. Here, from the Place de l'Étoile to the Place de la Concorde, the great German victory fiesta was in full swing.

In the Place de l'Étoile more guns faced down the avenues, the band played on, troops still marched past in close phalanx. Above it all, the German flag flaunted its swastika from the Arc de Triomphe. A crowd of Parisians, larger than in the morning, watched apathetically. Past the swastika-crowned hotels of the Champs-Élysées sped German cars, some carrying bundles of Nazi flags to be hoisted on more buildings. In a café near the Rond Point, German officers drank champagne. At a garage on the corner of the rue de Berri, soldiers were painting German army numbers on commandeered French vehicles. The Champs-Élysées itself was now lined with watchers, mostly silent and a few in tears. Here and there brittle laughter erupted, the result of taut nerves. In a spurious gaiety, young girls were sporting ribbons in their hair. Across the Place de la Concorde floated the strains of music from another band; and on the square stood two recently landed Messerschmitts.

But the center of German celebration, formal and informal, was the Arc de Triomphe. All day it drew the Germans like a magnet. Officers and troops alike filed past it, photographing it, gazing at the list of victories chiseled on its stone, paying homage to its Tomb and Flame. A German general, deeply moved, was seen to remove his cap and kneel before the Tomb in prayer. For Hitler's press chief, Otto Dietrich, the Arc was the showplace in the tour of conquered Paris on which he led newly arrived foreign journalists in the afternoon.

The morning ceremony at the Arc de Triomphe had been witnessed with particular grief by one Frenchman, M. Gaudin. A wounded veteran of World War I, Gaudin held the honored position of guardian of the Eternal Flame. Through the morning and into the afternoon he stayed beside the Flame, watching the Germans move past it. Gaudin was deeply concerned that on the previous day he had been told to extinguish the Flame on the

German entry. He now sought advice about this from a member of the Committee of the Flame, Edmond Ferrand, who joined him at his post under the Arc. They agreed to defer a final decision until 6:30. At that hour, as no countermanding instruction had been received, they took the drastic step. In their military uniforms, hands on swords, Gaudin and Ferrand solemnly put out France's Eternal Flame while the watching Germans stood to attention. Then they signed their names in the register. The flame, lit on November 11, 1920, had burned uninterruptedly for five months short of twenty years.

That evening the one place in Paris where people were gathered in any numbers was the Arc de Triomphe. Now Parisians were making their own pilgrimage there—the weeping wives and mothers, many of them in mourning, the children and old men. An American reporter who arrived in the capital shortly before dusk found the rest of central Paris silent and deserted. On the street corners stood a few Parisians, and a single German car was crossing the Place de la Concorde. The great hotels not requisitioned for the Germans, like the Scribe, were shuttered. Along the Champs-Élysées a solitary café was open. The restaurant of the Ritz, though not officially closed, was empty and unable to serve a meal to the hungry newspapermen who besieged it. As the 9 p.m. curfew descended, inertia gripped the whole city. Langeron, paying a late visit to his main police stations, got unanimous reports of empty streets, with no incidents. Never in peace or war had Paris, the traditionally gay capital, lain under such a cloud of gloom and sorrow.

The Paris police had spent a thankless and frustrating day. Wearing their distinctive red-and-white disks, they had conscientiously attempted to perform their usual duties and also been at the beck and call of the Germans. What rankled most with them was having to salute German officers. The orderly behavior of the Parisians had made their task easier, and Von Studnitz had kept his word not to interfere with the police if the security of his troops was not threatened. But four guns mounted around the Prefecture warned Langeron that he was prepared to be ruthless if necessary. The only sign of trouble appeared late that evening. Returning to the Prefecture from his tour of the stations, Langeron was informed that his Director of Information, Jacques Simon, had been ordered to German headquarters for questioning.

Langeron at once drove to the American Embassy to see

Bullitt and request his help. Bullitt had already proved a tower of strength that day. Earlier he had telephoned Langeron to say that he wished the representatives of the French government to feel that they were not alone, and that the ambassador of the great republic was close behind them. Now he sent his Councilor, Robert Murphy, to the Hôtel Crillon to make plain to Von Studnitz that if he persisted in violating his assurances, given that morning, no one could be answerable for maintaining order in Paris. Simon was immediately released.

In the Invalides, General Dentz and his Chief of Staff had been under close constraint all day. Late that night they were roused and driven through darkened Paris to Von Studnitz's headquarters at the Hôtel Crillon. Von Studnitz ordered Dentz to hand over his *consigne*—his instructions from the French High Command. Dentz stood erect and self-possessed. "I have no *consigne* to pass to an enemy army," he answered calmly. "My mission was to maintain order until your arrival. It is now completed." "Your mission now completed?" burst out Von Studnitz. "All I've got to do is give you your liberty? You who have broken the undertakings of your government on the firing of petrol dumps, in order to hold up our advance? This is an act of war for which you will have to make account before a German court-martial!" Dentz coolly replied that the dumps were outside the Paris boundaries and thus no hostile act had been committed in Paris itself. He and his Chief of Staff were escorted back to the Invalides.[1]

For their eventual release, General Dentz and his staff had to thank the intervention of Bullitt. Confined in the Invalides for the next four days, they were then to be moved to Maisons-Laffitte, outside Paris. From there, as a result of the U.S. ambassador's vigorous protests, they were to be taken after a further week to the demarcation line and freed.

In Germany that evening there was wild rejoicing over the fall of Paris. All over the country, on Hitler's orders, the bells rang out a fifteen-minute peal of triumph. The shock and dismay that were widely felt elsewhere were voiced in next day's London *Times*. "One of the great lamps of civilization has been darkened, though it

---

[1] A. Laffargue: *Le Général Dentz* (1954), p. 16.

will never be quenched" ran an editorial in that paper. "The pollution of the great city will strike grief, as the fall of no other capital could do, in the hearts of men all over the world."[2]

Under its first night of occupation, Paris slept uneasily. Far worse was to come, starting with the arrival of the Gestapo on the morrow. But the swastika banners and the troops and guns were already there to signal a domination that would last four years. Among the tragedies of June 14 in Paris were the suicides, reports of which trickled into the police headquarters throughout the day. These were typified by the death of the noted brain surgeon, Professor Thierry de Martel, who had declared earlier that he could not go on living if Paris were occupied. That morning De Martel took strychnine, leaving a letter that said it would be useless to try to revive him. His farewell note contained the despairing phrase: "*Je ne peux pas.* (I can't . . .)."[3] But as the capital faced its bleak future, two small events offered Parisians a gleam of comfort. That evening the Germans hauled down the swastika flag from the Arc de Triomphe; and next day, just twenty-four hours after its extinction, the Eternal Flame was ceremonially relit.

---

[2] *The Times* (London), June 15, 1940, p. 7.
[3] P. Audiat: *Paris pendant la Guerre: juin 1940–août 1944* (1946), p. 17.

Chapter 19

>>>>>>>>>>●<<<<<<<<<

THE CHAOS OF TOURS

"The war is irretrievably lost."
(General Weygand)

T HE OLD CITY OF TOURS, on its twin rivers the Loire and Cher, had never known such crowds. For days refugees from Paris and northern France had poured into its narrow streets. Now, on the night of June 10–11, as the government retinues began arriving from Paris, congestion reached its peak. Conditions bordered on the chaotic. Whatever reception plans existed proved wildly inadequate. Typical of the confusion was the siting of the Censorship Bureau and Ministry of Information in two cramped, dilapidated old buildings in the obscure rue Gambetta. Many departments and living quarters were located outside the town at Langeais, Azay-le-Rideau, Ligneuil, and a dozen other places. The various requisitioned premises—many of them châteaux—had no direct telephone link. The Foreign Ministry, lodged in the Château de la Chataigneraie, near Langeais, possessed a single line to the Langeais post office. In a nearby château British Ambassador Sir Ronald Campbell had wisely equipped himself with a radio set. Less fortunate was the French President, in a lonely state at the Château de Cange, standing in its elegant grounds on a hill dominating the Cher, 12 miles from Tours. Visiting him from Langeais on the afternoon of the eleventh, Paul Baudouin found him "depressed and overcome," without news from Reynaud or Weygand. No one had made contact with him since his arrival there with his wife and Secretary-General, M. Magré, the day before.[1] Reynaud and Weygand

---

[1] P. Baudouin: *The Private Diaries (March 1940 to January 1941)*, trans. Sir Charles Petrie (1948), p. 95.

themselves had a telephone problem. Quartered in the Château de Chissay, near Montrichard—a huge, unprepossessing Renaissance mansion of massive walls and heavy-beamed, sparsely furnished rooms—the Premier and his party[2] had only a hand-operated telephone to the small local exchange. A hundred miles away at the Château du Muguet, Briare, Weygand's one instrument was in the bathroom. When officers wanted news of the battle, they rang the local operator. Commented one writer: "The Government is camped rather than installed."[3]

Scattered over the Touraine countryside, Reynaud's government struggled to maintain a control that was rapidly slipping. For the next seventy-two hours strained and harassed ministers and army chiefs hurried between the Tours Prefecture and outlying châteaux, along choked and unfamiliar roads, without proper communications, short of news, prey to rumor, often ignorant as to where their colleagues were. And now, as total defeat loomed near, they were fundamentally divided among themselves. Under increasing pressures and with time against them, they argued and wrangled over the fate of France in a series of tense and often stormy meetings.

The meetings were almost continuous. From the eleventh to the thirteenth the Council of Ministers convened five times in all, and the Supreme Council twice. In the latter—which were the last Franco-British conferences to be held before the French capitulation—one figure, as always, dominated the scene: Winston Churchill. Determined, and sympathetic, the British Premier strove to shore up the Frenchmen's faltering spirit, and pledged that, whatever happened, Britain would fight on. For some days, in increasing alarm at the French situation, he had been urging an inter-Allied meeting; and on the morning of the eleventh he readily answered a call from Reynaud to fly to Briare.

Late that afternoon Churchill's Flamingo aircraft landed at a deserted nearby airfield, carrying, besides the British Premier, Anthony Eden and Generals Dill and Ismay. They drove to the Château du Muguet—in Spears's description "a large monstrosity of red lobster-coloured brick, and stone the hue of unripe Camem-

---

[2] Included in the party was Reynaud's intimate and influential friend, the Comtesse de Portes.

[3] H. Bidou: *La Bataille de France, 10 mai–25 juin 1940* (1941), p. 196.

bert."[4] At seven the meeting started in the mansion's large dining room. The French party consisted of Reynaud, Pétain, Weygand, De Gaulle, and two of Reynaud's staff, Captain de Margerie and Colonel de Villelume. Spears was one of the British group. The atmosphere was funereal. As Spears noted, the French "sat with set white faces, their eyes on the table."[5] Only De Gaulle showed any strength and confidence. Churchill's opening words solemnly affirmed the British resolve to continue the struggle. He went on to announce the forthcoming arrival of two Allied divisions, and promised up to twenty-five divisions by spring 1941, if France could hold out until then. Next, Weygand detailed the military position. His report carried an air of calamity. "It is a race between the exhaustion of the French troops, who are almost at the end of their powers, and the enemy's breathless state," he declared.[6] At Churchill's request, General Georges appeared. Georges endorsed Weygand's statement. Some twenty-five divisions had been lost since June 5, he said. French fighter strength was reduced to 170 or 180 planes. "We are literally at the end of our tether," was Georges's dismal summation.[7] The crucial matter of British air support arose. During an exchange between Reynaud and Churchill, with Georges intervening, Reynaud declared—in answer to Churchill's explanation of why Britain could not commit the entire R.A.F. to the battle—"history will undoubtedly say that the Battle of France was lost through lack of aircraft."[8] Churchill raised the question of the Breton redoubt—or, failing that, the possibility of waging guerrilla warfare in various parts of France. From Weygand came a quick reaction on the redoubt plan: he explained concisely why he did not think it would work. Now Pétain made a rare interjection. Guerrilla warfare, he said, would mean the destruction of France. Less categorically, Reynaud agreed. The conference ended with a stirring exhortation from Churchill, who restated his conviction that Hitler would fall.

---

[4] E. L. Spears: *Assignment to Catastrophe* (1954), Vol. II, p. 138.
[5] Ibid., Vol. II, p. 139.
[6] M. Weygand: *Recalled to Service*, trans. E. W. Dickes (1952), p. 149.
[7] P. Reynaud: *In the Thick of the Fight*, trans. J. D. Lambert (1955), p. 485.
[8] Weygand: *Recalled*, p. 151.

De Gaulle had said little during the meeting. "Thinking of what was to come," he wrote later, "I had a full sense of how empty and conventional these palavers were, since they were not directed towards the one valid solution: to re-establish ourselves overseas."[9] Churchill appeared to him "imperturbable, full of vitality." The British Premier, as De Gaulle recorded, had one clash with Pétain. Attempting to rally the marshal out of his pessimism, he chided him mildly: "Come, come, *Monsieur le Maréchal!* Remember the battle of Amiens in March, 1918, when things were going so badly. I visited you then at your HQ. You outlined your plan to me. A few days later the front was re-established." "Yes, the front was re-established," Pétain answered tartly. "You, the English, were done for. But I sent 40 divisions to rescue you. Today it's we who are smashed to pieces. Where are your 40 divisions?"[1]

Dinner was served at the conference table. Captain Beaufre recalls the scene beforehand—Reynaud walking up and down, "broken with fatigue," Pétain looking "Olympian," Darlan "solid and shrewd," Eden "delicate," Churchill "forceful as usual, firmly enthroned in an arm-chair."[2] As they went to dine, the British Premier was talking so animatedly with De Gaulle that he insisted on his sitting next to him—creating havoc with the carefully arranged table plan. The council resumed briefly next morning, and at its close Churchill asked Reynaud to call him and his colleagues back "if there was any change in the situation" and "before they took any final decisions." When about to leave the château he singled out Admiral Darlan for a final word. "Darlan," he said, "you must never let them get the French fleet." Darlan, as Churchill recorded, gave his promise.[3]

Afterwards, in the hall, Spears talked to General Georges. The Frenchman was sunk in dejection and repeated that the French Army was finished. He drew a gruesome picture of the plight of General Besson's troops—overwhelmed by enemy aircraft and armor. Then Spears spoke at length with Pétain. The old marshal

---

[9] C. de Gaulle: *War Memoirs.* Vol. I: *The Call to Honour,* trans. by J. Griffin (1955), p. 71.

[1] Ibid.

[2] A. Beaufre: *Le Drame de 1940* (1965), p. 261.

[3] Churchill: *Second World War,* Vol. II, p. 140.

was equally hopeless. "An armistice is inevitable," he said, brushing aside Spears's appeal that France must fight on.[4] Meanwhile Weygand and Doumenc were at Georges's headquarters nearby, examining the position with Georges. Later they were joined by Reynaud and Pétain. The reports coming in were uniformly disastrous—so much so that Weygand now directed Georges to execute a drastic provisional order he had given him the previous day: to withdraw his forces to a line Caen–Tours–the middle Loire–Clamecy–Dijon–Dôle–the forests of Doubs. Almost the whole of northern France had gone. "So our last line of defence was cracking everywhere," wrote Weygand. ". . . The Battle of France was lost. . . . My resolve was unshakably formed. In a few hours I should ask the Government to conclude an armistice."[5]

At Tours, bewildered ministers had been waiting for twenty-four hours, virtually without news or instructions. "What decisions have been taken at Briare?" asked Baudouin late on the eleventh. "What is happening on the battlefield? Where are the German troops?"[6] Several times they had met informally, in nervous uncertain conclave: now, about 7:30 p.m. on Wednesday, the twelfth, they trooped into the vast drawing room of the Château de Cange for the first full assembly of the Council of Ministers. (Several ministers were late: in the prevailing chaos they had called at the wrong château. Weygand himself was delayed, negotiating the refugee-thronged roads from Briare.) The usual stiff protocol of the Élysée was notably missing. The salon, with its wide bay windows looking out over the valley, contained no table. Roughly placed along its sides stood two facing rows of hard and soft chairs. Seating priority was dispensed with. In random order, ministers took their places at the window end of the room, the President on the right of the bay with Reynaud near him; and opposite them, Chautemps, Pétain, Mandel. Most were assembled when the gray tapestry covering the door was pulled aside and Weygand marched in. He saluted the President and seated himself on his left.

The Prime Minister asked Weygand to report. Ranged around

---

[4] Spears: *Assignment*, Vol. II, p. 174.
[5] Weygand: *Recalled*, pp. 154–5.
[6] Baudouin: *Private Diaries*, p. 96.

the great salon, the ministers listened tensely as the Commander in Chief made his appreciation. Recalling that when he assumed command the Meuse front was already broken and the French forces retreating in disorder, Weygand explained the current situation in clear and uncompromising terms. Then he added with careful emphasis: "I will of course continue to resist the enemy, if the Council so orders me. But it is my duty to tell you bluntly that from this moment fighting should cease. The war is irretrievably lost. On the other hand, as Commander in Chief of the Army and as a loyal Frenchman, it is for me to maintain order in the country. I am not willing that France should slide into anarchy which always threatens to follow a military defeat. That is why —though it breaks my soldier's heart to say so—I repeat that an armistice must be sought immediately."[7]

The words fell amid a deathlike silence. The issue was now starkly in the open. Having made his declaration—and added that all the army commanders were behind him in his request for an immediate armistice—Weygand offered to leave the room while the council discussed the matter; but he remained on Pétain's insistence. Various members replied—all rejecting Weygand's proposal. Reynaud took the lead. In an unusual show of emotion he pleaded for France to honor her obligations. Even if the army were defeated, he urged, France still had her fleet and her empire: the government's plain duty was to resist. None of the following speakers contested Weygand's purely military arguments, but all opposed his conclusions. At one point Weygand, catching a murmured remark that the Commander in Chief could not give up the fight, was provoked into a heated outburst. "If I were only considering my feelings as a soldier," he exlaimed, "I wouldn't be thinking of anything else but getting killed at the head of the last defenders. This is the greatest humiliation of my life—I'm ending my career in dishonour."[8]

Dusk crept over the salon. A servant who came in to light the lamps was dismissed. The debate continued in twilit gloom. One after another, ministers were now declaring their position.

---

[7] J. Thouvenin: *Une Année d'Histoire de France* (1941), p. 8.
[8] A. Kammerer: *La Vérité sur l'Armistice* (1944), p. 80.

Most stood by Reynaud, urging no laying down of arms at any price. Among these were Marin (Minister of State); Mandel (Interior); Rollin (Colonies); Campinchi (Military Marine); Dautry (Armaments); Monnet (Blockade); Laurent-Eynac (Air); Ybarnegaray (State). Some like Queuille (Agriculture); Rivière (Pensions); and Chichery (Commerce) were doubtful and uncommitted. Only Pétain—possibly supported by Prouvost (Information)—spoke for Weygand's proposition. The marshal produced a prepared statement, which he read to the meeting. Any delay in asking for an armistice would be criminal, he asserted. It was a question of saving what still survived of France and working for the country's reconstruction. He urged the ministers to think of the men who were fighting and the millions of refugees. After others had spoken, Reynaud referred to Franco-British unity. An armistice would destroy this, he pointed out; "but France must never be separated from England and the United States."[9] Then he mentioned his promise to Churchill not to take any far-reaching decision before consulting him, and said he would invite him to France next day to meet the government. Once again the Breton redoubt issue was raised, livening up the tired discussion as almost every minister pronounced against it, siding with Pétain and Weygand. "A mere fantasy," scoffed Weygand: there were no troops to defend it.[1] Reynaud had been intending that the government should move forthwith from Touraine to Quimper, Finistère's capital, but now this plan was abandoned: like their predecessors in 1914, Reynaud and his colleagues would, when the moment came, take the road south to Bordeaux. The meeting broke up at 11 p.m. Over the weary ministers, as they dispersed, still hung the question of France's fate. They would wait to hear the British Prime Minister's views next day.

Driving with Reynaud to the Château de Chissay, Baudouin tried to shake the Premier's faith in the Breton redoubt. He claimed that it "would hardly be tactful" for the government to retreat to a remote stronghold, leaving the rest of France open to invasion. He also showed him a report from Darlan stating that the redoubt was indefensible: German aircraft could effectively prevent the landing of vital supplies and reinforcements by sea. Reluctantly,

---

[9] Baudouin: *Private Diaries,* p. 99.
[1] Ibid.

Reynaud appeared to agree. Then—on the assumption that the Premier still planned to transfer the government to North Africa —Baudouin sought to move him on the all-important armistice question. Churchill, he said, must be induced to consent to an immediate request for a cease-fire: it would be unwarrantable to leave France without a government. This plea the Premier flatly rejected.[2]

One absentee from the council had been De Gaulle. He had been busy all day at the neighboring Château de Beauvais, working with General Colson on plans for a withdrawal to North Africa. De Gaulle was a staunch pro-Brittany advocate, seeing the redoubt —which he knew could not be held for long—as a steppingstone to Algiers. Differing radically from Weygand on this and every other basic issue, he had become increasingly convinced that the Commander in Chief must be replaced. As Weygand's successor he favored Huntziger, now commanding the Fourth Army Group. On the eleventh, with Reynaud's consent, he had visited Huntziger at his headquarters at Arcis-sur-Aube, 55 miles south of Reims. Huntziger was in the midst of handling a heavy panzer assault against his forces on the Champagne front. De Gaulle was impressed by his steadiness. Having sketched out the general situation to him and explained that it was proposed to carry on the fight in Africa, he intimated that Weygand was not the right man for the task. "Would you be the man?" he asked. "Yes," replied Huntziger simply.[3] That afternoon he reported Huntziger's answer to Reynaud at Briare. But the Premier was immersed in other affairs and no longer seemed interested. Meanwhile, De Gaulle was keeping up his pressure for the move to North Africa, and thus for the interim stand in Brittany. Now, late on the twelfth, he hurried to the Château de Chissay to urge on the Premier the firm adoption of the Quimper plan—only to find it was canceled in favor of Bordeaux. In a testy midnight discussion in the château's lofty dining hall he failed to dissuade Reynaud, and the matter was left.

Overnight Parçay airfield, near Tours, had been bombed. Landing on its cratered surface early on the afternoon of the

---

2 *Ibid.*, p. 100.
3 De Gaulle: *Memoirs*, Vol. I, p. 69.

thirteenth, Churchill's Flamingo brought him to France for the final Franco-British meeting. This time his chief colleagues were the contrasting figures of Lord Halifax, tall and gaunt, and squat, dynamic Lord Beaverbrook—respectively Foreign Minister and Minister of Aircraft Production. The airfield seemed deserted: there was no one to meet them. In a borrowed car they drove to the city Prefecture, again finding no reception. Hungry, they continued to the Grand Hôtel for lunch. Here Baudouin, briefed by a telephone call from Mandel (whose offices were in the Prefecture), hastily joined them. At Churchill's request he reported the gist of Weygand's armistice ultimatum of the night before, adding his own view that the French Army was beaten.[4] Then, at 3:30, he escorted the British back to the Prefecture for the meeting. The setting for this grave assembly was almost casually informal. The council chamber was a modest first-floor room with hard and easy chairs and a single desk—in fact, Mandel's office, which he hurriedly vacated, carrying his lunch tray, when the British entered. Moreover, as a Supreme Council it was strangely one-sided: the only French representatives were Reynaud and the comparatively junior Baudouin. (De Gaulle joined the conference later.) In attendance with the three British Ministers were Sir Alexander Cadogan (Permanent Under-Secretary for Foreign Affairs), General Spears, Captain Berkely, the interpreter, and three others. But there was no mistaking the momentous nature of the meeting. Two Allies faced each other, the one on the brink of defeat, the other virtually unable to help. Before them was the question—building up ever since the Meuse breakthrough in mid-May—that now demanded immediate decision: Should France sever her links with Britain and seek a separate armistice, or should she abandon metropolitan soil and fight on in North Africa?

But now a new element entered into the problem. This became clear as Reynaud opened the proceedings. After referring to the plight of the French Army, he said with feeling: "I told General Weygand that England and America would be the end of Ger-

---

[4] Suspicious of Baudouin's attitude, Churchill later asked Spears about him—to be told (Spears: *Assignment*, Vol. II, p. 199) that Baudouin was "now doing his damndest to persuade Reynaud to throw up the sponge."

many. America is our hope; without her we are powerless."[5]
Reynaud had already addressed at least two appeals for aid to
President Roosevelt, the latest on the tenth. This he read to the
meeting, adding that he intended sending the President a further,
more urgent plea. "Our only chance of victory," he reiterated, "is
the prompt entry of the United States into the war. President
Roosevelt must realise this and accept the responsibility."[6] But
Reynaud admitted that this did not alter the position as between
France and Britain. Declaring that France could no longer continue the fight, he put to the British the blunt question: "Will
Great Britain release France from her promise?"[7] In an eloquent
reply, Churchill acknowledged the sufferings that France had
undergone and pointed out that Britain's turn was coming. But the
sole thought of Britain was to win the war. Britain must fight on—
and she must ask France to do the same. If the French Army broke,
its formations should form guerrilla bands. Large-scale guerrilla
warfare would wear down the German Army. But, whatever happened, Britain would fight until Hitler's Germany was destroyed.
It was a stirring speech, but failed to answer Reynaud's question
precisely. Now he framed this again. Must France, he asked, prolong a struggle that had become hopeless? Would Britain be surprised if France were forced, on account of her sufferings, to
request permission to conclude a separate armistice—while still
maintaining the link between herself and Britain?

To this, Churchill's response was unequivocal. Spears, who
was carefully noting every nuance of the meeting, records his
words. Having said that Britain would never indulge in "reproaches
and recriminations," Churchill added sternly: "But that is a very
different matter from becoming a consenting party to a peace made
in contravention of the agreement so recently concluded."[8] But,
above all, Churchill was fighting for time. Now he too invoked the
United States. He endorsed Reynaud's suggestion for an immediate
French appeal to President Roosevelt, and promised that the British would back this with a message of their own. Reynaud expressed his gratitude. Churchill answered with a warning: if the

---

5 Baudouin: *Private Diaries,* p. 102.
6 Ibid.
7 Ibid.
8 Spears: *Assignment,* Vol. II, p. 209.

war continued—as it inevitably would—the British blockade would damage France as well as Germany. This shocked Reynaud. He said he feared that such a calamity, should the British let it happen, might badly strain Franco-British relations and create a new and serious situation in Europe. The close, hard bargaining continued. Churchill's main object now was to defer the crucial French decision until Roosevelt's reply to the Franco-British plea had been received. The meeting briefly adjourned, easing the tension in the room. Churchill and his colleagues paced the damp Prefecture garden, deep in conversation. Reynaud and Baudouin moved to the next room to confer with the presidents of the Senate and the Chamber, Jules Jeanneney and Édouard Herriot, who were waiting there with Mandel. Reporting on the discussion, he was heatedly assailed by all three—like Mandel, both presidents were opposed to an armistice—for suggesting that France might seek a separate peace. Herriot was so moved, recorded Baudouin, that he broke into tears. The members filed back to resume the conference. Churchill, cigar in mouth, looked grave and pensive. Little further remained to be said. Reynaud asked Churchill for suggestions on how he should approach Roosevelt. "Be very frank and blunt," replied Churchill. ". . . You must ask him for all the American air force and the fleet, in short for every help he can give us except an expeditionary force. After he has replied our two Governments will examine the position."[9] Whatever comfort the hope of American aid offered Reynaud, he closed the meeting on an ominous note. If Roosevelt's answer was unfavorable, he said, he must warn Churchill of the "serious questions that would have to be settled between France and England."[1]

The conference ended at 5:50 p.m. Reynaud took the British into the next room to meet Jeanneney, Herriot, and others. As they talked, De Gaulle, as he himself relates, went up to Reynaud and demanded brusquely: "Is it possible that you are thinking of France asking for an armistice?" "Certainly not!" Reynaud replied. "But we must give the British a shock, to get more help out of them."[2] De Gaulle was skeptical. Leaving the Prefecture amid an

---

[9] Baudouin: *Private Diaries*, p. 105.
[1] Ibid.
[2] De Gaulle: *Memoirs*, Vol. I, pp. 75–6.

anxious crowd of deputies and journalists, Churchill murmured to the tall, unresponsive Under-Secretary: *"L'homme du destin."*[3] The British party then drove straight back to Parçay to fly to England.

Next day, at 1 p.m., Reynaud directed his latest and strongest plea to President Roosevelt. In the course of it he said:

> At the most tragic hour in her history France has to make a choice. Is she to continue sacrificing her youth in a hopeless struggle? Should her Government leave national territory to avoid surrendering itself to the enemy and to be able to continue the struggle on sea and in North Africa? . . . Or shall she ask Hitler's conditions for an armistice?
>
> We can only choose the first path, that of resistance, if the chance of victory appears in the distance, if a light shines at the end of the tunnel. . . .
>
> Henceforth, France can only continue to fight if American intervention reverses the situation by making victory for the Allies certain. The only chance of saving the French nation . . . is to throw the weight of American strength into the scales. This very day. This is also the only chance of avoiding an attack by Hitler against America. . . .
>
> I know that a declaration of war does not lie within your hands alone. But I have to tell you in this hour which is a grave one in your history as in our own, that, if you cannot give France in the coming days a positive assurance that the United States will come into the struggle within a short space of time, the destiny of the world will be changed.
>
> You will then see France go under like a drowning person after having thrown a last look towards the land of liberty from where she was expecting salvation.[4]

More promptly, Churchill had dispatched his note to Roosevelt late on the thirteenth. Speaking of the Tours meeting, he said:

> I cannot exaggerate its critical character. They [the French] were very nearly gone. . . . I did not hesitate in the name of the British Government to refuse consent to an armistice or separate peace. I urged that this issue should not be discussed until a further appeal had been made by Reynaud to you and the United States, which I undertook to second. . . .
>
> Reynaud felt strongly that it would be beyond his power to

---

[3] Churchill: *Second World War*, Vol. II, p. 162.
[4] Reynaud: *Fight*, p. 509.

encourage his people to fight on without hope of ultimate victory, and that that hope could only be kindled by American intervention up to the extreme limit open to you . . .[5]

Across 3,000 miles of ocean, President Franklin D. Roosevelt had been watching the triumphant German progress with mounting dismay. From mid-May on, as French resistance began to fail, he and his advisers had asked themselves anxiously how they could help the Allies. Although the United States was benevolently neutral—with its leaders convinced that an Allied victory was vital to the security of the United States—the strong isolationist element in and out of Congress was opposed to any intervention in Europe. And even if this political difficulty were overcome, there was the practical question of exactly what war material America could send the Allies and how soon it could be delivered. Through late May and into June, reports from William Bullitt and Joseph P. Kennedy, U.S. ambassador to Britain, stressed the Allies'—and especially France's—increasingly dangerous situation. At home, Roosevelt strove to alert Americans to the German menace by asking large additional arms credits. But the Allied position began to seem so precarious that on May 26 he and his Secretary of State, Cordell Hull, sent notes to the French and British governments calling on them not to let their fleets fall into German hands. Meanwhile Reynaud was looking to the United States in desperate appeal. On May 18 he had had to be dissuaded by Bullitt from sending a personal plea to Roosevelt to get Congress to declare war on Germany. Ten days later he proposed to Bullitt that the U.S. Atlantic Fleet be sent at once to the Mediterranean. More sober, though equally disquieting, were the messages Roosevelt was receiving from Churchill—characteristically signed "Former Naval Person."

By the beginning of June, Roosevelt and Hull had, on all the evidence available to them, come to the conclusion that France was—as Hull put it—"finished." There could no longer be any question of trying to send her war material, when this might quickly fall into German hands. Stirred by Churchill's solemn "We shall never surrender" speech to the House of Commons on June 4,

---

[5] Churchill: *Second World War,* Vol. II, p. 163.

they were now placing their faith in Britain alone. To Britain, they decided, would go henceforth what support America could provide. During the previous week arrangements already had been made to ship American planes to Europe via Canada. The President further resolved to send Britain half a million rifles, massive stocks of artillery and machine guns, and several hundred more planes originally intended for France. Consent was also given for American pilots to join the Canadian air force under certain conditions. All this the United States was prepared to do, but the ultimate step she would not take. When Australian Minister Robert Casey visited Cordell Hull in Washington on June 6, he urged that the United States declare war. "That," Hull replied, "is unthinkable in the present situation."[6] Hence, in answer to Reynaud's heartfelt plea to Roosevelt, dated the tenth, the President could only reply: "Your message has moved me deeply. As I have already stated to you and to Mr. Churchill, this Government is doing everything in its power to make available to the Allied Governments the material they so urgently require. . . . I am, personally, particularly impressed by your declaration that France will continue to fight on behalf of Democracy, even if it means a slow withdrawal, even to North Africa and the Atlantic . . ."[7]

Reynaud would glean little further cheer from Roosevelt's response to his even more powerful appeal of the fourteenth.

The President, ministers, and General Weygand were impatiently patrolling the terrace of the Château de Cange. A ministerial council had beeen arranged for 5 p.m., and since then an hour had passed. They were awaiting not only Reynaud but Winston Churchill, who was understood to be coming straight from the Tours conference to attend the council—the meeting at which the momentous armistice question would finally be decided. When Reynaud's car drove up, with no sign of Churchill, there was consternation. Ministers excitedly asked where he was. "He has gone back to London," Reynaud told Chautemps, who broke into angry protests.[8] Once more the ministers moved into the confer-

---

[6] C. Hull: *The Memoirs of Cordell Hull*, (1948), Vol. I, p. 776.

[7] Churchill: *Second World War*, Vol. II, p. 162.

[8] Baudouin: *Private Diaries*, p. 106.

ence room. A murky, rain-filled sky threw the great salon into semi-darkness. The meeting began in what Baudouin describes as "a glacial atmosphere."[9] Reynaud's colleagues—their nerves already frayed by days of stress and suspense—were bitterly incensed at being cheated of the British Prime Minister's attendance, when Reynaud had undertaken to arrange this the previous evening.

There was an outcry at the start as Reynaud reported on the conference with the British. Bouthillier indignantly accused him of misrepresenting to Churchill the conclusions reached by yesterday's ministerial council concerning an armistice. Only one decision had been reached, said Bouthillier—namely, to ask Britain's advice on the request for an armistice. The embarrassed Reynaud explained that he had not had the chance to ask Churchill—who was in a hurry to return to England—to address the council at Cange. He added that the sole agreement arrived at with Churchill was to send an urgent appeal to Roosevelt. Only after Roosevelt had replied could the French government decide whether or not to seek an armistice. Amid mounting commotion Weygand described the military position. His account was bleak: German armored units were advancing toward Chartres in the west and Romilly in the east, and the French forces in the center were in a state of exhaustion. Emphatically he repeated his previous demand for a speedy armistice. Further, he proposed that, before negotiations were begun, the French fleet be sent to North Africa. Three ministers objected that Germany would never grant an armistice on these terms. Interruptions grew louder, recriminations rang round the salon. Finally Weygand stormed out of the room, complaining angrily that Mandel had smiled. Later, at Riom, Monnet would recall that ministers could hear him shouting before the secretaries in the anteroom: "They sit with their backsides in their armchairs, and they don't give a damn that, all this time, the French Army is in the process of being massacred!"[1]

Then—as on the last occasion—Pétain rose to read a prepared memorandum. The old marshal dismissed the Breton redoubt plan once more—there being no French troops in a condition to organize any defenses. He went on to broach another theme.

---

[9] Ibid.
[1] Reynaud: *Fight,* p. 504.

"It is impossible for the French Government, without emigrating, without deserting," he said, "to abandon French territory. The duty of the Government is, whatever may happen, to stay in the country, under the penalty of no longer being recognised as the Government. . . . It is necessary to wait for a French renaissance by remaining on the spot. . . . I am, therefore, of the opinion that we should not leave French soil. . . . I shall stay amongst the French people to share her pains and miseries. An armistice is to my mind the necessary condition for the perpetuity of an eternal France— *la pérennité de la France éternelle.*"[2] The marshal sat down. In the silence that followed, Reynaud declared solemnly: "This is contrary to the honour of France."[3]

Ministers jumped up one by one to testify for or against an armistice. Among new speakers in favor were Pomaret (Works) and Pernot (Public Health); among those against were Rio (Merchant Marine) and Sérol (Justice). A notable convert to the Pétain-Weygand view was Ybarnegaray, who yesterday had backed Reynaud. Years later (when on trial in the High Court in 1946) he was to admit: "When I heard Weygand . . . say, 'We can no longer fight on. We are defeated'; when I saw Pétain rally to this view, my resistance completely collapsed. I asked Weygand, 'Have we no reserves?' He answered me bluntly, 'Yes, 800,000 men in depots, but nothing with which to arm them!' Then, yes, I did vote for an armistice."[4] The lamentable debate wore on until Frossard (Public Works) asked the meeting not to come to a division for, as all members would agree, a final decision must be deferred pending a reply from Roosevelt as to how far he was prepared to pledge American aid. Tired and frustrated, ministers left the château at 8:30 p.m. Still unresolved was the agonizing dilemma. Reynaud, at the least, had made a grave tactical error in not bringing Churchill to the meeting. Had the British Prime Minister had the chance to convince Reynaud's colleagues that Britain was dedicated to fighting on at all costs, whatever Roosevelt's answer, wavering spirits might have been fortified and the future course of events influenced.

---

2 Kammerer: *La Vérité,* p. 316.
3 Ibid., p. 306.
4 Reynaud: *Fight,* pp. 503–4n.

On that evening of the thirteenth, from the Prefecture at Tours, Reynaud broadcast a speech directed at Americans as well as Frenchmen. From the Americans it appealed for aid, stressing—doubtless as a further reminder to Roosevelt—what America now owed France. For the French it carried a warning of ordeals to come, tempered with a note of dour exhortation. "We have always," declared Reynaud, "thrown back or subjugated the invader."[5] France needed hope at that moment. The "invader" had already swarmed over some ten departments, and in a dead and darkened Paris two million citizens awaited his imminent arrival with dread.

---

[5] Ibid., p. 508.

Chapter 20

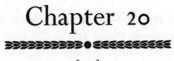

REYNAUD RESIGNS

"I returned to Downing Street with a heavy heart."
(Winston Churchill)

THE FRENCH ARMIES were retreating in a ragged line from the channel to Nancy. On either side of captured Paris the leading German tank columns were racing south into open, undefended country. In the west they had breached the 10th Army positions around Évreux; and in the east they were outflanking Huntziger's Fourth Army Group to press on past Troyes and Neufchâteau in the direction of Dijon. Farther east still, they were launching an assault on the steel-and-concrete bastions of the Maginot Line itself. At Orléans, on June 12, a despairing French officer had told a British staff officer: "We have 35 divisions. Some hold a 20-mile front: five miles is the normal maximum. Some are good divisions, but others are bad. What can you do? The Germans have 80 divisions with every superiority in equipment. *Que voulez-vous?*"[1]

Now, ahead of the advancing Germans, lay the great river line of the Loire—the curving waterway that guarded the heart of France. Within four days of its move to Briare, on the river's north bank 50 miles southeast of Orléans, French GHQ was once more in danger of being overtaken by the approaching battle. On the fourteenth—the day Paris fell—it pulled out for Vichy, 120 miles to the southeast. But its retreat would not stop there. Before the end it would move back two more stages, to Mont-Dore and finally to distant Montauban, in the Tarn-et-Garonne Department well south-

---

[1] *The Diary of a Staff Officer at Advanced Headquarters North, B.A.F.F., 1940* (1941), p. 68.

east of Bordeaux. By then—a mere skeleton headquarters with little further function—it would reflect the total disaster that had overtaken the French Army. As the long convoy moved out of Briare across the Loire Bridge, swarms of Stukas were dive-bombing the small town of Gien, five miles away. Even now, as Captain Beaufre relates, the role of this mobile GHQ was reduced to asking the military and civil authorities, during its steps, whether they were fighting or withdrawing. Both alternatives struck Beaufre as equally nonsensical. At Vierzon, between Briare and Bourges, a tank commander preparing to defend the town was killed by the population, who wanted to avoid its destruction. Later, at Clermont-Ferrand, the garrison was ordered to parade in its barracks and surrender to the Germans while its commanding general withdrew alone.

Early on the fourteenth General Alan Brooke, back in France as Commander in Chief of the B.E.F., called on Weygand at GHQ, Briare, to consult with him on the use of the British forces in Brittany. He found him looking "very wizened and tired."[2] In a candid talk Weygand admitted that the French Army was no longer effectively resisting and was splintering into disconnected groups. Moreover, he had no reserves. With Weygand, Brooke then visited General Georges at his nearby headquarters. On the way he told the astonished Brooke: "This is a terrible predicament that I am in. . . . Yes, I had finished my military career which had been a most successful one."[3] General Georges—"very tired and haggard, but as charming as usual"—showed them a large wall map marked with the latest information. Chalked in red were several alarmingly deep German panzer penetrations. Georges, too, with a hopeless gesture, confessed he had no reserves, "not a man, vehicle or gun left."[4]

Discussing the employment of the British troops, Weygand and Georges both agreed that the Breton redoubt plan was a pure fantasy. Brooke himself calculated that the front to be defended would be about 90 miles, necessitating at least fifteen divisions— which were not available. The British, he judged, could muster a maximum of four divisions. Nonetheless, Weygand maintained that, on the orders of the Allied Supreme Council, he must make a show

---

[2] A. Bryant: *The Turn of the Tide* . . . *F. M. Viscount Alanbrooke* (1957), Vol. I, p. 167.
[3] Ibid.
[4] Ibid., Vol. I, p. 168.

of implementing the plan. The two French generals and Brooke thereupon drew up and signed a directive—"within the framework of the decision of the British and French Governments to organise a redoubt in Brittany"[5]—involving the British forces in the scheme.[6] Even as it was signed this was a dead letter. Soon there would not be enough French troops to make an effective defense anywhere.

Like the French Army, much else in France was disintegrating. A prime casualty was civil order and authority, swamped under the vast and unprecedented tide of refugees. Various estimates put the number of these at between eight and twelve million. Since May 10, from Belgium, Luxembourg, and the French northern provinces, the displaced populations had surged south in ever-growing numbers. Abandoning whole communes in panic and disorder, they herded in miles-long columns along the roads of France. On their laborious journey, laden with whatever goods they could push or carry, they suffered ordeals of bombing and machine-gunning far worse than if they had stayed at home. It was a mass migration impossible to control, causing havoc in the towns and villages that lay in its path. It worked like an avalanche, picking up more refugees as it progressed. From the military aspect, it actively helped the Germans by blocking the highways to urgently needed troops and supplies en route to the front. The problem had been greatly accentuated by a lack of planning beforehand. When the offensive broke no general scheme existed to deal with it; and local officials in the north, whose areas were immediately flooded with fugitives, had no idea whether to keep them or send them on. In addition, among these refugees might well be German agents. Some officials, unable to get in touch with Paris, hurried there themselves to ask what to do. Bombed and crowded roads prevented them getting back—and so their local populations were left without instructions. Elsewhere, different communities were given different orders, increasing the confusion. In some cases, German agents issued false directions and sent more terrified villagers onto the packed highways.

Weygand, on taking over command, was horrified at the

---

[5] M. Weygand: *Recalled to Service,* trans. E. W. Dickes (1952), p. 167.
[6] On the night of the fourteenth, Brooke was ordered by London to withdraw the 150,000 men of the B.E.F. from France, and he was released from French command.

hordes of evacuees choking the Flanders and Picardy roads. He issued orders restricting them to the use of certain routes at fixed times, but this measure soon broke down under the unmanageable press of refugees. When the evacuation intensified in northern France, he blamed the government for not ensuring that officials appointed by them stayed at their posts exercising control. Within the Zone of the Armies he again attempted to handle the traffic himself: movement was authorized only when ordered by army commanders and dictated by military necessity. But with the start of the Battle of France, nothing could stem the further rush of refugees. From the Seine-Inférieure, Somme, Oise, Seine-et-Oise, Eure, Aisne, and Marne departments they joined the great trek, many converging on Paris. On June 12 it was taking twenty hours to travel from Paris to Étampes, 35 miles southwest, along a road solid with three lines of loaded cars and a dense flux of cyclists and pedestrians. That day, 60 miles farther south, General Spears found similar conditions on every southbound road as he struggled across country from Briare to Tours. Elsewhere, on all main routes from the north, it was the same story. In these June days half the nation seemed on the move—a nation of leaderless people, resigned to defeat.

Wedged in the great rout, on Friday, the fourteenth, the long government convoys trailed out of Touraine, bound for their final destination—Bordeaux. Reynaud's official car sped southwest along main roads cleared for its passage: other transports tried to avoid the worst congestion by taking minor thoroughfares. That evening the President, ministers, and their staffs moved in, like a miniature army, to all the city's public buildings, from the Prefecture and law courts to university and school premises and the Chamber of Commerce headquarters. The confusion of Bordeaux surpassed that of Tours. Into this bustling provincial capital on the Garonne was flocking, along with senators, deputies, officials, pressmen, a great concourse of fugitives: 360 miles south of Paris, Bordeaux was the meeting place of several refugee streams. Not a room was to be had in the city. People slept in hotel chairs or on floors; used their cars, which were massed in the tree-shaded squares: even lay on the pavements. The full emergency of war had come unexpectedly to Bordeaux: in the wide square of the Allées d'Orléans, as a British journalist noted, stood the unfinished, abandoned pavilions of a fair. Aimless crowds filled the streets, anxious for news and guidance. The lobbies of the Hôtel Splendide and the tables of the famous Chapon Fin restaurant were thronged with speculating politicians and pressmen. Nobody seemed to know what was happening. Bordeaux seethed with suspense, rumor, and intrigue. As the armies faced destruction in the north, here the cliques and factions gathered—the ministers and their hangers-on, plotting, lobbying, and jockeying for power in the pro-armistice government that, it was clear, would replace Reynaud's at any moment.

Sixty-nine-year-old President Lebrun remembered Bordeaux in happier days—when he had attended its gay Wine Festival in 1938. Now, in the isolation of the Prefecture, he summed up gloomily: "The atmosphere of the town is bad." He was alarmed at the growing activities of the *"cinquième colonne."* "The deputies who have arrived from their various provinces are surrounded, button-holed, lectured," he noted. "They are shown the uselessness of the struggle and told *'il faut en finir.'* "[7] In the evenings Lebrun was glad to take the air on the quays, where he tried to catch the remarks of passers-by and gauge their state of mind.

At the center of it all, in his office at the headquarters of the 18th Military Region, rue Vital-Carles, and in the council room of the Bordeaux Prefecture, the care-worn Paul Reynaud was waging a losing battle for his proclaimed "fight-on-from-Africa" policy. Through June 15 and 16 he was in almost ceaseless conference— with British and United States representatives, the President, the presidents of the Senate and Chamber, senators, deputies, ministers, service chiefs, all with their pleas and arguments to carry on or end the struggle. Reynaud knew that there was no longer any question of the French Army continuing resistance: for him it was now a matter of how that resistance would be terminated. On this he clashed violently with General Weygand on the afternoon of the fifteenth. Weygand himself had just reached Bordeaux, tired and irascible, after a sixteen-hour train journey from Vichy. Following a brief talk with Pétain and others, he called on Reynaud. The Premier put it to him that he wished to stop the fighting in France, but would not request an armistice, and if necessary would leave

---

[7] A. Lebrun: *Témoignage* (1945), p. 80.

France. He therefore proposed that Weygand should capitulate with his army like the Dutch Chief of Staff, and even offered to give him a written order to this effect. Weygand hotly refused. "I would never agree to bring such disgrace on the flags of the French Army," he exclaimed.[8] The quarrel flared again that evening after the close of the first ministerial council, held in the city Prefecture. Meeting Weygand in the antechamber of the council room, Reynaud said to him: "You are going to have to make the army capitulate, General." "There is no power in the world," Weygand burst out, "that would make me sign the capitulation of an army that has just fought as the French Army has!" "You will do it if I give you the order!" "Never," snapped Weygand. "You won't find one French officer who'd accept such a humiliation." "You are here to obey," retorted Reynaud. "I'm here to defend the honour of the army," Weygand shouted. "You and the President are trying to evade your responsibility! The Government took the responsibility of declaring war—it must shoulder the responsibility for the armistice!"[9]

In London, Churchill and his colleagues were remaining adamant on keeping France to her agreement, signed on March 28, not to make a separate peace. Sir Ronald Campbell, accompanied by General Spears, visited Reynaud on the evening of the fourteenth to stress anew the British attitude. Calling again next morning, the two Britons learned with satisfaction from Reynaud that he had decided to install part of the government overseas. But while this concession—with its implication that the French fleet would be moved beyond German reach—pleased the British, the pro-armistice group within and outside Reynaud's own Cabinet were increasing their pressure. At the Council of Ministers meeting on the afternoon of the fifteenth, Chautemps—a leading armistice advocate— put forward the shrewd and plausible proposal that France should, as an initial step, ask Germany for her armistice conditions: if unacceptable, these could be rejected. Most of the council, including President Lebrun, approved—but Reynaud stubbornly objected, declaring that this was incompatible with France's pledge to Britain. He even offered to resign but was dissuaded by Lebrun.

---

[8] Weygand: *Recalled*, p. 169.
[9] Y. Bouthillier: *Le Drame de Vichy* (1950), p. 25.

Finally, he reluctantly agreed that France should ask British permission to inquire from Germany what her armistice terms would
be. Meanwhile, he advised the council to await Roosevelt's reply
to his latest appeal.

As to this, Reynaud's hopes were soon dashed. Late that
night, while conferring with Campbell and Spears, he received the
American President's answer. "As he read it," Spears records, "he
grew still paler, his face contracted, his eyes became just slits. . . .
'Our appeal has failed,' he said in a small toneless voice, 'the
Americans will not declare war.' "[1]

Sympathetic, diplomatic, politely but uncompromisingly negative, Roosevelt's message ran as follows:

". . . May I, first of all, repeat to you the increasingly deep
admiration of the American people and its Government for the
striking courage which the French armies are showing on French
soil in their resistance to the invader."

It went on to point out that America had helped to equip the
Allied armies in recent weeks and would continue to do so as long
as resistance was maintained; and it concluded:

"I know you will understand that these statements do not
imply any pledge of a military nature. Congress alone has power
to enter into such engagements."[2]

Reynaud had lost his last bargaining counter with the armistice
seekers. No inducement he could now offer would withstand their
demands for an immediate cease-fire approach to Germany,
coupled with a refusal to contemplate the government's withdrawal
to North Africa. Weygand having declined to head a military capitulation, it was now a matter of a government-sponsored armistice
request. He knew that there was a heavy majority in favor of this:
during the council meeting on the afternoon of the fifteenth he had
jotted down the names of ministers thought to be for and against,
and passed the list to Lebrun. His reckoning showed fourteen ministers in support and six opposed. If—as he had maintained that
he would—he refused to initiate an armistice request and offered
his resignation, he knew that ready and waiting to step into his place

---

[1] E. L. Spears: *Assignment to Catastrope* (1954), Vol. II,
p. 265.
[2] P. Reynaud: *In the Thick of the Fight* (1955), p. 535.

was Marshal Pétain, backed by the Chautemps clique, Weygand, and the sinister figure of Deputy Pierre Laval, now emerging from the background of the Bordeaux cafés in which he had been busily plotting on the marshal's behalf.

As Reynaud contemplated disaster in the early hours of Sunday, the sixteenth, De Gaulle was across the Channel, speeding by train from Plymouth to London. De Gaulle had been happily spared the intriguings of Bordeaux. He was in England to arrange for British transport aid in the projected French move to North Africa. Leaving Bordeaux late on the fourteenth, he had made one notable farewell. At dinner in the Hôtel Splendide he saw Pétain, and went over to him to pay his respects. The marshal shook his hand in silence. "I was not to see him again, ever," wrote De Gaulle, of this figure who was the archopponent of everything he was fighting for.[3] Now DeGaulle was to enter dramatically into the struggle to counter the peace moves headed by Pétain.

In the Hyde Park Hotel he met two compatriots, M. Corbin, the French Ambassador, and M. Monnet, a minister and member of the French Economic Mission in London. They told him of a startling plan now being formulated at the Foreign Office—nothing less than a proposal for a complete Anglo-French Union. De Gaulle examined a draft of it and was impressed. While he appreciated that it was essentially a long-term project, his main thought was that it might help Reynaud to prolong French resistance here and now. He raised the matter with Churchill and others at lunch at the Carlton Club. The British Premier, hearing of the plan for the first time, was cautious: he realized the vast implications and difficulties of such a union. However, he was partly won over by De Gaulle's enthusiasm. They went together to Downing Street, De Gaulle to wait in an anteroom with Corbin while the proposal was discussed by the Cabinet. After two hours the British ministers emerged to tell De Gaulle they were agreed on adopting the plan. He at once telephoned the news to Reynaud at Bordeaux. The delighted Reynaud asked De Gaulle to hurry the wording of the text through so that he could submit the plan to the Council of Ministers timed for 5 p.m. Soon after, De Gaulle telephoned again, and dictated the

---

[3] C. de Gaulle: *War Memoirs,* Vol I: *The Call to Honour,* trans. J. Griffin (1955), p. 78.

draft. Reynaud "was transfigured with joy," noted Spears, who was present in the Premier's office as Reynaud scribbled down De Gaulle's words.[4] In London, Churchill himself took the receiver from De Gaulle to confirm the proposal. Reynaud's own later comment was: "It was to give me a new argument for keeping France in the alliance."[5]

Leaving aside the practicalities, the British gesture was inspiring and imaginative. In default of planes, tanks, guns, and men, at that crucial moment it carried a message of hope and faith to a faltering ally. France and Britain, ran the sense of the proposal, should henceforth be a single nation. There would be joint organs of defense, foreign, financial and economic policies. French and British nationals would enjoy common citizenship. Both countries would share the responsibility for repairing war damage in their territories, their common resources being employed for the purpose. For the duration of the war there would be a single War Cabinet, with all Anglo-French forces under its direction. The two Parliaments would enter into a formal association. France would keep all her available forces fighting. Finally, the Union would bring all its power to bear against the enemy, wherever the battle might be.

Earlier that day, the sixteenth, Reynaud had been feeling ill-used by the British. Sir Ronald Campbell and General Spears had called to tell him that the British government agreed to his request of yesterday that Germany be asked about the nature of armistice terms—provided that the French fleet sailed at once for British waters. Reynaud was incensed. "What a very silly thing to . . . ask," Spears records him as saying.[6] Protesting that such an action would expose the French North African coast to Italian attack, he intimated that the British proviso was unacceptable. But later, after Reynaud had received two confirmatory telegrams, Campbell and Spears called again to announce that the British government had reversed its decision and to ask for the return of the telegrams. As Reynaud subsequently learned, the British had judged that the situation was radically altered by the Union proposal.

---

[4] Spears: *Assignment,* Vol. II, p. 291.
[5] Reynaud: *Fight,* p. 537.
[6] Spears: *Assignment,* Vol. II, p. 284.

Pétain, Chautemps, and their followers were fuming with frustration at what they considered Reynaud's delaying tactics. To force the Premier's hand, at that morning's brief council meeting the old marshal dropped a carefully prepared bombshell. Amid a tense silence he rose and read a letter of resignation.

"The gravity of the military situation, increasing daily," recited Pétain, "convinces me of the need for the Government to bring hostilities to an immediate end. This measure is the only one capable of saving the country. The enemy advance, if it is not brought to an end, will lead to the total occupation and destruction of our territory. The result will be a reduction of the nation's food resources, in conditions which will make famine inevitable in a very short time. The daily deliberations of the Government seem to me to be pure procrastinating manoeuvres which will result in the final abdication of French sovereignty. I cannot associate myself with this. I therefore tender you my resignation from the functions of Minister of State and Vice-President of the Council."[7]

As Pétain finished, President Lebrun, deeply moved, exclaimed in protest. The marshal made as if to leave the room: other ministers, according to Baudouin, were ready to follow him. Reynaud dryly suggested that since Pétain had made his resignation in writing, he should at least await his (Reynaud's) formal reply. He added that Britain should be given time to answer the French request of yesterday. The President supported Reynaud. Pétain hesitated, and sat down. Pocketing his letter of resignation, he grudgingly accepted an adjournment of the council until five that afternoon—but said he would wait no longer.

Meanwhile the Germans continued to drive down into central France. Along most of the crumbling battle front the three French army groups were being steadily cut to pieces or outflanked. Only on a line south of Paris, where the German pressure was lightest, were the French retreating in any sort of order. On the left the remnants of Altmayer's 10th Army were being chased from the Risle (a Seine tributary) due southward in the direction of Poitiers. East and southeast of Paris, where part of Touchon's 6th Army, and Requin's 4th, had virtually ceased all resistance, Verdun had

---

7 Reynaud: *Fight,* p. 531, (facsimile letter).

fallen and a German spearhead had reached Chaumont, deep in the Haute-Marne Department. And—symbolically the worst reverse of all—in France's eastern marches the impregnable Maginot Line had been taken in the rear, and the men of Prételat's armies were in full retreat, threatened by encirclement from German forces that on the fifteenth had penetrated to Gray and Vesoul in the Saône Valley. The three army group headquarters had been forced back to points almost as far south as French GHQ at Vichy. Weygand, returning to Vichy from Bordeaux early on the sixteenth, heard this news from Doumenc and Georges at his headquarters in the Hôtel du Parc. Georges—whose calm and self-control impressed Weygand—added that all the senior commanders had stressed the impossibility of continuing the battle.

For Weygand this clinched the matter. An immediate cease-fire was imperative. Flying back to Bordeau, he was at the Prefecture by midday. The ministers were emerging from that morning's council meeting. Weygand approached the President, who was in an anteroom with Reynaud and others, and told him that if hostilities did not stop at once, the army faced total disintegration. Capitulation, he added, would be contrary to the honor of the flag. "If capitulation is written into the armistice convention," asked Reynaud, "would you oppose it as against the army's honour?" "I will tell you that when the time comes," Weygand retorted. "No," interposed Lebrun, "you must tell us now." Reynaud then proposed to give Weygand a written order, thus relieving him of the responsibility for capitulating. Weygand curtly refused.[8]

At 5 p.m. on Sunday, June 16, twenty-four solemn and anxious ministers moved into the council room of the Bordeaux Prefecture. Under the chairmanship of President Lebrun, the day's second Council of Ministers session began. Weygand waited in an adjoining room in case he was called. Everyone sensed that this was a crucial meeting. For six days the ministers had havered and quarreled while the French Army slid toward collapse: now the great decision must finally be made. To stress the military crisis, during the conference a message was passed to Lebrun, originating from General Georges at Vichy, and dated 5 p.m. It reported

---

[8] A. Lebrun: *Témoignage* (1945), p. 82.

further serious setbacks and ended: "It is absolutely vital to reach a decision."[9] The Pétain-Chautemps group hardly needed this added evidence: their hand was powerfully strengthened by the first item on the agenda—Roosevelt's answer to the latest French appeal. Reynaud read the President's message to a stony-faced audience. Lebrun mildly described the common reaction as "somewhat depressing."[1] The reply gave the Pétainists an angry satisfaction, stirring Ybarnegaray to call for an armistice. Equally ill-received was Reynaud's next statement, on Britain's withdrawal of consent to the seeking of armistice terms. Worse still, his announcement of the Anglo-French Union proposal—just received so enthusiastically by Reynaud from London—was greeted with surprise, then skepticism.[2] To puzzled ministers it seemed irrelevant to France's needs at this dire moment. "I was completely alone in supporting the proposal," mournfully wrote Reynaud.[3] As Lebrun noted, had the offer come sooner, allowing time for careful study, it might have been welcomed: "but, falling like a bomb in the midst of such an unpropitious atmosphere, it met a very cool response."[4] In fact, it immediately came under fierce attack. Pétain talked insultingly about "fusion with a corpse."[5] "France," cried Ybarnegaray, "would be nothing more than a dominion." Chautemps voiced heated objections and harped again on his armistice proposal. "I prefer to collaborate with my allies rather than my enemies!" Reynaud rejoined. Supporting him, Mandel shouted: "Would you rather be a German colony?"[6]

The sorry debate veered to the matter of France's obligations to Britain. Marin asked Reynaud: "Do you really judge, according to your conscience as head of the Government, that the honour of France is involved in pursuing the struggle at the side of our allies?" "Yes, absolutely and entirely," replied Reynaud.[7] The room echoed to charge and countercharge as Mandel and Chautemps broke into

---

[9] Ibid., p. 83.
[1] Ibid.
[2] If some pro-Reynaud ministers were surprised, Reynaud's opponents had apparently been forewarned: the Premier later claimed that news of the plan had been leaked through a tapped telephone.
[3] Reynaud: *Fight*, p. 541.
[4] Lebrun: *Témoignage*, p. 84.
[5] Kammerer: *La Vérité*, p. 142.
[6] Ibid., p. 143.
[7] Ibid., p. 144.

dispute on the armistice issue. "There are some who want to go on fighting," exclaimed Mandel, "and others who don't!" "No!" Chautemps retorted, "there are only Frenchmen here who are all equally conscious of the great suffering which her military reverses have caused France, and who want to find the best means of saving her!"[8] Tired to the point of exhaustion and his resolve almost spent, Reynaud now saw before him an irreconcilably divided council. Although backed by De Gaulle, Mandel, Marin, and others, he was opposed by a powerful group headed by Pétain and Chautemps (both vice-presidents of the council)—itself formidably reinforced from outside by Weygand, Laval, and others. In these circumstances, one thing was clear to him: he no longer had a mandate to lead the government. He rose to his feet and addressed the assembly: "Only a minority of the Council now shares my point of view.[9] I no longer consider myself as qualified to intervene in London in order to secure the release of France from her obligations. Perhaps one day you will again have need of the man who based his policy on the Franco-British alliance."[1] Then he formally offered the President his resignation and designated his successor—Marshal Pétain. After weeks of battling to hold his government together and keep France in the war, this courageous figure was admitting failure and stepping down from the center of French affairs.

There seemed a doubt as to whether Reynaud had actually resigned. Meeting Campbell and Spears after the council, "he said he had not," according to Spears, "but intended doing so." Spears was struck by Reynaud's mood: he seemed almost a different man —experiencing sheer relief at the thought of being freed from his crushing burden.[2] In any case his resignation was confirmed at 10

---

[8] Lebrun: *Témoignage*, p. 84.

[9] Reynaud appears to have gained supporters since the previous afternoon, so that he now actually had a majority. Although no votes were taken, according to Kammerer (*La Vérité*, p. 155), ministers against an armistice on the sixteenth—including Reynaud himself—totaled 13 (or 15, if 2 absent ministers, De Gaulle and Monnet, are included), and those in favor totaled 11. Reynaud's supporters at the meeting were Mandel, Marin, Rio, Campinchi, Laurent-Eynac, Delbos, Dautry, Rollin, Thellier, Jullien, Queuille, Pernot. Reynaud's opponents were Pétain, Chautemps, Baudouin, Prouvost, Bouthillier, Ybarnegaray, Frossard, Pomaret, Chichery, Rivière, Sérol.

[1] Kammerer: *La Vérité*, p. 147.

[2] Spears: *Assignment*, Vol. II, p. 299.

p.m. at a meeting with the President and Pétain. With his ready-made list of ministers in his briefcase, the marshal emerged from the presidential salon as France's new Prime Minister—pledged to end the fighting with an immediate armistice.[3] He wasted no time. At 12:30 a.m. Baudouin, Pétain's Foreign Minister, saw Señor Lecquerica, the Spanish ambassador, and set in motion the armistice request to Germany. Meanwhile Winston Churchill had been about to make a last effort to keep France in the war. At seven that evening he was on the point of leaving London to meet Reynaud in Brittany next day, when he received a message from Campbell in Bordeaux reporting a "ministerial crisis" and canceling the meeting. Churchill returned to Downing Street "with a heavy heart."[4]

---

[3] Pétain's government was as follows: Chautemps (Vice-President of the Council); General Weygand (National Defense); General Colson (War); General Pujo (Air); Admiral Darlan (Marine); Frémicourt (Justice); Pomaret (Interior); Baudouin (Foreign Affairs); Bouthillier (Finance and Commerce); Rivière (Colonies); Rivaud (National Education); Frossard (Public Works); Chichery (Agriculture); Février (Works); Ybarnegaray ("Anciens Combattants et Famille"). Laval was appointed a Minister of State on June 22.

[4] Churchill: *Second World War*, Vol. II, p. 186.

Chapter 21

ARMISTICE

*"Whatever happens, the flame of French resistance
must not and shall not be extinguished."*
(General de Gaulle)

STILL THE REFUGEES streamed south. The chaos and confusion—
and sometimes the horror—of the pilgrimage reached their
peak at the Loire bridges. At Sully, Gien, Orléans, vast bottlenecks
formed as the crowds herded onto the narrow river crossings.
Laboring pedestrians were pinned against the parapets by the
pressure of the wheeled traffic. The turmoil was increased by the
columns of retreating troops with their trucks and gun limbers. The
bridges being primary German targets, these slow-moving hordes
often had to run the gauntlet of German bombing. Under a hail of
bombs, terrified refugees threw themselves into the water, others
stampeded over the bodies of the dead and dying. Almost equal
alarm was caused when French sappers blew the bridges, and the
procession, stopped short at the approaches, broke up in a desperate
bid to find other ways across. The mining was done so hurriedly that
it would cut off half a contingent of troops, leaving it on the north
bank with the last gun of a battery. Among the worst was the experience of fugitives struggling over the bridges of Nantes. On June
18 rumors that the bridges were to be destroyed started a panic
flight from the great seaport city. So dense was the crush that it
took an hour to cross the first bridge. The mob then fought its
way amid massed traffic to the second bridge[1]—in a frenzy to get

---

[1] Nantes, standing on several branches of the Loire, had its
bridges over each branch.

clear before the explosions. This crossing took as long as the first. Carried helplessly along in the surge was André Soubiran, a medical officer attached to a tank unit. Later he wrote: "I knew the true face of panic."[2]

Hunger was another ordeal for the refugees. Pushed off the roads by advancing motorized units, on the nineteenth a mass of fugitives to the east of Mâcon faced starvation. Hearing of this, General Freydenberg, commanding the remnants of the retreating 2nd Army, wanted to send a food convoy north to feed them. He dispatched a German-speaking officer in a white-pennanted car to intercede with the local German commander. The envoy was stopped and disarmed at Villefranche-sur-Saône and taken to the divisional command post, where he put his request to a German general. "As a man, I am heart-broken to refuse," said the general, "but tomorrow at daylight I shall need all the roads in my zone."[3] The French officer begged him to put his appeal to a higher echelon, hoping that the refugees could be reached through another route. "I'll ask, but it's very unlikely," the general replied. Soon after, the answer came back—a refusal. The disappointed envoy left to report to Freydenberg.[4]

Now, to mark the final stage of France's dissolution, civilians and soldiers were swarming down the French roads together. Mingled with the refugees were thousands of troops, haggard and disheveled, on the run from the broken armies. Disintegration went even further than this. The rear areas were full of men who had apparently not been in action. On his journey from Tours to Bordeaux on the fourteenth, President Lebrun noted with puzzled dismay the crowds of idle servicemen in the towns and villages. Weygand himself had admitted that there were nearly a million men in the camps and barracks, with no arms. Yet at the Riom trials allegations were to be made of masses of equipment and material lying unused in the depots—tanks, antitank guns, shells by the million. In the free zone of France and North Africa there were said to be 5,000 aircraft—1,700 of them front-line planes—of which 2,500 were never flown.

---

[2] A. Soubiran: *J' Étais Médecin avec les Chars* (1943), p. 297.

[3] E. Ruby: *Sedan, Terre d'Epreuve* (1948), p. 246.

[4] Ibid., p. 247.

As the French formations melted away—for want of men or weapons, or both—the German armies bit still deeper into the French hinterland. The confused and fragmentary reports flowing into French GHQ, now at Mont-Dore, completed the picture of defeat. The Germans were racing down the Channel coast, splicing through Altmayer's broken 10th Army to take Cherbourg and Rennes on the eighteenth; meanwhile the British were hastily evacuating from their Brittany bases. In the center, the Loire Line had gone, and on the night of the eighteenth–nineteenth Besson's Third Army Group started withdrawing to the Cher. To the east, in the Loire and Saône valleys, German armored columns were on a curving line Roanne-Mâcon-Bourg-Pontarlier, threatening to cut off Second Army Group and the Army of the Alps. "Especially poignant," as Weygand described it, was the fate of the Maginot Line armies, the 3rd, 5th, and 8th, isolated by the German thrusts in their rear.[5] On the eighteenth Georges issued imperative orders to their commander, General Condé, to fight his way out. "It was heartbreaking," wrote Weygand, "to have to order our fortress troops to abandon the fortifications which they had prepared to defend with such confidence and which some did defend . . . with stubborn heroism."[6]

On June 17 at Petain's residence in the boulevard President Wilson, Bernard Serrigny talked to the marshal's Chief of Staff, General Bineau. The old general was in the depths of gloom. "The enemy tanks," he told Serrigny, "are cruising through our countryside with their bonnets decked with flowers, while their crews proclaim their love of the French!"[7] He then proceeded to give Serrigny a succinct sketch of the situation as seen from his chief's viewpoint. For eight days, he said, the parleys had followed one after another. The Reynaud-Mandel clique wanted to shift the government to Algeria and leave France without a leader, to struggle under the German grip. Pétain had different ideas. He was not going to abandon his compatriots to their fate at any price. In agreement with Weygand, he therefore called for the negotiation of an armistice through Roosevelt. Much could be hoped from

---

[5] M. Weygand: *Recalled to Service,* trans. E. W. Dickes (1952), p. 180.
[6] Ibid., p. 181.
[7] B. Serrigny: *Trente Ans avec Pétain* (1959), p. 174.

this. But Reynaud and his group were exaggerating this request into an appeal for America's entry into the war. This was a purely theatrical gesture, for the benefit of the electorate. Reynaud knew better than anyone that the United States would not declare war! Bineau went on to echo Pétain's resentment against Churchill—who in the last week had twice seen Reynaud without inviting the marshal to their talks. The British Premier was insisting that France should hold fast: naturally he promised powerful aid for the future, but was meanwhile recalling his troops and withholding the use of his planes. And while the talks went on, the army was falling back, losing each day more of its capacity to resist. Now that the position had become catastrophic, Reynaud had passed the responsibility to Pétain, who now had to correct the failures in the worst possible conditions.

Meanwhile, in his first public act as Premier, Pétain was bringing heavy tidings to his people. At 12:30 that day, from a microphone in Bordeaux, he broadcast to the nation:

> Frenchmen, At the request of the President of the Republic, I am assuming as from today the direction of the French Government.
>
> Sure in the affection of our admirable army . . . , sure that by its magnificent resistance it has fulfilled its obligations to our allies, sure of the support of the old fighting men whom I have been proud to command, sure of the trust of the whole nation, I am giving myself to France to mitigate her misfortune.
>
> . . . It is with a sad heart that I tell you today that we must cease the fight.[8] I approached the enemy last night, to ask him if he is ready to seek with me, as between soldiers, after the struggle and in all honour, the means of ending hostilities . . .[9]

Frenchmen heard the news with stupefaction and grief. At General Brooke's headquarters in Brittany, one of his French liasion officers, Captain Méric, broke into his room "and collapsed in a chair," as Brooke records, "shaken from head to foot with sobs."[1] Many stout-hearted French refused to credit it. Some de-

---

[8] Pétain's colleagues immediately challenged this phrase as being misleading and premature, and likely to weaken the continuing resistance of the troops. It was modified in subsequent foreign broadcasts to: "the moment has come to try to stop the fight" (A. Kammerer: *La Vérité sur l'Armistice* [1944], p. 174).

[9] Kammerer: *La Vérité*, pp. 173–4.

[1] A. Bryant: *The Turn of the Tide . . . F. M. Viscount Alanbrooke* (1957), Vol. I, p. 181.

clined to accept it. Admiral Traub, Maritime Prefect of Brest, had posters stuck on the town's walls proclaiming that France was going on fighting. But Pétain's declaration dealt a cruel blow to the wavering morale of the troops who were still valiantly resisting. In London a dour War Cabinet considered the implications of the new position. That evening Churchill broadcast to the British nation, in words addressed also to the French. "The news from France is very bad," he said, "and I grieve for the gallant French people. . . . Nothing will alter our feelings towards them or our faith that the genius of France will rise again. What has happened in France makes no difference to our actions and purpose. . . . We are sure that in the end all will come right."[2] Earlier Churchill had sent Pétain and Weygand—now Minister of National Defense as well as Commander in Chief—a warning not to hand over the French fleet to the Germans. In Washington too, shocked and dismayed at the tidings from France, this was one of the first preoccupations. Along with the British—who sent three top-level representatives to Bordeaux on the nineteenth—the United States ambassador in Bordeaux, Anthony J. Drexel Biddle, Jr., now redoubled his efforts to ensure the salvage of this great asset.

On the afternoon of Wednesday, June 20, against the unending flood of southbound traffic on the Tours-Bordeaux road, one small convoy was struggling north. Ten French staff cars flying flags of truce were heading for Tours. Near the Loire they would cross the enemy lines into German-held France—their final destination a clearing in the Forest of Compiègne. The French armistice delegation was en route to play out the last act of the drama.

Through June 17 and 18 Pétain and his Cabinet had anxiously awaited the German reply to their armistice overtures. This reached Señor Lecquerica in Bordeaux at 6:25 a.m. on the nineteenth. It demanded to know the names of the French "plenipotentiaries." At nine o'clock, Pétain, Weygand, Darlan, Baudouin, and other colleagues met in the marshal's office in the rue Vital-Carles to select the envoys. "Why don't you go yourself?" Baudouin somewhat tactlessly asked Weygand. The general replied that he was for any personal sacrifice, but recalled that in 1918 the Ger-

---

[2] W. S. Churchill: *The Second World War*, Vol. II: *The Call to Honour*, p. 191.

mans had not sent their Commander in Chief or any top-ranking general to Rethondes.[3] Pétain proposed Chautemps to head the delegation; but largely on Weygand's recommendation, a soldier —General Huntziger—was finally chosen for this hard role. Having known Charles Huntziger in the Middle East, Weygand was impressed by his "shrewdness and firmness in negotiation."[4] The rest of the delegation comprised Léon Noël, former ambassador to Poland; Rear Admiral LeLuc, deputy Naval Chief of Staff; General Parisot, recently Air Attaché at Rome; and Air Force General Bergeret. Huntziger, then at his Fourth Army Group command post at Châtel-Guyon, near Clermont-Ferrand, was called to Bordeaux immediately. Arriving that afternoon, he learned of his mission at a brief interview with Weygand. "It went to my heart," recorded Weygand.[5]

At 5 a.m. on the twentieth, the Germans radioed Bordeaux approving the delegation. Just before noon they radioed again to detail travel orders. The envoys were to present themselves after 5 p.m. "on the Loire bridge near Tours." Firing would be suspended across the Poitiers-Tours road and along the river as they passed. After a last briefing from Pétain, Baudouin, and Weygand —in which Huntziger was authorized to break off negotiations immediately if the Germans demanded the surrender of the fleet or the occupation of French colonial territory—the ten-car delegation started off at two o'clock. From Bordeaux to Tours was about 200 miles, but a terse German message to Bordeaux just before midnight reported that the delegation had still not arrived at the Loire Bridge. Caught in endless traffic jams, Huntziger and his colleagues did not reach this first rendezvous until the early hours, when the Prefect of Indre-et-Loire accompanied them a few miles east to less congested Amboise. From there, under German escort, they traveled on northward through the night, without sleep or a proper meal, to reach Paris at 7 a.m. Still unrested, they were ordered to drive on to Compiègne, 50 miles northeast of the capital. They arrived at Rethondes—the final rendezvous—at 3:15 p. m., hungry and dazed with fatigue. Here, in its sunlit clearing, was

---

[3] Kammerer: *La Vérité*, p. 213.
[4] Weygand: *Recalled*, p. 184.
[5] Ibid.

the historic railway coach in which the Germans had signed the armistice in November 1918, and where the terms would now be dictated to the French. Nearby were a tent for the French delegates and the stone commemorating the Allied victory in 1918— covered by a German flag. Over it flew Hitler's own standard.

Hitler, the Iron Cross adorning his plain uniform, had arrived at Rethondes fifteen minutes before. With him in the fleet of German cars were his service chiefs, Göring, Keitel, Brauchitsch, Raeder; and Ribbentrop and Hess, Deputy Party Leader. Followed by his entourage, he marched up to the granite block and read the inscription. American correspondent William Shirer, watching through binoculars from the cover of the pines, saw him turn away contemptuously and execute a little gesture of scornful triumph. The Führer led the way into the coach. The Germans were seated at its long narrow table when the French delegates entered. They stood stiffly at the Nazi salute, and then the whole party took their places, Huntziger facing Hitler. Keitel rose and read a short preamble disowning German responsibility for World War I and charging the Allies with perjury. Then he came to the present war. The Allies, he said, had again declared war on Germany, without the slightest reason. "Now," he went on, "arms have pronounced their verdict. France is beaten. . . . If the Forest of Compiègne has been chosen for the communication of the armistice conditions, this is because of the wish to efface once for all, by an act of reparatory justice, a memory that was for France an inglorious page of history and was felt by the German people as the deepest shame of all time. After a heroic resistance, and conquered in an uninterrupted series of bloody battles, France is broken. That is why Germany has no intention of imposing on the armistice conditions or negotiations a character that would humiliate a valiant adversary."[6] He concluded by stating that the object of the German claims was to prevent a resumption of fighting, to afford Germany all the guarantees necessary for her pursuit of the war against Britain, and to create the conditions necessary for the establishment of a new peace whose essential aim was the righting of wrongs committed against Germany. At 3:30, as Keitel finished, Hitler got up, gave the Nazi salute, and left the coach,

---

[6] Kammerer: *La Vérité*, pp. 323–4.

followed by all except Keitel and the secretarial staff. They stalked off down the avenue to the patriotic strains of a German band.

With Keitel now presiding, copies of the armistice were distributed. Article by article the document was read out in French by Schmidt, the German interpreter. No discussion was permitted. After some ten minutes the French envoys retired to their tent to study the text. There they remained until six o'clock, returning then to the coach with certain queries, which they put to Keitel. But to every inquiry Keitel retorted flatly: "All details as to application will be arranged by an Armistice Commission."[7] Back the Frenchmen went to their tent, where they were served with a frugal meal. They worked on exhausted until the early hours and were then driven to Paris for the rest of the night. Telephone communication had been established between Compiègne and Bordeaux, and at 8:30 Huntziger had telephoned the anxious Weygand to report the armistice terms. Over the faulty line he read the 24 Articles, describing them as "very harsh." Moreover, continued Huntziger's tired voice, the German government expected the French reply by 9 a.m. next day, the twenty-second. At 1 a.m. the Cabinet assembled in the President's quarters for a tense three-hour meeting. Ministers heard the terms with consternation. President Lebrun, overcome, declared with head in hands that they were "unacceptable."[8] All that the ministers could do was frame a number of requests for modifications. After a second Cabinet assembly at 8:30 a.m., these—together with the government's acceptance in principle of the terms—were telephoned by Captain Gasser to Huntziger, now back at Compiègne.

At Bordeaux the Cabinet sat almost permanently through the day. And in the clearing at Rethondes the envoys' feverish deliberations went on, with the Germans inflexibly refusing to discuss anything but minor modifications. Shouting over an infuriatingly unreliable telephone line, several times Huntziger called Bordeaux for advice and instructions. The envoys were further harassed by the constant German supervision that allowed them no private discussion. A time extension had been given for the French answer; but at 6 p.m. Keitel, chafing at the delays, sent Huntziger a written order for a final reply within the hour. Even at this solemn moment,

---

[7] Ibid., p. 216.
[8] Ibid., p. 218.

minor chaos worried the government in Bordeaux. As Weygand notes, the President and certain ministers could not be found, so Pétain, himself and nine other members took on themselves to accord the fateful assent; and Weygand immediately dispatched this telephone message to Rethondes: "Order is given to the French delegation under General Huntziger to sign the Armistice Agreement. Report when done . . ."[9]

From their tent the envoys filed back into the Rethondes railway coach. At 6:50 p.m. on this Saturday, June 22, the Franco-German armistice was signed, Keitel appending his name for Germany and Huntziger for France.[1] The stress and humiliation had borne heavily on all the delegates—on none more than the soldierly Charles Huntziger, who had already tasted his share of defeat with the breaking of the 2nd Army at the Meuse. Now, as he signed, Huntziger said in a voice choked with grief: "Before carrying out my Government's order, the French delegation deems it necessary to declare that in a moment when France is compelled by fate of arms to give up the fight, she has a right to expect that the coming negotiations will be dominated by a spirit that will give two great neighbouring nations a chance to live and work once more. As a soldier you will understand the onerous moment that has now come for me to sign." Keitel listened, stern-faced, and after the signing he asked all present to rise, and made a brief formal speech: "It is honourable for the victor to do honour to the vanquished. We have risen in commemoration of those who have given their blood for their countries."[2]

Two evenings later, in Rome, Huntziger signed the armistice agreement with Italy. In its way this was an even deeper humiliation. Italy had been an unworthy foe, entering the lists only when France was already virtually defeated. Moreover, in June 1940, she was singularly ill-prepared for war. Her air force, army (which possessed no more than about ten first-line divisions), and navy were all poorly equipped and her fighting men apathetic. Her effort against France was, in fact, weak and unimpressive. No large-scale

---

[9] Weygand: *Recalled,* p. 201.
[1] For armistice terms see Appendix, page 373.
[2] H. F. Armstrong: *Chronology of a Failure: the Last Days of the French Republic* (1940), p. 142 (quoted from a German source).

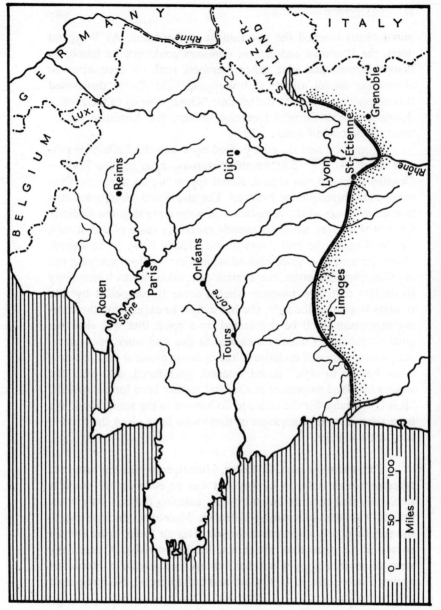

4. *The French positions at cessation of hostilities on June 24, 1940.*

offensive had been launched until June 20, and then it was held along the French advanced line except at Lanslebourg, in the Savoie Department, and Mentone, on the Mediterranean seaboard. The main danger to General Olry's depleted Army of the Alps came not from the Italians but from the southward-driving German forces, which threatened to take the French in the rear.

Hostilities were ordered to stop in all theaters at thirty-five minutes past midnight on Tuesday, the twenty-fifth. After forty-six days of Hitler's main offensive in the West, France was beaten. Despite the unceasing efforts of Paul Reynaud, despite the powerful exhortations and assurances of Winston Churchill, and the certainty of eventual massive aid from the United States if she held firm, her troops had been forced to give up the fight. At the moment of the cease-fire, the Germans stood on a line stretching from the Atlantic coast at Royan, to Clermont-Ferrand, Saint-Étienne, Tournon on the Rhône, Aix-les-Bains, and thence north to the Swiss border. They occupied well over half of France. The French toll of casualties amounted to 100,000 dead, 120,000 wounded, and a million and a half prisoners. Forty thousand officers were killed, wounded, missing, or prisoner—and among the captured were 130 generals. Losses of equipment and material were immense. But as the battered French armies laid down their arms, in one zone the troops refused to accept the news of the armistice. Isolated in the forts of the Maginot Line, over 20,000 men stubbornly battled on for five days until ordered to surrender by the French High Command.

On the twenty-fifth—day of national mourning on which the President, the diplomatic corps, and members of the government attended a solemn service in Bordeaux Cathedral—Weygand issued his last order to the French Army. "After an uninterrupted series of furious battles," he said, "the order is given to you to end the struggle. The fortune of war has gone against us, but at least you responded magnificently to the appeals I addressed to your patriotism, your bravery, and your tenacity. . . . Honour is safe. . . . Remain united and trust your leaders. Continue to submit to a strict discipline. . . . Wherever you may be, your task is not ended. . . . Keep up your spirits, my friends. *Vive la France.*"[3]

---

[3] Weygand: *Recalled*, pp. 206–7.

Shortly afterwards, at three crossroads between Bordeaux and Clermont-Ferrand, Weygand was to inspect the remnants of Besson's Third Army Group—the troops of Hering's, Frère's, and Touchon's armies. "Commanders, officers and soldiers stood proudly," he recorded, "with sad faces, but with the steady look of men who had done their duty to the end."[4] These troops had been beaten by circumstances too strong for them, as had their chief, Maxime Weygand. Called back to command at the age of seventy-three, he inherited a military situation in which the battle was already lost beyond recovery. Fiery, rigid, prejudiced, a soldier and authoritarian first and foremost, he believed that, in the final resort, the country could be saved only by saving the army.

"*Viva la France,*" Weygand had proclaimed in his last order to his troops. France might live on, but the Third Republic was dead. Born in high hopes seventy years before, now it failed to surmount this greatest ordeal and collapsed under its weight of errors and weaknesses. While these extended deep into French roots and reached far beyond the military sphere, in her second confrontation with Germany since 1870 the immediate factors leading to France's defeat were nothing other than military. For too long the General Staff and High Command had clung to old ideas and methods, ignoring the formidable new war machine being shaped by Hitler's Germany. When the clash came, the result was a foregone conclusion. One French writer, Colonel de Bardies,[5] summed up the direct causes of the military collapse as: lack of the right material and equipment; the wrong kind of training; absence of strong command, as exemplified by General Gamelin—a soldier of high intelligence but without the necessary drive and dynamism; the reliance on a defensive instead of an offensive doctrine (which itself dictated the choice of equipment and type of training). Underlying these, added de Bardies, was a want of morale and an ignorance of the reasons why France was fighting. Of such defects the French Army, despite tough and heroic resistance by many units, reaped the full harvest in the fateful days of mid-May, on the banks of the Meuse—the battle ground that made its ultimate

---

[4] Ibid., p. 207.
[5] R. de Bardies: *La Campagne 39–40* (1947), pp. 293–4.

eclipse certain. As another French writer, M. Richecourt, put it: "On the 15th May the outcome of the struggle was settled. The efforts of our troops could no longer alter a result written in history before the attack. The 15th May was the debacle; and France was beaten by herself rather than by the enemy."[6]

Much of the wrong military thinking stemmed from Marshal Philippe Pétain—the once great leader whose aged voice now enjoined discipline, austerity, and submission in somber broadcast addresses to the French people. But another voice was speaking to France—a voice from London. General Charles de Gaulle had returned to troubled Bordeaux on the night of the sixteenth. He learned that Reynaud had just resigned. Knowing what this meant, he promptly decided to leave France again for Britain. By the good offices of General Spears, he evaded possible arrest by his political enemies and secured a seat in the plane that was taking Spears home early on the seventeenth. In De Gaulle's mind his mission was clear. At 6 p.m. on the eighteenth, as France bowed under the news of the armistice request, he spoke to Frenchmen from the BBC in London. "Has the last word been said?" he asked. "Must all hope vanish? Is the defeat final? No. . . . I, General de Gaulle, now in London, invite French officers and soldiers who are in British territory or will be coming to British territory, with or without arms, I likewise invite engineers and specialist armament workers, to get in touch with me."

"Whatever happens, the flame of French resistance must not and shall not be extinguished . . ."[7]

---

[6] Richecourt: *La Guerre de Cente Heures—1940* (1944), p. 319.
[7] Kammerer: *La Vérité*, p. 322.

APPENDIX

THE TERMS of the Franco-German Armistice, based on the official German text issued in Berlin on June 25, 1940 (as quoted in H. F. Armstrong: *Chronology of Failure* [1940], pp. 142–7).

ARTICLE 1: The French Government directs a cessation of fighting against the German Reich in France as well as in French possessions, colonies, protectorate territories and mandates, as well as on the seas. It directs the immediate laying down of arms of French units already encircled by German troops.

ARTICLE 2: French territory north and west of the line Geneva, Dôle, Châlon-sur-Saône, Paray, Moulins, Bourges, Vierzon, thence to 20 kms east of Tours, thence south parallel to Angoulême Railway to Mont-de-Marsan and St.-Jean-Pied-de-Port, will be occupied by German troops. Those areas which are to be occupied and which are not yet in control of German troops shall be turned over to them immediately.

ARTICLE 3: In the occupied parts of France the German Reich exercises all rights of an occupying Power. The French Government obligates itself to support with every means the regulations resulting from the exercise of these rights and to carry them out with the aid of the French administration. . . . It is the intention of the German Government to limit the occupation of the west coast, after ending hostilities with England, to the extent absolutely necessary. The French Government is permitted to select the seat of its government in unoccupied territory, or, if it wishes, to move to Paris. In this case, the German Government guarantees the French Government and its central authorities every necessary alleviation so that they will be in a position to conduct the administration of unoccupied territory from Paris.

ARTICLE 4: French armed forces on land, on the sea and in the air are to be demobilised and disarmed in a period still to be set. Excepted are only those units which are necessary for maintainence of domestic order. Germany and Italy will fix their strength. The French armed forces in the territory to be occupied by Germany are to be hastily withdrawn into territory not to be occupied and be discharged. These troops, before marching out, shall lay down their weapons and equipment at the places where they are stationed at the time this treaty becomes effective. They are responsible for orderly delivery to German troops.

ARTICLE 5: Germany may demand the surrender, in good condition, of all guns, tanks, planes, means of conveyance and ammunition of French units which are still resisting and which at the time this agreement becomes effective are in the territory not to be occupied.

ARTICLE 6: Such of the above war materials as are not allocated to French use are to be stored under German or Italian control. The manufacture of new war material in the unoccupied territory is to be stopped immediately.

ARTICLE 7: Land and coastal fortifications in the occupied territory are to be surrendered to the Germans undamaged, together with the plans of these fortifications.

ARTICLE 8: The French war fleet is to collect in ports to be designated more particularly, and under German and (or) Italian control, there to be demobilised and laid up—with the exception of those units released to the French Government for protection of French interests in its colonial empire. The peacetime stations of ships should control the designation of ports.

The German Government solemnly declares to the French Government that it does not intend to use the French war fleet which is in harbours under German control for its purposes in war, with the exception of units necessary for the purposes of guarding the coast and sweeping mines. It further solemnly and expressly declares that it does not intend to bring up any demands respecting the French war fleet at the conclusion of a peace.

All warships outside France are to be recalled to France, with the exception of that portion of the French war fleet which shall be designated to represent French interests in the colonial empire.

ARTICLE 9: The Germans are to be given the exact location of all mines, and may require that French forces sweep them away.

ARTICLE 10: The French Government is obligated to forbid any portion of its remaining armed forces to undertake hostilities against Germany in any manner.

The French Government also will prevent members of its armed forces from leaving the country and prevent armaments of any sort, including ships, planes, etc., being taken to England or any other place abroad.

The French Government will forbid French citizens to fight against Germany in the service of States with which the German Reich is still at war. French citizens who violate this provision are to be treated by German troops as insurgents.

ARTICLE 11: No French merchant shipping may leave port until further notice without the approval of the German and Italian Governments. French merchant vessels will either be recalled by the French Government or instructed to enter neutral ports.

ARTICLE 12: No airplane flights may be made over French territory without German approval. Airfields in the unoccupied territory shall be placed under German and Italian control.

ARTICLE 13: The French Government must turn over to German troops in the occupied region all facilities and properties of the French armed forces, in undamaged condition; also harbours, industrial facilities and docks; also transportation and communications facilities. Further, the French Government shall perform all necessary labour to restore these facilities, and will see to it that the necessary technical personnel and rolling stock of the railways be retained in service, also other transportation equipment, to a degree normal in peacetime.

ARTICLE 14: Further transmission from all French wireless stations is prohibited. Resumption of wireless communication from unoccupied France will require special permission.

ARTICLE 15: The French Government must convey transit freight between the German Reich and Italy through unoccupied territory.

ARTICLE 16: The French Government, in agreement with the responsible German officials, will carry out the return of the population into occupied territory.

ARTICLE 17: The French Government is to prevent transfers of economic valuables and provisions from the occupied to the non-occupied territory or abroad without German permission. In that connection, the German Government will consider the necessities of life of the population in unoccupied territory.

ARTICLE 18: The French Government will bear the costs of maintenance of German occupation troops on French soil.

ARTICLE 19: All German war and civil prisoners in French custody, including those under arrest and convicted, who were seized and sentenced because of acts in favour of the Reich, shall be surrendered immediately to the German troops. The French Government is obliged to surrender upon demand all Germans designated by the German Government in France, as well as in the French possessions, colonies, protectorate territories and mandates. . . .

ARTICLE 20: French troops in German prison camps will remain prisoners of war until conclusion of a peace.

ARTICLE 21: The French Government is responsible for the security of all objects whose surrender is demanded in this agreement, and is required to make compensation for any damage or removal contrary to the agreement.

ARTICLE 22: The Armistice Commission, acting in accordance with the direction of the German High Command, has authority to regulate and supervise the carrying out of the armistice agreement. The French Government will send a delegation to the seat of the German Armistice Commission to present French wishes and to receive rulings with regard to them.

ARTICLE 23: This agreement becomes effective as soon as the French Government has also reached an agreement with the Italian Government. Hostilities will cease six hours after the Italian Government has notified the German Government of conclusion of such an agreement.

ARTICLE 24: This agreement is valid until conclusion of a peace treaty. The German Government may terminate this agreement at any time with immediate effect if the French Government fails to fulfil the obligations it assumes under the agreement.

NOTE ON SOURCES

U SE HAS BEEN MADE of a wide range of mostly French material, embracing official records, background works, general
and specialized histories, military studies and treatises, biographies,
topographical accounts, journals and diaries of both soldiers and
civilians, memoirs and commentaries of leading politicians and
commanders. This material has been supplemented by a number
of English and American works. In Part I the sources were mainly
employed to give a general survey of the events of seventy years
in a fairly brief space, though these events have been presented
through the eyes of as many participants and commentators as
possible. In Part II, the main portion of the book, in which the
events of a few months are covered at length, a more detailed
treatment was aimed at. In order to describe the parallel happenings at the front, at various military headquarters, and in Paris and
elsewhere, full recourse was had to journals, diaries, and eyewitness accounts. Documentation of the May–June campaign itself
is plentiful and includes the valuable study by Captain Goutard,
and the works of various senior commanders—like Generals Doumenc, Roton, Prioux, Grandsard, Ruby, Menu—and other officers
who directed operations. As comprehensive day-to-day records that
cover the battle front and also the political background in France
and abroad, the books of Benoist-Méchin and Kammerer are indispensable, as is the American chronicle of H. F. Armstrong.
Among personal narratives of regimental officers, those of Captain
Barlone and Soubiran can be mentioned; while the accounts of
Colonel Minart and Captain Beaufre throw an informative light
on events at different centers of French GHQ (though Minart's
accuracy is disputed by General Gamelin). For happenings in Paris
and elswhere behind the Army Zone there are, notably, the chroni-
cles of Senator Bardoux and Langeron, the Paris Police Prefect,
and observers like Audiat, Amouroux, and others, reinforced by
the English account of Alexander Werth.

Finally, there are the copious memoirs of the leading politicians and service chiefs. While these take us to the heart of the

drama, almost inevitably they are colored by the great controversies
that surround the collapse of France. In matters of high policy and
military planning and strategy, figures such as Paul Reynaud,
Prime Minister, and Generals Gamelin and Weygand, the successive Commanders in Chief, are at pains to present their side of
the case and justify their own motives and actions. Hostilities are
revealed, like that of Reynaud for Gamelin (whose plan for the
Allied advance into Belgium he mistrusted) and Daladier. Sometimes truth is distorted, as when Reynaud wrongly condemns King
Leopold of the Belgians for betraying the Allies by his surrender.
Conflicting versions in other ministerial memoirs make it hard to
determine what was said, and by whom, at Cabinet meetings, on—
for instance—the vital question of an armistice. Gamelin insists
that his interpretation of his functions as Supreme Commander,
under which he left General Georges responsible for the operational direction of the battle, was the correct one. Weygand forcibly
argues that Reynaud and his supporters, who wanted to fight on,
were wrong, and he and Pétain, in pressing for a cease-fire, were
right. Of all the reportage of what went on inside and outside the
government council rooms, the diaries of Paul Baudouin, Secretary
of the War Cabinet and Under-Secretary of State in Reynaud's
administration, are perhaps the most illuminating. They give a
graphic day-to-day account of the tensions and disputes building
up within the Cabinet, and between Reynaud and Weygand, as
defeat draws near. The memoirs of General de Gaulle, appointed
Under-Secretary of State for National Defense by Reynaud, are
obviously of major importance. Valuable too is the testimony of
President Lebrun, and the records of Bouthillier and others. In
general, if this whole group of sources often lacks objectivity,
collectively it demonstrates well the crisis and confusion that over-
took French leadership in May and June 1940.

Outstanding among the English sources that reinforce the
French material at this level are the works of Sir Winston Churchill,
Sir Arthur Bryant, and Sir Edward Spears, whose *Assignment to
Catastrophe* provides an intimate picture of the political scene,
together with closely drawn portraits of many of the chief French
personalities.

BIBLIOGRAPHY

THE FOLLOWING are the principal sources consulted:

Allard, Paul: *La Vérité sur l'Affaire Corap*. Paris, 1941.

Amouroux, Henri: *La Vie des Francais sous l'Occupation*. Paris, 1961.

Armstrong, Hamilton Fish: *Chronology of Failure: the Last Days of the French Republic*. New York, 1940.

Aspinall-Oglander, Cecil: *Roger Keyes*. London, 1951.

Audiat, Pierre: *Paris pendant la Guerre: juin 1940–août 1944*. Paris, 1946.

Baedeker, Karl: *The Rhine from Rotterdam to Constance*. London, 1900.

Bainville, Jacques: *Bismarck et la France*. Paris, 1907.

Barbusse, Henri: *Ce Qui Fut Sera*. Paris, 1930.

————: *Paroles d'un Combattant*. Paris, 1920.

Bardoux, Jacques: *Journal d'un Témoin de la Troisième . . . 1940*. Paris, 1957.

Barlone, Daniel: *A French Officer's Diary, 23 August 1939–1 October 1940*, trans. L. V. Cass. London, 1942.

Barrès, Philippe: *Charles de Gaulle*. London, 1941.

Baudouin, Paul: *The Private Diaries (March 1940 to January 1941)*, trans. Sir Charles Petrie. London, 1948.

Beaufre, André: *Le Drame de 1940*. Paris, 1965. Now available in English under the title *1940: the Fall of France*, trans. Desmond Flower. New York: Alfred A. Knopf, 1968.

Benoist-Méchin, Jacques G. P. M.: *60 Jours qui Ebranlèrent l'Occident*. 3 vols. Paris, 1956.

Bidou, Henry: *La Bataille de France, 10 mai–25 juin 1940*. Geneva, 1941.

Bloch, Marc: *L'Etrange Défaite*. Paris, 1946.

Bois, Élie J.: *Truth on the Tragedy of France*, trans. N. S. Wilson. London, 1941.

Bonnal, Henri: *L'Art Nouveau en Tactique*. Paris, 1904.

Bordeaux, Henry C.: *Histoire d'une Vie*, Vols. VI and VIII. Paris, 1959, 1962.

Bourget, P.-A.: *De Beyrouth à Bordeaux.* Paris, 1946.

Bourret, Victor: *La Tragédie de l'Armée Française.* Paris, 1947.

Bouthillier, Yves: *Le Drame de Vichy.* 2 vols. Paris, 1950.

Brogan, Denis William: *The Development of Modern France (1870–1939).* London, 1940.

Bryant, Arthur: *The Turn of the Tide, based on the War Diaries of F.-M. Viscount Alanbrooke.* 2 vols. London, 1957.

Bullock, Alan: *Hitler: a Study in Tyranny.* London, 1952.

Butler, Harold: *The Lost Peace: A Personal Impression.* London, 1941.

Carré, Henri: *Les Grandes Heures du Général Pétain.* Paris, 1952.

Chartier, Émile Auguste: *Mars, ou la Guerre Jugée.* Paris, 1921.

Churchill, Winston S.: *The Second World War.* Vol. II: *Their Finest Hour.* London, 1949.

Clemenceau, Georges: *Grandeur and Misery of Victory.* London, 1930.

Cobban, Alfred: *A History of Modern France.* Vol. 3: *1871–1962.* London, 1965.

Contamine, Henry: *La Revanche, 1871–1914.* Paris, 1957.

Corday, Michel: *The Paris Front: an Unpublished Diary, 1914–18.* London, 1933.

Cru, Jean: *Témoins.* Paris, 1929.

Daily News, The (London): *Correspondence of the War between Germany and France, 1870–71.* London, 1871.

D'Arman, R.: *La Garde à la Frontière.* Paris, 1913.

Dauvergne, Robert: *Campagne de 1939–1940.* Paris, 1947.

Davis, Shelby Cullom: *The French War Machine.* London, 1937.

De Bardies, R.: *La Campagne 39–40.* Paris, 1947.

De Gaulle, Charles: *War Memoirs.* Vol. I: *The Call to Honour, 1940–42,* trans. J. Griffin. London, 1955.

————: *France and her Army,* trans. F. L. Dash. London, 1945.

De Gontaut-Biron, Charles Armand: *Les Dragons de Combat: Journal de Marche du 2 Dragons, Campagne 1939–45.* Paris, 1945.

De Grandmaison, Loyseau: *Deux Conférences, Février 1911.* Paris, 1912.

De La Gorce, Paul-Marie: *The French Army: A Military-Political History,* trans. Kenneth Douglas. London, 1963.

De La Tour, J.: *Le Maréchal Niel.* Paris, 1912.

De Maricourt, André: *Foch.* Paris, 1920.

De Pierrefeu, Jean: *French Headquarters, 1915–1918,* trans. C. J. C. Street. London, 1924.

De Polnay, Peter: *Death and Tomorrow.* London, 1942.

De Vibraye, Tony: *Avec mon Groupe de Reconnaissance Aug/39– Aug/40.* Roanne, Loire, 1943.

Debeney, Marie-Eugène: *La Guerre et les Hommes.* Paris, 1937.

The Diary of a Staff Officer at Advanced Headquarters North, B.A.F.F., 1940. London, 1941.

Doumenc, A.: *Histoire de la Neuvième Armée.* Grenoble, 1945.

Downing, Rupert: *If I Laugh.* London, 1940.

Draper, Theodore: *The Six Weeks' War: France, May 10–June 25, 1940.* London, 1946.

Duruy, Victor: *A Short History of France,* trans. M. Carey. 2 vols. London, 1927.

East, Cecil Jones: *The Armed Strength of France.* London, 1877.

Encyclopaedia Britannica (14th edition). 24 vols., *passim.*

Engerand, Fernand: *Le Secret de la Frontière.* Charleroi, 1918.

Eon, Joseph Marie: *Bataille de Flandres.* London, 1943.

Éparvier, Jean: *À Paris sous la Botte des Nazis.* Paris, 1944.

Fabre-Luce, Alfred: *Journal de la France: mars 1939–juillet 1940.* Trévoux, Ain, 1940.

Falls, Cyril: *The First World War.* London, 1961.

Fisher, Herbert A. L.: *A History of Europe,* Vol. III. London, 1935.

"The Flight from Paris." *Fortnightly Review,* Vol. CLIV (London, 1940), pp. 131–7.

France—État-Major de l'Armée: *Les Armées Françaises dans la Grande Guerre,* Tome V, Vol. II; Annexes, Vol. I. Paris, 1937.

————: *Révue Historique de l'Armée,* Vol. I *et seq.* Paris, 1945 *et seq., passim.*

Fuller, John F. C.: *The Second World War, 1939–45: a Strategical and Tactical History.* London, 1948.

Gamelin, Maurice: *Servir.* 3 vols. Paris, 1946–7.

Gibbs, Philip: *European Journey.* London, 1934.

Goutard, Adolphe: *The Battle of France, 1940,* trans. A. R. P. Burgess. London, 1958.

Grandsard, C.: *Le 10ᵉ Corps d'Armée dans la Bataille, 1939–1940.* Paris, 1949.

Greenwall, Harry J.: *When France Fell.* London, 1958.

Guderian, Heinz: *Panzer Leader,* trans. Constantine FitzGibbon. London, 1952.

Hamp, Pierre: *La Peine des Hommes: le Travail Invincible.* Paris, 1918.

Herbillon, Émile: *Du Général en Chef au Gouvernement.* 2 vols. Paris, 1930.

Hibbert, Christopher: *Mussolini: A Biography.* London, 1962.

History of the Second World War, U.K. Military Series. L. F. Ellis: *The War in France and Flanders.* London, 1953.

Horne, Alistair: *The Price of Glory: Verdun.* London, 1962.

House of Commons: Parliamentary Debates, 5th Series (1940).

Houssaye, Henry: *La Patrie Guerrière.* Paris, 1913.

Hull, Cordell: *The Memoirs of Cordell Hull.* 2 vols. London, 1948.

Ironside, Edmund: *The Ironside Diaries.* London, 1962.

Jacques [pseud.]: *A French Soldier Speaks.* London, 1941.

Jaurès, Jean: *L'Armée Nouvelle.* Paris, 1915.

Joffre, Joseph Jacques Césaire: *Memoirs,* trans. T. Bentley Mott. 2 vols. London, 1932.

Jordan, William M.: *Great Britain, France and the German Problem, 1918–39.* London, 1943.

Journal of the Royal United Services Institute: "Musketeer." Paris 1870 and 1940. Vol. XCIX (1954), pp. 412–18.

Jubert, Raymond: *Verdun.* Paris, 1918.

Jucker, Ninetta: *Curfew in Paris: A Record of the German Occupation.* London, 1960.

Kammerer, Albert: *La Vérité sur l'Armistice.* Paris, 1944.

Kernan, Thomas: *Report on France: 'Paris in the Dark.'* London, 1940.

Keyes, Roger: *The Private Papers of Lord Keyes.*

Knight, W. Stanley MacBean, ed.: *The History of the Great European War, its Causes and Effects.* 10 vols. London, n.d.

Kuntz, François: *L'Officier Français dans la Nation.* Paris, 1960.

Labusquière, Jean: *Vérité sur les Combattants: Grandes Batailles de Mai–Juin, 1940.* Lyon, 1941.

Laffargue, André: *Justice pour Ceux de 1940.* Paris, 1952.

————: *Le Général Dentz.* Paris, 1954.

Langeron, Roger: *Paris, Juin 1940.* Paris, 1946.

Laure, Auguste M. E. *et al.: Pétain.* Paris, 1942.

Lavedan, Henri: *Les Grandes Heures.* 5 vols. Paris, 1915–20.

Lebrun, Albert: *Témoignage*. Paris, 1945.

Leroy, Maxine: *L'Alsace-Lorraine*. Paris, 1914.

Lévy, Louis: *The Truth about France,* trans. W. Pickles, Harmondsworth, Herts, 1941.

Liddell Hart, Basil H.: *The Remaking of Modern Armies*. London, 1927.

———: *Reputations*. London, 1928.

———: *The Other Side of the Hill*. London, 1951.

Lockner, L. P.: "*Germans Marched into a Dead Paris*." *Life* (New York), Vol. IX, No. 2 (1940), pp. 22, 23, 74, 75.

Lyet, Pierre: *La Bataille de France, mai–juin, 1940*. Paris, 1947.

MacDonald, William: *Reconstruction in France*. London, 1922.

Madelin, Louis: *Le Chemin de la Victoire*. 2 vols. Paris, 1920.

Margueritte, Victor: *Au Bord du Gouffre*. Paris, 1919.

Masefield, John: *The Nine Days' Wonder (The Operation Dynamo)*. London, 1941.

Maurois, André: *The Battle of France,* trans. F. R. Ludman. London, 1940.

———: *Tragédie en France*. New York, 1940.

———: *Why France Fell,* trans. Denver Lindley. London, 1941.

Menu, Charles Léon: *Lumière sur les Ruines*. Paris, 1953.

Messimy, Adolphe: *Mes Souvenirs*. Paris, 1937.

Millerand, Alexandre: *Pour la Défense Nationale*. Paris, 1913.

Minart, Jacques: *P. C. Vincennes, Secteur 4*. 2 vols. in one. Paris, 1945.

Montgomery, Bernard Law: *Memoirs*. London, 1958.

Muirhead, Findlay: *Belgium and the Western Front*. London, 1920.

——— and Monmarché, M.: *North-Eastern France*. 2nd edn. London, 1930.

Newman, Bernard: *The Lazy Meuse*. London, 1949.

Pages Actuelles, No. 30 (Paris, 1915). Blanchon, Georges: "Le Général Pau."

Pertinax [pseud.]: *Les Fossoyeurs*. 2 vols. New York, 1943.

Pétain, Henri Philippe: *La Bataille de Verdun*. Paris, 1929.

———: *Messages aux Français*. Paris, 1942.

Petges, Jean Pierre: *Bataille d'Amiens, 1940*. New York, 1943.

Peyrefitte, Roger: *La Fin des Ambassades*. Paris, 1954.

Picht, Werner: *La Fin des Illusions: l'An 1940*. Brussels, 1940.

Plumyène, Jean: *Pétain.* Paris, 1964.

Prioux, R.: *Souvenirs de Guerre.* Paris, 1947.

Revue des Deux Mondes (Paris): "Le Rôle Social de l'Officier." Vol. 104 (1891), pp. 443–59.

Reynaud, Paul: *La France a Sauvé l'Europe.* 2 vols. Paris, 1947.

———: *In the Thick of the Fight,* trans. J. D. Lambert. London, 1955.

———: *Mémoires.* 2 vols. Paris, 1960.

Ribet, Maurice: *Le Procés de Riom.* Paris, 1945.

Richecourt: *La Guerre de Cent Heures—1940.* Paris, 1944.

Romains, Jules: *Verdun.* London, 1962.

Rommel, Ervin: *The Rommel Papers,* ed. Basil H. Liddell Hart, trans. Paul Findlay. London, 1953.

Roton, G.: *Années Cruciales.* Paris, 1947.

Rowe, Vivien: *The Great Wall of France: the Triumph of the Maginot Line.* London, 1959.

Ruby, Edmond: *Sedan, Terre d'Epreuve.* Paris, 1948.

Samné, Georges: *Raymond Poincaré.* Paris, 1933.

Serrigny, Bernard: *Trente Ans avec Pétain.* Paris, 1959.

Shirer, William L.: *Berlin Diary.* London, 1941.

Siegfried, André: *France: A Study in Nationality.* New Haven, 1930.

Simond, Émile: *Histoire de la Troisième République de 1899 à 1906: Presidence de M. Loubet.* 3 vols. Paris, 1913–21.

Somervell, David Churchill: *Modern Europe, 1871–1939.* London, 1940.

Soubiran, André: *J'étais Médecin avec les Chars.* Paris, 1943.

Spears, Edward L.: *Liaison 1914.* London, 1931.

———: *Prelude to Victory,* London, 1939.

———: *Assignment to Catastrophe.* 2 vols. London, 1954.

Stembridge, Jasper H.: *The Oxford War Atlas, Sept. 1939–Sept. 1941.* Oxford, 1941.

Strategicus [pseud.]: *The War for World Power.* London, 1940.

Suarez, Georges: *Le Maréchal Pétain.* Paris, 1940.

Taylor, Telford: *The March of Conquest: the German Victories in Western Europe, 1940.* London, 1959.

Tharaud, Jérome and Jean: *La Vie et la Mort de Déroulède.* Paris, 1925.

Thoumin, Richard L.: *The First World War: Accounts of Participants,* trans. Martin Kieffer. London, 1963.

Thouvenin, Jean: *Une Année d'Histoire, 1940–1941.* Paris, 1941.

Times, The (London), June 1940 and *passim.*

Tint, Herbert: *The Decline of French Patriotism.* London, 1964.

Tissier, Pierre: *The Riom Trial.* London, 1943.

Tony Revillon, M. M.: *Mes Carnets (juin–octobre 1940).* Paris, 1945.

Trevor-Roper, Hugh R., ed.: *Hitler's War Directives, 1939–1945.* London, 1964.

Tuchmann, Barbara W.: *August, 1914.* London, 1963.

Waterfield, Gordon: *What Happened to France.* London, 1940.

Watt, Richard M.: *Dare Call It Treason.* London, 1964.

Werth, Alexander: *The Last Days of Paris.* London, 1940.

Weygand, Maxime: *Mémoires.* 3 vols. Paris, 1950–7.

———: *Recalled to Service,* (Vol. III of *Mémoires*), trans. E. W. Dickes. London, 1952.

——— and Weygand, Jacques: *The Role of General Weygand: Conversations with his Son,* trans. J. H. F. McEwen. London, 1948.

Young, Desmond: *Rommel.* London, 1950.

INDEX

A NOTE ABOUT THE AUTHOR

JOHN WILLIAMS, an English military historian, served in the
Royal Artillery during World War II and was subsequently,
for ten years, librarian at the Administrative Staff College.
He is the author of a notable account of the French Army
mutinies in the First World War, *Mutiny: 1917,* published
in Great Britain. *The Ides of May* is his first book to appear
in the United States. Mr. Williams was born in 1908, is
married, and is the father of three daughters. He lives in
St. Leonards-on-Sea in the county of Sussex, England.

A NOTE ON THE TYPE

—————

THE TEXT of this book was set on the Linotype in a face called TIMES ROMAN, designed by Stanley Morison for *The Times* (London), and first introduced by that newspaper in 1932.

Among typographers and designers of the twentieth century, Stanley Morison has been a strong forming influence, as typographical adviser to the English Monotype Corporation, as a director of two distinguished English publishing houses, and as a writer of sensibility, erudition, and keen practical sense.

This book was composed, printed, and bound by the Haddon Craftsmen, Inc., Scranton, Pennsylvania.

Typography and binding design by

WARREN ⌗ CHAPPELL